Consumer Culture Theory

Edited by

Eric J. Arnould & Craig J. Thompson

Consumer Culture Theory

$\circledS$SAGE

Los Angeles | London | New Delhi
Singapore | Washington DC | Melbourne

Los Angeles | London | New Delhi
Singapore | Washington DC | Melbourne

SAGE Publications Ltd
1 Oliver's Yard
55 City Road
London EC1Y 1SP

SAGE Publications Inc.
2455 Teller Road
Thousand Oaks, California 91320

SAGE Publications India Pvt Ltd
B 1/I 1 Mohan Cooperative Industrial Area
Mathura Road
New Delhi 110 044

SAGE Publications Asia-Pacific Pte Ltd
3 Church Street
#10-04 Samsung Hub
Singapore 049483

Editor: Matthew Waters
Editorial assistant: Jasleen Kaur
Production editor: Sarah Cooke
Copyeditor: Elaine Leek
Proofreader: Fabienne Pedroletti-Gray
Indexer: Elizabeth Ball
Marketing manager: Alison Borg
Cover design: Francis Kenney
Typeset by: C&M Digitals (P) Ltd, Chennai, India
Printed in the UK

Library of Congress Control Number: 2018932204

British Library Cataloguing in Publication data

A catalogue record for this book is available from the
British Library

ISBN 978-1-526-42071-8
ISBN 978-1-526-42072-5 (pbk)

At SAGE we take sustainability seriously. Most of our products are printed in the UK using responsibly sourced
papers and boards. When we print overseas we ensure sustainable papers are used as measured by the
PREPS grading system. We undertake an annual audit to monitor our sustainability.

CONTENTS

ABOUT THE AUTHORS

Eric Arnould is Visiting Professor of Marketing at the Aalto University Business School, Finland. He has been on faculty at four European universities and several in the United States. He has pursued a career in applied social science since 1973, receiving a PhD in social anthropology from the University of Arizona in 1982. Aalto University awarded him an honorary doctorate in 2016. Early ethnographic research in West Africa inspired his approach to contemporary market-mediated society. He is senior editor at the *International Journal of Research in Marketing*, and associate editor at the *Journal of Retailing*. Current interests include collective consumer creativity, human branding, sustainable business practice, visual representations, and digital mobility.

Zeynep Arsel is Research Chair in Consumption and Markets at Concordia University, Montreal, Canada. Her research investigates consumption, taste, space, and the culture(s) of the market(s). Her work has been published in the *Journal of Consumer Research*, *Journal of Marketing*, and *Journal of the Association for Consumer Research* and has been funded by SSHRC, FRQSC, ACR, and MSI. She is associate editor at the *Journal of Consumer Research* and *Consumption Markets & Culture*. Arsel has been featured in mass media outlets including the *Wall Street Journal*, *Harper's Magazine*, *Vice*, *Globe and Mail*, and *Wired*. She is the co-editor of *Taste, Consumption and Markets* (Routledge, 2018).

Fleura Bardhi is a Professor of Marketing at Cass Business School, City, University of London, UK. As a consumer researcher, Fleura examines how socio-historical transformations of modernity shape our contemporary consumption. Her research examines liquid consumption, access and sharing, global branding and mobilities, and life transitions. She approaches her research from a consumer culture theory (CCT) perspective. Fleura's work has been published in the *Journal of Consumer Research*, *Harvard Business Review*, *Sloan Management Review*, *International Marketing Review*, *Consumption Markets & Culture*, *Psychology and Marketing*, *Journal of Consumer Behaviour*, etc. Fleura is a member of the editorial review board for *Journal of Consumer Research*, and *Consumption Markets & Culture*. Her work has received attention and was cited in the *Wall Street Journal*, *The Financial*

Times, The Economist, The Guardian, Boston Globe, etc. She is a Visiting Professor at Lund University, Sweden.

Jonathan Bean is Assistant Professor of Architecture, Sustainable Built Environments, and Marketing at the University of Arizona, USA. His research on taste and consumption spans the fields of consumer research, human–computer interaction, architecture, and design. He is the author of the Consuming Tech column for *ACMInteractions* magazine and is completing a multi-year immersive study of market transformation in the United States building market. He has received grants from the Social Sciences and Humanities Research Council of Canada, the National Institute for Transportation and Communities, and others. His work on IKEA hacking was featured on an episode of the 99% Invisible podcast.

Shona Bettany is Professor of Marketing and Associate Dean for Research, Liverpool Business School, UK. Her research focuses on ethnographic studies of consumption cultures, particularly related to the family, technology and sexualities. Her work also encompasses critical studies employing feminist and post-humanist approaches. She has published in the *European Journal of Marketing, Journal of Business Research, Marketing Theory, Journal of Marketing Management, Advances in Consumer Research* and *Consumption Markets & Culture*.

Marylouise Caldwell is Associate Professor at the University of Sydney Business School, Australia. Her research has focused on the influence of cultural capital on life-style activities, celebrity worship, and more recently stigmatization of HIV sufferers. Her work had been published in journals such as *Marketing Theory, Journal of Business Research, European Journal of Marketing, Consumption Markets & Culture*, and *Psychology and Marketing*.

Gokcen Coskuner-Balli is an Associate Professor of Marketing at Argyros School of Business and Economics, Chapman University, California, USA. Her research explores the cultural and political shaping of consumer–market interactions and offers theorizations for politics of consumption, institutional legitimacy, market creation and evolution. Her work has been published in the *Journal of Marketing, Journal of Consumer Research, Marketing Theory, Journal of Consumer Culture*, and *Journal of Consumer Behavior*.

Bernard Cova is a Professor at Kedge Business School, Marseilles, France and a Visiting Professor at the Bocconi University in Milan, Italy. Since the early 1990s, he has participated in postmodernist streams of consumer research and marketing, focusing on a tribal approach. He is also a B-to-B marketing researcher, primarily in the field of project marketing.

David Crockett is Associate Professor of Marketing at the Moore School of Business, University of South Carolina, USA. His primary research interest is in sociological aspects of consumer behavior and marketing, particularly the consequences of social inequality. His research investigates social inequality in the marketplace and addresses public policy and social movement initiatives designed to alleviate it. His research has appeared in leading marketing journals, including the *Journal of Consumer Research, Journal of Public Policy and Marketing,* and *Consumption Markets & Culture,* as well as journals in sociology and public health.

Samantha Cross is an Associate Professor of Marketing in the Debbie and Jerry Ivy College of Business at Iowa State University, USA. Her research examines how diverse entities, identities, perspectives, and beliefs co-exist in consumers, households, and society. She incorporates innovative multi-method approaches in her research, which has been presented in several national and international forums. Her work has been accepted for publication in top marketing journals, including the *Journal of Marketing, International Journal of Research in Marketing, Journal of Public Policy and Marketing, Journal of Advertising, European Journal of Marketing,* and *Consumption Markets & Culture.*

Amber Epp is an Associate Professor of Marketing at the University of Wisconsin-Madison's School of Business, USA. Her research focuses on understanding collective phenomena, including the interplay of family and relational identities, collective goals, network agency, and group decision-making. Her work has been published in the *Journal of Consumer Research* and *Journal of Marketing,* and she has co-authored book chapters on qualitative data analysis, family consumption behavior, and assemblage theory. Professor Epp also serves on the editorial review board for the *Journal of Marketing* and *Journal of Consumer Research,* and is a member of the JCR Policy Board.

Burçak Ertimur is an Associate Professor of Marketing at the Silberman College of Business at Fairleigh Dickinson University, New Jersey, USA. Her research examines value co-creation and its sociocultural dynamics with implications for marketing strategy, brand management, and market dynamics. She has published in the *Journal of Marketing, Marketing Theory, Journal of Business Research,* and *Journal of Interactive Marketing.* Her work on consumer-generated advertising has been supported by the Marketing Science Institute and received recognitions by the Society for Marketing Advances and the Academy of Marketing Science.

Markus Giesler is a consumer sociologist and ethnographer specializing in the study of dynamic market systems. He is an Associate Professor of marketing at York University's Schulich School of Business in Toronto, Canada. He has published in the *Journal of Marketing, Journal of Consumer Research,* and *Marketing Theory.* Giesler is an editorial review board member at the *Journal of Marketing, Journal of Consumer Research, Consumption Markets & Culture, Marketing Letters,* and *Business and Society.* His research has been featured in *The New York Times, Time Magazine, BusinessWeek, Wired,* and a TEDx talk. He blogs about his research at bigdesignlab.com.

Robert Harrison III is an Associate Professor of Marketing at Western Michigan University's Haworth College of Business, USA. His research examines gender, racial, and family identities, qualitative and mixed methodologies, and consumption and organizational rituals. His work has been accepted for publication in the *Journal of Consumer Psychology, Journal of Advertising, Journal of Business Research, Consumption Markets & Culture*, and others. Before pursuing his academic career, Harrison worked as a business news reporter.

Paul Henry is Associate Professor at the University of Sydney Business School, Australia. His research focuses on social class and consumption. He has also examined the relationship between political ideology and consumer rights. This work has been published in journals such as the *Journal of Consumer Research, Marketing Theory, European Journal of Marketing, Consumption Markets & Culture*, and the *Journal of Public Policy and Marketing*.

Elif Izberk-Bilgin is Associate Professor of Marketing at the University of Michigan-Dearborn. Her research focuses on consumer activism, religious ideology in the marketplace, Islamic marketing, and sociological aspects of consumerism in emerging countries. Her work has been published in the *Journal of Consumer Research, Journal of Academy of Marketing Science*, and *Consumption Markets & Culture*. She is the recipient of the 2015 Journal of Consumer Research best paper award and 2012 Sidney J. Levy research award.

Eminegül Karababa is an Associate Professor of Marketing at the Middle East Technical University, Turkey. Her research interests include historical development markets and consumer cultures, and value creation processes in markets. She is currently researching sustainable consumption of Nature Based Solutions as part of a large competitive European Commission grant. Eminegül's research is published in journals such as *Economic History Review, Journal of Consumer Research, Marketing Theory, Consumption Markets & Culture*, and *Journal of Historical Research in Marketing*. She serves as the editor-in-chief for the *Journal of Historical Research in Marketing* and an associate editor for *Consumption Markets & Culture*.

Marius K. Luedicke is a Reader in marketing at Cass Business School, City, University of London, UK. His research explores dynamics of consumer culture its brands with a particular focus on consumer conflicts and moralism. His work has been published in journals such as *Consumption Markets & Culture, Psychology and Marketing*, and the *Journal of Consumer Research*, of which he is also an editorial review board member. His research has been discussed in various international media, including the *New York Times, Huffington Post, The Guardian*, and *Wired*.

Debbie MacInnis is the Charles L. and Ramona I. Hilliard Professor of Business Administration and Professor of Marketing at USC's Marshall School of Business, Los Angeles, USA. Her work focuses on the role of emotions in consumer behavior and branding. She has received the *Journal of Marketing*'s Alpha Kappa Psi and Maynard Awards for the papers that make the greatest contribution to marketing thought and the Long-Term Contribution Award from the *Review of Marketing Research*. She has also been named as a Fellow of the Association for Consumer Research and a Fellow of the Society for Consumer Psychology. She has served as co-editor of the *Journal of Consumer Research*, and associate editor at the *Journal of Consumer Psychology* and the *Journal of Marketing*.

Pauline Maclaran is Professor of Marketing and Consumer Research in the School of Management at Royal Holloway, University of London, UK. Her research interests focus on cultural aspects of contemporary consumption, particularly in relation to gender issues. She is a co-editor in chief of *Marketing Theory*, a journal that promotes alternative and critical perspectives in marketing and consumer research.

Dominique Roux is Professor of Marketing at University of Reims Champagne-Ardenne, France. Her main research interests focus on four main areas: alternative retail channels, collaborative consumption, consumer resistance, and consumer protection. She has coordinated the ANR/NACRE international project (New Approaches to Consumer REsistance). She served as guest editor of a special issue (2011) on Anti-Consumption and Consumer Resistance in the *European Journal of Marketing*. Her research has appeared in the *Journal of Retailing*, *Journal of Business Research*, *Marketing Theory*, *Journal of Macromarketing*, *Consumption Markets & Culture*, *Recherche et Applications en Marketing*, of which she is an editorial board member, and *Décisions Marketing*, for which she serves as associate editor.

Daiane Scaraboto is Assistant Professor of Marketing at Pontificia Universidad Católica de Chile. Her research projects converge around examining the multiple roles consumers assume in markets – and that lead to the creation, shaping, or destruction of consumption opportunities for themselves and for others. Her work has been published in the *Journal of Consumer Research*, *Journal of Macromarketing*, and *Journal of Marketing Management*, among others.

Hope Jensen Schau is Eller Professor of Marketing at The University of Arizona, USA. She earned her PhD from the University of California, Irvine. Her research focuses on the impact of technology on the marketplace and has appeared in top-tier journals including the *Journal of Consumer Research*, *Journal of Marketing*, *Journal of Retailing*, *Journal of Public Policy and Marketing*, and *Journal of Advertising*. She is academic fellow leading the Filene Institute's Center for Excellence in Consumer Decision Making.

Avi Shankar is Professor of Consumer Research in the School of Management at the University of Bath, UK. His research interests fall within two of CCT's major domains: studies of marketplace cultures and consumer identity projects. He is currently exploring process-orientated approaches to reimagine core concepts in marketing and consumer behavior theory.

Zahra Sharifonnasabi is a Lecturer in Marketing at the School of Business and Management, Queen Mary, University of London, UK. Her research explores the impact of globalization on different aspects of consumers' lives, particularly, consumer mobilities, consumption of global brands, and consumer empowerment. Zahra's research tends to be multidisciplinary in nature and have implications regarding everyday consumers' lives, including consumers' relation with places and consumer markets, consumer identity, and consumption taste.

Kevin D. Thomas, PhD is an educator, analyst, and activist scholar. His research focuses on the socio-political impact of marketing communication and consumer behavior. Dr Thomas explores how identity markers (i.e. race, gender, class, and sexuality) are represented in marketing and experienced in the marketplace. Kevin's research is informed by 10 years of industry experience as a market researcher. His research is featured in the *Journal of Public Policy and Marketing, Journal of Advertising, Consumption Markets & Culture*, among others. He is co-founder of Food for Black Thought, the Black Media Council, and co-organizer of the Race in the Marketplace Network (RIM).

Tandy Chalmers Thomas is an Assistant Professor of Marketing at the Stephen J.R. Smith School of Business at Queen's University, Kingston, Canada. Her research, encompassing a variety of methodological techniques, examines how the social contexts in which individuals are embedded, as well as their individual and collective identities, influences their consumption behaviors. Her work is published in the *Journal of Consumer Research* and the *Journal of Advertising* and has been presented at numerous international conferences. Tandy is also a member of the editorial review board for the *Journal of Consumer Research* and serves as an ad hoc reviewer for several additional marketing and consumer behavior journals.

Craig J. Thompson is the Churchill Professor of Marketing at the University of Wisconsin-Madison, USA. He has published in a wide range of marketing, consumer research, and sociological journals. He has co-authored the book *The Phenomenology of Everyday Life* and co-edited *Sustainable Lifestyles and the Quest for Plenitude: Case Studies of the New Economy*. Craig has served as an associate editor for the *Journal of Consumer Research* and *Journal of Consumer Culture*. Craig is the current president of the Consumer Culture Theory Consortium. Craig was the Society for Marketing Advances 2014 Distinguished Marketing Scholar. In 2017, he was named an Association of Consumer Research Fellow.

Ela Veresiu is an Assistant Professor of Marketing at York University's Schulich School of Business, Toronto, Canada. Her research, which focuses on understanding the political dynamics of markets and consumption, has been funded by the Schulich School of Business and the European Research Council, published in the *Journal of Consumer Research and Marketing Theory*, and featured by, among others, *Fast Company, Pacific Standard*, the *Globe and Mail*, and *Huffington Post*. Veresiu is a reviewer for the *Journal of*

Consumer Research, Consumption Markets & Culture, and *Journal of Business Ethics*, among other journals.

Luca M. Visconti is Professor of Marketing at USI – Università della Svizzera italiana, Lugano, Switzerland and Affiliate Professor at ESCP Europe, Paris, France. A CCT scholar, his research covers consumer vulnerability and wellbeing, luxury brand management, and brand storytelling. His work has appeared in *Consumption Markets & Culture*, *Industrial Marketing Management*, the *Journal of Advertising*, *Journal of Consumer Research*, *Journal of Macromarketing*, and *Marketing Theory*, among others. His latest edited book is *Marketing Management: A Cultural Perspective* (with L. Peñaloza and N. Toulouse). He is also Visiting Professor at Università Bocconi, Milan, and Adjunct Professor at Sciences Po and at IFM – Institut Français de la Mode, Paris.

Michelle Weinberger is Associate Professor at the Medill School of Journalism, Media, Integrated Marketing Communications at Northwestern University, Illinois, USA. Her research focuses on how people use consumption to create and span symbolic boundaries through analyses of substantive arenas such as collective rituals, gift giving, and social class. A second stream of research examines how marketing communications create meaning for stakeholders and consumers and the effects of these communications. Weinberger's research is published in the *Journal of Consumer Research*, *European Journal of Marketing*, *International Journal of Advertising*, and *Journal of Advertising Research*. She serves on the board of the Consumer Culture Theory Consortium.

INTRODUCTION

What Is Consumer Culture Theory?

Eric J. Arnould, Aalto University
Business School, Helsinki
Craig J. Thompson,
University of Wisconsin–Madison

This textbook systematically explores the rich mosaic of consumer culture and the ways it affects personal identity, social interactions, and affiliations, and not to be overlooked, behaviors in the commercial marketplace. Most fundamentally, *Consumer Culture Theory* addresses how these interrelations are manifested across a wide range of consumption contexts and brings to light core commonalities, revealing points of distinction, that help us better understand why consumers do what they do and why consumer culture takes the forms it does. To begin this exploration, let us consider two quite different consumption contexts in which consumers pursue a common quest to transcend constraints on their identities and forge meaningful connections with others who share common passions. In both cases, consumers enlist commercial products, services, experiences, and ideals towards their individual and collective ends.

TOUGH MUDDER

We paraphrase below a journalistic account from *The Atlantic* magazine (Khazan 2017).

Most office workers sit for 10 hours a day, but if they sign up for the Tough Mudder, a military-style obstacle course, they'll certainly be on their feet – running through live electrical wires. They'll also be on their hands, swinging from treacherous-looking monkey bars, and on their stomachs, crawling through the mud. And yet, millions of people have paid about $100 each for the privilege.

Rebecca Scott, a lecturer at Cardiff Business School in Wales, sought to explore this paradox when she was working on her PhD dissertation. Initially focused on the psychology of hedonism and pleasure, she was interviewing competitive offshore yacht racers in Sydney,

Australia, when one day a skipper mused to her, 'Why do people want to sit on a boat for days and get pummeled with weather?' as she recalled. That, she decided, was a more interesting question: Why would comfortable Westerners want to pay for physical pain?

For a new study, Scott and her co-authors, Julien Cayla at Nanyang Business School in Singapore and Bernard Cova at the Kedge Business School in France, participated in Tough Mudders, interviewed 26 participants, and read online forums created by the Tough Mudder community to try to understand what motivates people to run these races.

In their conversations with Scott and each other, the participants emphasized how painful it was to train for and compete in the Mudder – and how rewarding that pain felt in the end. Here's how a man named James described the 'Arctic Enema' obstacle, in which participants slide into a dumpster full of ice water, on his blog: 'I can't breathe. My legs aren't working. My head is going to explode! My arms are too cold to drag me out. That was horrendous.'

As the event wore on, many participants described dissociating from their thoughts, as though in a zen state of unity with their mud-caked bodies. A man named Mike said, 'I wasn't feeling bad, but I wasn't feeling good, I don't know how to explain it, I wasn't in shock, I wasn't worried, I wasn't in pain, but I wasn't all there, I was a bit rattled.'

Scott and her colleagues argue that 'Mike's experience of not being "all there" is consistent with past research arguing that extreme pain obliterates "the contents of consciousness"'. The intense pain helps them to forget, temporarily, the hyper-mental concerns of their daily lives as cubicle drones.

Scott argues that, in a way, Tough Mudders and other painful forms of exercise allow people to 'rediscover' their physical bodies, as revealed in participant comments like, 'I hurt in places I didn't even know existed' (Khazan 2017).

COSPLAY

All over the world, cosplay fans gather at conventions and parties to share their appreciation of and affection for anime and manga. These fans, who also refer to themselves as *otaku*, wear detailed makeup and elaborate costumes modeled after their favorite anime, manga, and related video game characters. Cosplayers spend immeasurable amounts of money and hours constructing or purchasing the components of costumes, learning signature poses and dialogue, and performing at comics conventions and parties, as they transform themselves from 'real world' identities into chosen (fictional) characters. This is the essence of cosplay, or *kosupure* (Winge 2006).

Cosplay also refers to the activities, such as masquerades, karaoke, and posing for pictures with other *otaku*, that are associated with dressing and acting like anime, manga, and video game characters. While the term cosplay encompasses various types of costumed role-playing, such as science fiction, fantasy, horror, mythology, fetish, and so forth, Japanese and North American cosplay related to Japanese anime, manga, and video games perhaps enjoys the widest popularity (Allison 2014).

The game designer Takahashi Nobuyuki coined the term *cosplaying* in the 1980s when he encountered the costuming practices of American science fiction fans on a visit to the United States. In Japan, cosplay has become very prominent. Many Western fans nowadays learn about costuming not through science fiction or fantasy genres, but through Japanese fiction. As a fan practice, cosplay is associated with Japanese anime (cartoons), manga (comics), and games. Fans usually wear their costumes in specific settings, such as during particular events at conventions (e.g. competitions, fashion shows), or as props for fan videos (Lamerichs 2011).

To the uninitiated, cosplay can seem like little more than a glorified costume party, a Halloween dress-up parade at the wrong time of the year. But where a costume party ensemble is picked simply to amuse, many cosplayers feel a deeper connection with their chosen character that elevates the experience from mere dress-up to a more profound experience. They don't just don the same outfit as a beloved character; they adopt the same mannerisms, posture and accent, embodying the character rather than just imitating (Bastow 2014).

Cosplay is a highly competitive field with an almost endless supply of opportunities to accumulate social status and prestige among fans and other cosplay participants. Constructing costumes and expertly performing characters as well as making costumes for others as a small business, enrich the experience. Thus, cosplay is an emotionally rewarding practice that combines intrinsically pleasurable DIY costume crafting with intoxicating identity play at conventions. Cosplay participants experiment not only with the performance of fictional entities' character but may also experiment with the performance of gender in male-to-female and female-to-male transformations into the iconic media characters. To do so, participants make complex investments in emotional labor and skill building (Seregina and Weijo 2017).

This book aims to help you make sense of spectacular consumer behaviors like these but also the mundane practices that make up our lives in a market-driven, global consumer culture.

CONSUMER CULTURE THEORY: WHAT IS IT?

Consumer culture theorists are fascinated by phenomena such as Tough Mudder and cosplay. They seek to unravel their secrets and, in so doing, provide a more robust and nuanced understanding of global consumer culture and the market-mediated society that molds our lives as consumers within this world. This book aims to share and help the reader develop a consumer culture perspective of their own. In the following pages, we define consumer culture theory, outline its general contours with the help of some recent examples, and finally outline the book itself.

Consumer culture theory (CCT) is a field of inquiry that seeks to unravel the complexities of consumer culture. Rather than viewing culture as a fairly homogenous system of collectively shared meanings, ways of life and unifying values shared by a member of society (e.g. Americans share this kind of culture, Japanese share that kind of culture), CCT explores the heterogeneous distribution of meanings and the multiplicity of overlapping cultural groupings that exist within the broader socio-historical frame of globalization and market capitalism. From a CCT standpoint, consumer culture is as a dynamic network of boundary spanning material, economic, symbolic, and social relationships or connections. Consumer culture is what consumers do and believe rather than an attribute of character. Similarly, 'being a consumer' is an identity intrinsic to market capitalism, our dominant global economic system, and the two evolve and develop in tandem. Concretely, as Don Slater (1997) proposes, consumer culture denotes a social arrangement in which markets either directly or indirectly mediate the relationships between lived experiences, that is, between meaningful ways of life and the symbolic and material resources like brands on which they depend.

Again, following Don Slater, the consumption of market-made commodities and desire-inducing commercialized symbols is central to consumer culture. At the same time, the perpetuation and reproduction of this system is largely dependent upon the exercise of personal choice in the private sphere of everyday life, that is, the choice to choose among commercialized offerings. The term consumer culture also conceptualizes an interconnected system of commercially produced images, texts, and objects that groups use – through the construction of overlapping and even conflicting consumption practices, identities, and meanings – to make collective sense of their environments and to anchor and orient their members' experiences and lives.

Arnould and Thompson's (2005) CCT framework is a heuristic mapping of CCT research along for four key, interrelated theoretical dimensions. These four dimensions, in a somewhat modified form, have also provided the organizing template for this book. They are (1) Consumer Identity Projects; (2) Marketplace Cultures; (3) The Socio-historic Patterning of Consumption; and (4) Mass-Mediated Marketplace Ideologies and Consumers' Interpretive Strategies (see Arnould and Thompson 2005).

These theoretical dimensions highlight systematic commonalities among CCT studies that manifest diversity in terms of methodological orientations (e.g. ethnography, phenomenology, multiple schools of textual analyses, historical methods, web-based methods) and they encompass an array of theoretical traditions (variously drawing from sociology, anthropology, literary criticism, critical theory, and feminist studies to name a few). And of course, CCT researchers deploy this theoretical system to explicate substantive issues emanating from the acquisition, use, and disposition of commercially circulated products, services, knowledge, images, and experiences by groups and individual actors.

To explain these four clusters of theoretical and practical interests in a bit more detail, consumer identity projects align CCT with the cultural studies focus on identity work and the negotiation of cultural contradictions through the marketplace, as well as the commodification of cultural rituals and emotions. Researchers ask questions like: Why is identity such an issue in consumer culture? How do consumers pursue their identity projects? How do they use commercially circulated products, services, knowledge, images, and experiences to construct identities? What meanings do consumers pursue? How does a sense of selfhood form in market-mediated societies? What problems does globalization of consumer culture pose to individuals in diverse cultural contexts?

To take one example, Jafari and Goulding (2008) analyze the different meanings of consumption and consumer identities for young adult Iranians in their home country and, subsequently, in their expatriate locales in the UK. In the former case, study participants described using consumption to resist theocratic restrictions imposed on their identity practices. Participation in Western consumer culture became a risk-laden expression of defiance and liberty (see the recent trend among Iranian women to post 'uncovered' selfies on social media sites). Once ensconced in the UK, however, these immigrant consumers struggled to address the overwhelming array of 'free' market choices and the unnerving obligation to construct an 'authentic' identity that often conflicted with internalized Iranian moral codes. But, they also used consumption to enact a visible degree of Westernization and thereby ease suspicions that they might be a threat to the civic order. In both settings, these consumers experienced themselves as the subjects of panoptic social surveillance, though taking different forms. Facing these contrasting and potentially disempowering conditions, their consumption practices sought freedom from theocratic restriction (which could afford a more expressive identity project) and, later, freedom to live in anonymity, rather than as subjects of perpetual suspicion.

Over time, CCT research has expanded its initial theoretical focus on consumer experiences and their practices of identity construction through the use of marketplace resources. Beginning in the late 1990s, CCT researchers became increasingly interested in the question of how processes of social structuration – gender and class-based socialization, collective social and cultural formations, naturalized cultural ideologies, and enduring inequities in the distribution of capital – shape and are shaped by consumption practices and consumer individual and collective identity projects. This turn has animated three other clusters of research in consumer culture theory.

The socio-historic patterning of consumption aligns CCT with sociological and historical research on the role of class, gender, and ethnicity as structural influences on marketplace behaviors and vice versa. Researchers ask questions like: How do consumers use consumption to express and remake sociological categories like gender, age, ethnicity, and nationality? How do immigrants assimilate through consumption? How does consumption reinforce or challenge social boundaries? How does market-mediated society assimilate diverse peoples to the contemporary 'consumer' template? Who or what is a consumer?

To take an example, David Crockett (2017) investigates and illuminates the intersection of race, class, culture, and consumption. He historicizes 'the politics of respectability', which has been a prominent feature of middle-class African American culture since their emancipation from slavery in 1863. He further analyzes the contemporary influences exerted by this multifaceted ideology. Through the politics of respectability middle-class African American consumers make a claim to legitimate citizenship (and thereby seek to rebuke disparaging racial stereotypes). Their legitimating, de-stigmatizing practices of racial uplift draw from the Protestant work ethic, Christian piety, and an ethos of self-discipline that embody principles of comportment and decorum characteristic of a professional class work milieu. Crockett further argues that this uplift strategy aligns with the twin practices of entrepreneurial self-development and oppositional respectability, whereby African Americans use the marketplace and conspicuous consumption practices to reclaim selected aspects of black culture from negative associations circulated by dominant racialized institutional discourses in popular media.

The interest in marketplace cultures aligns CCT with anthropological studies on material culture and the role of everyday practices and rituals in creating institutional forms of social and familial solidarity. Research on brand communities, for example, highlights the way in which technology and market structures facilitate new forms of communal organization and rituals of solidarity. At the same time, a new generation of studies has explored specific tensions between local and global meanings systems and institutions. Researchers ask questions like: How do communities form in market-mediated society? What forms does community take in market-mediated society? How do 'taste' cultures emerge? How do consumers participate in, or precipitate market emergence? How do consumers create value through collective association?

To take another example, Sandıkcı and Ger (2010) detail the emergence of the market for *tesettür* fashion, which involves an intersection of political Islam, familiar market channels, and the strategic use of economic and cultural capital. *Tesettür* began as metropolitan professional women appropriated a dressing practice that had formerly been associated with the impoverished and less educated rural sector of Turkish society. These formerly secular women embraced political Islam and sought to destigmatize veiling practices. Leveraging their economic capital and the cultural capital acquired through their middle-class upbringing, formal education, and, most of all, lifelong immersion in the sphere of secularized consumer culture, assisted by profit-seeking market intermediaries, these women remade the once stodgy and unflattering *tesettür* style of dress into a more urbane, appealing, and hybridized fashion style. These aestheticizing transformations led to the emergence of an upscale *tesettür* market of designers, retailers and middle-class clientele that not only legitimated this mode of public presentation but also further mainstreamed political Islam as a countervailing ideology to the secular legacy of Kemal Atatürk, the Turkish nation's founding father.

Mass-mediated ideologies and consumers interpretive strategies aligns CCT with the critical theory tradition that examines the ideological bases of consumer culture and resistance thereto, and contemporary media studies research on the active and creative media user. Consumer culture theorists argue that consumers creatively and constructively rework mass media and advertising messages in ways that often run against the grain of their corporate encoded meanings. This stream of research examines how consumers exert agency and pursue identity goals through a dialogue (both practical and narrative) with the cultural frames imposed by dominant commercial ideologies. Researchers ask questions like: What are the ideological underpinnings of consumer societies? How do consumers make sense of these ideologies? How do resistant and divergent consumer ideologies form? How do such ideologies take material form in consumer goods and services? How do new technologies and markets become legitimate objects of consumer desire?

CCT studies have explored the power relations manifest in consumption and market-mediated relationships, such as the cultural discourses and systems of classification that normalize certain consumer identities and practices while casting others as problematic or deviant. Thus, some of this work looks at how body weight has become entangled with moral judgments of good and bad that deeply stigmatize some consumers. More broadly this research looks at how recent consumer ideology inculcates in us particular self-management models such that consumers who fail to take 'responsibility' for their diets, physical fitness, and health are deemed to threaten the moral order and everyday standards of propriety.

Mapping the diversity of empirical research into four clusters of theoretical interest provides an orienting device. It is a useful framework for organizing the materials presented in this book. It can also help a masters or doctoral student researcher identify a subset of CCT research questions and findings that have the most relevance for his/her given study, or reciprocally to discern important questions; identify boundary conditions; re-think research contexts as venues for programmatic theoretical contribution; and more broadly, to identify domains of theoretical concern that have not been addressed by prior CCT studies.

WHERE DID IT COME FROM?

CCT emerged as a corrective to the overly rationalistic and utilitarian view of the consumer that predominated in business schools up until the 1980s. This conventional orientation was based on the idea that consumers were rational decision-makers, most concerned with the functional benefits of goods, and maximizing subjective utility. Consumer research based on these rational-utilitarian assumptions invested considerable effort in studying how factors, such as pricing, product assortments, retailing systems and formats, and information presentation in advertising and public relations, for example, influenced consumers' decision-making strategies. This substantial body of research had little to say about what fascinated early CCT researchers: consumers' desires, the consumption experiences that arose after purchases or the ways in which consumers meaningfully integrated brands and commercial services into their personal and social lives. For example, one of us conducted research on American Thanksgiving Day celebrations, which is the most widely celebrated holiday in the United States. We discovered that through this consumption ritual people perform important ideas about American social life. They celebrate the specific beliefs about family pooling and redistribution of resources, women's nurturing role in the household, and a belief in the abundance of basic consumption opportunities for all. At Thanksgiving, family members often make heroic efforts to come together across time and space, even though members may experience considerable mutual ambivalence during most of the year. Participants vigorously recollect the past, imagine the future, and negotiate their relationships in the kitchens and around the dining tables and games that bring together families and even strangers 'with nowhere else to go' on Thanksgiving Day. Through cooking and following what they claim are old family recipes, people celebrate skills and in turn are celebrated. They work out their dietary preferences and establish just what a 'homemade' meal actually means. They often believe they celebrate just like everyone else although we found quite a variety of distinctive ways of celebrating this holiday. It is a very busy event (Wallendorf and Arnould 1991).

In the early 1980s, the scholars who formed the nexus of what would become CCT drew on distinctive theoretical and methodological sources to address these overlooked topics (Arnould 1989; Belk 1988; Hirschman 1986; McCracken 1988a; Sherry 1983). Whereas traditional consumer and marketing research had been inspired by economic and psychological theory, the nascent CCT field drew upon anthropology, design, history, literary criticism, semiotics, sociology, and social psychology. Owing to fundamental differences in the subject matter of interest, that is, the whole cycle of consumption, and the theoretical orientations chosen, CCT scholars pursued methods designed to understand what people were up to in their consumption activities. Thus, the approaches adopted relied on qualitative methods such as existential phenomenological inquiry if the focus was on individual action and on ethnographic methods if the focus of interest was collective action. In both cases, the goal was understanding how consumption experiences were shaped by webs of cultural meanings and the symbolic value that consumption goods (and the practices that put them into use) served in consumers' personal and collective life projects.

LOOKING TO THE FUTURE

Though CCT has an academic origin, its approach has found application in the managerial sphere, as brand managers realized that cultural meanings, consumer collectivities and social affiliations, and consumer identity projects, are integral to the market success of brands (Atkin 2004; Fournier and Lee 2009; Holt 2004; McCracken 2009). This is why nowadays anthropologists and designers inspired by cultural insights find positions in many companies and in successful consulting firms like the Practica Group, ReD Associates, Stripe Partners, or the :Anthropik network. Moreover, the cultural approaches inspired by CCT have lead a number of scholars to apply them to the task of reimagining marketing management from a cultural perspective, as for instance in Sunderland and Denny (2007), Holt and Cameron (2010) or Madsbjerg and Rasmussen (2014).

Doug Holt (2017) has proposed an approach to research that he terms Consumer Culture Strategy to drive substantive engagements with significant real world problems – climate change, poverty, inequality, shortfalls in the distribution of health care services. Holt's consumer culture strategist would pursue his/her project by building expertise in the social problem domain; designing and conducting research that can address gaps in practice and building problem-solving models that can redress those gaps. For a CCS-oriented researcher, theory becomes a means to the larger end of combatting the larger social/policy problem. Holt (2017) also suggests that research following a consumer culture strategy should be diffused through platforms such as books, blogs, think tank white papers, and practitioner-oriented journals. A good example of this type of approach is that adopted by Linda Scott, a contributor to foundational feminist CCT scholarship (Scott and Penaloza 2006). In recent years, she has devoted her efforts to the promoting and publicizing what she calls the XX economy, a gynocentric vision of economic relations, with special focus on the developing world. Her network manifests a blog, aggregates projects devoted to women's empowerment, engages in advocacy directed to governmental and intergovernmental organizations, and develops teaching cases on women's empowerment (see www.doublexeconomy.com/). Consumer Culture Theorists might also take inspiration from the Ethnographic Praxis in Industry Conference (EPIC) group composed primarily of practitioner ethnographers and designers. EPIC has begun to develop just such a platform as Holt proposes (see www.epicpeople.org/).

ABOUT THIS BOOK

Consumer culture theory is an exciting world of research and reflection on the 'what?' 'when?', 'where?' and 'how?' of consumer behavior set in its global and socio-historic context. It aims to unpack the secrets of spectacular phenomena like Tough Mudder and cosplay described above. But as you will find in these pages consumer culture research offers insight into both the deeper historical roots of consumer culture and the everyday experiences of navigating our market-mediated world as consumers. So welcome to the world of CCT scholarship. The remainder of this introduction briefly outlines the sections and chapters and provides a rationale for inclusion of these topics. What you will find in this book are 14 chapters each authored by a unique team or individual specialist in the topics covered. Thus, each chapter has a slightly different style, a slightly different feel particular to the authors, although they all include similarly formatted content. As you read you are looking over the shoulders of the experts who with their research collaborators and industry, civic society, and government partners are actively making the field of consumer culture theory.

The first three chapters address a phenomenon that is simultaneously a central feature of contemporary consumer society, a prime topic of study in consumer culture theory, as well as the imagined target of global marketing apparatus – the consumer or more accurately, the identity of the consuming human being. As we said earlier, economists and many policy-makers presume the consuming subject is the active source of choices and behaviors that produce and reproduce consumer society over time and across space. We know from important scholarly work (Colin Campbell 1987; Marcel Mauss 1985/1938; Marshall Sahlins 1976, 1996; Max Weber 2003/1920) that the modern individual, you and us included, is a relatively recent and unique historical product. Nowadays, the consumer self is globalized throughout the world although taking different forms that reflect regional and local socio-historical shaping forces. The perpetuation of a market society depends on an endlessly proliferating stream of commercial offerings. In turn, consumer culture embeds individual selves in a logic in which selfhood depends upon we consumers asserting our distinctive selfhood through acquiring, rejecting or discarding these commercial offerings. Chapter 1 by Hope Schau offers an extended inquiry into Western conceptions of, and the implications of these conceptions for, consumer culture theory. The reader can find further reflections on the consumer self in Chapter 11 that traces out how contemporary neoliberal political and economic ideas shape our understanding of our consumer selves and our 'responsibilities' as consumers. Similarly, Chapter 10 on global mobilities discusses how massive flows of goods, ideas, images, and people produce different ways people think of themselves and their consumption. Meantime, Chapter 2 by Amber Epp and Tandy Chalmers Thomas, develops a point of which we all are aware, that individuals' identities and senses of self form and reform over the life course by way of our interaction with intimate others in households. Moreover, these identities are also co-created in a material nexus of commercial commodities and things that have been personalized through family members' interaction among themselves and with these things during important life events. Chapter 3 by Michelle Weinberger and David Crockett provides a critical perspective on consumer identity work. Much consumer research, whether of an economic, psychological or cultural bent, focuses on a consumer who is presumed to be agentic; that is, a being who can and does make choices in the furtherance of her own interests. However, agentic acts of consumption are subject to social influences and constraints in ways that people do not readily recognize. There are dominant, that is, socially approved, consumer identities and there are subordinated consumer identities. The latter are sometimes negatively sanctioned or stigmatized on the basis of demographic or cultural characteristics. That relationship between dominate and subordinate consumer identities is the theme of Weinberger and Crockett's contribution.

The second part of the book focuses on marketplace cultures. In Chapter 4, Bernard Cova and Avi Shankar outline the nature of these collectivities in consumer culture. Anthropology and history are adorned with examples of human groups larger than the family through which people express their humanity, their dreams, their fears, and their creative ambitions. From Australian totemic groupings, to Amazonian tribes, from Sierra Leonian secret societies to ancient Greek Dionysian cults, from schools and movements in art, music, and sculpture to poetic and literary traditions, people have expressed their affiliations in innumerable ways. So too, as Cova and Shankar reveal, consumer culture is cross-cut with consumer subcultures, tribes, communities and publics. They show that each of these forms of social life develop distinctive relationships to commercial market offerings, and how in turn these relationships inevitably affect what marketers bring to the marketplace. Particularly notable with the rise of Web 2.0, an aspect of everyday life of which all readers of this text must be deeply aware, is the heightened influence of consumers on the marketplace. If from the late 18th to the late 20th century, consumers' economic role was to choose among offerings made available by producers, Web 2.0 has changed this dynamic. Thus, in Chapter 5, Eminegül Karababa and Daiane Scaraboto trace out the emergence of contemporary markets and the active role that consumers take in forging and forming new markets, market forms, and offerings. Indeed, their work leads us to ask whether this old 18th century distinction between producer and consumer – or between supply and demand as economists term it – is still meaningful in contemporary consumer culture. Unique to our era is the truly global extension of market-based society and consumer culture. Building on this idea, Chapter 6, co-authored by Gokcen Coskuner-Balli and Burçak Ertimur, discusses the effects of this pan-global globalization on consumer culture. They point out how the interaction between a consumer culture that took full form in Euro-American contexts inevitably produces global-local, or glocal, hybrids as it takes root in regions of the world with dramatically different socio-historical experiences such as West, South and East Asia, for example. Of course, globalization is not a one-way street; it is constituted of global flows of ideas, things, people, money, and consumer practices of all sorts. Thus, they provide compelling examples of how market society trans-forms local activities into global consumption goods on an accelerating scale.

Part Three, the third and longest section of our text, addresses the socio-historic patterning of consumption. This section explores in detail how market-mediated society and consumer culture has modified and even produced, as well as been affected by, distinctions of gender, ethnicity, and class. Further, authors develop the theme of globalization to suggest how globalized consumer culture 'liquefies' some of these seemingly solid groupings. Chapter 7, contributed by Paul Henry and Marylouise Caldwell, dives into the topic of social class. Their work builds on the classic foundation provided by Karl Marx showing how capitalist market society divides people into groups based on their economic status, basically those who have labor and those who have capital. But, their analysis then goes on to build on more contemporary understandings of market-mediated society which suggest that our social relationships and cultural knowledge likewise become assets that we use to obtain and make use of market offerings in building our identities and connecting with, or disconnecting from, groups that are significant to us.

Every society makes use of gender to organize many aspects of economic and social life. Beliefs and practices concerning biological sex and gender are deeply ingrained cultural constructs. Consumer culture is no different, as Chapter 8, co-authored by Luca Visconti, Pauline Maclaran, and Shona Bettany elaborates. The authors remind us that because markets thrive on change and diversity, in consumer culture gender roles are always in flux. The authors develop the ways in which marketing intersects with gender. They discuss the troubles that unfold due to gender stereotyping in marketing practice and marketing communications. They discuss the ways in which consumption is implicated in performing, resisting, and reformulating gender roles. They point out that branded products and services are strongly linked to gender roles, and gender affects how people respond to marketing practices.

Chapter 9, co-authored by Kevin D. Thomas, Samantha N.N. Cross, and Robert L. Harrison III, illuminates the complex relationships between consumer culture, race, and ethnicity. The authors show how these terms all refer to socially constructed characteristics of particular groups, but the implications of these social constructions differ markedly both in consumer culture and society more generally. The construct of race focuses heavily on the visible, physical characteristics of people. Ironically, while race is the most superficial and least differentiating of these three social constructions, it is, as these authors demonstrate, an influential and divisive marketplace identifier that groups and separates people on the basis of quite arbitrary distinctions. Crockett's (2017) work, as we discussed above, shows that consumers adopt distinctive strategies to contend with racial marketplace identifiers.

Following classic theories from social science, consumer theorists have tended to treat subculture, ethnicity, race, and social class as stable structural factors influencing consumers' behaviors. Chapter 10, co-authored by Fleura Bardhi, Marius Luedicke, and Zahra Sharifonnasabi, provides a more contemporary perspective on how globalization accelerates the movement of people, products, ideas, and images, not to mention money, which can dramatically upend local social structures. Global mobilities can take different forms from economic and political migration to global nomadism. Global nomads are pioneers in what the authors term liquid consumption, a kind of hyper-cosmopolitan consumer lifestyle that prioritizes flexibility and adaptability in consumption practice. For consumers, global mobility can be a source of capital accumulation, potential social mobility, as well as empowerment. However, global mobilities are challenging and can also result in feelings of homelessness, and may lead to social isolation and challenge one's sense of personal security. Some migrant consumers use what is called compensatory consumption to cope with these feelings whereas locals may resist their efforts. Owing to these social tensions and conflicts, consumption may not always bring the sense of completion migrant consumers may want.

The last three chapters in this book reflect consumer culture theorists' defining interest in the role of ideology in shaping consumer behavior and in turn as shaped by consumers' creative employment of commercial resources. Ideology consists of values, norms, beliefs, meanings, symbols, and customs; it is a common framework of understanding of 'how we do things around here', or a worldview. Ideology is a common horizon, an intellectual heritage, and set of shared beliefs linked to social practices and integrated into key political and economic institutions (Press et al. 2014: 104). An essential reference point for this discussion is Chapter 11, co-authored by Ela Veresiu and Markus Giesler, neoliberalism and consumption. The chapter traces out the history and implications of neoliberal ideology, one of the dominant ideologies of our time. They show that neoliberalism complements market capitalism by presenting the satisfaction of individual interests through consumption as a responsibility, a right and the lynchpin of the market economy. These ideas resonate with those presented in Chapter 1. The authors also review some examples of responses to neoliberal ideology such as consumer activism and consumer resistance, a theme developed further in Chapter 13. Furthermore, they show how neoliberal ideology produces responses to major social problems that imagine their solution lies in providing consumers with market-based alternatives.

Chapter 12, co-authored by Zeynep Arsel and Jonathan Bean, is an excellent illustration of how consumers contribute to market formation in consumer culture through the development of taste regimes, which are a kind of aesthetic ideology. The famous 'Danish design' is a useful example. These authors also foreground the ways in which complements of objects produce what McCracken (1988b: 118ff) calls Diderot effects, the feeling that some things just go together. Theorists and philosophers have long seen taste as trickling down from the attitudes and behaviors of the upper classes. This chapter provides an overview of how social mobility, globalization, and digital culture is transforming taste in contemporary consumer culture. A key takeaway from this chapter is that taste is not purely individual. Instead, a host of inescapable social influences shapes taste. These influences range from your upbringing in a particular social class milieu to the aesthetic norms and ideals that members of the social cohorts and consumption community share, and in which individual consumers participate and seek to gain acceptance and status.

In Chapter 13 Dominique Roux and Elif Izberk-Bilgin explore the important topic of consumer resistance. Resistance means standing up against what a person or group perceives as a power, a pressure, an influence, or any attempt to act upon one's conduct. Marketing practice and communications can impose norms, prescribe certain behaviors, and convey ideologies that consumers resist. In turn, consumer resistance can be transformative, mobilizing for change in marketplace meanings, practices, and power relationships that enable particular factions of consumers to combat social inequities or collective feelings of disempowerment or injustice.

Chapter 14 provides an afterword to the book. In this concluding chapter, Craig Thompson, Debbie MacInnis, and Eric Arnould offer a perspective that bridges interests of consumer culture theorists and consumer behavior researchers. If the former primarily focus on meso and macro levels of analysis, consumer behavior researchers have tended to focus on micro-level issues related to consumer choice and decision making. The resource perspective bridges these points of view. For example, consumer culture theorists are likely to view economic, cultural (knowledge and taste) and social capital (educational attainment and interpersonal networks) as resources. Consumers use these resources to build identities they think of as authentic, as described in Part One of this book, or link them through authoritative custom and ritual to collectives of the kinds describe in Parts Two and Three of this book (Arnould and Price 2000). Consumer behavior researchers are inclined to think of cognition and memory as precious resources, but also to focus on how people use time and money to make meaningful decisions. Consumer behavior researchers tend to conceive of both time and money as scarce resources. Similarly, a significant body of consumer decision research examines social inclusion, comparison, and exclusion, in other words, the effects of social resources on decision-making and choice (Dahl 2013). Increasingly, these researchers, like consumer culture theorists, are interested in how people make choices that increase meaningfulness and even wellbeing (Aaker 2014).

REFERENCES

Aaker, Jennifer (2014) 'Curation: Meaningful choice', *Journal of Consumer Research*, (Autumn), https://academic.oup.com/jcr/pages/meaningful_choice.

Allison, Peter Ray (2014) 'Cosplay: "It is fun to be someone entirely different"', *The Guardian*, 13 May. www.theguardian.com/lifeandstyle/2014/may/13/cosplay-sci-fi-weekender-dressing-up-fantasy-characters.

Arnould, Eric J. (1989) 'Toward a broadened theory of preference formation and the diffusion of innovations: Cases from Zinder Province, Niger Republic', *Journal of Consumer Research*, *16* (September): 239–67.

Arnould, Eric J. and Price, Linda L. (2000) 'Authenticating acts and authoritative performances: questing for self and community', in S. Ratneshwar, David Glen Mick, and Cynthia Huffman (eds), *The Why of Consumption: Contemporary Perspectives on Consumers Motives, Goals, and Desires*. New York and London: Routledge. pp. 140–63.

Arnould, E.J. and Thompson, C. J. (2005) 'Consumer culture theory (CCT): Twenty years of research', *Journal of Consumer Research, 31* (4): 868–82.

Atkin, Douglas (2004) *The Culting of Brands: Turn Your Customers into True Believers*. New York: Portfolio.

Bastow, Clem (2014) 'Cosplay: It's more than just "a glorified costume party"', *The Guardian*, 8 July www.theguardian.com/culture/australia-culture-blog/2014/jul/08/cosplay-its-more-than-just-a-glorified-costume-party.

Belk, Russell W. (1988) 'Possessions and the extended self', *Journal of Consumer Research, 15* (September): 139–68.

Campbell, Colin (1987) *The Romantic Ethic and the Spirit of Modern Consumerism*. Oxford: Basil Blackwell.

Crockett, David (2017) 'Paths to respectability: Consumption and stigma management in the contemporary black middle class', *Journal of Consumer Research, 44* (3): 554–81.

Dahl, Darren (2013) 'Curation: Social influence and consumer behavior', *Journal of Consumer Research*, (Spring), https://academic.oup.com/jcr/pages/social_influence_and_consumer_behavior.

Fournier, Susan and Lee, Lara (2009) 'Getting brand communities right,' *Harvard Business Review*, April, 105–11.

Hirschman, Elizabeth C. (1986) 'Humanistic inquiry in marketing research: Philosophy, method, and criteria', *Journal of Marketing Research, 23* (3): 237–49.

Holt, Douglas B. (2004) *How Brands Become Icons: The Principles of Cultural Branding*. Boston, MA: Harvard Business Press.

Holt, Douglas B. (2017) 'Consumer culture strategy'. Available at www.academia.edu/15574357/Consumer_Culture_Strategy.

Holt, Douglas B. and Cameron, Douglas (2010) *Cultural Strategy: Using Innovative Ideologies to Build Breakthrough Brands*. Oxford: Oxford University Press.

Jafari, Aliakbar and Goulding, Christina (2008) '"We are not terrorists!" UK-based Iranians, consumption practices and the "torn self"', *Consumption Markets & Culture, 11* (June): 73–91.

Khazan, Olga (2017) 'Escaping office ennui through painful exercise: A study explores how Tough Mudders allow the "cognitariat" a break from the tedium of sedentary work', *The Atlantic*, 25 March. www.theatlantic.com/health/archive/2017/03/breaking-the-ennui-of-office-work-through-painful-exercise/520746/.

Lamerichs, Nicolle (2011) 'Stranger than fiction: Fan identity in cosplay,' *Transformative Works and Cultures, 7*. http://dx.doi.org/10.3983/twc.2011.0246.

Madsbjerg, Christian and Rasmussen, Mikkel (2014) *Moment of Clarity*. Boston, MA: Harvard Business School Publishing.

Mauss, Marcel (1985/1938) 'A category of the human mind: The notion of person; the notion of self' (trans. W.D. Halls), in Michael Carrithers, Steven Collins and Steven Lukes (eds), *The Category of the Person: Anthropology, Philosophy, History*. Cambridge: Cambridge University Press. pp. 1–25.

McCracken, Grant (1988a) 'Diderot unities and Diderot effect: Neglected cultural aspects of consumption', in *Culture and Consumption*. Bloomington and Indianapolis: Indiana University Press. pp. 118–29.

McCracken, Grant (1988b) *Culture and Consumption*. Bloomington and Indianapolis: Indiana University Press.

McCracken, Grant (2009) 'Getting past guru' and 'Stealth CCOs', excerpt from *Chief Culture Officer: How to Create a Living, Breathing Corporation*. New York: Basic Books. pp. 5–40.

Press, Melea, Arnould, Eric J., Murray, Jeff B., and Strand, Katie (2014) 'Ideological challenges to changing strategic orientation in commodity agriculture', *Journal of Marketing*, *78* (November): 103–19.

Sahlins, Marshall (1976) *Culture and Practical Reason*. Chicago, IL: University of Chicago Press.

Sahlins, Marshall (1996) 'The sadness of sweetness: The native anthropology of Western cosmology', *Current Anthropology*, *37* (June): 395–428.

Sandıkcı, Özlem and Ger, Güliz (2010) 'Veiling in style: How does a stigmatized practice become fashionable?', *Journal of Consumer Research*, *37* (June): 15–36.

Scott, Linda M., and Lisa Peñaloza (2006) 'Matriarchal Marketing: A Manifesto', *Journal of Strategic Marketing*, *14* (1): 57–67.

Seregina, Anastasia and Weijo, Henri A. (2017) 'Play at any cost: How cosplayers produce and sustain their ludic communal consumption experiences', *Journal of Consumer Research*, *44* (June): 139–59.

Sherry, Jr, John F. (1983) 'Gift giving in anthropological perspective', *Journal of Consumer Research*, *10* (September): 157–68.

Slater, Don (1997) *Consumer Culture and Modernity*. Malden, MA: Blackwell.

Sunderland, Patricia L. and Denny, Rita M. (2007) *Doing Anthropology in Consumer Research*. New York: Routledge.

Wallendorf, Melanie and Arnould, Eric J. (1991) '"We gather together": The consumption rituals of Thanksgiving Day', *Journal of Consumer Research*, *18* (June): 13–31.

Weber, Max (2003/1920) *The Protestant Ethic and the Spirit of Capitalism*. Mineola, NY: Dover Books.

Winge, Theresa (2006) 'Costuming the imagination: Origins of anime and manga cosplay', *Mechademia*, *1*: 65–76.

PART ONE

Consumption and Identity

1

IDENTITY PROJECTS AND THE MARKETPLACE

Hope Jensen Schau,
The University of Arizona

CHAPTER OVERVIEW

- Identity is complex, volitional and relational, consisting of four major constructs: personality, self-concept, identity project, and self-presentation.
- Identity is constructed in the imagination.
- Imagination enables people to conceptualize realities of self, collectives, and materiality.
- Identity projects are strategic configurations of objects, symbols, scripts, and practices to claim particular identity positions.
- Identity projects become manifest as context-driven self-presentations, or identity performances within social settings,
- Consumer imagination is when people use the marketplace and market-mediated objects, symbols, scripts, and practices to enact identity projects, or self-present.

INTRODUCTION

Identity is a complex phenomenon. It encompasses: (1) personality, the set of features that comprise a given person's character, which is thought to be relatively stable and scaffolded by genetically determined traits; (2) self-concept, a collection of beliefs one has about one's self; (3) identity project, the strategic configuration of objects, symbols, scripts, and practices to claim particular identity position; and (4) self-presentation, the performance of an identity project within a social context. In this chapter, personality is set aside as a broader identity construct; for now we leave this to psychologists. Self-concept is addressed insofar as it illuminates identity projects. Here, identity projects are focal, specifically highlighted is how identity projects are enabled by the marketplace and are performed via self-presentation.

Consider how you act across different face-to-face social situations: holidays with family, out on the town with friends, at the gym, engaging in sport (basketball, football, surfing), attending classes, performing on stage (actors, magicians, dancers, musicians), on a job interview. Add to that the ways in which you enact your identity across media: email, text, Skype, Instagram, Pinterest, Reddit, Tinder, Snapchat, YouTube, thredUP, fan forums, blogs. Some may participate in team sports, hobby groups, fan communities, fantasy leagues, and/or cosplay events. What elements of yourself stay constant and what elements change? What different goals are operating across these settings? What props (objects, symbols, scripts, practices) are needed to perform these identity projects? How does the market support your identity performance?

This chapter lays the foundations for examining consumption and its importance in people's lives. The focus, here, is on identity projects, where identity is recognized as volitional, that is, a matter of choices, and that imagination is the process of forming identity. Of central importance is how the market supports identity projects.

ROLES, PERPETUAL BECOMING, AND SELF-NARRATIVE

Identity is not accidental. Even the most seemingly casual or haphazard of identity performances is volitional: created with intention and guided by purpose. Identity projects are complex sets of behaviors and affiliations carried out daily and affected by social context. To move through this complicated world, people have multiple identity projects in play that they juggle depending on context and social role. A social role is a set of connected behaviors, rights, obligations, beliefs, and norms people inhabit in a social situation. A given person holds multiple roles: son/daughter, lover, friend, employee, co-worker, citizen, gamer, music fan, movie buff, and athlete. Roles are multiple, simultaneously or cyclically enacted. The social context determines which role is, or roles are, dominant. In a given day, a person cycles through distinct social roles that require subtle and even dramatic role-related shifts in their identity performances: from student to employee, from athlete to gamer and from son/daughter to lover. Likewise, a person performs more occasional identity work that might cross social roles and that is dependent on evolving circumstances: comic relief, sage advisor, unwitting accomplice, bold hero, enthusiastic storyteller, reluctant patient, frustrated commuter, impatient shopper, distracted diner, and even elevator rider. At times, these social roles harmoniously connect and reinforce one another. At other times, these roles collide, creating contradiction, conflict, and chaos. People struggle to define and redefine themselves amidst dynamic external forces (time, weather, economy, politics, science, technology).

Just when one thinks they have 'it' all figured out, circumstances shift, sometimes cosmically, and one rebuilds their self on ever-shifting ground. Identity is manifest as a continuous orchestrated performance. Identity evolves over time, taking on new challenges and editing scripts, or the series of behaviors, actions, and consequences that are expected in a particular situation. People deftly weave together identity projects into relatively cohesive self-narratives: their unique stories. The idea of identity as a project refers to the ongoing creation of narratives of self-identity relating to our perceptions of the past, present, and hoped-for future.

In contemporary consumer culture, people strategically construct their identities across time and space in a constant state of becoming. Often identity projects are aided and even enabled by the market, offering a set of props and practices that can be deployed separately or in combination to self-present, or perform identity. For example, to be an athlete in training requires a combination of activity appropriate clothes, shoes, food and drink, and equipment, as well as the performance of calisthenics and strategic maneuvers using these props. Likewise, to be a student necessitates access to educational texts, technology, and a virtual or physical campus, the use of backpacks or messenger bags to organize and transport materials, and the performance of reading, analyzing, writing, and discussing. These roles are made manifest through the marketplace where objects, symbols, scripts, and practices are on offer to support identity performance. Athlete and student are social roles and identity projects that contribute to an identity and elements of grand self-narratives, or ongoing, introspective recountings of personal development. In other words, social roles drive identity projects and identity projects are supported by and performed with marketplace offerings. Taken together, identity projects and self-presentation form self-narratives and self-narratives organize identity projects and performances into relatively cohesive, holistic identities. This perpetual recursive loop is what makes each person unique. How does the loop begin? Philosophers posit that identity is constructed through the process of imagination.

THE PROCESS OF IMAGINATION

Arguably, humans are distinct from many other living beings due to their ability to create and communicate knowledge. Knowledge begins when beings understand themselves as distinct from the world around them. People have the capacity to understand themselves and their environment, and to transmit this understanding to one another. In essence, humans have identities. Throughout history humans have struggled to understand themselves and their place in the world. Their quest for self-discovery involved exhaustingly complex mental gymnastics. One term repeatedly emerges: imagination.

Although the term imagination has many colloquial and academic connotations, it can be traced to the ancient Greek philosopher Plato's (424/423–348/347 BC) notion of phantasia as a synthesis of sensory perception and rational thought resulting in knowledge (from his dialogue entitled *Theaetetus* [Plato 1953]). Many centuries later, philosopher Immanuel Kant (1724–1804) asserted imagination defines and shapes human experience (Kant 1956). This influenced Benedict Anderson's contemporary theory that our imagination became commodified via print capitalism, enabling collectives beyond those that meet face-to-face to form (Anderson 1983). Print capitalism refers to the consequences of Gutenberg's printing press (invented 1440) that permitted texts produced in a given language to be distributed widely within a language community, thereby forming collectively shared ideas or common frames of reference. Consider how media capitalism (television and streaming services) expands communities, as people around the world access programming like reality television and become acquainted with *Keeping Up with the Kardashians*. This program details the exploits of the Kardashian-Jenner clan and their lifestyles of excess and trite melodrama. The Kardashian-Jenners, a once relatively obscure American family cobbled together from a lawyer at the center of a celebrity murder trial, a former Olympian, a fame-seeking matriarch and her photogenic offspring, becomes a global symbol of wealth, social success, and the American dream.

The concept of imagination yields two primary themes relevant to the study of consumption: (1) imagination links corporeality (the body and physical sensations) and abstract reasoning (thought) to yield knowledge (intelligence), and (2) imagination is central to the construction and expression of identities and realities. While philosophers expend significant brainpower on the first theme, we focus more on the second: the creation and performance of identity.

Plato introduces the term imagination to explain how sensory perception is combined with interpretation, to create knowledge. In essence, Plato asserts that imagination enables people to make sense of sensation. Put simply, Plato contends that imagination transforms sensation into knowledge. From Plato's perspective, the mind cannot apprehend sensory stimuli as they are presented to the senses; the mind must attach meanings to the perceptions that can then be ordered by rational thought into understanding (from his dialogues *Philebus* [Plato 1982], 39b; *Theaetetus*, 195d, 193b). Therefore, all knowledge, truth itself, is filtered through imagination; nothing can be humanly known that cannot first be imagined. Imagination is a central capacity: the knowledge factory. This means that everything that comprises our intellect is the work of imagination. We imagine art (paintings, sculpture, fiction, music, dance, etc.), science (biology, chemistry, astronomy, mathematics, etc.), and at times, the hair's breadth difference between the two.

The ancient Greek philosopher Aristotle (384–322 BC) builds on Plato, making a subtle distinction between sensation and imagination. In sensing, the object itself is present to the senses, while in imagination sensation is prolonged past the presence of the object (*On Dreams* [Aristotle 1941], 459a). Sensation is the process of perceiving, and imagination is abstracted sensation. In other words, sensation is what we do when confronted with a stimulus and imagination is where we attach meaning to a stimulus so it can remain in our minds after the stimulus has disappeared. These meanings become unmoored from the stimuli that inspired them, expanding human intellect far beyond bodily experience. Aristotle explains how we imagine what has never before been sensed: scientific breakthroughs, like disease cures and novel art forms, like fantasy fiction.

In contrast to Plato and Aristotle, René Descartes (1596–1650) positions the imagination solely in the bodily realm, and renders it inessential to the self (Descartes 1955). The imagination is disassociated from the essential self (located in Cartesian terms in the abstract/intellectual realm) because the abstraction created by the imagination originates within the physical realm (is tainted by corporeality). In *Meditation VI*, Descartes definitively states, 'imagination is nothing but a certain application of the faculty of knowledge to the body which is immediately present to it' (Descartes 2008: 49). Because the imagination is in Descartes' terms completely reliant on, and tainted by physical experience, imagination is not infinite; it is inextricably dependent upon what the body has experienced. In short, Descartes argues that imagination is limited to what at least once, we have sensed. We can only imagine permutations of what we have experienced firsthand. This means that truly novel ideas can only arise if they are the compilation of previously experienced phenomena. Descartes might say that we imagined human aviation from examining birds in flight and extrapolating to what we know about gravity and speed. Descartes might explain a technology like Skype as the reconstitution of face-to-face interactions with telephonic transmission and live videography – a novel pairing of experienced technologies.

The British philosopher David Hume (1711–1776) provides a hybrid understanding of imagination. Hume concurs with Plato and Aristotle that imagination is the central intellectual endeavor, however, the specifics of how the imagination works are omitted, or taken for granted, and given a mystical or magical nature within the proverbial black box of the mindscape (Hume 1962, *Treatise*). Despite the supernatural quality of the imagination, Hume echoes Descartes that imagination is grounded in sensation and limited. Hume states, 'nothing we imagine is absolutely impossible' (*Treatise*, I, ii, 2). Because the imagination (1) represents material phenomena and (2) acts upon sensory representations, it cannot create inherently impossible ideas. In other words, if we can imagine something, it is possible. For example, Hume might say that color-changing clothing, like that made by Del Sol, is enabled by people who imagined humans could become like chameleons changing colors according to environmental factors. To make the seemingly impossible possible, human ingenuity introduced clothing that mimicked chameleon's chromatophores (the cells that change color), reacting to heat to modify the color palette of the clothes.

Further, Hume brings a social component to imagination. We have all heard someone say that they didn't want to 're-invent the wheel'? Good news, they don't have to! People can create wheels, document the process, and pass the instructions to other people to build more wheels, or to modify the designs and create specialized or enhanced wheels.

But, how a did person identify the need for a wheel and how did they envision the first wheel. Imagination is responsible for closing the loop, or for creating strategies to communicate the abstractions in representational tools to be included as sense data in subsequent perceptions, carrying meaning across people. Hume asserts that reality is not a universal truth external to us, but rather a multiple, and layered product of independent and communal understandings of the external world and social relationships. Reality is a social construct built from shared individual physical experiences. Hume contends that realities cannot be constructed without individual and shared conceptions of materiality (understood as relationships between people and things that simultaneously constitute human experience and give coherence to the world of objects) and social relations. In this way, Hume refutes Plato's claim that imagination leads to knowledge and truth that form stable realities. For Hume, reality, based on truths, is historically and culturally variable and is socially defined, that is to say, by convention. The anthropologist Daniel Miller has examined consumption and people's relationships with market-mediated objects extensively (Miller 1987, 1998, 2008, 2012) exploring how meanings are socially and historically constituted and how important these meanings are in creating and signaling identity via ownership, proximity, and association. Miller asserts that the relationship between people and consumption is meaningful and identity-centered. People consume to establish who they are and where they fit in the social world.

Kant builds on Hume, refining the explanation of the process of imagination and elaborating on its social component. Kant distills imagination into two primary forms: (1) reproductive (pre-experiential intuition summoned spontaneously), and (2) productive (the location of knowledge construction) where syntheses take place and understanding results (Kant 1956). Hence, imagination is dependent upon sensible objects (both tangible like a physical brand and intangible like a service or online game), the intellect, and their interrelationship. For Kant, understanding and imagination are not independent forces; rather they are interdependent and together produce realities that can be empirically experienced. Thus, imagination is only limited by each person's interpretation of experience, their individual mental faculties and the socio-cultural system in which the experience and the individual are embedded. Put simply, Kant agrees with Hume that a person's imagination is constrained by their social network, their culture. Communicating knowledge is an imaginative endeavor. To take a simple illustration, in the Disney film *The Little Mermaid*, Ariel, aided by Scuttle, believes the fork at Prince Eric's table setting is a hair comb and identifies it by the name dinglehopper. In this way, the audience understands that the meaning of the fork is not shared by those that live under the sea, and is reconstituted in both name and function.

Political scientist Benedict Anderson (1983) identifies imagination as an integral component of community formation, specifically nations as a social category: 'All communities larger than primordial villages of face-to-face contact (and perhaps even these) are imagined' (Anderson 1983: 6). He is the first theorist to directly apply imagination to consumption by depicting the inaugural commodification of imagination through the rise of print capitalism and its impact on identity and social relations (Anderson 1983). In Anderson's account, the emergence of print technology allowing large-scale dissemination of written material fostered a sense of national community not previously experienced. Print capitalism gave national citizens consumable tools to imagine and build shared experience. Through reading, people became united in language communities roughly overlapping with geographic boundaries. For Anderson, ideas, images and ideologies became the building blocks of imagined identities. Anderson's notion of imagination is premised on the act of consuming (buying and deciphering written texts) which led to new identity configurations, new industries, new markets, and new social realities (Anderson 1983). As noted above, Anderson's notion of print capitalism can be updated to include global media and the proliferation of programming like *Keeping Up with the Kardashians* or alternatively, brands like *Harry Potter* and *Game of Thrones*. These commercial platforms span media (print, film, Internet streaming) to form common vocabularies for understanding worlds beyond what any person has physically experienced. Likewise, the advent of the Internet gave rise to global imagined communities centering on commercial brands (Muniz and O'Guinn 2001; Muniz and Schau 2005; Schau et al., 2009). In these brand-based collectives, brand enthusiasts collaborate to create value by enhancing brand-oriented experiences through creating and performing practices related to the brand and to the collective brand-related engagement. In this way, *Game of Thrones* becomes more valuable via collective practices of engaging in fan theories regarding the trajectory of characters or cosplay events where fans dress as favored *Game of Thrones* characters. Similarly, through global communications, the experience of Mini Cooper is enhanced via collaborative use rituals like Mini Drives and shared consumer customization practices, and LEGO brand experience is enhanced through fan collaboration to construct block representations of iconic architectures (Tower of Pisa), adventure scenes (*Indiana Jones*), science fiction characters (*Star Wars'* R2D2), and fantasy era environments (LEGO Castle).

Developing Anderson's premise, anthropologist Arjun Appadurai (1996) considers imagination the manipulation of signs, symbols, commercial products, and their respective meanings to visualize human potential and limitations. From Appadurai's perspective, imagination is a mundane practice and an inherently social process, belonging to all people. Consider seasonal holiday displays. People around the world delight in the vicarious consumption of others' displays of holiday-themed decorations. The delight stems from shared imagination about what the particular holiday means.

Appadurai is concerned with imagination as the way in which ordinary people derive meaning and create identity and community. Appadurai finds 'imagination has become a collective social fact ... the quotidian mental work of ordinary people' (Appadurai 1996: 5).

Further, 'ordinary people have begun to deploy their imaginations in the practice of their everyday lives' (Appadurai 1996: 5). In this way, imagination is not only the realm of impassioned scientists, gifted artists or even hyper-enthusiastic fans, but rather imagination is how all people envision their identity projects and devise ways to enact them. Through omnipresent social media, people routinely assert their association with market-based offerings via symbolic appropriation, visually representing branded symbols and market-oriented phenomena to perform identity projects, becoming what they post (Schau and Gilly 2003). Thus, for example, on Instagram people document their consumption journeys posting pictures of themselves at performances of the Broadway play *Hamilton* or of the Blue Apron subscription meals they constructed. Similarly on Sheng Li, Chinese tourists snap photos of their every experience in Finnish Lapland, from reindeer sledging to Santa Claus village, Rovaniemi.

To recap our quick tour of imagination theories, experience, both individual and collective, is understood, or made knowable, through the work of imagination. The imagination is composed of abstractions and conceptual frameworks, which evolve into knowledge and understanding. This evolution occurs when the frameworks are consistently able to sustain relationships among stimuli. Knowledge and understanding based on these coherent conceptual frameworks become larger intellectual projects known as identity and reality. Imagination is influenced and shaped by social networks and ultimately culture. Social possibilities (orders, communities, social infrastructures) are products of the imagination infused with conventions used to maintain and perpetuate individual and shared notions of space, objects, self, and other. Imagination is where the notions of self, community, and materialism develop and are maintained. People define themselves in terms of their relationship to things, other people, and existing social groups. Often people turn to the market for props to imagine and realize identity projects and construct lived reality.

Box 1.1: Critical Reflection

Creativity and imagination

Philosophers have posited that humans are unique in their capacity to fathom and strategically enact identity. Further, based on the writings of prominent philosophers, identity is the cornerstone of knowledge: we understand the world in relation to our identity. This chapter reveals imagination as the process that underlies identity. Philosophers of experience argue about the limits of imagination, asserting that imagination is the translation of sense data into meaning and meaning into knowledge. Therefore, humans cannot imagine the impossible because it is beyond sensation. Our imaginations are limited by what we have experienced. How does this notion of imagination differ from imagination as the site of infinite creativity, a place where the improbable and even the impossible can be envisioned? Think of narrative brands like Marvel comics that have a stable of characters that exist outside the parameters of everyday experience possessing capacities far beyond any human who has ever lived. Is this evidence of infinite imagination? There is ample evidence that even superheroes are beholden to the real world in some way. They are inspired by contemporary circumstances. Conversely, science fiction often presents novel realities (self-driving cars and live video conferencing) that inspire real-life innovations and become reality. What do these premonitions reveal about imagination?

Agency and Self-Presentation

Above we learned that the concept of imagination crosses many disciplines (e.g. philosophy, anthropology, political science, and cultural studies) and the meanings and conceptual nuances are not stable among the disciplines and even contested within them. In other words, imagination is complicated and scholars have not agreed on precisely what it is and how it works. Yet, there is consensus that it underlies identity.

In general, philosophers seek to understand how people translate the stimuli their bodies are exposed to into higher-level reasoning, and how higher-level reasoning inspires purposeful, replicable behavior in order to assert their identity projects and communicate with one another. Replicable behavior is socially enabled by the creation and dissemination of behavioral recipes or action templates.

Action templates are blueprints for action, or codified, insight-driven, manifest manipulations of patterned meaning for a specified purpose. They are formulas for replicable behaviors. For example, how does a person realize they are hungry, locate a kitchen, concoct a set of edible ingredients, perhaps add heat, decide it was an enjoyable and satisfying meal, document the recipe and share it with others? In general, the question becomes: how do you turn cues from the physical world (sensation) into meaning and derive insight patterns (knowledge) that can be turned into action (behavior)? The answer may surprise you. You need imagination to know who you are and how you relate to the world around you. You need identity projects with action templates to guide your self-presentation. You need agency to achieve volition, or will.

Psychoanalysis is based on the psychology of will. Psychoanalytic theorists recognize humans as agentic beings capable of exerting free will. They emphasize the voluntary nature of identity that we experience within levels of consciousness and bring into being through introspection. Beginning with the philosopher Schopenhauer (1788–1860) who finds human will to be mastery of the intellect, identity is freed from the confines of bodily experience (Schopenhauer 1970) but bound by states of intellectual awareness.

For Schopenhauer, identity is more than lived experience and people exert considerable thought toward identity. Similarly, philosopher Frederic Nietzsche (1844–1900) recognizes will and intentionality in human identity, as freeing human intellect from dependence on external divinity (deities) (Nietzsche 1977, 1986). Nietzsche posits that people are the masters of themselves and their destinies rather than acting on the whims of gods.

Building upon Schopenhauer and Nietzsche, the founder of psychoanalysis Sigmund Freud (1946) introduces multiple levels of identity (the super ego, the ego, and the id). These three concepts account for the intentionality of will and simultaneously provide an explanation for why people are not always aware of exercising their will (Freud 1962). Freud argues that the id is governed by instinctive impulses. The superego is responsible for moral behavior and enforcing norms. The ego imposes rationality on action, mediating between the super ego and the id. For example, a student's id might drive one to succeed on a test, even if that means cheating. The student's super ego asserts that cheating is outside the normal rules of the game and provides an unfair advantage over other students. The student's ego considers cheating on the test but decides it is wrong and opts to take the test according to the rules the professor sets.

Freud argues that tension arises among the three levels of identity and that people temper their free will, suppressing their instincts in the favor of social expectations. Together, Schopenhauer, Nietzsche, and Freud recognize people have free will but may not act on it because they fluidly move across levels of awareness (consciousness) which focus on different elements of identity. Through introspection or actively contemplating identity, one can recognize their free will, and wield it via action templates. For example, someone may want to enact a superhero identity project so they locate a cape pattern online, go to a fabric store to purchase raw materials, create the cape from the selected cloth, couple the cape with a leotard and purchase a ticket to a comicon event at which they will socially perform their superhero identity. Perhaps less dramatically, one might imagine a runner's identity project: purchase running shoes, running-appropriate attire, a belt to house their mobile phone and keys, as well as an easy-to-carry water bottle to maintain hydration (Thomas et al., 2013).

The psychoanalysts describe introspection that leads to identity and is translated into action templates but do not illuminate the social nature of these action templates. The sociological tradition has yielded theories of identity that emphasize humans' fundamentally social nature. Sociologists see order in human behavior, which is based on causal incidents and motive complexes (interwoven desires and goals). Social actors behave according to the operating cultural logics of their society (Durkheim 1950). The process of people collectively using effectively identical assumptions in interpreting each other's actions may be termed cultural logic (Enfield 2000). That is, we hypothesize as to motivations and intentions in our use of objects, symbols, and practices. Our individual behaviors, like each household offering up a similar holiday display, when found in aggregate trends, become social facts (Durkheim 1950). Thus, through consistent consumer display, we show and we know that we are the kind of people who celebrate Halloween, the Day of the Dead, or the Midsummer festival. The individual identity is akin to a cell-level entity of a larger social organism. From the perspective of Durkheimian sociology, while Americans may vary greatly in behavior, they share an underlying belief in democracy and equality, where each person has the capacity to influence institutions like government and rules like laws. In essence, psychoanalysts describe the introspective nature of imagination and sociologists explicate the aggregation of individual imagination to form social facts like belief in democracy and equality. In this way, members of a community recognize the cape wearer at comicon as a superhero not a gothic aristocrat, and the person struggling and sweating along on the side of the road as a fitness buff rather than a person in imminent danger fleeing a violent perpetrator.

Also utilizing a sociological lens, sociologist Erving Goffman (1922–1982) introduces theories of self-presentation and social performance (Goffman 1959) to our understanding of identity and creates an explicit link to consumption. The basic premise of Goffman's thesis is that self-presentation is the intentional, tangible component of identity. Social actors engage in complex intra-self negotiations to outwardly project a desired impression (Goffman 1959). Maintenance of the desired impression comes from a cohesive set of complementary behaviors consistently performed in order to sustain external perceptions (Schlenker 1975, 1980; Schneider 1981). Goffman terms this process impression management (Goffman 1959). Therefore, impression management is embodied, or relies on what Marcel Mauss (1934/1973) terms body techniques to communicate the desired self. The social actions requisite for self-presentation are consumption-oriented because they are dependent upon individuals consuming signs, symbols, brands and practices to communicate the desired impression (Williams and Bendelow 1998). The art of self-presentation is at once the manipulation of meaningful signs (Willey 1969) and embodied representation of self and experiencing as a self (Brewer 1998). Put simply, people consume to perform their identities. The Red Hot Chili Peppers fan may signal their band allegiance by wearing band t-shirts, create sharable playlists of recorded RHCP songs, and emblazon a RHCP sticker on their computer, skateboard or car. Perhaps more extreme, a Harley–Davidson rider or enthusiast may tattoo the brand on their neck (Schouten and McAlexander 1995).

Identity, Self-Presentation, and Consumption

Consumption is central to the construction and expression of individual and collective identities. Social theorists assert that consumption plays 'a central role in the way the social world is constructed' (Elliot 1997: 285). As McCracken (1988) states, 'the meaning of consumer goods and the meaning creation accomplished by consumer processes are important parts of the scaffolding of our present realities' (p. xi). Consumption is a productive, social, and communicative endeavor. Consumers are social actors who (re)configure ideas, images, symbols, and commercial products into meaningful identity projects: 'it is in acquiring, using, and exchanging things that individuals come to have social lives' (Lury 1996: 12). Anderson (1997) emphatically asserts 'consumption is now inseparable from identity' (p. 189). In essence, consumers deliberately acquire things and engage in consumption practices to achieve a pre-conceived notion of their essential self(ves) (Campbell, 1993). Every consumer, alone and/or in conjunction with groups with whom we associate, aspires to locate the self(ves) within the socio-material world by aligning their identity(ies) with certain objects and practices, while simultaneously distancing their identity(ies) from others. Zaltman (1995) acknowledges imagination as the underlying construct of meaning creation and knowledge, which Zaltman utilizes to justify the importance of metaphor in consumption practices. As Fiske contends, 'commodities are not just objects of economic exchange; they are goods to think with, goods to speak with' (Fiske 1989: 31). Thus, in contemporary consumer culture, through consumers' representational and communicative practices, material items are infused with meaning(s) that extend(s) far beyond the producers' intent (McCracken 1986).

The CCT (consumer culture theory) perspective adopts a socio-cultural notion of consumption focusing on 'the manner in which people convert things to ends of their own' (Strathern 1994: X). Consumption is procuring, appreciating, and using things as utilitarian objects, signs, and enablers of the identity projects. A considerable amount of scholarship in consumer research examines the role of consumption in identity (Arnould and Wilk 1984; Belk 1988, 1992; McCracken 1986, 1988). The central tenets of this work rest on the assumption that consumers are what they consume, and conversely that consumers consume to communicate what they are; Belk asserts, 'this may be the most basic and powerful fact of consumer behavior' (Belk 1988: 160). The relationship implicit in the above statement is that identity directly translates into consumption, and that consumption is capable of revealing identity. Put simply, consumers transform goods into possessions.

Box 1.2:   Critical Reflection

Consumption and life transitions

At every stage of life, consumers imagine their identity. They use material, symbolic, and experiential resources to enact personal and collective identities. Consumption patterns facilitate social differentiation (rings may signify marital status, a minivan might signal parenthood). Changes in identity inspire new modes of consumption:

adolescence, adulthood, parenthood, graduation, marriage, divorce, career switching, geographic relocation, drug rehabilitation. How do people in adolescence, adulthood, and parenthood engage in self-presentation? What consumption objects do they use, what consumption practices do they perform? How do people who recently graduated, married, and divorced engage in self-presentation? What consumption objects do they use, what consumption practices do they perform? How does switching careers, relocating or rehabilitating from substance abuse impact consumption?

Following the CCT tradition, consumer identity projects are 'social arrangement[s] in which relations between lived culture and social resources, and between meaningful ways of life and the symbolic and material resources on which they depend, are mediated through markets' (Arnould and Thompson 2005: 869). A basic premise of this research is that 'the marketplace has become a preeminent source of mythic and symbolic resources through which people, including those who lack resources to participate in the market as full-fledged consumers, construct narratives of identity' (2005: 871). The following is a brief review of some of the pioneering consumer researchers to have addressed the link between identity and consumption at the individual and collective level.

Belk (1988) demonstrates that material items act as extensions of the self and communicate personal and group-level identity. Belk asserts that consumers seek to make tangible their intangible beliefs and values through consumption: '[p]eople seek, express, confirm, and ascertain a sense of being through what they have' (Belk 1988: 146). He shows that possessions assist in self-perception and actually become, usually figuratively, or symbolically, but less often literally, or physically, part of the consumer body (Belk 1988). Belk argues, 'It seems an inescapable fact of modern life that we learn, define, and remind ourselves of who we are by our possessions' (1988: 160). Belk contends that possessions help to express collective identities as well: 'we exist not only as individuals, but also as collectivities. We often define family, group, subculture, nation and human selves through various consumption objects' (1988: 152).

Likewise, Belk asserts that consumers imagine themselves and their relationship to groups and social institutions individually and in concert with other consumers through common symbols, buildings and monuments. Further, artifacts associated with various group levels of identity 'provide a sense of community essential to group harmony, spirit, and cooperation' (1988: 160).

Similarly, Wallendorf and Arnould (1988) find favorite objects to be repositories of personal meanings and symbols of experiences. Through interviews, informants were encouraged to share object histories and to highlight object significance within their lives. Favorite possessions are shown to be meaning containers, or material signs, through which abstract identities and social ties are made concrete. Objects help situate possessors within the socio-material world through affiliation and association. By examining materialism at the level of lived experience and contextualizing object attachment, Wallendorf and Arnould (1988) demonstrate how possessions are signifiers of identities and manifestations of self-expression.

O'Guinn and Belk (1989) describes a Christian fundamentalist theme park, where the attendees see their consumption of the park experience as a pilgrimage and a tangible affirmation of their commitment to their religious identity. Items acquired at the theme park (cosmetics, handbags, statuettes) are accorded sacred status due to an imagined proximity to the consumers' deity by virtue of their availability in theme park stores.

Wallendorf and Arnould (1991) examine Thanksgiving consumption rituals and how consumers imagine identity through the celebration of material surplus. Although they do not use the concept of imagination, they demonstrate how consumers make sense of tradition and family relationships through overt material excess and how this identity is reinvigorated through annual ritual observation.

Belk (1992) discusses the meanings Mormon migrants ascribed to the possessions these internal American migrants brought west to the Utah territory from their homes in the east, and how the ascribed symbolism worked to imagine community and familial bonds in accordance with their religious faith. During the Mormon migration, the uprooted believers gained strength from sacrificing certain material things and used possessions to recreate their fractured identities and form a new community in the 'promised land'. Along the same thread, Mehta and Belk (1991) discuss how Indian immigrants use objects to imagine affinity with India and to stand in for the geographic locale of India. Totemic objects, emblems of their Indian origin, within migrants' American households were designated signifiers of socio-cultural and physical India. In addition, shrines representing emigrated family members were also placed in Indian homes. In both sets of households physical proximity was imagined through material objects.

In Arnould and Price (1993), a river rafting expedition is said to yield magical experience. A rock is transformed into a spiritual object with signification obtained through the rafting adventure. In essence, it may be said the translation is the work of imagination. The rock as sense data is given spiritual significance through a shared imagining. Furthermore, the rock grounds the abstractions of the consumers, or makes tangible their belief structures and enables overt, observable consumption and self-expression. Group members symbolically enact their affiliation to each other and the experience by touching the rock.

Consumption collectives such as brand communities are tightly linked to identity (see Chapter 4 for more discussion on this point). One such collective is a brand community defined as 'a specialized, non-geographically bound community, based on a structured set of social relationships among admirers of a brand' (Muniz and O'Guinn 2001: 4). Brand communities can be complex entities with their own cultures, rituals, traditions, and codes of behavior. Muniz and O'Guinn (2001) examine the brand communities centered

MLM

on Ford Bronco trucks, Macintosh computers and Saab automobiles and demonstrate that members of these communities derive an important part of the brand consumption experience from membership in these communities. Moreover, members appear to derive an aspect of personal identity from their membership and participation in these communities. Schouten and McAlexander (1995) detail a set of consumers and their relationships to Harley–Davidson motorcycles. They show that consumers enact identity projects through the use of the motorcycles and the interaction among brand enthusiasts.

Conversely, consumers derive a sense of being from what they have and do not have. People create identities from those things in their socio-material context: 'goods are a means of making visible and stable the basic categories by which we classify people in society' (Lury 1996: 13). Further, consumers may rely on the marketplace to establish oppositional brand associations that signal identity projects where consumers self-present as not a Starbucks consumer (Kuo and Hou 2017; Thompson and Arsel 2004).

These early efforts to link consumption and identity yield significant insights into consumption motives and practices. Still, consumer identities often also consist of intentionally intangible abstractions. We are sometimes what we choose not to have, as in voluntary consumption abstinence. Sometimes our identities reflect a lack of resources. We cannot afford to consume what would potentially make our identities tangible. Sometimes our identities reflect a denial. We choose not to make tangible aspects of identity in order to hide their presence. Sometimes our identities are not prone to tangible expression. We cannot locate strategies to express complex facets of our identities. In other words, we may indeed be what we have self-presented, but our identities exceed what is expressed through consumer goods either tangible (brands) or intangible (experiences). Consumers selectively express aspects of identity and mute other identity elements.

Box 1.3:   Critical Reflection

We are what we consume

Identity is volitional, people act with intention toward a purpose. Through consumer imagination, goods, symbols, experiences, and services are transformed into knowledge and consumer identity projects. We are what we consume. The converse is also true: we are what we do not consume. As such and to paraphrase Shakespeare, to consume or not to consume is a choice. Consider ways in which people enact their identity by not consuming certain objects and not engaging in specific practices. Make a list of your own choices to consume and not to consume. What does this list reveal about your identity?

Consumer Imagination

Using the theories associated with imagination and a socio-cultural notion of consumption, imagination is revealed as a fundamental construct in consumption. The market is a social structure that scaffolds imagination and the performance of identity. In other words, the market structurally supports consumer imagination and the self-presentation of identity projects. People try to become the being they desire to be by consuming the items they imagine will help create and sustain their ideas of themselves, their image, their identity (Bocock 1993: 68). That is to say, consumers consume to make identities created in the imagination tangible, or put another way, consumption is a manifestation of imagination. A concept of consumer imagination (Schau 2000) emerges as the transformation of goods, symbols, and services into knowledge and consumer identity projects. It is where consumers make sense of consumption objects and practices. Consumers create identities within consumers' imagination as they situate themselves with respect to consumer goods, symbols, services, and experiences. Consumer self-expression is the manipulation of goods, symbols, and services to communicate consumer identity projects generated within the imagination. Since imagination is not instantly recognized as a manifest behavior, consumer self-expression contains strategies for articulating the intangible consumer identities. Consumer imagination is an individual and collective process, which through time becomes a social fact, providing consumers with the realm of social and technical possibilities that are the building blocks for lived, material reality.

Box 1.4: Real World Scenario

Social media

Technology influences consumer imagination. Within social media, consumers are able to create and perform identity unimpeded by resources constraints. Often, just as in the physical world, this is done through association with and use of brands, market-offerings and consumption practices. Consider Facebook, Instagram, Pinterest and Snapchat. Consider the avatars adopted in World of Warcraft. How do consumers present their identities, their selves in each of these social media platforms? How do the features of the technology modify our identity projects? How are brands and market offerings used in each of these platforms? Would we expect identity to be imagined in these technology-mediated environments differently than in the physical world? Why or why not?

Box 1.5:   Real World Scenario

Video games

People crave amusement. Play is an imaginative endeavor. Since consumption is the enactment of identity, how does playing video games reflect identity projects? What identity projects do video games support? Consider games that are anchored in the real world but perhaps not the real world of a given consumer. For example, Call of Duty, a military-themed video game, enables consumers to experience combat situations that they may never have encountered in their lives. How does playing Call of Duty support identity projects? Likewise, how does a game like Grand Theft Auto, a game themed after criminal activity, support identity projects? Both of these examples are anchored in real life, with human actors taking on relatively possible physical circumstances. Turn now, to games that reflect less probable real life circumstances. Mario Brothers games present actors in a relatively simplistic or stripped-down set of life circumstances. There is a discrete goal and it is repetitive. How does mastery of this game reflect identity projects? Conversely, games like World of Warcraft and Assassins' Creed are premised on complex goals and anchored in environments that do not reflect consumers' everyday lives. How do these games support identity projects? How do these game-based identities influence consumers' everyday identities? How do they influence your sense of self?

CONCLUSION

In summary, identity is intentional. Imagination is the process translating sensation into meaning, meaning into knowledge, and knowledge into replicable purposive action. The market provides fodder for consumers to enact imagined identify projects. The essence of imagination from a consumer research perspective is that imagination is a creative production of the mind (alongside calculation, reason, and memory), where identities (self and communal, physical, and psychic) are constructed and later communicated. Consumer imagination as a useful construct is the individual and communal process of combining socio-cultural tools (commercial products, signs, and symbols) to self-present identity projects.

RESEARCH DIRECTIONS

This chapter reviews existing theories about human identity, focusing on consumer imagination and volitional identity behaviors, or identity projects. Within marketing and consumer research, studies reveal that identity projects implicate the market. The market provides access to products, symbols and services, which people buy and use to stake and perform their social roles related to their identity project (Campbell 1993). Even the most mundane products help us enact our social identities (Kleine et al. 1993). The market enables the performance and may also provide a stage for the enactment to take place, such as retail stores (Borghini 2009; Peñaloza 1998), service encounters (Underwood et al. 2001), and webspace (Schau and Gilly 2003). This suggests three fruitful research areas: (1) the interplay of identity project consumption strategies, (2) marketplaces as identity stages, and (3) the impact of technology on consumer imagination.

Research is needed to understand the interplay of identity projects within consumer lives. Identity projects within a single consumer may not be entirely consistent with one another and may inspire conflicting consumption strategies. How do consumers reconcile their identity projects and potentially conflicting consumption strategies? For example, a consumer may be performing an environmentally conscious identity project that conflicts with their identity as a coffee enthusiast who uses Nespresso pods that are not readily recycled across geographical regions. The market may identify the coffee pod–environmental tension and derive a strategy to reconcile them. To address the tension, Nespresso offers consumers who buy in bulk a pre-paid bag to return the used pods to be properly recycled. How can tensions between and among identity projects be identified? How can markets offer tension resolution?

Marketplaces are often the sites of identity project performances. Research to identify how marketplaces can best support identity work and further identity projects can provide insights on how to inspire consumer engagement. Large indoor malls with department store anchors and an array of specialty shops were extremely popular in prior decades. With the rise of the Internet and consumers' appetites for sophisticated product and service comparisons, mall patronage has declined. Mall owners and managers struggle to breathe new life into these spaces and to find new arrays of products and services that will re-ignite consumer patronage by tying the malls to relevant consumer identity projects. Research can inform marketers on the best use of these marketspaces as entertainment meccas and experiential retail spaces that support contemporary consumer identity projects.

A fruitful area for further research is the advent of technology-enabled immersive environments such as video games and simulations. How do these immersive environments impact consumer imagination and identity projects? These new spaces may impact consumer imagination, modifying and expanding both identity projects and identity performances. For example, consumers may explore identities unmoored from their physical bodies reducing the restrictions of age, gender, ethnicity, health, and physical abilities. These environments themselves may be marketplaces as consumers can personalize their avatars, in-game props, and adventures. How do consumers enact identity projects in tech-enabled environs and how does this identity play impact the array of identity projects within consumers' lives?

REFERENCES

Anderson, Benedict (1983) *Imagined Communities: Reflections on the Origin and Spread of Nationalism*. London: Verso.

Anderson, Walter Truett (1997) *The Future of the Self: Inventing the Postmodern Person*. New York: Penguin Putnam Inc.

Appadurai, Arjun (1996) *Modernity at Large: Cultural Dimensions of Globalization*. Minneapolis, MN: University of Minnesota Press.

Aristotle (1941) *The Basic Works of Aristotle* (trans. G.R.G. Mure, ed. Richard McKeon). New York: Random House.

Arnould, Eric and Price, Linda (1993) 'River magic: Extraordinary experience and the extended service encounter,' *Journal of Consumer Research*, (June).

Arnould, Eric J. and Thompson, Craig J. (2005) 'Consumer culture theory (CCT): Twenty years of research', *Journal of Consumer Research*, 31 (4): 868–82.

Arnould, Eric and Wilk, Richard (1984) 'Why do Natives wear Adidas?', in T. Kinnear (ed.), *Advances in Consumer Research*, Vol. 2. Provo, UT: Association for Consumer Research.

Belk, Russell W. (1988) 'Possessions and the extended self', *Journal of Consumer Research*, 15 (September).

Belk, Russell W. (1992) 'Moving possessions: An analysis based on personal documents from the 1847–1869 Mormon migration', *Journal of Consumer Research*, 19 (December).

Bocock, Robert (1993) *Consumption*. London: Routledge.

Borghini, Stefania, Diamond, Nina, Kozinets, Robert V., McGrath, Mary Ann, Muniz Jr, Albert M., and Sherry Jr, John F. (2009) 'Why are themed brandstores so powerful? Retail brand ideology at American Girl Place', *Journal of Retailing*, 85 (3): 363–75.

Brewer, Bill (1998) 'Bodily awareness and the self', in Eilan Bermudez Marcel (ed.), *The Body and the Self*. Cambridge, MA: MIT Press.

Campbell, Colin (1993) *The Sociology of Consumption*. London: Routledge.

Descartes, René (1955), *Descartes Selections*, ed. Ralph M Eaton, New York, NY: Charles Scribner's Sons.

Descartes, René (2008) *Meditations on First Philosophy*. Oxford: Oxford University Press.

Durkheim, Emile (1950) *The Rules of Sociological Method*. Glencoe, IL: Free Press.

Elliot, Richard (1997) 'Existential consumption and irrational desire', *European Journal of Marketing*, 31 (3/4): 285–96.

Enfield, Nick J. (2000) 'The theory of cultural logic: How individuals combine social intelligence with semiotics to create and maintain cultural meaning', *Cultural Dynamics*, 12 (1): 35–64.

Fiske, John (1989) *Reading the Popular*. Boston, MA: Unwin Hyman. Inc.

Freud, Sigmund (1946) *An Autobiographical Study*. London: Hogarth Press.

Freud, Sigmund (1962) *The Ego and the Id*. London: Hogarth Press.

Goffman, Erving (1959) *The Presentation of Self in Everyday Life*. New York, NY: Doubleday.

Hume, David (1962) *Hume on human nature and the understanding; being the complete text of An inquiry concerning human understanding, together with sections of A treatise of human nature, An abstract of a treatise of human nature, and two biographical documents* (ed. Anthony Flew). New York, NY: Collier.

Kant, Immanuel (1956) *Critique of Pure Reason* (trans. Norman Kemp Smith). York: St Martin's Press.

Kleine, Robert E., Kleine, Susan Schultz, and Kernan, Jerome B. (1993) 'Mundane consumption and the self: A social-identity perspective', *Journal of Consumer Psychology*, *2* (3): 209–35.

Kuo, Ying-Feng and Hou, Jian-Ren (2017) 'Oppositional brand loyalty in online brand communities: Perspectives on social identity theory and consumer-brand relationship', *Journal of Electronic Commerce Research*, *18* (3): 254.

Lury, Celia (1996) *Consumer Culture*. New Brunswick, NJ: Rutgers University Press.

Mauss, Marcel (1973) 'Techniques of the body', *Economy and Society*, *2*: 70–88.

McCracken, Grant (1986) 'Culture and consumption: A theoretical account of the structure and movement of the cultural meaning of goods', *Journal of Consumer Research*, *13* (June).

McCracken, Grant (1988) *Culture and Consumption*. Bloomington, IN: Indiana University Press.

Mehta, R. and Belk, R.W. (1991) Artifacts, identity, and transition: Favorite possessions of Indians and Indian immigrants to the United States', *Journal of Consumer Research*, *X*: 398–411.

Miller, Daniel (1987) *Material Culture and Mass Consumption*. Oxford: Basil Blackwell.

Miller, Daniel (ed.) (1998) *Material Cultures: Why Some Things Matter*. Chicago, IL: University of Chicago Press.

Miller, Daniel (2008) *The Comfort of Things*. Cambridge: Polity.

Miller, Daniel (2012) *Consumption and its Consequences*. Cambridge: Polity.

Muniz, Albert M. and O'Guinn, Thomas C. (2001) 'Brand community', *Journal of Consumer Research*, *27* (March): 412–32.

Muniz, Albert M. and Schau, Hope Jensen (2005) 'Religiosity in the abandoned Apple Newton brand community', *Journal of Consumer Research*, *31* (March): 737–47.

Nietzsche, Friederich (1977) *A Nietzsche Reader* (trans. and introduction R.J. Hollingdale). Harmondsworth: Penguin Books.

Nietzsche, Friederich (1986) *Human, All Too Human*. Cambridge: Cambridge University Press.

O'Guinn, Thomas and Belk, Russell W. (1989) 'Heaven on earth: Consumption at Heritage Village, USA', *Journal of Consumer Research*, *15* (3, September): 227–38.

Peñaloza, Lisa (1998) 'Just doing it: A visual ethnographic study of spectacular consumption behavior at Nike Town', *Consumption Markets & Culture*, *2* (4): 337–400.

Plato (1935) *Plato's Theory of Knowledge: The Theaetetus & the Sophist of Plato* (trans. Francis Macdonald Cornford). New York: Harcourt, Brace and Co.

Plato (1982) *Philebus* (trans. Robin A.H. Waterfield). Harmondsworth: Penguin Books.

Schau, Hope Jensen (2000) 'Consumer imagination, identity and self-expression', in Stephen J. Hoch and Robert J. Meyer (eds), *Advances in Consumer Research*, 27: 50–6.

Schau, Hope Jensen and Gilly, Mary C. (2003) 'We are what we post? The presentation of self in personal webspace,' *Journal of Consumer Research*, *30* (4): 385–404.

Schau, Hope Jensen, Muniz, Albert M., and Arnould, Eric J. (2009), 'How brand community practices create value', *Journal of Marketing*, *73* (September), 30–51.

Schlenker, B.R. (1975) 'Self-presentation: Managing impression of consistency when reality interferes with self enhancement', *Journal of Personality and Social Psychology*, *32*: 1030–7.

Schlenker, B.R. (1980) *Impression Management: The Self-Concept, Social Identity and Interpersonal Relationships*. Monterey, CA: Brooks/Cole.

Schneider, D.J. (1981) 'Tactical self-representations: toward a broader conception', in J.T. Tedeschi (ed.), *Impression Management Theory and Social Psychological Research*. New York: Academic Press.

Schopenhauer, Arthur (1970) *Essays and Aphorisms* (trans. and introduction by R.J. Hollingdale). Harmondsworth: Penguin Books.

Schouten, John W. and McAlexander, James H. (1995) 'Subcultures of consumption: An ethnography of the New Bikers', *Journal of Consumer Research*, *22* (1): 43–61.

Strathern, M. (1994) 'Foreward: The mirror of technology', in R. Silverstone and E. Hirsch (eds), *Consuming Technologies: Media and Information in Domestic Spaces*. London: Routledge.

Thomas, Tandy Chalmers, Price, Linda L., and Schau, Hope Jensen (2013) 'When differences unite: Resource dependence in heterogeneous consumption communities', *Journal of Consumer Research*, *39* (5): 1010–33.

Thompson, Craig J., and Zeynep Arsel (2004) The Starbucks brandscape and consumers' (anticorporate) experiences of glocalization', *Journal of Consumer Research*, *31* (3): 631–42.

Underwood, Robert, Bond, Edward, and Baer, Robert (2001) 'Building service brands via social identity: Lessons from the sports marketplace', *Journal of Marketing Theory and Practice*, *9* (1): 1–13.

Wallendorf, Melanie and Arnould, Eric J. (1988) '"My Favorite Things": A cross-cultural inquiry into object attachment, possessiveness, and social linkage', *Journal of Consumer Research*, *14* (March): 531–47.

Wallendorf, Melanie and Arnould, Eric J. (1991) '"We gather together": Consumption rituals of Thanksgiving Day', *Journal of Consumer Research*, *18* (1): 13–31.

Willey, Basil (1969) *Coleridge on Imagination and Fancy*. Folcroft, PA: The Folcroft Press.

Williams, Simon J. and Bendelow, Gillian (1988) *The Lived Body: Sociological Themes and Embodied Issues*. New York: Routledge.

Zaltman, Gerald (1995) 'Amidword: Anthropology, metaphors, and cognitive peripheral vision', in J.F. Sherry, Jr, *Contemporary Marketing and Consumer Behavior*. Beverly Hills, CA: Sage.

2

FAMILY AND COLLECTIVE IDENTITY

Amber M. Epp, University of Wisconsin–Madison
Tandy Chalmers Thomas, Queen's University, Kingston

CHAPTER OVERVIEW

- Relationships between the marketplace and family life can be contentious.
- Cultural discourses guide family behavior.
- Socialization practices teach families how to be consumers but also reproduce inequitable family structures, including social class and gender norms.
- Examining families' stuff (their material culture) reveals insights about their identities, relationships with others, and patterns of everyday life.
- Marketers need to move beyond stereotypes and attend to the evolving notion of family.

INTRODUCTION

The pull of family life, among consumers' many other influences, powerfully directs our attention and orders our motivations. Thus, family acts as a key organizing force that shapes our behaviors and experiences in the marketplace. Further, families' identities – meaning the unique character, qualities, and attributes that are constituted in practices, narratives, and everyday interactions – both inform consumption choices and rely on the marketplace as a resource (Epp and Price 2008). In this way, family is a practical and embodied aspect of daily life. It houses consumers' most intimate behaviors and is inevitably dynamic and complex on a micro-level. However, the universality and cultural impact of family also make it a dominant cultural institution. Many cultural battles are fought over how to define family and the implications of these definitions as they evolve.

Given its pervading influence, family research taps into intersecting interests of scholars, managers, consumers, and policy-makers.

In this chapter we provide an overview of family research that directly considers its immersion in, and contributions to, consumer culture. To begin, we examine the boundaries between family life and the marketplace to build an understanding of how the two interact in both productive and destructive ways. We then elaborate on how cultural discourses of family shape parents' consumption choices and their evaluations of themselves and one another in relation to cultural ideals and normative beliefs about parenthood. Next, we consider the role of family in the social reproduction of certain cultural structures (e.g. gender roles) through socialization and family routines. Finally, we highlight how the material culture of family – our stuff – enables and constrains family action. We pay particular attention to how objects gain and retain meanings that keep them relevant to families. We conclude with some directions for future research in the family domain.

MARKET AS FRIEND OR FOE TO FAMILY LIFE?

Consumer culture is pervasive. Everywhere we turn, we are immersed in a world of brands, products, and marketplace interactions. Yet, family life is heralded by some as a sacred and insulated space – one kept separate from the capitalist notions of the market – where families spend intimate time together building memories and life skills. Perhaps paradoxically though, much of this time together takes place in the marketplace, or at least involves market resources. For example, families make annual treks to spectacular vacation destinations – Disneyworld, the Great Barrier Reef, or Mediterranean beach resorts. Even routine activities around town such as attending local children's museums, zoos, aquariums, or favorite restaurants exemplify the intertwined nature of family life and the marketplace. The market interacts with family across all life stages, from dating couples to young families to elderly families who seek help with care provision. As such, the market often facilitates intimate family relations, providing a site for connection, expertise, and common experience. Thus, the question arises, is the market friend or foe to family life?

As a general rule, family researchers express ambivalence toward social relations between family and the market, while also acknowledging the tensions that emerge when the market and family life intersect. That is, the market is a site of both destructive and productive relationships with family; it both incites and relieves tensions within the family (Epp and Velagaleti 2014). These tensions emerge from the basic understanding that family exists in the intimate sphere, governed by a logic of intimacy, love, and self-sacrifice, whereas the market exists in the economic sphere, governed by a logic of monetary exchange, profit motives, and competition. Often referred to by sociologists as the hostile worlds view, this latter perspective pits the market and intimate relations against one another (Hochschild 2003). Within this view, the market encroaches on family life.

Contemporary family life offers numerous examples of market encroachment. The invasion of market logics into the parenting domain provides a poignant illustration. For example, competitive parenting is evident in children's birthday parties as parents create increasingly elaborate party themes, complete with Pinterest-inspired decorations, professional cakes, and expensive favors. One could argue that the transparency of parenting activities – made more accessible via social media – adds to the pressure for families to compete, and even more challenges for those who lack the socio-economic resources to compete. Of course, social competitions have always existed (e.g. getting into the best schools, sending kids to elite summer camps, dressing in branded clothing), but advocates for the hostile worlds perspective argue that the market is increasingly intrusive into once sacred domains of family life (see Box 2.1: Corporatization of education and Box 2.2: Outsourcing parenting).

Another illustration of market encroachment on the boundaries of family life considers the power of technologies to transform once taken-for-granted family routines. Common across many contemporary households are daily battles over whether and when technology should be integrated or isolated from family activities. Nowhere is this battle more evident than at the family dinner table. Here, the mantra of Sherry Turkle's book *Alone Together* (2010) rings true. She documents the phenomenon of being emotionally dislocated from those physically in our presence as intimate life shifts to our devices. Around the dinner table, kids are streaming their favorite TV shows on their iPads, teens are texting with friends, and parents are responding to work emails. The risks of this type of isolation, according to proponents of the hostile worlds view, is a loss of the art of conversation and devaluing of the essential task of connecting with family members. This is becoming an increasing concern across the world. In 2015, for example, the Center for Psychological Research, Shenyang – a government body focused on raising awareness around social issues and causes in China – launched an ad campaign that highlighted the way that smartphones can negatively affect family life and relationships (Bologna 2015). Thus, technology encroaches on family time.

Certainly, if we adopt the opposite view and frame the market as an active partner in family life, the role of technology in facilitating family relations becomes readily apparent. For example, for long-distance families where parents commute for work or grandparents live far away from their grandkids, technology allows for intimate connection to those separated by time and space (Epp et al. 2014). Technology also plays a crucial role in helping families in developing countries stay connected as parents leave home to be migrant workers. For example, research conducted in Ecuador, China, and Kenya, shows that the children of migrant workers use technology to create a private mode of communication with their parents that allows the family to remain emotionally bonded

(Cheong and Mitchell 2015). With so many ways to connect, families remain in constant contact, afffording them opportunities to be present in the lives of others, even when they are physically absent. In this way, market technologies preserve family time and ease some of the encroachment tensions.

Similarly, consumer researchers and sociologists often examine compatibilities between the market and family life (Zelizer 2011). Not only is the market a site of intimate family relations that provides resources for connection, but it also eases tensions within families directly. The market and its transactional exchange logics can alleviate tensions, especially when tensions of control and reciprocity make it difficult to lean on family members, such as when parents have strict guidelines for child or eldercare or when one is moving to a new house and does not want to overburden family (Epp and Velagaleti 2014; Marcoux 2009). Further, market and intimate relations sometimes coexist when considering family definitions. Families often think of care providers in particular (e.g. nannies, eldercare nurses) as family members (Barnhart et al. 2014). This speaks to defining family through interactions rather than through bloodlines, which opens the door for the blurring of market and family relations.

Box 2.1:   Extended Case Study

Corporatization of education

Protection of childhood from market influence animates critics to take action against corporate encroachment. The case of corporate funding for public education is no exception. As some public school systems suffer from extensive state budget cuts paired against the realities of educational costs, they face tough choices about cutting essential programs and forgoing necessary resources. In the United States, for example, beginning around 2008, low or slow economic growth – coupled with high unemployment rates and neoliberal policies that favored privatized market options over social welfare programs (see Chapter 11 by Veresiu and Giesler) – forced budget cuts that disproportionately impacted state and local governments. 'Coincidentally, state and local governments provide about 90.0% of primary and secondary education funding, so this caused growth in education funding to slow below 1.0% annually after 2008. Between 2010 and 2013, government spending on education declined moderately in real terms' (IBISWorld Business Environment Report 2016). In these restrictive environments, corporations often filled the budget gaps through sponsorships or donations, and in turn, garnered an audience with the youngest consumers. Consider the following examples:

- Coca-Cola helped fund field trips and school newspapers
- American Girl developed an anti-bullying curriculum for Grades 3–5

(Continued)

(Continued)

- Corporations donated sponsorships for naming rights to stadiums, gyms, cafeterias, auditoriums, and other educational spaces (e.g., Kohler donated $45,000 to name kitchens in two Wisconsin high schools)
- Apple offered free computer recycling to schools
- McDonald's sent 'brand ambassadors' to speak at schools across the country about nutritional choices

These examples represent a diverse array of product types, extent of involvement with the schools, and age ranges of children. Corporate involvement, such as that exemplified in these cases, incites debate over the types of relationships that should be allowed between school systems and corporations and calls to the public's attention the long-term ramifications of using corporate funds to cover the shortfall of public investment in education. Importantly, this debate is not only restricted to the United States – Canadian schools, for example, have found themselves embroiled in similar debates.

Schools, like family life, are viewed as sacred places where children are free to learn, grow, and discover. But, corporate involvement with education potentially changes schools from 'pure' educational institutions to another form of marketing. While children are routinely involved with the marketplace (e.g. they interact with healthcare services during checkups; they accompany their parents to the grocery store for basic provisioning starting in their first few months of life; and they are regularly exposed to advertising messages and cartoon characters promoting their favorite foods, toys, and games), many of these interactions are regulated.

Regulation of advertising to children, for example, falls within the purview of multiple oversight groups, including but not limited to the Federal Trade Commission, Food and Drug Administration, Congress (i.e., Children's Television Act – enforced by FCC), State Legislatures, The Children's Advertising Review Unit (the children's advertising review arm of the ad industry's self-regulatory system), and private trade groups. A primary concern of these regulators is children's vulnerability to advertising messages presented by familiar characters, their abilities to discern persuasion efforts, and their understanding of marketers' motivations. Although specific age estimates vary, the general consensus among child development experts is that children younger than 7–8 years old have difficulty comprehending the persuasive intent of commercials (Danovitch and Mills 2009). This research, however, has predominately been conducted in television mediums, rather than in the diversity of ways children are exposed to marketing efforts. Thus, understanding how children evolve into astute consumers also concerns school boards and policy-makers when it comes to children's exposure to products and brands within an educational environment. This debate becomes especially important given the amount of time children spend in school as well as the fact that their attendance is compulsory.

Questions

1. In what ways would you consider corporations as friends or foes of family life in this context?
2. How should companies interact with public schools? What factors should schools consider when making decisions about whether or not to accept corporate investment?
3. Discuss the tradeoffs schools make when they accept corporate funding. What are the positive and negative outcomes for schools? What are the positive and negative outcomes for corporations? What are the short- and long-term consequences of corporate investment in public education?

Box 2.2:   Critical Reflection

Outsourcing parenting activities: market as friend *and* foe

Hire a babysitter from Nanny in the Clouds to sit with your kids on an upcoming flight, so you can relax. Visit Nordstrom's shoe department and drop off your kids for a shoe-tying clinic while you complete your shopping. Go Kid Go will pick your child up from school and transport them to their activities (sports, dance, karate, etc.). Not a fan of removing head lice? Hair Whispers will do the dirty work for you. Alongside all of the traditional care providers such as daycares and nannies, parents can now outsource almost anything they could imagine.

Turning these activities over to other people outside of the immediate family, however, often raises tensions for parents related to intimacy, control, and substitutability. The marketplace, in particular, tends to increase intimacy and substitutability tensions, while alleviating control tensions (Epp and Velagaleti 2014). That is, parents want the market to show care for their children, but not overstep and get too close for comfort. This tends to threaten a parent's own intimate relationship with their child (fear that the child feels closer to a care provider than to the parent). Parents also often want the market to carry out activities in the same way the parent would, but they worry about a service provider replacing the parent in their child's memories of iconic childhood activities (e.g. learning to ride a bike or throwing birthday parties). In other words, they want providers to be 'like me' but 'not me'. Finally, when it comes to control, parents find no conflicts telling service providers exactly what to do and giving specific direction because they are paying for care. In this way, the market resolves tensions around control in ways that are not possible when accepting help from other resources (e.g. friends, relatives, neighbors) where

(Continued)

(Continued)

ongoing relationships are at stake. It proves to be much more of a challenge to request that a neighbor feed your child a specific food, follow a strict routine, and reinforce your rules when they are doing you a favor.

Marketers often recognize the benefits they offer in avoiding control tensions in tag-lines, such as those for kids' birthday party planners, which emphasize parents' ability to customize the party and add their personal touches. Companies seem less aware, though, of the substitutability and intimacy tensions they may create when marketing childcare activities. For example, a kids transportation service in Broward Country, Florida, boasts the following tagline: *Discover the same caring transportation for your kids that you'd give them yourself.*

Although this sentiment captures the idea that the providers genuinely care for the child and instills confidence that kids will be treated well, it also may remind parents that someone else is substituting for them. As we all know, family car rides move beyond the pure functionality of getting from place to place, and instead, typically entail intimate con-versations, adventures together, and concerns about protection and safety. Sometimes, it's hard for parents to give these things up.

CULTURAL DISCOURSES OF FAMILY

Given that family life dominates much of our time and motivation as consumers, a general understanding of family ideals and where they originate is useful for making sense of fam-ily behavior. Cultural discourses of family provide some initial clues. Cultural discourses are broadly defined as dominant narratives that guide behavior and shape our interpreta-tions of the world. These discourses are historically instantiated, politically motivated, and socially articulated (Bristor and Fischer 1993). For example, motherhood discourses, such as those projected through Mother's Day celebrations, engender a romanticized image of mothers who are maternal, virtuous, selfless, and feminine (Jones 1980). Push back from women's organizations in the early 1900s that decried the implications of cel-ebrating women's social roles as mothers as opposed to the 'whole of a woman's potential' paired with heated debates among legislators over the merits of a Mother's Day resolution and a lackluster response from businesses to promote it resulted in an inauspicious begin-ning (Jones 1980: 179–80). It wasn't until the endorsement from Sunday schools years later that the holiday, and its associated discourses celebrating the romanticized images of motherhood, gained favor as a national custom.

As Schmidt (1991) discusses, the emergence of Mother's Day as an almost universally celebrated national holiday also received a significant boost from the aggressive promo-tional efforts of the floral industry which sought to integrate the purchase and display of flowers into established cultural rituals, such as weddings, and new ones that were consistent with their product's domestic and feminine associations; hence, Mother's

Day proved to be a perfect cultural match. Soon after, the greeting card industry – with Hallmark being a key player – also began the idea that a sentimental card should be an integral part of the holiday. Once these commercial footholds were established, the array of goods and services ritually associated with Mother's Day began to expand. While a personal mission led by Anne Jarvis to honor the memory of her mother coupled with support from religious leaders helped pioneer the holiday, we should not underestimate the role of commercialization in its longevity. This alliance between the celebration of motherhood (as a romanticized ideal) and the ritualization of consumption (via flowers, cards, candies, meals out for mother) ensured that this holiday attained and maintained its cultural significances. As Schmidt (1991: 904) explains, 'Without the systematic, sustained campaign of commercial florists (and eventually other industries as well), Mother's Day would certainly have been a smaller observance and might well have remained a parochial event; it might even have gradually withered away like other Protestant days of the early twentieth century such as Children's Day or Temperance Sunday.'

Once instantiated, however, cultural discourses prove consequential in their ability to both guide notions of ideal behavior and exert forms of social control (e.g. Potter and Wetherell 1987). For families, cultural discourses of parenthood, childhood, motherhood, and fatherhood abound. For example, as noted above, cultural discourses of motherhood tend to emphasize caring, nurturing, and sacrifice as ideals. To align with these ideals, consuming in the proper way using the appropriate props becomes part of demonstrating that one is a 'good' mother and a moral parent (Bradford 2015; O'Donohoe et al. 2014). Examples range from everyday consumption products such as buying the safest, top-of-the-line car seat to prescriptions about women's bodies including how women should give birth and feed their babies. Although what constitutes a 'good' mother varies across cultures and contexts, the certainty of moral judgments regarding how one measures up to these ideals universally exists. In this way, cultural discourses legitimate certain family forms or relations over others and structure what it means to be a 'good' parent in the moral economy.

Collectively, religious, educational, political, and marketplace institutions are among the primary authors of cultural discourses. In comparison to other institutional forces, the marketplace contributes to the production and evolution of cultural discourses most directly through advertising and media portrayals of family (see Box 2.3). When a family's behavior does not match what is expected, they continuously engage with and contest cultural discourses as they make sense of and assign meaning to their own consumption choices and behavior. As you might imagine, marketers aim, either implicitly or explicitly, to situate their product or service as solutions that can alleviate the tensions between the realities of family life and the ideals according to the cultural discourses they helped advance, especially as these tensions often take the form of anxiety, risk-aversion, and guilt (Theodorou and Spyrou 2013). Consider, for example, that marketers commonly depict convenience products as an escape for parents from the daily drudgery of laundry, cleaning, or meal preparation by suggesting that the product affords parents some respite and much-needed family time (where of course kids are joyfully playing with siblings and parents minus the inevitable arguments and whining). When we weigh our every-day experiences against cultural ideals, we almost always fall short. Thus, consumption is presented as a means of coping with tensions and providing solutions to close the gap between real and ideal family life.

Importantly, families do not always blindly accept cultural discourses. In particular situations, consumers become more reflexive about cultural discourses and how they do and do not match their view of family. Family transitions, for example, represent a time when cultural discourse tends to be especially powerful, as the vulnerability of uncertain circumstances takes hold. When having children, for example, consumers actively think about how they want to parent and what kind of parent they want to be. In doing so, they often critically engage with cultural discourses as they navigate through this new life-stage. Likewise, cultural shifts in what constitutes family (e.g. the increasing acceptance of same-sex marriage) and gender roles (e.g. more and more fathers are choosing to be stay-at-home dads) prompt consumers to contemplate their own underlying assumptions about family and family life.

Box 2.3:   Real World Scenario

Marketers redefining family in ads

As a cultural medium, the marketplace affords legitimacy to particular forms and images of family by portraying them as normal, as an unremarkable case of family life. Marketing campaigns often act as a site of political struggles over definitions of family that challenge dominant cultural discourses (Velagaleti and Epp 2017). When companies engage in this reconstitution, they are typically met with both support and backlash from across consumer (as well as other stakeholder) groups. Consider the following examples:

- **General Mills** featured a biracial family in an advertisement for Cheerios in the United States. According to Adweek, although the ad received three times as many likes compared with dislikes among viewers, the racist backlash was so severe that it closed down the comments section on YouTube (Nudd 2013). The company responded by bringing back its famous biracial family in a 2014 Super Bowl spot created by Saatchi & Saatchi.
- **Honey Maid** made similar gestures to broaden the definition of family through its 'This is Wholesome' campaign featuring blended, interracial, immigrant, and same-sex families. In a statement made to Adweek by Mondelez International, senior marketing director Gary Osifchin explained the campaign received an overwhelmingly positive response and concluded, 'We're holding a mirror up to America and celebrating all-American families. We're on a journey here where we are very much showing America who they are. ... It's reality' (O'Leary 2014).

- Starting in the mid-1990s, IKEA has launched several ads supporting same-sex couples in both Europe and North America. For example, as part of a broader campaign in 2016 that attempted to redefine the American Dream, IKEA launched a series of ads in North America featuring the tagline 'all homes are created equal' alongside a same-sex, mixed-race couple (Figure 2.1). According to Leslie Stone, director of strategic services for Ogilvy – the firm responsible for the creative – IKEA's goal was to capture the diversity of family forms and create a more realistic portrait of family life (Klara 2016). This ad is similar to one launched in Europe in 2007 that also featured a mixed-race gay male couple and their daughter in an IKEA-furnished living room.

Figure 2.1   IKEA advertisement: 'All homes are created equal', 2016 (*credit to come*)

- **Wells Fargo** ran a television ad that showed a lesbian couple adopting a child with a hearing impairment. The company faced criticism from some religious groups, including the Billy Graham Evangelistic Association which pulled its accounts to protest the ad. In response, Wells Fargo stated that they stand by their ad, as supporting the LGBT community is aligned with their company values. Spokesperson Valerie Williams stated, 'We were not naïve to think that there would be no negative responses' but noted that the response to the ad was 'overwhelmingly positive' (Wattles 2015).
- **Ariel**, a laundry detergent brand, launched a 'Share the Load' campaign directed toward men in India to encourage them to do more housework. The brand also partnered with clothing brands (tags that read 'This fabric can be washed by both men and women') and dating sites (incorporating #sharetheload as part of women's selection criteria) to promote the slogan. According to Business Insider, the campaign succeeded in doubling its sales targets (Rath 2017).

FAMILY AS SOCIAL REPRODUCTION

As an institution, family provides our earliest immersion in the development of tastes, preferences and social skills through socialization. It is thus a dominant force in the smooth functioning of society, and in a consumer society part of this socialization specifies appropriate relationships between the family and the marketplace that results in learning to be consumers. Beyond explicit instruction from parents, children learn about consumption patterns that align with cultural norms by participating in family practices and routines (e.g. dinner, household functioning, shopping, discipline, leisure activities, etc.).

In particular, family practices pass along and reinforce aspects of families' idiosyncratic collective identities (Epp and Price 2008). For example, in their everyday interactions with commercial media and technologies (e.g. parental rules around appropriate use), families fortify norms about how and when they should connect with one another. In addition, participation in certain consumption pastimes such as sports, music, gaming, or outdoor adventures provides a foundation for communicating a family's identity. Similarly, families promote and transmit their core values through consumption practices such as when they choose volunteer vacations to emphasize civic responsibility or when they engage in water conservation at home to emphasize commitment to sustainability. Across these consumption contexts, part of the goal is to reproduce family values – reinforcing what is meaningful to a particular family – across generations.

While social reproduction does serve to reproduce important family values, this comes with some unintended consequences, such as the reproduction of limiting gender roles. The family meal offers a revealing example. Who does the provisioning, shopping, preparation, cooking, presentation, and clean up? How are these responsibilities divided (or not) among family members? Traditionally, these consumption responsibilities fall under the umbrella of motherhood, with acknowledgement of the sacrifices mothers make that tend to reinforce gender inequities (Cappellini et al. 2014; Miller 1998). Enactment of such basic consumer routines tends to reflect and reproduce taken-for-granted notions of gender roles, unless explicitly challenged. For instance, evolving notions of the division of labor within households (i.e., which family members perform which tasks within the household), and particularly, of the role of the father in the domestic sphere (see Box 2.4), have the potential to disrupt families' interactions over time. The updated version of Richard Scarry's *Best Word Book Ever* provides a subtle illustration of the importance of everyday enactments and images of family life in reproducing – and updating – gender roles (see Figure 2.2).

Thus, if the family is a site of social reproduction, then it is also a site of political struggle and social change. On a micro-level, it is the earliest foundation from which we build our perspectives. As such, whether through gender ideologies that push the boundaries of tradition – such as stay-at-home dads, notions of volitional family, or moms as primary

Figure 2.2   Richard Scarry's *Best Word Book Ever.* Left: 1963 version of family kitchen. Right: Modern day version of family kitchen

"Illustrations" from RICHARD SCARRY'S BEST WORD BOOK EVER by Richard Scarry, copyright © 1963 and renewed 1991 by Penguin Random House, LLC. Used by permission of Golden Books, an imprint of Random House Children's Books, a division of Penguin Random House LLC. All rights reserved.

Reprinted by permission of HarperCollins Publishers Ltd Amber Epp 975 University Ave 4253 Grainger Hall Madison, WI 53706 16-04-2018 © (originally published 1963, new edition 2013) (Scarry).

breadwinners – or through the micro-politics of navigating decisions about division of labor and childcare, the family becomes a space for potential transformation. Even minor shifts in families' everyday routines and interactions, then, may offer insights into global challenges related to health and environmental concerns. For example, researchers investigating the childhood obesity epidemic facing the United States place family squarely at the center of the problem (Moore et al. 2017). In part, they uncover patterns of eating and activity within the family that socialize children into a life trajectory toward or away from obesity.

Box 2.4:   Critical Reflection

Breaking the 'Doofus Dad' stereotype

A common critique of marketers when targeting both moms and dads is that they tend to portray parenthood using outdated and one-dimensional stereotypes. That is, the default in advertising is to maintain the status quo related to gender roles – mothers as thoughtful and dedicated caregivers and fathers as playmates, at best, and incompetent 'Doofus Dads' in other portrayals.

(Continued)

(Continued)

However, research indicates that gender roles are more fluid in contemporary families: 60% of US men who live with a partner prepare all or most of the meals for their family (Roper Report US study); 43% of men are the primary grocery shoppers for their families compared to only 11% in 2002 (The Hartman Group and MSLGROUP 2015); and men today spend triple the amount of time in the kitchen compared to what they did in 1970 (Mintel 2010). Men are also embracing their roles as fathers. The number of men in the United States who regularly care for children under the age of 5 increased to 32% in 2010 compared to only 19% in 1988 (US Census 2011). In addition, in the United States, almost 2 million fathers were stay-at-home dads (Pew Research Center, Livingston 2014) while 7 million identified as the primary caregivers (US Census 2011). In Canada, the number of stay-at-home dads has increased 161% since 1976 (Statistics Canada 2017) and, in Britain, the number of stay-at-home dads has doubled since 1993 (Office for National Statistics 2014).

Despite these trends and changes in gender roles and dynamics, many marketers still fall back on outdated stereotypes when communicating with their customers, especially with narrow portrayals of dads (Gentry and Harrison 2010). Huggies diapers, for example, launched an ad campaign, 'Dad Test', in 2012 that described dads taking care of their babies as 'the toughest test imaginable'. The ads depicted fathers as inattentive and neglectful caregivers who would rather watch sports on television than care for their babies. The ads were instantly met with outrage from fathers, and mothers, who viewed the ads as offensive and outdated. Parents loudly expressed concerns about the portrayal of fathers across blogs, social media, and through petitions. Consumers were outraged at both the negative depiction of fathers but also the influence of the ads on young boys and girls who are still forming their views and expectations of both genders.

Huggies executives quickly took action and withdrew the ads, replacing them with more nuanced versions that showed fathers attentively caring for their babies. A Huggies spokesperson stated: 'We have listened and learned. The company has already made changes to the campaign to better reflect the true spirit of the campaign – putting the performance of Huggies diapers and baby wipes to the test ... We also realize that a fact of life is that dads care for their kids just as much as moms do and in some cases are the only caregivers. The intention of our Huggies TV ad was to illustrate that dads have an opinion on product performance just as much as moms do' (ABC News 2012).

Recently, advertising standards groups have started to take note of the detrimental effect these types of ads can have on consumers. In July 2017, the UK's Advertising Standards Authority released a set of guidelines that, if implemented, would ban advertisements that portray traditional gender stereotypes. The author of the report, Ella Smillie, stated, 'Our review shows that specific forms of gender stereotypes in ads can contribute to harm for adults and children. Such portrayal can limit how people see themselves, how others see them, and limit the life decisions they take. Tougher standards in the areas we've identified will address harms and ensure that modern society is better represented' (Sweney 2017).

THE MATERIALITY OF FAMILY RELATIONS

We often do not give enough credit to the powerful influence of objects in our lives. The stuff that surrounds us provides the scaffolding for everyday life. Family objects and living spaces, in particular, reveal a material culture of family life that has the potential to intensify, limit, and transform family identity (Price 2012). Consider the diversity in family homes, especially in the configuration of common versus separate spaces that structure families' interactions. To illustrate, in most North American and Australian cities, the norm is for moderate-income families to live in single-family homes that allow space for family members to spread out. In contrast, given the population and close living quarters, Korean families typically dwell in apartment blocks that feature multi-purpose spaces. The structure of our living spaces not only reflects the cultural norms of family activity, but also shapes families' interactions (see Box 2.5).

Reciprocally, how families arrange their spaces, or order their possessions, directly implicates their priorities and identity claims (Csikszentmihalyi and Rochberg-Halton 1981). You can learn a lot about families by spending time in both their public and private living spaces, observing how families use and arrange their consumption objects. Photojournalist Peter Menzel did just this in the mid-1990s when he traveled the world and photographed families with their homes and possessions to learn about the daily lives of families, as represented by their stuff. The resulting images display a stunning array of objects, from the sacred texts held by a family in Bhutan to a Japanese family watching television around their dinner table, that characterize the similarities and differences across cultures.[1] Other photographers, such as Michele Crowe, took on a comparable pilgrimage more recently as an attempt to underscore the evolving universality of family by photographing diverse families – including gay parents, adoptive, child-free, and single parents – from across the globe in their homes. Within academic research, in his book *The Comfort of Things* (2008), anthropologist Daniel Miller visited 30 households on an ordinary street in London and uncovered the ways material objects provide a glimpse into the nature of relationships. We can learn a tremendous amount about families by examining what things they choose to buy, how they arrange and use them, and which things they are willing to part with, or not. These consumption artifacts not only reflect the identity of a family but also allow us to observe how varying levels of socioeconomic status and access to marketplace resources affect the ways in which families build and enact home. Overall, it is important to recognize that a family's objects are not a random assortment, but rather a curated collection, appropriately ordered to embody and facilitate relationships.

---

[1] You can view the image gallery from Menzel's Material World project here: http://menzelphoto. photoshelter.com/gallery-collection/Material-World-A-Global-Family-Portrait-by-Country/C0000d 0DI3dBy4mQ

Inevitably, ideas of designing spaces in the home and generating a sense of family togetherness are intimately linked. Across our own studies, we frequently hear tales about how the family kitchen and eating areas, such as the family table or breakfast bar, epitomize the hub of family life. Certainly, other objects also serve these functions such as the family car, cuddling up on the couch together for movie night, technological platforms, or other gathering spaces. While objects certainly help to facilitate and strengthen family relationships, they can also sometimes lead to clashes within families when members disagree over how to use shared spaces, when clutter disrupts family practices, or when family members disagree over who 'owns' various possessions (Dion et al. 2014).

Beyond the arrangement of existing possessions, another key question of interest to consumer researchers and to marketers who manage family-oriented brands is how do objects gain prominence and meanings within the family to remain relevant over time? The answer to this question, in part, lies in understanding family heirlooms – objects passed from generation to generation – that hold the potential to transfer meanings and identity to preserve family legacies (Curasi et al. 2004). These objects are considered sacred and kept from the marketplace as they are imbued with a family's history. By tracing an object's biography, we get a sense of how that object was initially pulled into the family's setting, the meanings and emotionality it took on, its uses and challenges, and its states of disrepair and possible rejuvenations (Kopytoff 1986). Although heirloom objects typically are regarded as vessels of family continuity, the objects themselves often require substantial change to remain relevant to subsequent generations as family values and practices shift, potentially displacing the heirloom (Epp and Price 2010; Ture and Ger 2016).

Similarly, brands face this same potential fate as they interact with particular families. If you ask college students why they buy a certain brand of peanut butter or laundry detergent, for example, they often reply that it's just what they remember from growing up in their households. These brands enjoy a history not afforded to competitors. To remain relevant, however, marketers must recognize the ways their brands are embedded within not only family relations, but also within other material environments and evolving consumption practices. Thus, an object's history might afford it some agency, meaning the ability to impact family relations and practices, but history alone will not ensure its place in the family over the long term.

To understand how material objects remain relevant to families, it is not enough to explain keeping behaviors. As such, substantial research also has investigated disposition processes to provide insights into why and how families get rid of their once-valued possessions (or disrupt brand loyalties) and to make sense of the emotional world that accompanies disposition. We often grow attached to the objects that surround us and facilitate our relationships, so letting go can prove a painful endeavor. Families create all sorts of strategies to lessen the ambivalence and guilt over parting with once-loved objects (Lastovicka and Fernandez 2005). They move objects into storage spaces to provide some distance before discarding. They find like-minded others to pass objects on to who they trust will care for, use, enjoy, and preserve the meaning of the objects in a similar fashion. Sometimes they photograph items to retain the sentiments before selling or discarding them, transferring the memories to the image rather than the object. Often, fierce nego-tiations occur within families over which objects can and cannot be discarded. In all of these cases, we find further evidence that objects embody relationships – to others, to activities, to family, to experiences – that require families to engage in emotional work in disposition processes.

Box 2.5:   Real World Scenario

Sustainability solutions start in the home

Families use their homes and material objects to express and enact their family identi-ties and values. For many families, a key value they want to enact in their daily family practices revolves around issues of sustainability and being environmentally conscious. In doing so, families transform their practices and material objects into sustainability solutions.

As the home becomes the center of sustainability efforts, consumers adopt both high- and low-tech solutions to problems of pollution, energy and water conservation, and healthfulness. Over the years, we have seen an uptake in consumers integrating sustainability solutions into their daily routines. For example, in our own research on new parents we see families striving to create a more environmentally friendly set of practices for their babies – this includes the use of cloth diapers (sometimes even home-made cloth diapers), bio-degradable diapers, home-made laundry detergent, and using glass/bpa free breastmilk storage solutions (Thomas and Epp 2017). Family meals have also become a focal site for families to adopt sustainability practices. Families are now much more aware of where their food is coming from and have focused on con-suming locally produced organic foods with about 1 in 3 US households now growing some of their own food (National Gardening Association 2014) – a movement called Urban Gardening. Families often supplement their home-grown harvest with that from local farms that they support through Community Supported Agriculture (CSA) pro-grams. Families also adopt water conservation practices, such as collecting rain water to water their gardens.

In contrast to these 'low-tech' solutions to sustainability, we also see families adopt-ing high-tech solutions that are becoming more prolific in the marketplace. Companies, such as Tesla, are building an entire portfolio of products that allow consumers to turn their homes into sustainable energy centers. Tesla, for example, has introduced solar roofs (roof shingles that are also solar panels) that work with Tesla's Powerwall home

(Continued)

(Continued)

battery that allow consumers to turn their homes into a sustainable personal utility center that reduces reliance on fossil fuels. This model of home-based power generation also seamlessly integrates with Tesla's electric cars. And, with the introduction of the lower-priced Model 3, it is now possible for middle-class families to integrate this particular sustainable product into their family's portfolio of material objects. As noted in *Scientific American*, Tesla is helping consumers 'harness the power of sunlight' (Hsu 2017). This remarkably low-tech idea is enabled by extremely high-tech solutions that help make the home the center of a family's sustainability efforts.

CONCLUSION AND RESEARCH DIRECTIONS

If we acknowledge the pervasive nature of family and the ways consumer culture provides resources for constituting family identity, then we can appreciate the force with which it matters. In this chapter, we covered the entanglements between family life and the marketplace that can sometimes spark controversy as well as reinforce the necessary connections between the two. We also considered dominant cultural discourses of family that underpin and legitimize certain family forms over others and shape ideals related to parenthood and childhood. With this notion in place, we recognized the stabilizing family practices that reproduce culture, both in its smooth functioning and in its structural inequalities. In the final section, we examined the material culture of families – the way objects, and how they are ordered, not only reflect cultural norms and personal relationships, but also structure family interactions.

In general, family consumer research historically has focused on relatively stable notions of family and how it is reinforced and reproduced, while noting the inherent inequities, contradictions, and constraints faced by families. It is beginning, however, to acknowledge the evolution of family life on both the macro-level, considering broad cultural shifts in the diversity and meanings associated with family as an institution, and on the micro-level, contemplating the implications of changes within households and families' everyday lives. As the marketplace and family life become more entwined, questions relating to families that lack the resources to engage with the marketplace take on even more importance. Families with limited socio-economic resources and those in emerging economies will inevitably form different relationships with the marketplace that reflect their unique position in both global and regional economies. Future research should adopt a more emergent lens to consider contemporary disruptions to family domains (e.g. evolving family life, global mobility, integrated technologies, cultural shifts, and access to resources; see Table 2.1) and their implications for consumer behavior.

Table 2.1 Future research directions

Research area	Central issue	Key questions
Evolving family types	What constitutes family is fluid and multidimensional, moving beyond traditional stereotypes.	How should marketers talk to and address the needs of a broader range of families such as single parent families, biracial families, LGBT families?
		How can marketers target their products to also meet the needs of dads, moving away from the idea that 'moms' are the primary shoppers and caregivers in families?
		What kinds of social, marketplace, and institutional barriers are inhibiting the ability of a more diverse range of families and caregivers to engage fully with the marketplace?
Global mobilities	Global mobilities spark new flows of objects and people that change consumers' relationships with home and family.	Urban millennials tend to live in small downtown apartments and view home as a place to store stuff and sleep rather than as the hub of family life. What does this mean for consumers' views of access vs. ownership of material goods?
		With consumers placing less value on objects and more value on experiences, what does this mean for branding practices and the role of brands as purveyors of consumer and family identity?
		Global mobility means that consumers often live in countries that differ from the homelands of their parents (i.e., Third Culture Kids). What impact does this merging of culture and nomadic lifestyle have on consumers' identities and associated relationship with material possessions?
Family and technology	Technologies are becoming increasing embedded in family life and practices.	How do new technologies both enhance and disrupt family life?
		Does the use of mobile technologies infringe on families spending quality time together?
		What kinds of technologies can be used to better integrate families?
		How can marketers bridge the gap between consumers' simultaneous desires for low-tech interactions and family practices (e.g. home-cooked meals) and their reliance on high-tech solutions for communications, information search, and entertainment?
Cultural shifts	Cultural shifts are often politically divisive with multiple views of what is considered appropriate.	How should companies interact with growing niche groups that tend to be politically divisive?
		How and when should companies engage with these groups?
		How do the actions of a company toward niche markets impact their broader appeal?
Access to Resources	Lower-income consumers and those in developing economies have limited access to marketplace resources.	How should companies adapt their offerings to meet the needs of lower-income consumers?
		What role should companies play in establishing consumption opportunities in developing economies?
		How does a lack of access to the marketplace influence family relations?
		What roles can, or should, governments play in improving consumers' access to marketplace resources?

RECOMMENDED READING

Coskuner-Balli, Gokcen and Thompson, Craig J. (2013) 'The status costs of subordinate cultural capital: At-home fathers' collective pursuit of cultural legitimacy through capitalizing consumption practices', *Journal of Consumer Research*, *40* (June): 19–41.

Cross, Samantha N. and Gilly, Mary C. (2014) 'Cultural competence and cultural compensatory mechanisms in binational households', *Journal of Marketing*, *78* (3): 121–39.

Epp, Amber M., Schau, Hope Jensen and Price, Linda L. (2014) 'The role of brands and mediating technologies in assembling long-distance family practices,' *Journal of Marketing*, *78* (May): 81–101.

Epp, Amber M. and Velagaleti, Sunaina (2014) 'Outsourcing parenthood? How families manage care assemblages using paid commercial services', *Journal of Consumer Research*, *41* (Dec): 911–35.

Ture, Meltem and Ger, Guliz (2016) 'Continuity through change: Navigating temporalities through heirloom rejuvenation', *Journal of Consumer Research*, *43* (June): 1–25.

REFERENCES

ABC News (2012) 'Huggies pulls ads after dads insulted', 14 March. http://abcnewsradioonline.com/business-news/huggies-pulls-ads-after-dads-insulted.html (accessed 24 January 2018).

Barnhart, Michelle, Huff, Aimee Dinnin, and Cotte, June (2014) 'Like a member of the family: Including and excluding paid caregivers in performances of family', *Journal of Marketing Management*, *30* (15–16): 1680–702.

Bologna, Caroline (2015) 'Powerful ads show what your child sees when you're addicted to your phone', *Huffington Post*, 10 July. www.huffingtonpost.ca/entry/powerful-ads-show-what-your-child-sees-when-youre-addicted-to-your-phone_us_559fd64be4b096729155ec27.

Bradford, Tonya Williams (2015) 'Beyond fungible: Transforming money into moral and social resources', *Journal of Marketing*, *79* (2): 79–97.

Bristor, Julia M. and Fischer, Eileen (1993) 'Feminist thought: Implications for consumer research', *Journal of Consumer Research*, *19* (March): 518–36.

Cappellini, Benedetta, Marilli, Alessandra, and Parsons, Elizabeth (2014) 'The hidden work of coping: Gender and the micro-politics of household consumption in times of austerity', *Journal of Marketing Management*, *30* (15–16): 1597–624.

Cheong, Kakit and Mitchell, Alex (2015) 'Kwento: Using a participatory approach to design a family storytelling application for domestic helpers', in Julio Abascal et al. (eds), *Human–Computer Interaction – INTERACT 2015*. New York: Springer International. pp. 493–500.

Csikszentmihalyi, Mihaly and Rochberg-Halton, Eugene (1981) *The Meaning of Things: Domestic Symbols and the Self*. New York: Cambridge University Press.

Curasi, Carolyn Folkman, Price, Linda L., and Arnould, Eric J. (2004) 'How individuals' cherished possessions become families' inalienable wealth', *Journal of Consumer Research*, *31* (December): 609–22.

Danovitch, Judith H. and Mills, Candice M. (2009) 'Children's vulnerability to advertising messages from familiar characters', *Proceedings of the Consumer Culture and Ethical Treatment of Children Conference*, pp. 72–82.

Dion, Delphine, Sabri, Ouidade, and Guillard, Valérie (2014) 'Home sweet messy home: Managing symbolic pollution', *Journal of Consumer Research*, *41* (October): 565–89.

Epp, Amber M. and Price, Linda L. (2008) 'Family identity: A framework of identity interplay in consumption practices', *Journal of Consumer Research*, *35* (June): 50–70.

Epp, Amber M. and Price, Linda L. (2010) 'The storied life of singularized objects: forces of agency and network transformation', *Journal of Consumer Research*, *36* (5): 820–37.

Epp, Amber M., Schau, Hope Jensen, and Price, Linda L. (2014) 'The role of brands and mediating technologies in assembling long-distance family practices', *Journal of Marketing*, *78* (May): 81–101.

Epp, Amber M. and Velagaleti, Sunaina (2014) 'Outsourcing parenthood? How families manage care assemblages using paid commercial services', *Journal of Consumer Research*, *41* (Dec): 911–35.

Gentry, James and Harrison, Robert (2010) 'Is advertising a barrier to male movement toward gender change?' *Marketing Theory*, *10* (1): 74–96.

Hochschild, Arlie R. (2003) *The Commercialization of Intimate Life: Notes from Home and Work*. Berkeley, CA: University of California Press.

Hsu, Jeremy (2017) 'Will Tesla's tiles finally give solar shingles their day in the sun?', *Scientific American*, 18 May. www.scientificamerican.com/article/will-tesla-rsquo-s-tiles-finally-give-solar-shingles-their-day-in-the-sun/.

IBISWorld (2016) 'IBISWorld Business Environment Report: Government funding for primary and secondary education', IBISWorld Inc.

Jones, Kathleen W. (1980) 'Mother's Day: The creation, promotion, and meaning of a new holiday in the progressive era', *Texas Studies in Literature and Language*, *22* (2): 175–96.

Klara, Robert (2016) 'Ikea says the American dream is about more than just buying stuff', *Adweek*, 26 September. www.adweek.com/brand-marketing/ikea-says-american-dream-about-more-just-buying-stuff-173683/.

Kopytoff, Igor (1986) 'The cultural biography of things: Commoditization as process', in Arjun Appadurai (ed.), *The Social Life of Things*. Cambridge: Cambridge University Press. pp. 64–94.

Lastovicka, John L. and Fernandez, Karen V. (2005) 'Three paths to disposition: The movement of meaningful possessions to strangers', *Journal of Consumer Research*, *31* (March): 813–23.

Livingston, Gretchen (2014) 'Growing number of dads home with the kids', Pew Research Center, 5 June. www.pewsocialtrends.org/2014/06/05/growing-number-of-dads-home-with-the-kids/.

Marcoux, Jean-Sebastien (2009) 'Escaping the gift economy', *Journal of Consumer Research*, *36* (December): 671–85.

Miller, Daniel (1998) *A Theory of Shopping*. Ithaca, NY: Cornell University Press.

Miller, Daniel (2008) *The Comfort of Things*, Cambridge: Polity.

Mintel (2010) 'Marketing to Dads – US' – August 2010. http://store.mintel.com/marketing-to-dads-us-august-2010.

Moore, Elizabeth S., Wilke, William L., and Desrochers, Debra M. (2017) 'All in the family? Parental roles in the epidemic of childhood obesity', *Journal of Consumer Research*, *43* (February): 824–59.

National Gardening Association (2014) *Garden to Table: A 5-year Look at Food Gardening in America*. Vermont: National Gardening Association. Available at: https://garden.org/special/pdf/2014-NGA-Garden-to-Table.pdf.

Nudd, Todd (2013) 'It's 2013, and people are still getting worked up about interracial couples in ads', *Adweek*, 30 May. www.adweek.com/creativity/its-2013-and-people-are-still-getting-worked-about-interracial-couples-ads-149889/.

O'Donohoe, Stephanie, Hogg, Margaret, Maclaran, Pauline, Martens, Lydia, and Stevens, Lorna (2014) *Motherhoods, Markets, and Consumption*. London: Routledge.

Office for National Statistics (2014) 'Stay-at-home fathers double in 20 years', *Mail Online*, 31 March. www.dailymail.co.uk/news/article-2593027/Stay-home-fathers-double-20-years-229-000-look-children.html

O'Leary, Noreen' (2014) 'Honey Maid didn't test its "This Is Wholesome" campaign before it launched', *Adweek*, 22 September. www.adweek.com/brand-marketing/honey-maid-didnt-test-its-wholesome-campaign-it-launched-160256/.

Potter, Jonathan and Wetherell, Margaret (1987) *Discourse and Social Psychology: Beyond Attitudes and Behavior*. London: Sage.

Price, L. (2012) 'Family stuff: Materiality and identity', in Russell Belk and Ayalla Ruvio (eds), *The Routledge Companion to Identity and Consumption*. New York, NY: Routledge. pp. 302–12.

Rath, Julien (2017) 'Inside the 11 best advertising campaigns of the last year', *Business Insider*, 12 March. www.businessinsider.com/the-11-best-advertising-campaigns-of-2016-2017-3/#ariel-share-the-load-2.

Schmidt, Leigh Eric (1991) 'The commercialization of the calendar: American holidays and the culture of consumption, 1870–1930', *The Journal of American History*, *78* (3): 887–916.

Statistics Canada (2017) 'Changing profile of stay-at-home parents'. www.statcan.gc.ca/pub/11-630-x/11-630-x2016007-eng.htm.

Sweney, Mark (2017) 'Standards body unveils plan to crack down on sexist advertisements', *The Guardian*, 17 July. www.theguardian.com/media/2017/jul/18/new-measures-announced-to-crack-down-on-sexist-adverts.

The Hartman Group and MSLGROUP (2015) 'New study reveals growing influence of the male shopper'. Press release 10 February. www.prnewswire.com/news-releases/new-study-reveals-growing-influence-of-the-male-shopper-300033494.html.

Theodorou, Eleni and Spyrou, Spyrus (2013) 'Motherhood in utero: Consuming away anxiety', *Journal of Consumer Culture*, *13* (2): 79–96.

Thomas, Tandy Chalmers and Epp, Amber M. (2017) 'The best laid plans: Consumer responses to betrayals', Working Paper, Queen's University, Kingston, ON.

Ture, Meltem and Ger, Guliz (2016), 'Continuity through change: Navigating temporalities through heirloom rejuvenation', *Journal of Consumer Research*, *43* (June): 1–25.

Turkle, Sherry (2010) *Alone Together: Why We Expect More from Technology and Less from Each Other*, New York: Basic Books.

US Census (2011) 'One-third of fathers with working wives regularly care for their children'. Press Release. 5 December. www.census.gov/newsroom/releases/archives/children/cb11-198.html.

Velagaleti, Sunaina and Epp, Amber M. (2017) 'From symbolic violence to revolution: How social change impacts consumer legitimacy in the marketplace'. Working paper, University of Wisconsin–Madison.

Wattles, Jackie (2015) 'Wells Fargo's gay couple ad sparks evangelist protest', *CNN Money*. http://money.cnn.com/2015/06/09/news/companies/franklin-graham-lgbt-wells-fargo/index.html.

Zelizer, Viviana (2011) *Economic Lives: How Culture Shapes the Economy*, Princeton, NJ: Princeton University Press.

3
CRITICAL REFLECTIONS
ON CONSUMER IDENTITY

Michelle F. Weinberger, Northwestern University
David Crockett, University of South Carolina

CHAPTER OVERVIEW

- Some aspects of identity take material form in markets, which offer *marketplace resources* useful for doing identity work.
- In a broad sense, the market provides an *interpretive lens* for understanding our own preferences (and others') for certain objects (e.g. action movies or documentaries), affinities, and interests.
- *Legitimate and stigmatized identities* and *identity practices* are socially constructed and reinforced by representations (or, *what is communicated*) in advertisements, social media communications, and retail displays.
- Marketing researchers and practitioners debate the extent to which consumers' identity work is shaped by cultural and sociological forces beyond their volitional control, such as those that limit their access to marketplace resources or constrain their imagination about which identities are possible or legitimate.
- Practitioners create *representations of dominant identities* based on marketing and branding strategy and disseminate them through media. Taken as a whole these representations communicate both what is normal (*mainstream identity*) and what is normative (*aspirational identity*).
- Practitioners also create *representations of non-dominant identities* based on marketing and branding strategy and disseminate them through media. These representations correspond to four basic strategic types, or models: (1) the United Nations Model, (2) the Cultural Appropriation Model, (3) the Normalization Model, and (4) the Effortful Accommodation Model.
- *Consumer resistance* to identity representations occurs when they use marketplace resources for social change (e.g. 'buycotts', boycotts, protest, etc.) or they reject the market as a legitimate provider of resources useful for identity work (e.g. voluntary simplifiers).

INTRODUCTION

Suppose someone said to you, 'Tell me about yourself. But, do it without referring to anything that you bought or that was bought for you.' You could not talk about being a huge music or movie fan. Nor could you talk about your affinity for yoga, running or cycling, skateboarding or snowboarding, fashion, gaming or e-sports, hunting, collecting, shopping, or cosplaying. It is even challenging for ethnic/national, gender, and religious identities such as being Jewish, French, or female. Each of these aspects of your identity is accompanied by an array of necessary goods and services that come from the marketplace. How coherent could your description of yourself be without references to any of them? We suspect the answer is 'not very coherent'. The marketplace is deeply implicated in how we see the world and how we see ourselves in it. Yet we typically understate the importance of *marketplace resources* to the work of building identity until we are asked (or compelled) to do such work without those resources.

A central debate in marketing is about the extent to which building identity is a fully *agentic* activity; that is to say, entirely within an individual's control. Among practitioners, like advertisers whose job involves tapping into and influencing identity work, this debate goes right to the heart of marketing strategy. In this chapter, we trace how identity work became a focus of marketing strategy through mass market consumption. We also introduce core concepts to help readers understand the role of the mass market and marketing strategy in constructing *dominant representations* of identity. We also show that even agentic consumption is subject to social influences and constraints in ways that people do not readily recognize.

WHEN SOCIAL IDENTITY MET THE MASS MARKET

Think back to high school. Were you and your friends jocks? Were you nerds or geeks (math, science, computer, band, or chorus)? Were you preps, hippies, goths, or fashionistas? Each of these adolescent social identity archetypes comes with its own easily recognizable pattern of consumption, especially (but hardly limited to) a sense of style and dress. Many if not all of these archetypes would be instantly familiar to your parents or even grandparents, despite the fact that styles have changed. Each identity (and the styles associated with it) is widely recognizable despite emerging in particular places under particular historical conditions. Each is learned and legitimized such that generations of adolescents come to look and act in ways that are fairly true to a theme while simultaneously displaying a seemingly limitless number of expressions based on that theme.

We tend to think of identity as entirely personal because expressions of style have so few absolute limits, but prior to the Industrial Revolution (c.1760–1840) much of our social identity was ascribed to us at birth. Social roles, assigned based on family, location, religion, gender, occupation, etc., largely fixed boundaries around what identity could be and how much status a given identity could have (Fowles 1996). As long as society remained relatively stable, it tolerated few departures from set social roles. But, moments of instability could generate tremendous anxiety about social roles while freeing people to construct identities more proactively and self-consciously in ways that departed from established norms.

Global trade, which long preceded the Industrial Revolution, also created much of the infrastructure necessary to facilitate individual identity work. It developed the expansive distribution networks required to broaden access to the goods for sale in the market-place (e.g. sugar, tobacco, textiles, etc.) that would become material markers of identity. As consumer demand slowly replaced subsistence as a primary motive behind production, producers began to differentiate their offerings. They attempted to gain competitive advantage by appealing to what would come to be known as 'segments' of consumers with different needs. Re-sellers and shopkeepers, who dealt directly with customers, began to implement strategies to help fuel demand by making shops and shopping more customer-friendly. They also began to promote products in ways that helped tie identity to marketplace consumption. Consider for example the advertisement for men's wigs that appeared in the Montgomery Ward & Company 1895 Catalog & Buyer's Guide (Figure 3.1). At a time when producers mostly touted the product's technical advantages and resulting functional benefits, this ad by contrast offers 'cosmopolitanism' as a symbolic product benefit. Then it communicates a fear-based appeal, where cosmopolitanism is threatened by balding, which is likened to deterioration (peeling paint). The hairpiece subdues the threat by ensuring a proper presentation of the self.

As the culture of mass consumption emerged in earnest during the late 19th century, the marketing practitioners of that time created representations of 'the good life', including what that looked like, who it was for (and not for), how it was enacted, and what goods it involved. They disseminated these representations through mass media, which included books, magazines, newspapers, and catalogues. These representations provided examples to people who used them as aids to construct a social identity and that associated the good life with consumption (Fowles 1996). According to US historian Lizbeth Cohen (2004), consumption was at the heart of what it meant to be a full social and cultural citizen, because it comprised one of the very few routes to attain higher status for people not born into those positions. By the turn of the 20th century it had become the primary (but not the only) way to display social identity, and it served to distinguish traditional elites from the garish nouveaux riches, and them from the lower classes (see Veblen 1899).

As the 20th century progressed, the relationship between consumption and identity became more nuanced, especially in the decades following World War II. The notion that consumption plays a role in identity development became more commonplace,

Men's Wigs.

Directions for measuring the head for a wig, to insure a good fit. Mention number of inches.

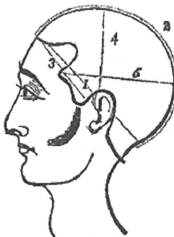

No. 1.   The circumference of the head.
No. 2.   Forehead to nape of the neck.
No.   3.   Ear to ear, across the forehead,
No. 4.   Ear to ear, over the top.
No. 5.   Temple to temple, around the back.

TO MEASURE FOR A

TOUPEE.

Cut a piece of paper the exact size and shape of the bald spot; also the measure around the head, and mention which side the parting is on.

Each

17730   Men's Toupee, weft foundation.........$ 5.50
17733   Men's Toupee Wigs, ventilated foundation........ 10.00
17735   Toupee Paste, for keeping the same in place.   Per stick... .50
17737   Men's Full Wigs for street wear, weft seam, with crown cotton foundation........ 8.00
17730   Men's Wigs, silk foundation, vegetable net seam.... 12.00
17755   Men's Wigs, silk foundation, gauze net seam...... 15.00
17758   Men's Wigs, silk foundation, hair lace ....$18.00 to 21.00
Extra shades will be charged according to color.
17704   Minstrel Wigs. Each.................$0.75
NOTE.—In addition to above list of men's wigs, we can furnish all kinds of wigs for either ladies or men, for stage, masquerade or character purposes.
17768   Grease Paints, 8 colors in a box, for make-up purposes. Per box,.............$1.00

WHAT would you think of a city man if he let the paint peel off his house?

What do you suppose the city man thinks of you under the same circumstances?

Figure 3.1   Advertisement for men's wigs in the 1895 Montgomery Ward & Co. Catalog & Buyer's Guide

Life was just one diaper after another until Sarah got her new Mustang. Somehow Mustang's sensationally sophisticated looks, its standard-equipment luxuries (bucket seats, full carpeting, vinyl interior, chiffon-smooth, floor-mounted transmission) made everyday cares fade far, far into the background. Suddenly there was a new gleam in her husband's eye. (For the car? For Sarah? Both?) Now Sarah knows for sure: Mustangers have more fun!

Best year yet to go Ford

MUSTANG!
MUSTANG!
MUSTANG!

Figure 3.2   Advertisement for 1965 Ford Mustang

and by the 1960s producers and consumers began to shift their focus to exploring how to participate in a culture of mass consumption (Holt 2002). For example, the Mustang ad from 1965 (Figure 3.2) makes a fundamentally similar kind of fear appeal as the Men's Wigs ad. (It may come as a surprise to some readers that the Ford Mustang – the quintessential American muscle car – originally targeted female drivers.) At a time when Americans were flocking to suburbs, and thereby becoming two-car households, the ad highlights the 'domestic feminine' and the threat posed to women by drudgery and boredom ('... one diaper after another'). Where the wig ad claims to ward off the critical gaze of others, the Mustang ad claims to reduce anxiety ('everyday cares fade far, far into the background'). The promise of more fun extends to those Mustangers, like Sarah, who have the sophistication to choose, use, and properly appreciate the product. This shift towards highlighting the traits of the product user, increasingly at the expense of details about the product, is so widespread that by the turn of the 21st century it was no longer notable.

DOING SOCIAL IDENTITY WORK IN THE MARKETPLACE

Social identity is intersubjective. In other words, it consists of how a person thinks of herself (internal identification) as well as how others think of her (external identification), and both are important. The marketplace puts social roles, objects, and relationships – and by extension internal and external identification – in a constant dialogue. As an example, consider adults who engage in what we usually consider child-focused hobbies, like collecting and building LEGOs. The dialog between internal and external identification may normally be harmonious for the adult LEGO enthusiast who works as an architect, but you can imagine how it might quickly turn dissonant when he says to a first date that his hobby is building LEGOs. This occurs across a range of identity categories, for example gender (I feel male but am visually identified by others as female) and ethnicity (I feel American but am visually identified by others as Mexican; I am not Jewish, but I have a Jewish sounding last name).

People inevitably use consumption to emphasize some aspects of identity while relegating other aspects to the background, striving to balance the innate human need to 'fit in' and belong with an equally natural desire to reinforce personal identity. People are very much aware that the markers of identity they put on display, which include how they carry themselves, what they consume and how they talk about it, are constantly being interpreted by others. Consequently, at moments they feel compelled to make tradeoffs between the conflicting goals of fitting in to a broad (often ill-fitting) social identity versus reinforcing personal identity. For instance, Weinberger (2015) examines people in the United States who do not celebrate Christmas because of their religious identities and/or beliefs. She explores how choices about engaging in Christmas celebrations take on heightened importance for this small minority because of the holiday's key role in reinforcing social ties. She finds that non-celebrants often opt in, choosing to attend parties and give gifts, effectively pushing their own identity to the background in order to reinforce their ties to members of the dominant group. They often see this as necessary but not desirable because other celebrants don't recognize, never consider, or would refuse to endorse their non-dominant identity practices. This was most often a problem on the job, where the consequences of opting out are worse for those with non-dominant identities.

Under some circumstances, even dominant identities can come to be discredited if they come to be perceived as abnormal in the eyes of others. For that to occur, some personal attribute must be associated with negative stereotypes. Such an association discredits (or 'spoils') identity, a process commonly referred to as *stigmatization* (Goffman 1963/2009; Mirabito et al. 2016). Once stigmatized, identities are not merely perceived to be different. They are viewed as abnormal and thus subject to marginalization, which has consequences that range from trivial to quite severe. Stigmatization is commonly experienced as an assault on a person's sense of self-worth. The stigmatized are perceived by others to lack legitimacy and status, and to be morally deserving of varying degrees of ostracization (Lamont et al. 2016). For example, Natalie Ross Adkins and Julie Ozanne (2005) observe that low literate adults are commonly stigmatized as irredeemably unintelligent, and deserving of derision rather than simply lacking a crucial skill. Stigma commonly accrues to traits that are not freely chosen, like race and ethnicity. For instance, black identity has historically been stigmatized and is widely regarded as low in social status. On this basis, blacks in the United States, along with other racialized minorities, experience significant discrimination and ostracization. To wit, sociologist Maria Krysan and colleagues have found across numerous studies that task people with constructing their 'most desired' and 'least desired' neighborhoods that among whites, even after controlling for the effects of socio-economic status, the 'most desired' neighborhoods routinely have a very small proportion of black neighbors (Chang 2017).

A significant part of identity work involves creating meaningful *boundaries* that reliably distinguish between 'just the right amount' of some trait, too much of it, or not enough. More broadly, boundaries help differentiate *us*, the legitimate or possibly even valorized, from *them*, the illegitimate and stigmatized. Boundaries are important because they reveal the nature of the social interactions that construct and reinforce legitimate and stigmatized identities inside boundaries and between them (see Lamont and Molnar 2002). A study by Luedicke (2015) illustrates these boundary-marking interactions. The author found that indigenous locals initially welcomed immigrant newcomers, whom they framed as industrious and hard-working. However, locals also ridiculed and resisted the immigrants' efforts to thoroughly integrate into the community while at the same time expressing resentment about their efforts to retain aspects of their original culture, such as language, dress, and religious identity. Put differently, the locals erected boundaries that were both permeable and rigid. This allowed locals to think of immigrants as simultaneously 'like us' and 'not like us'. The marketplace plays an especially important role in such interactions by representing what is (and is not) legitimate through marketing communications and products that valorize (or stigmatize) particular identity practices.

USING MASS MARKET RESOURCES IN IDENTITY WORK

Marketers craft imagery and tell particular stories in order to appeal to their targeted ideal consumer segments. Those segments are associated with particular identities. Consider the multitude of brand advertisements, catalogs, store mannequins and displays, and brand websites that you are exposed to every day. What identities are represented?

Think about the types of products sold in stores where you shop. Whose identities do those products reference? In much of the Western world, certain identities are overwhelmingly positioned as having unquestioned legitimacy. A person who is defined as white, middle-class (or better), cosmopolitan, thin, cisgender, and a politically moderate Protestant living in a traditional nuclear family household (or demographically similar young adults in non-family households) is in most respects the targeted ideal. This set of demographic descriptors constitutes the *dominant identity representations* in the mass market. Most identities not on this list experience varying degrees of stigmatization.

To be clear, these dominant identities are not inherently any better or worse than others. Rather, marketers and many consumers usually take for granted that they are both normal (*mainstream*) and normative (*aspirational*). They are the identity categories against which others are commonly compared. Obviously, the entire mass market also includes other identities. However, their associated stigmas exclude them from the categories of reference and often signal that these are not the identities of the targeted ideal consumer. To the extent that consumption is important to building identity, exclusion influences what is imaginable and what is legitimately possible for everyone – not just the stigmatized.

Box 3.1:   Critical Reflection

Consumer discrimination and profiling

Kayla Phillips, a 21-year-old African American woman, was falsely accused of credit card fraud by employees of Barneys, an upscale Manhattan retailer, in 2013. Later that same year, Trayon Christian was also unjustly accused of fraud after purchasing an item at the same Madison Avenue location. In 2014, Barneys agreed to pay $525,000 to settle nearly a dozen allegations of consumer racial profiling, or what some referred to as 'shop and frisk' (Smith 2014).

Although companies often target specific identity-based consumer segments, trying to appeal to them based on marketing strategy, it is illegal to discriminate against particular consumers in the United States and many other parts of the world. That is, with few exceptions, customers should all have access to the firm's offering at the same list price. Nonetheless, the experiences of consumers with non-dominant identities in retail and service establishments makes abundantly clear that discrimination is part of their everyday experience. Gallup polls in the United States reveal that a substantial portion of whites (almost 40%) believe that racial profiling in the marketplace is widespread, but the majority of blacks and Hispanics believe this to be the case (Carlson 2004).

(Continued)

(Continued)

Many legal cases, academic studies, and reports focus on racially oriented discrimination, and a disproportionate number of incidents are racially oriented (Harris et al. 2005), but discrimination can occur based on class, gender, sexuality, religion, age, body type, or other group-based identity. Identity-based discrimination can sometimes involve restrictions on access to products or services, such as not being allowed to purchase a product, being refused service, or being sold at lower quality and/or higher prices (Harris et al. 2005). Or, it may involve differential treatment at the hands of employees (or even other patrons). Profiling may take various forms such as excessive surveillance without probable cause.

Identity-based profiling and discrimination can be overt or subtle. Many cases involve innocent shoppers who are viewed with suspicion and accused of theft or who are refused entry into an establishment. Take, for example, controversy over dress codes at bars and night clubs, which can be quite reasonable, but applied in a discriminatory fashion. Many have noted that these restrictions operate as a shorthand to deny entry in an illegal way (Selvam 2017). Some cases of exclusion are less overt. In an experiment with minority and white loan applicants at a bank, a study found whites were initially offered more information from the loan officer, while minorities were offered less information and asked to provide more supporting evidence for applications (Bone et al. 2014).

The outcomes of identity-based discrimination (whether based on exclusion or differential treatment) can obviously be quite harmful. Economically, victims are effectively paying more (or the same amount) for less of a product or a worse experience. Additionally, scholars have shown that the feeling of rejection, where one is not welcome, has long-term negative effects on self-esteem and agency (Bone et al. 2014).

Nevertheless, those with non-dominant, stigmatized identities must manage their identity positions. One approach to doing so is to downplay aspects of one's non-dominant identity to avoid stigma where possible. For example, some consumer research shows how African American consumers are careful to disassociate themselves from racial stereotypes when dining in mixed-race groups (Wooten 1995). In other words, not wishing to confirm negative racial stereotypes in a mixed-race setting, they were less likely to eat foods closely associated with black stereotypes, like fried chicken, that they might otherwise eat when dining in same-race groups. Additional research describes a closely related approach to managing identity, which involves actively affirming dominant identity taste practices to signal their legitimacy, while another involves actively disavowing stigma by expanding the boundaries of what is legitimate thereby destigmatizing aspects of non-dominant identity (Crockett 2017). Researchers studying stigma in a very different context question how successful these practices are in actually reducing stigma. For instance, one study shows that women who are chief household income earners must often engage in practices designed to protect the identities of their male partners who otherwise might fall into the heavily stigmatized category of non-providers (Commuri and Gentry 2005). It is not uncommon for those with non-dominant identities to feel compelled to undermine their identity just to engage in everyday social interactions.

Overall, the scope of mass-mediated identity representations that might act as marketplace resources for those with non-dominant identities is thought to be quite limited. For example, one study found that only a small percentage of advertisements that incorporate representations of black popular culture were actually designed to authentically represent and communicate with African Americans as target customers. Most ads lacked any blackness representations at all, or they featured people of color as part of a background ensemble solely to signal diversity to the mass market. In other instances, they used features of black popular culture (rather than black people) to represent ideas like coolness to the mass market (Crockett 2008). Despite this, at times marketers make use of non-dominant identity representations. Later in this chapter, we spotlight four strategic approaches (or 'models') for how non-dominant identities are represented in mass media.

Dominant identities are often made to appear unchanging and unchangeable. However, they do change. One means by which they change is through the incorporation of non-dominant identities into marketing communications. This happens when they gain enough legitimacy to be pursued by marketers as distinct segments or niches. This can be the result of organized campaigns by marketers or consumer-led social movements that stimulate shifts in the way society (and firms) think. For example, organized efforts by advertising entrepreneurs from Cuba and later Mexico resulted in the creation of a Hispanic market segment, which incorporates a variety of different nationalities, cultures, and languages into a single group (Mora 2014). Similarly, brand managers have created numerous regional Asian brands reliant on a globalization motif and an imagined Asia that is urban, modern, and multicultural (Cayla and Eckhardt 2008).

A somewhat different way that dominant identities change in the market is when non-dominant identities are incorporated into the mass market entirely. That is, when the boundaries of the mass market expand to incorporate the previously excluded. For instance, since 2015 (when same-sex marriage became legal throughout the United States) the wedding industry has begun to incorporate LGBTQ couples (Bonos 2016). Additionally, since the early 2000s clothing designers have been more intentional about offerings products to plus-sized shoppers (Scaraboto and Fischer 2013). Marketers of all types now portray single and stay-at-home fathers as competent parents and consumers (Coskuner-Balli and Thompson 2013). Expanding the boundaries of the mass market and its 'hailed viewer' ultimately provides a broader set of identity resources for consumers to draw on as they perform identity work. Although these trends are clearly hopeful, we note that perceptions about stigmatized identity can be quite stubborn and difficult to change. In their study of plus-sized fashion bloggers (who called themselves 'fatshionistas'), researchers found that the women successfully garnered positive market attention for women who had been woefully underserved in the market. But, they were only marginally successful in destigmatizing representations of plus-sized women in the mainstream market (Scaraboto and Fischer 2013).

To sum things up on identity work, consumers are *agentic* in many ways. They carefully use consumption to construct identities, and carefully use marketplace resources (e.g. *identity representations*) to communicate them. Their identity projects are very much tied to the marketplace, which provides not only material and symbolic resources for constructing identity but a stage on which to enact it. Many (if not most) consumers are quite creative identity builders, configuring market offerings in both obvious and unexpected ways. However, most consumers are also largely unaware of underlying limits on the resources made available to them for doing identity work. Sometimes these limitations, like stigmatized non-dominant identities, leave people feeling invisible and powerless. At other times, people use their individual and collective power in the marketplace to bring attention to their exclusion and misrepresentation, and to stretch the boundaries of what is possible and legitimate. For marketers to keep up they must develop a nuanced understanding of their role in identity construction, particularly how consumers interpret and use products and mass-mediated communications.

REPRESENTATIONS OF NON-DOMINANT IDENTITIES

Given that the marketplace partially provides legitimacy to and resources for non-dominant identity projects, it is important to understand some of the primary representational strategies used in marketing campaigns and entertainment media. We identify four basic strategies (or models) firms commonly use for representing non-dominant identities.

(1) The United Nations Model (Multiculturalism). In what we call the 'United Nations Model', several non-dominant and dominant identities are represented in the same communication (typically advertisements). This depiction of a proverbial rainbow of skin tones, religious markers, or genders, etc. is a strategy whose goal is to signal that the company or organization recognizes and values members of those varied identities. For instance, in his content analysis of a large sample of ads, Crockett (2008) found that roughly 90% of ads that utilized any sort of representation of blackness did so to highlight multiculturalism to the audience. This form of inclusion is a step towards legitimization, but advertisers are still making choices about which non-dominant identities to represent, which to exclude, and how. Moreover, these advertisements do not always communicate that non-dominant identity-holding consumers are the target. Rather, they deliver a message to their target that the organization values diversity. To illustrate, the advertisement for Esteé Lauder in Figure 3.3 shows three leading models with different ethnic backgrounds. The ad signals that the firm values diversity. Note that the white model, flanked by non-white models, is the visual focus, which commonly occurs in these types of ads.

Nevertheless, this strategy can be successful for attracting consumers with diverse identities and allows those who assume cosmopolitan identities to feel good about the values of the brands they purchase. In one example, the cable television network Home & Garden Television (HGTV), whose programming features real families house hunting and doing home renovations, increased the racial and ethnic diversity on its show and saw a marked increase in viewership by those represented groups (Montagne and Ulaby 2011).

Figure 3.3   Estée Lauder advertisement

(2) The Cultural Normalization Model. In the 'Cultural Normalization Model', non-dominant identities are visually represented in the exact same way as those with dominant identities. Their identity is not the focus of the ad and the content contains no specific appeals to identity. A Cheerios advertisement (Figure 3.4) aired in 2014 depicts an interracial couple telling their daughter that they are expecting another child. (You can access the full advertisement on YouTube at www.youtube.com/watch?v=jLAYkUHnvWw.) This advertisement could have been executed in an identical way utilizing virtually any couple at any identity position. In this way, it serves to normalize the identity of the hailed viewer who can presumably see him or herself in the ad. Like the UN Model, the Cultural Normalization Model signals the firm's valuation of diversity, which appeals to those who similarly value it, as well as those longing to see their own identities so recognized. However, this model typically limits notions of identity to what can be represented visually. Further, it does not generally recognize the unique identity practices of specific groups. For instance, in Velagaleti and Epp's

(2016) study of lesbian weddings, their informants are critical of a Target advertisement using Cultural Normalization. It depicts what is ostensibly a lesbian couple in a kitchen (Figure 3.5). Although these consumers are in fact the intended target market, some see the couple in the ad as a simple visual substitution for a heterosexual couple rather than an accurate representation of lesbian couples.

Figure 3.4   Still from a 2014 Cheerios advertisement depicting an interracial family

Figure 3.5   Target advertisement featuring a same-sex couple

(3) The Cultural Appropriation Model. In the 'The Cultural Appropriation Model', marketers makes use of authentic representations of non-dominant identities for rhetorical purposes to communicate to the hailed viewer (Crockett 2008). Often, advertisers appropriate or borrow stereotypical representations of non-dominant identities. They then use these symbols to craft messages designed to appeal to a viewer who is not a member of the identity group. That is, advertisers make use of cultural materials to craft and deliver messages to an audience located outside that culture – for example, the advertisement for Domtar, a North American sheet paper producer, in Figure 3.6 depicts an Asian boy holding up his A+ graded test paper. It uses the 'model minority' stereotype that describes Asian American cultures as hyper-focused on academic achievement. The advertiser is not targeting Asian American customers, instead it is trying to sell more copy paper to the mass market by prevailing on this commonly understood stereotype.

Figure 3.6 'Model minority' stereotype in a 2010 'Paper Because' (Domtar) advertisement

(4) The Effortful Accommodation Model. The concept of 'Effortful Accommodation' comes from linguistics where native speakers view non-native speakers who put more effort into the communication more positively. Koslow, Shamdasani, and Touchstone (1994) translate this model to marketing. In it, advertisers develop deep, nuanced understanding not only of language use, but also other cultural practices to target non-dominant identities with messages that resonate. When marketers get it right, effortful accommodation is perceived as an authentic attempt to develop a relationship with hailed viewers who are often underserved in the marketplace. To illustrate, in an award-winning campaign, Pampers diapers conducted research with Hispanic mothers-to-be and found that they

worried that their children would not appreciate their heritage. They invited pregnant mothers to a concert for them and their babies that celebrated their heritage, providing them with special headphones for their bellies. It was an enchanting experience for the mothers delivered to them by a brand that wanted to signal that they cared about this particular identity and their unique concerns at this life stage. This strategy can backfire though when the sell is too hard and when the organization fails to deeply understand the identity practices represented.

CONCLUSION

In Western consumer culture, people often pay little attention to the social aspects of identity. They generally think of themselves as builders of their personal identities. This is certainly true in many notable ways. It is also true that the market's role in their social identity appears to them as naturalized or entirely neutral. In their identity work, consumers select from combinations of seemingly limitless options, but the menu from which they select is nevertheless created and cultivated by the surrounding culture. Marketers shape the universe of options for building identity and contribute to the construction of legitimate and dominant identities by providing product offerings, retail platforms, and *servicescapes* for particular identity projects and creating marketing communications depicting particular identities. The servicescape includes everything that potentially impacts customer and employee experience. It is the stage on which all service encounters occur (Bitner 1992). Certainly, marketers take their cues about how to build the servicescape from culture. But, they also play a central role in amplifying and morphing what culture makes available for use in identity work at a given moment. Consider the examples of themed servicescapes like Las Vegas casinos, Disney, or American Girl Place. These complex built environments are designed around a theme in order to interact with identities as they are in the process of being constructed and they provide a stage for people to enact them. For instance, American Girl Place is a metaphorical stage on which mothers, daughters, and other female family members enculturate young girls into a particular kind of womanhood (Sherry 2009).

For those in stigmatized identity positions, cognizance of marketers' actions in the role of brand (stage) manager is a must because they must wrestle with how to respond to what is offered (and how it is communicated). Notably, some in non-dominant and stigmatized identity positions look to the market as a site for instituting social change campaigns through collective action, such as consumer boycotts to bring attention to unfair treatment, and co-creation efforts to coax businesses to attend to otherwise underserved groups. Others resist the market and try to disentangle its role in facilitating (hindering) their social identity projects and legitimizing certain identity positions.

Box 3.2: Extended Case Study

'Pepsi Moments'

In 2017, Pepsi released a highly choreographed and well-funded YouTube-based advertisement as part of its 'Pepsi Moments' campaign that evoked widespread rebuke, forcing
the company to delete the spot. What did this Pepsi ad do to generate such an outcry?
In this mini-case study, we first provide you with some context to help you interpret consumer
reactions. After you carefully view the advertisement, answer a series of questions that
analyze what went wrong and generate strategic recommendations for Pepsi Co.

Background

As with most advertising and audience understanding analyses, it is essential to first
understand the social and cultural context in which the advertisement was created. It
was released following a surge of political protest marches in the United States and
across the globe. Although some protests emerged in the aftermath of Donald Trump's
election to the presidency, others had origins in ongoing dissent over the deaths of
unarmed black people at the hands of local law enforcement and federal immigration agents. Media coverage relied heavily on depictions of lines of law enforcement
personnel clad in riot gear squaring off against lines of protesters. The shootings and
subsequent protests made institutional racism salient for many. Put differently, the
actions of law enforcement in interacting with those who hold minority identity positions made apparent the ways that institutions (schools, housing authorities, banks,
stores, zoning boards, hospitals, the military, law enforcement, etc.) create and perpetuate inequality.

In addition, the 2016 American presidential election exposed deep cultural tensions.
Candidate Donald Trump's most ardent supporters largely embraced a nativist campaign platform that privileged a closed borders approach to immigration and economic
protectionism. Candidate Hillary Clinton's supporters favored a campaign platform that
privileged certain aspects of multiculturalism, specifically a less openly nativist stance
toward immigration and support for marriage equality. The first few months of Trump's
presidency featured a women's march on the Washington DC Capitol Mall, reputed to be
the largest of its kind in the nation's history. Marchers characterized the administration
as having a misogynistic orientation and a goal of undermining women's reproductive freedom. A separate nationwide campaign brought together protesters incensed
about what they perceived to be denial of climate change science by the administration. Additionally, another nationwide campaign saw millions of protesters participate
in a series of marches against the administration's bans on immigration and travel from
numerous Muslim countries.

(Continued)

(Continued)

Some marketing context is helpful as well. Historically, Pepsi has positioned itself as the younger, cooler brand to nostalgia-laden Coca-Cola. It has a legacy of aggressively pursuing this segment of young (and young-at-heart) consumers. Consider Pepsi Co. brand Mountain Dew's long-running, youth-oriented 'Do the Dew' campaign as one illustration of this legacy. Many reports describe highly sought-after 'millennial' consumers as socially conscious, activism-oriented, and seeking 'authenticity' from brands. Notably, prior high profile advertisements, some airing during the widely watched American Super Bowl football game, have met with success using social activist messages.

The Ad

Smart brands create ads that understand the cultural context, and develop resonance for consumers by connecting with something in their lives so that the brand becomes a resource for telling their personal story (Holt 2004). Readers should find and watch the Kendall Jenner 'Pepsi Moments' advertisement. The ad depicts a female photographer wearing a hijab, a passionate musician with phenotypically Asian characteristics, and Jenner wearing a blond wig at a photo shoot. They are each in their own spheres focusing on their work. Meanwhile, a large march is occurring outside with an attractive, diverse group of seemingly lighthearted marchers carrying signs bearing symbols such as a peace sign, a heart, and 'join the conversation'. The artists and Jenner join in the march, interacting with the various participants. The crowd encounters the police, who have stern looks on their faces. Jenner, smiling, grabs a Pepsi from a tub, steps forward from the crowd and seductively hands a Pepsi to one of the officers, who drinks the Pepsi

Figure 3.7 Still from the 2017 'Pepsi Moments' advertisement

and smiles. Members of the crowd cheer, exchange high fives, and embrace. The phrases: 'Live Bolder. Live Louder. Live for Now. Pepsi' appear on the screen. While the ad is no longer provided by Pepsi, it was widely reposted by a range of media outlets. As readers will see in searching for the ad, there were many media interpretations. We recommend readers ignore those. We would like readers to carefully watch the advertisement and interpret it using the concepts introduced in this chapter and other chapters.

Figure 3.8   Still from the 2017 'Pepsi Moments' advertisement featuring Kendall Jenner

Questions

1. What advertising model(s) were used in this advertisement? Use evidence from the advertisement and concepts from the chapter to make the argument.
2. Why did Pepsi use the model(s) that they used? Use the concepts from the chapter and evidence from the advertisement. Consider more than one model. Address the role of the joint usage of these models with reference to the four-fold typology of representations presented earlier.
3. Why did this advertisement generate widespread condemnation and an apology from Pepsi? Who might have been at the forefront of these condemnations? How might identity concerns have affected some viewers? There are many ways to interpret the ad. Here, we would like readers to make arguments using concepts from this chapter and evidence from the advertisement.
4. Imagine there was an opportunity to remake the Pepsi ad, should it be remade? If yes, what changes should be made to make it successful? How could the new version be developed to avoid the same criticism the original ad attracted?

RESEARCH DIRECTIONS

Academic research on consumer culture and identity falls into a body of literature that explores 'the socio-historic patterning of consumption' (Arnould and Thompson 2005: 874). This involves the ways that consumption is consistently used as a vehicle for identity work over time and the implications of that identity work for relationships of status, power, and notions of consumer agency. This research also focuses on institutions, specifically their role in constructing identity resources, as well as how collective action by identity groups can create institutional change.

Several avenues for future research remain open for inquiry. A key avenue is the global marketplace. Because the bulk of research on the marketplace, identity, and agency is grounded in Western concepts and focused on Western markets, we know far less about market-oriented societies in the rest of the world. What are the implications for consumption and identity when we focus on consumers who constitute the majority of the global marketplace? How do advertisers and brand managers see their segmentation strategies *vis-à-vis* identity projects and representation? What does this mean for current theories that structure what we know?

One topic for continuing inquiry that we highlight in some detail here is *intersectionality*. As an area of study, it has grown considerably since its introduction as a conceptual innovation by black feminist scholars Patricia Hill Collins (1990/1999) and Kimberlé Crenshaw (1989, 1991). We summarize it here only briefly, relying extensively on ongoing research in sociology. We point interested readers to the Recommended Reading section at the end of the chapter as well.

In brief, intersectionality is the recognition that multiple systems of inequality (e.g. gender, race, social class) may be analytically distinct. However, they are experienced simultaneously by people and thus they are linked together. In sociology (the academic discipline most closely associated with studying systems of inequality), Choo and Ferree (2010: 131) describe three ways that intersectionality can be thought about in project design and used for analysis:

1. *inclusion-centered* – focuses on including (or its absence) granting special importance to the perspectives of multiply-marginalized people, especially women of color.
2. *process-centered* – focuses on the 'multiplier' or 'interacting' effects of experiencing multiple independent strands of inequality; and
3. *system-centered* – focuses on how multiple institutions produce complex configurations of inequality rather than simply 'extra' inequality for multiply-marginalized people.

The key insight of the *inclusion-centered* approaches to intersectionality is to draw attention to those who are marginalized as well as to the nature of marginalization. Intersections are like metaphorical street corners where independent systems of inequality meet. That is, some identity positions, notably for women of color, are at the corner of racism and sexism. They also draw attention to those 'unmarked' dominant identities that serve as taken-for-granted standards against which all other identities are compared (and usually found wanting). *Process-centered approaches* depart from this street corner metaphor in that they are less interested in specific identity locations *per se*. Instead, they seek to compare experiences of inequality at various locations to draw attention to the dynamic social forces (processes) that underlie and transform systems of inequality. So, for instance, Lamont et al. (2016) compare resistance to racial stigma in different locations around the world, including African Americans in the United States, blacks in Brazil, and Palestinians in Israel. They show that different national and local political systems and cultural repertoires help shape the extent to which stigma is internalized by its targets and the amount (if any) and type of resistance that occurs. *System-centered approaches* operate in fundamentally similar ways but allow for greater complexity. They also draw attention to social forces that transform systems of inequality. But, rather than being strictly comparative, these approaches conceptualize the experience of inequality in ways that allow for both action and reaction that combine to produce something new, like in a chemical compound. To illustrate, consider the processes of acculturation that newcomers engage in when they migrate to a new culture. As Luedicke (2015) shows, both the newcomers and so-called indigenes are transformed through their interactions. A system-centered intersectional approach would draw attention to the entirely new understandings of citizenship, culture, and country that might be co-produced through intra- and inter-group interaction.

In marketing and consumer research, the concept of intersectionality is only now gaining attention by researchers in its role as a theoretical frame, in research design, and in the practice of marketing communications. Those interested in understanding the role that the marketplace plays in identity work, will find that using the lens of intersectionality will produce a more complex, but also richer, more robust, and more accurate understanding of consumption. Beyond application, consumer researchers can uniquely speak to and build on the intersectionality literature in sociology by foregrounding the role of the market and consumption in intersectional identity work, inequality, and social action.

RECOMMENDED READING

For those interested in reading consumer research that explores identity using a sociological lens, the reference section of this chapter and the pieces listed below provide some starting points.

Charron-Chénier, Raphaël, Fink, Joshua J., and Keister, Lisa A. (2017) 'Race and consumption: Black and white disparities in household spending', *Sociology of Race and Ethnicity*, *3* (1): 50–67.
This article uses data from the Consumer Expenditure Surveys (US) to examine racial differences in spending. The results show that racial disparities in consumption exist independently of other economic disparities and may be a key unexamined factor in the reproduction of racial inequality.

Gopaldas, Ahir (2013) 'Intersectionality 101', *Journal of Public Policy and Marketing*, 32, (special issue): 90–94.
This article provides background on and a marketing frame for understanding the challenges of holding more than one minority status within a society.

The Center for Consumer Equality. www.consumerequality.org/publications.html.
A curation of research articles focusing on consumer discrimination.

Thompson, Craig J. (2014) 'The politics of consumer identity work', *Journal of Consumer Research*, 40 (5): iii–vii; and associated articles.
Part of a series of 'curations' that bring together research articles in the *Journal of Consumer Research* on particular topics. This curation focuses on the interplay between the market, politics, and identity.

Visconti, Luca M. and co-authors (2014) 'Consumer ethnicity three decades after: A TCR agenda', *Journal of Marketing Management*, 30 (17–18).
This article reviews various ways that ethnicity is understood in the context of consumption and provides a research agenda for understanding wellbeing in the context of consumer ethnicity.

REFERENCES

Adkins, Natalie Ross and Ozanne, Julie L. (2005) 'The low literate consumer', *Journal of Consumer Research*, 32 (June): 93–105.

Arnould, E.J. (2007) 'Consuming experience: Retrospects and prospects', in A. Carù and B. Cova (eds), *Consuming Experience*. London: Routledge. pp. 185–94.

Bitner, Mary Jo (1992) 'Servicescapes: The impact of physical surroundings on customers and employees', *Journal of Marketing*, 56 (2): 57–71.

Bone, Sterling A., Christensen, Glenn L., and Williams, Jerome D. (2014) 'Rejected, shackled, and alone: The impact of systemic restricted choice on minority consumers' construction of self', *Journal of Consumer Research*, 41 (2): 451–74.

Bonos, Lisa (2016) 'LGBTQ and heterosexual weddings have a lot in common, survey finds', *Washington Post*, 29 June 29. www.washingtonpost.com/news/soloish/wp/2016/06/29/lgbtq-and-hetrosexual-weddings-have-a-lot-in-common-survey-finds/?utm_term=.ee2e86667eec.

Carlson, Daniel K. (2004) 'Racial profiling seen as pervasive, unjust'. www.gallup.com/poll/12406/Racial-Profiling-Seen-Pervasive-Unjust.aspx?g_source=racial+profiling&g_medium=search&g_campaign=tiles.

Cayla, Julien and Eckhardt, Giana M. (2008) 'Asian brands and the shaping of a transnational imagined community', *Journal of Consumer Research*, 35 (August), 216–30.

Chang, Alvin (2017) 'White America is quietly self-segregating: Everyone wants diversity but not everyone wants it on their street', Vox, 18 January. www.vox.com/2017/1/18/14296126/white-segregated-suburb-neighborhood-cartoon.

Choo, Hae Yeon and Ferree, Myra Marx (2010) 'Practicing intersectionality in sociological research: A critical analysis of inclusions, interactions, and institutions in the study of inequalities', *Sociological Theory*, *28* (2): 129–49.

Cohen, Lizbeth (2004) *A Consumer's Republic: The Politics of Consumption in Post-War America*. New York: Vintage Books.

Collins, Patricia Hill (1990/1999) *Black Feminist Thought: Knowledge, Consciousness, and the Politics of Empowerment*. New York: Routledge.

Commuri, Suraj and Gentry, James W. (2005) 'Resource allocation in households with women as chief wage earners', *Journal of Consumer Research*, *32* (September): 185–95.

Coskuner-Balli, Gokcen and Thompson, Craig J. (2013) 'The status costs of subordinate cultural capital: At-home fathers' collective pursuit of cultural legitimacy through capitalizing consumption practices', *Journal of Consumer Research*, *40* (1): 19–41.

Crenshaw, Kimberlé Williams (1989) 'Demarginalizing the intersection of race and sex: A black feminist critique of antidiscrimination doctrine, feminist theory, and anti-racist politics', *University of Chicago Legal Forum*, pp. 139–67.

Crenshaw, Kimberlé Williams (1991) 'Mapping the margins: Intersectionality, identity politics, and violence against women of color', *Stanford Law Review*, *43* (6): 1241–79.

Crockett, David (2008) 'Marketing blackness: How advertisers use race to sell products', *Journal of Consumer Culture*, *8* (2): 245–68.

Crockett, David (2017) 'Paths to respectability: Consumption and stigma management in the contemporary black middle class', *Journal of Consumer Research*, *44* (3): 554–81.

Fowles, Jib (1996) *Advertising and Popular Culture*. Thousand Oaks, CA: Sage.

Goffman, Erving (1963/2009) *Stigma: Notes on the Management of Spoiled Identity*. New York: Simon and Schuster.

Harris, Anne-Marie G., Henderson, Geraldine R., and Williams, Jerome D. (2005) 'Courting customers: Assessing consumer racial profiling and other marketplace discrimination', *Journal of Public Policy and Marketing*, *24* (1): 163–71.

Holt, Douglas B. (2002) 'Why do brands cause trouble? A dialectical theory of consumer culture and branding', *Journal of Consumer Research*, *29* (1): 70–90.

Holt, Douglas B. (2004) *How Brands Become Icons: The Principles of Cultural Branding*. Cambridge, MA: Harvard Business Press.

Koslow, Scott, Shamdasani, Prem N., and Touchstone, Eller E. (1994) 'Exploring language effects in ethnic advertising: A sociolinguistic perspective', *Journal of Consumer Research*, *20* (4): 575–85.

Lamont, Michele and Molnar, Virag (2002) 'The study of boundaries in the social sciences', *Annual Review of Sociology*, *28*: 167–95.

Lamont, Michèle, Moraes Silva, Graziella, Welburn, Jessica S., Guetzkow, Joshua, Mizrachi, Nissim, and Reis, Hanna Herzog Elisa (2016) *Getting Respect: Responding to Stigma and Discrimination in the United States, Brazil, and Israel*. Princeton, NJ: Princeton University Press.

Luedicke, Marius K. (2015) 'Indigenes' responses to immigrants' consumer acculturation: A relational configuration analysis', *Journal of Consumer Research*, *42* (June): 109–129.

Mirabito, Ann M., Otnes, Cele C., Crosby, Elizabeth, Wooten, David B., Machin, Jane E., Pullig, Chris, Ross Adkins, Natalie, Dunnett, Susan, Hamilton, Kathy, Thomas, Kevin D., Yeh, Marie A., Davis, Cassandra, Gollnhofer, Johanna F., Grover, Aditi, Matias, Jess, Mitchell, Natalie A., Ndichu, Edna G., Sayarh, Nada, and Velagaleti, Sunaina (2016) 'The stigma turbine: A theoretical framework for conceptualizing and contextualizing marketplace stigma', *Journal of Public Policy and Marketing*, *35* (2): 170–84.

Montagne, Renee and Ulaby, Neda (2011) 'If you're looking for a little diversity on television, try HGTV', www.npr.org/templates/transcript/transcript.php?storyId=135353192.

Montgomery Ward & Co. (1895) Catalog No. 13, *Spring and Summer*. Chicago, IL: Montgomery Ward & Co.

Mora, G Cristina (2014) 'Cross-field effects and ethnic classification: The institutionalization of Hispanic panethnicity, 1965 to 1990', *American Sociological Review*, *79* (2): 183–210.

Scaraboto, Daiane and Fischer, Eileen (2013) 'Frustrated fatshionistas: An institutional theory perspective on consumer quests for greater choice in mainstream markets', *Journal of Consumer Research*, *39* (6), 1234–57.

Selvam, Ashok (2017) 'Chicago bar slammed for allegedly racist dress code', *Chicago Eater*, 31 May. https://chicago.eater.com/2017/5/31/15719332/bottled-blonde-dress-code-racist-reddit.

Sherry, John (2009) 'The work of play at American Girl place', *Social Psychology Quarterly*, *72* (3): 199–202.

Smith, Greg B. (2014) 'Barneys agrees to pay $525g to settle racial profiling allegations', *New York Daily News*, 18 August. http://www.nydailynews.com/new-york/barneys-agrees-pay-525g-settle-racial-profiling-allegations-article-1.1899013.

Veblen, Thorstein (1899) *Theory of the Leisure Class: An Economic Study in the Evolution of Institutions*. New York: Macmillan.

Velagaleti, Sunaina R. and Epp, Amber M. (2016) *'From symbolic violence to revolution: the diverse destigmatization experiences of LGBT consumers'*, in Albert Haring Symposium, Bloomington, IN.

Weinberger, Michelle F. (2015) 'Dominant consumption rituals and intragroup boundary work: How non-celebrants manage conflicting relational and identity goals', *Journal of Consumer Research*, *42* (3): 378–400.

Wooten, David B. (1995) 'One-of-a-kind in a full house: Some consequences of ethnic and gender distinctiveness', *Journal of Consumer Psychology*, *4* (3): 205–24.

PART TWO

Marketplace Cultures

4

CONSUMPTION TRIBES AND COLLECTIVE PERFORMANCE

Bernard Cova, Kedge Business School, Marseilles
Avi Shankar, University of Bath

CHAPTER OVERVIEW

In this chapter, we will:

- highlight the logic behind the retribalization of society;
- explore how our understanding of marketplace cultures is underpinned by two key concepts – sociality and *communitas*;
- identify what and how value emerges for marketplace cultures; and
- sketch out the key characteristics of consumer tribes, brand communities, and brand publics.

INTRODUCTION

The study of marketplace cultures is one of the four original streams of CCT. Research into marketplace cultures focuses on understanding how consumers 'forge feelings of social solidarity and create distinctive, fragmentary, self-selected, and sometimes transient cultural worlds through the pursuit of common consumption interests' (Arnould and Thompson 2005: 873), and this has considerable implications for the practice of marketing.

Two important aspects of this definition are: (1) that consumption is situated within a logic of social processes and productive cultural practices; and (2) what consumers value, the 'why' of their consumption motivations, is its linking value. This means that what consumers' value is not primarily the object of consumption (the brand or leisure experience, for example) but the social relations and interactions with other like-minded consumers, enabled by the act of consumption, and the experiences it provides. This is in stark contrast to the dominant logic in marketing that views consumption as an individual process, and a consumer as an isolated processor of information, sealed off and separated from others in their own experiential world, seeking to extract and maximize utility from market offerings.

A plethora of terms have emerged to describe these marketplace consumption communities but three, consumer tribes, brand communities, and brand publics, have emerged as a central focus of research interest. A consumer tribe is defined as a co-consuming, heterogeneous group (in terms of demographic characteristics) of people, inter-linked by the same subjectivity, the same passion, and capable of taking collective action, often short-lived but intense. When these relations revolve around a specific brand then we call them a brand community defined as: a group of consumers that have a common interest in a specific brand and create a parallel social universe with its own myths, values, rituals, vocabulary, and hierarchy that the brand supports. Brand communities can be chronologically extended, with relations between people and brands lasting over decades. Brand publics, meanwhile, highlight the increasing role of social media in facilitating consumer–consumer–brand interactions and are defined as an organized media-space kept together by a continuity of mediation practices that have a specific brand as common focus. While distinct and different, the conceptual similarities underpinning the three outweigh their differences.

THE RE-TRIBALIZATION OF SOCIETY: CHALLENGING THE NORM

Historically, marketing inherited from its origins in the social sciences a tendency to analyze markets by dividing them into groups based on categories like age, class, gender, or nationality. They did, and still do this, to aid and simplify the marketing management process. The subsequent groups that emerge from this process, or market segments, are made up of a collection of individuals who share some global socio-cultural commonalities but whose specific consumer interests and goals could vary widely. In other cases, marketers sometimes conceptualized consumers in ways that drew from economic theory and assumed that they acted as autonomous agents who sought to maximize their own self-interest by making rational decisions, independent of each other.

Neither of these orientations is sufficiently sensitive to the interpersonal relations and desires for social connection that consumers often seek to realize through their marketplace behaviors. Inspired in part by the application of the tribal theory of French sociologist Michel Maffesoli (1996), many in the consumer research and marketing field are beginning to analyze the relations between producers and consumers in a different and far more socially oriented theoretical light. This emergent approach rejects an overly individualistic, information-processing view of the consumer. Rather, a variety of studies from both a North American anthropological tradition and a European micro-sociological tradition view human life as inherently social – people have a need to belong.

This orientation also means reimagining the assumption that market-based phenomena (and even non-market based ones too) are best analyzed through the top-down imposition of abstract categories (like class, age, gender etc.) in favor of what might be termed a bottom-up postmodern sociology (Maffesoli 1996). Social life is a rich, complex, kaleidoscopic mixture of emotional and cultural relations. In this view, the building blocks of human social life are not found in abstract categories that are applied to the analysis of social life. Instead, they are manifest in the multiplicity of social groupings that people participate in, knowingly or not, through the course of their everyday lives. Through re-tribalization, society appears therefore as a network of micro-groups, through which people migrate and to which they can experience strong emotional bonds, and share experiences and common passions – moments and spaces of shared identity. Of course, at different stages in people's lives some of these micro-groups will be more or less important than others.

These tribes are fundamental to people's experience of life in general. They differ from traditional anthropological tribes in one important way: people belong to multiple tribes at the same time – think of being a member of different fan communities – and are not exclusively tied to any single one. From this perspective the consumption of cultural resources circulated through markets (goods, brands, leisure experiences, etc.) should not be seen as the main priority of marketer; rather, marketers should see the products, brands or experiences they produce as a means to facilitate social relationships. For people in consumer tribes, 'links' (social relationships) are more important than things (products, services, and brands).

There is, therefore, an important collective dimension to consumption that traditional demographic approaches to market segmentation overlook. Two important facilitators to the proliferation of marketplace cultures have been, first, the advent of the Internet and then the emergence of social media platforms that facilitate consumer-to-consumer interaction. These technological innovations have afforded consumers with more and more resources to participate the re-tribalization of society. Perhaps most significantly, the digital dimension of tribalization enables people to participate in tribes beyond their immediate geographic location. This so-called de-territorialization of the social link contrasts to traditional tribal groupings that were and are geographically proximate. People all over the world are now able to connect with each other and contribute to events, campaigns, and other productive cultural practices mediated through the Internet and related social media. We can now witness people from different contexts communicate with each other and feel connected and even committed to each other under the umbrella of their common interests that could be tied to a product, service, brand, or a shared experience like a hobby or other leisure pursuit. The notion of the consumer has changed with this 'digital drive' and the resulting opportunities for social interaction. As a result, tribes and other consumption collectives assume an even greater role in people's lives and the digital domain becomes central for the process of learning about, and socialization and participation into, tribes.

Box 4.1:   Real World Scenario

Tribal entrepreneurship in rave culture

A defining feature of tribes, and other types of marketplace cultures, is their ability to produce culture for other members of the tribe. This is often because the market does not make available the cultural resources required for the tribe to engage in or support its collective rituals of identification. This is particularly the case with the rave tribe. Rave is one of the most generative forms of popular culture of recent years, with its influence felt across a wide variety of market sectors from the leisure through to the tourism, brewing, fashion, and, of course, the music industries.

The story of rave in the UK started in the late 1980s when a group of holidaymakers returned from the bohemian holiday island of Ibiza, having experienced a new musical genre, the Balearic Beat, and the island's relaxed attitudes to illicit drugs. Keen to replicate the experience in the UK they started the underground rave scene, utilizing the crumbling urban post-industrialized landscape as a site for their tribal rituals of collective identification. In its early incarnation rave was seen as an antidote to the harsh economic realities of late 1980s, a respite from high unemployment, and a response to the political and economic revolution that was being enacted by the government of Prime Minister Margaret Thatcher.

Ironically, however, the early rave organizers were also exhibiting entrepreneurialism, a defining feature of Thatcherism, in creating and sharing this new drug-fueled, dance culture. In 1990 the English football team released a song prior to the World Cup in Italy by the band New Order. Called 'World in Motion' and featuring a rap by England star John Barnes, it featured the chorus 'E is for England, Eng-er-land'. The E may well have been for England, but it was also E for Ecstasy. By the early 1990s rave had become the scourge of the right-wing press and it whipped up a moral panic, as hundreds and thousands of mainly young people descended on unregulated spaces, in the countryside, and outside of the crumbling inner cities, to engage in their drug-and-dance-fueled rituals of identification. This was viewed as a threat to the social order. By 1994, the Conservative government banned raves.

Rave culture didn't disappear – far from it. Rather, the pioneering DJs and club promoters exchanged the unlicenced, illegal, peripatetic, pop-up nature of rave for more traditional, regulated and legal clubs, to recreate the atmosphere and soundscapes of the original raves. However, unlike many countercultural practices that once coopted by the mainstream market lose their countercultural significance among a chorus of 'sold-out', rave in its new guise of clubbing did not. On the contrary, the shamen and women of the rave tribe, primarily the DJs and club promoters, became household names, as they leveraged their tribal status, and cashed it in, literally, as raving turned into clubbing and then entered the mainstream.

We also see evidence of entrepreneurialism in brand communities too. For example, Premium Cola is a soft drinks brand in Germany. It was launched by the Afri-Cola brand community in response to a change in the formula of the product. After protesting about the change in formula, to little effect, the anti-brand community turned itself into a new brand community and produced a cola-based drink to their own recipe (see Case Study).

SOCIALITY AND *COMMUNITAS* = ESCAPE

Two fundamental constructs underpinning the understanding of marketplace cultures are sociality and *communitas*. Sociality is a postmodern term used to describe communities in terms of the symbolic and emotional role they play in people's lives as 'a quality of diffuse, ephemeral, multiplicatus social aggregation' (Muniz and O'Guinn 2001: 414). By contrast, the term social refers to the anonymous 'modern communities' produced through the mechanical and instrumental aggregation of people into groups, such that these groups can be managed or organized in some way. This difference is important, as people find pleasure and emotional connection in sociality. Think of it like this: watching your favorite sports team on the television is a qualitatively different experience if you are alone than it is if you are watching with your friends, perhaps sharing a few beers and a pizza. And if you and your friends happen to be at the actual game watching with thousands of others then the experience will be different again. Alternatively, imagine you are at a gig or music festival, like Glastonbury, and you gather in front of the main stage to experience the headline act with thousands of others. You may be there with a few of your friends but you don't know personally the rest of the crowd. The feeling you all experience together, hands raised, waving, and singing along for the duration of the set, is *communitas*. Part of what makes the social experience different is this metaphysical, almost spiritual connection with others.

But why do we seek out these experiences? The argument goes something like this. With the advent of the Industrial Revolution in Europe at the end of the 18th century, and the resulting shift from rural to urban populations that, 250 years on, has produced an advanced, post-industrialized landscape, people have become alienated in the broadest sense of the term. Alienation refers to estrangement from our humanity. People have become alienated from themselves, especially their bodies, feelings and emotions, from each other as traditional forms of community have been eroded, from nature, and from social institutions that once provided order and structure to their lives. People also feel that many aspects of their lives have become overly rationalized (see Chapter 7). People have been turned into thinking subjects required to constantly make choices, and they have become the objects of economic and political management and organization. As Goulding et al. (2009: 759) state, marketplace cultures are 'transient social spaces where the often alienating and individualizing effects of everyday modern life in advanced industrialized societies can be temporarily ameliorated in favor of the effervescent excitement and energy of ritualistic, communal sociality and solidarity'.

Consumer researchers thus frame the contemporary quest for such communal experiences as a way to escape these rationalizing expectations and demands. People want respites from burdensome responsibilities, time-pressed daily routines, and, for some, the materialistic work–spend cycle, in search of more authentic, communal, often embodied, experiences. In this vein, Schouten and McAlexander (1995: 52) describe how members of the Harley–Davidson brand community see riding their bikes as the 'antithesis of all the sources of confinement (including cars, offices, schedules, authority, and relationships) that may characterize their various working and family situations'.

Studies that explicitly or implicitly reproduce this perspective are grounded in and indebted to the work of the British cultural anthropologist Victor Turner. Turner drew from anthropological studies of pre-modern societies in order to gain new insights into the nature of human desires and social needs in post-industrial society. In particular, he drew on van Gennep's idea of rites of passage. Briefly, rites of passage involve a movement in identity as people shift from one social identity category to another. A rite of passage is a three-stage process consisting of pre-liminal, liminal, and post-liminal rites. So a boy or girl leaves behind their childhood identity, enters a period when they are neither a boy nor a girl, engages in some kind of ritual that once successfully achieved means they move onto become an adult. You may be familiar with baptisms, confirmations, bar or bat mitzvah, fiesta de quinceañera, etc. Even college graduation functions as a rite of passage that affirms a transition from a still somewhat dependent, not fully adult status to being a fully fledged member of adult (working) society. Rites of passage generally involve significant consumption activity. Through rites of passage, people enter with one identity, shed that identity, and emerge with a new identity. Key then is the concept of the liminal, or in-between.

Turner (1974) develops the conceptualization of the liminal and introduces the term liminoid (or liminal-like) as a post-industrial alternative to the transitory liminal experiences of pre-industrial societies, because people now do not necessarily shed an identity permanently. The liminoid occurs within leisure settings, away from work and everyday responsibilities. Goulding et al.'s (2009) study of club culture shows how people temporarily leave behind their everyday identity, worker. They then engage in rituals of separation and transformation to inhabit a temporary identity, clubber, before engaging in rituals of reintegration and returning. From clubbing, they return rejuvenated to their prior identity, summed up in the title of a previous study, 'Working Weeks, Rave Weekends' (Goulding et al. 2002). During these liminoid periods, people can experience an escape from the pressures and demands of everyday life.

Theoretically, the related concepts of liminal and liminoid describe forms of antistructure (Turner 1969). According to Turner, antistructure refers to spaces and times that are separate from the ordinary routines and roles which constitute everyday life (i.e., Turner's structure). For Turner, religious experiences which unfold in sacred experiences were the quintessential case of antistructure but, numerous studies have shown that consumer culture provides other kinds of antistructure settings in intense feelings of community, magic, and other extraordinary experiences can arise. By immersing themselves in antistructure, people gain latitude for identity experimentation and to experience a sense of sacredness and extraordinariness that seldom arise in the flow of their normal, time-pressed routines. This structure–antistructure framework underpins many consumer research studies from Mountain Men rendezvous in the Rocky Mountains, to whitewater rafting on the Colorado River, and The Burning Man festival in the Black Rock Desert, through to studies of surfing, clubbing and Tough Mudder. By engaging in these activities and adopting liminoid identities of being a surfer, a clubber, and Burning Man pilgrim people commune with each other in an emotionally intensified way. In this antistructural space, they feel 'a sense of release from tyrannies – whether imagined or not' and in doing so 'liberate considerable creativity, to release repression, to fulfill some sense of people's hidden potential, to evoke self-expression, and to unleash the potential for self-transformation' (Kozinets 2002: 36). In others words people get immense pleasure and 'value' from their communal experiences. Because of the origin of marketing and consumer research theory in economic theory, we have a tendency to rationalize pleasure into value. Value, after all, can be measured, while pleasure is a more elusive concept. However, for Jeremy Bentham, an 18th-century political philosopher whose Utilitarianism underpins modern economics, the pursuit of pleasure and the negation of pain is foundational to living a Good Life.

LINKING VALUE AND VALUE CO-CREATION

As our discussion so far has articulated, a CCT approach considers marketplace cultures as sites for the creation of collective experiences. The symbolic (re)construction or (re)possession of meanings through shared experiences provides people with strong hedonic and emotional benefits. That means through consumption activities consumers can change the meanings of commercial brands to foster their identity projects or those of the communities to which they belong. The example of Turkish women's refashioning of the veil from a stigmatized garment into a fashion statement is a case in point (Sandıkcı and Ger 2010).

Many collective experiences (re)appropriate products and services from the market system. Reappropriation or the building of meaning through experience and shared emotions constitutes a daily occurrence in the creation, consolidation, and preservation of communitarian sentiment within groups. For example, working-class groups of bikers reappropriated Harley–Davidson motorbikes as the core symbol of outlaw biker subculture and, later, professional-class members of this brand community began to brandish this symbol of rebellion in a more ironic manner, and then later still women riders further transformed the meaning of the brand symbol, treating it as a symbol of female empowerment and gender metamorphosis (Martin et al. 2006; Schouten and McAlexander 1995). What these actions have in common is that they encompass experiences that help the brand, product or service evolve beyond its simple status as a commodity. These actions thereby enable consumers to live experiences that are not entirely commodified in nature while continuing to function within a marketized framework, i.e., one that is defined by the interactions that brands and companies have initiated.

Key to understanding this view is the concept of linking value (Cova 1997). Gone are the days when organizations wholly control the value-exchange process, although many still operate under a traditional economic view that their role is to create value by embedding utility into their products (goods and services) that is exchanged for money with consumers at the point-of-sale. Consumers thus extract utility (benefits) in exchange for their money. Linking value holds that the value of products lies in their ability to deliver socially meaningful experiences, to create *communitas* and sociality. This means that organizations should enable consumers to strengthen community links and foster a sense of tribal belonging, membership or 'we-ness' because linking value is as important, if not more so, than utility through exchange. Linking value therefore has two distinct yet complementary meanings. For consumers, it is the value (the fun, pleasure, satisfaction, usefulness, sociality, *communitas* etc.) inherent in communal relations, however ephemeral, fostered by the tribe or brand community. For the company, linking value is the value its products/services/brands have for the construction, development or maintenance of these communal relations (Cova 1997). So: How can organizations build and enhance a sense of 'we-ness', or build linking value?

Box 4.2:   Real World Scenario

Creating a brand community

There are five basic rules for cultivating and growing a brand community. The example below is the successful launch of Tough Mudder obstacle racing brand and the community of Mudders that it created (toughmudder.com). Since its launch in late 2010, nearly three million people worldwide have tested their stamina on an obstacle course designed first and foremost to be collaborative. By so doing, they have created their own community.

Rule no. 1: Leveraging on existing activity-related community

Carefully choosing the field of intervention is the first step. In some areas of activity – notably ones relating to sales of basic goods – the very idea of a community is absurd and ineffective. Conversely, there are other areas where communities already exist. For instance, before Tough Mudder was first launched there were already more than a million people in the US taking part in obstacle courses, which combines cross-country and military training. As such, when this company and brand were still in an embryonic stage, its community already existed. The goal then became to re-orient this non-commercial community to benefit the new brand. Hence a number of approaches made even before the company launch, seeking acceptance and recognition as a legitimate community member to avoid being seen as chancer from the outside. This initial work was done by Will Dean, the CEO and founder of Tough Mudder and an obstacle course enthusiast.

Rule no. 2: Offering linking value

Offering connections is more important than offering things.

This second rule for cultivating a community may be the most important. From the very outset of the company project, a 'tribal grain' must be sewn in the offer. To do this, the linking value must become a core principle in the branding model, defined as the value of what the brand is offering in terms of building or reinforcing connections (even ephemeral ones) between consumers. The aim here is to devise an offer not to cater to stereotypical isolated consumers – standard targets in traditional marketing – but to the people who will be living the brand's experience together. This can be exemplified by Tough Mudder's forcing fans to run their courses in teams where members help one another get over the obstacles – or as it says on the company website 'You can't run it alone'. Before the start, each participant swears to 'Put teamwork and camaraderie before [their] course time'. Teams can be comprised of old friends or made up on the spot, but in either case it is the experience itself that forges the communitarian connection. These are people living through something that they will want to discuss afterwards, creating online and offline interactions that can start to sustain their sense of community.

Rule no. 3: Encouraging interactions

The idea here is to allow a wide range of groups born out of the offer to link up and form what becomes a veritable community. Above and beyond the functional aspects of

(Continued)

(Continued)

developing all kinds of interactive platforms – a requirement for facilitating interactions – managers must also consider the symbolic aspects. For someone to be aware of belonging to a distinct group, it must have a name, in the same way as the brand itself. Tough Mudder consumers, for instance, are called mudders and encouraged to consider themselves part of a Mudder Nation. They flood Facebook with tales of the obstacles they faced and how they overcame them. The company itself focuses more on YouTube, which it uses to re-broadcast top fan videos.

Rule no. 4: Facilitating collaboration

Community consolidation is accelerated through collaboration. The more consumers collaborate with one another or with the people working for the brand, the greater their sense of belonging to a community. Each Tough Mudder course is located in a natural setting distant from urban environments and requires major logistics including participant registration, handing out kit, managing participant flows until they get to the starting point, supplying water, encouraging racers over obstacles, giving out ribbons at each completed stage, distributing beer and food at the end, etc. Consumers volunteer for some of these necessary tasks and help participants do the course. The CEO Will Dean never misses an opportunity to thank these 'brand volunteers' for their help and has said unambiguously on a YouTube motivation video that his 'business wouldn't work without volunteers'. This makes them feel like they are an integral part of the company's plans. The community is not detached from the company but a key part of its business model.

Rule no. 5: Relying on differentiation

The homogenizing syndrome where all community members are transformed into clones of one another must be avoided at any cost. What people want is a well-oiled community offering perpetual differentiation/de-differentiation. Within Tough Mudder, the first obstacle can be equated with a carnival where many participants come in disguise because they want to be different, before ending up covered in mud like everyone else. Online platforms are there to relay images of people in their disguises and the things that they achieve.

This task is not an easy one for managers because they are trained to control isolated consumers and anonymous market segments, rather than to support specific groups and their practices. Brandfests, such as the various celebrations and outings that Jeep, Harley–Davidson or Ducati owners have organized to encourage a festival experience, are popular types of brand–consumer–consumer engagement. These brand-related events are opportunities for consumers to have an embodied experience of the brand and enjoy direct contact with the staff and other consumers (McAlexander and Schouten 1998).

Riding and socializing with other Harley owners connects people of a similar mindset, congregating and engaging in a way of life that revolves around the consumption of Harley–Davidson. This collective experience involves the development and preservation of communitarian connections within an experiential context, thereby allowing mutual learning and shared emotions in a socio-experiential context.

CCT research identifies and delineates the co-creation of the collective service experience by demonstrating that 'one of the core services provided by market offerings is precisely implicit or explicit social links to groupings that are themselves products of the development of a market-mediated society' (Arnould 2007: 63). The focus on consumption practices fosters understanding of these collective experiences. Schau et al. (2009) use practice theory to show that brand community members co-create value through a set of practices. They identify four categories of value-creating, communal practices: social networking, like welcoming new members; impression management or converting people into the community; community management practices, like milestoning and badging, by commemorating consumer achievements; and product development, like creating after-sales add-ons.

Some studies have focused on value co-creation that takes place directly between firms and brand communities. Hatch and Schultz (2010) depict LEGO's managers and employees as 'co-consumers' and LEGO fans as 'co-producers', while Antorini et al. (2012) show how the LEGO group collaborates with its brand community members to innovate and enrich the brand. On this basis, value co-creation between a firm and a brand community is defined as an active, creative, and social process based on collaboration between organizations and participants that generates benefits for all and creates value for stakeholders. Brand community members play a dynamic role in the value co-creation process, 'by acting as providers and beneficiaries, thereby co-creating value for themselves, for brand communities, and for organizations' (Pongsakornrungsilp and Schroeder 2011: 320).

Although organizations may try to shape the collective experience of a brand, at the end of the day, it is a function of activities that people do together. The collective experience would not exist or would take a different form if people did not want it or did not enact it. Thus, the collective experience relies on the existence of practices that strengthen the collective identity and that structure the collective experience. Since the enactment of these practices depends on the community, rather than the company which sponsors the brand, there is an inherent unpredictability and unmanageability to these value co-creating practices and the resulting collective experiences. In the case of Harry Potter, for example, millions of enthusiast consumers have contributed to the collective experience. The tribute websites, podcasts, bloggers, chatrooms, fan conventions, LARPs (Live Action Role Playing), among many others, attest to the 'Potterphiles' co-creative prowess' (Brown and Patterson 2009: 525). However, this co-creation process by brand community members has not been without problems, including above all the issue of intellectual property. The creative and financial value of fictional and pictorial characters, such as Harry Potter, is captured in trademarks that can be licensed and are the legal embodiment of the brand that companies want to defend against any value slippage resulting from fan creativity. When Warner Bros acquired the Harry Potter brand, they attempted to apply traditional intellectual property rules by shutting down the tribute websites, issuing cease-and-desist letters to all. However, the community rose in revolt and threatened a boycott of tie-in merchandise and the company had to withdraw (Brown and Patterson 2009).

Box 4.3:   Critical Reflection

Exploitation of the collective performance of consumption tribes

Value co-creation has spurred debates among marketing researchers (see *Marketing Theory* 2006, 2011 and 2012 special issues). The intensity of these debates demonstrates how much is at stake – conceptually and politically – when the roles of consumer and producer become blurred, especially when consumers are gathered into consumption tribes.

On one hand, some researchers seem convinced that the typical consumer has shifted from being passive to active and creative. Researchers holding this and similar views laud consumer involvement in branding and production since it empowers consumers to create their own lives and contribute positively to companies (Schau et al. 2009).

On the other hand, other researchers see value co-creation practices as a way of shaping and disciplining consumers through the value co-creation marketing discourses (Shankar et al. 2006). Zwick and Cayla (2011: 8) argue that, through these discourses, consumers are urged 'to engage in proactive destabilization and permanent requalification of themselves'. From this perspective, it is suggested that 'work' offers the best description of consumer activity under the regime of value co-creation, and that consumers can be conceived as 'working consumers' (Cova and Dalli 2009). As such, consumer tribes incur the risk of being exploited by companies that could benefit from their unpaid contribution.

In between these two extreme positions, it makes sense to interpret consumer tribes as engaging in compromise (Cova et al. 2015). Consumers who make compromises do not have a naïve or romantic view of their involvement in value co-creation processes, as sometimes stated (Shankar et al. 2006). Aware that they are being manipulated, they freely choose the extent of their 'dupery' and involve themselves to exhaust the possibilities for individual and collective enjoyment. They are at the same time emancipated and exploited.

FORMS OF MARKETPLACE CULTURES: CONSUMER TRIBES, BRAND COMMUNITIES, AND BRAND PUBLICS

The marked interest of the two last decades for collective experiences in consumer research and marketing theory has generated different labels to describe divergent – and sometimes overlapping – forms of co-consuming groups (Goulding et al. 2013). We focus on three – consumer tribes, brand communities, and brand publics.

Consumer tribes (Cova et al. 2007) are naturally occurring groups where tribe members identify with one another (or alternatively they can be 'activated' and encouraged to be linked together by social media or marketing activities). They have shared experiences and emotions. They are capable of engaging in collective, though ephemeral, social action – that is, as members of the tribe consumers can 'do' things that they would not be able to do as non-members. A consumer tribe could form around any leisure-based activity, interest, hobby or passion. As Cova and Shankar (2012: 180) stated, 'if you are passionate about surfing, traveling, a TV show, snowboarding, running, reading books, a band or singer, knitting, fine wine, a film-star, music, international politics, fossil-hunting, or fishing, the rise of social media … means that you can search for and find other like-minded devotees and voilà you will have the basis of a tribe'.

A brand community is a specialized, non-geographically bound community, based on a structured set of social relations among admirers of a brand (Muñiz and O'Guinn 2001: 412). Consumer researchers use three constructs to identify the distinguishing features of these brand communities: (1) consciousness of kind, that is, the sense of belonging to an in-group, through a brand that is supported by all group members; (2) evidence of the rituals and traditions that surround the brand; and (3) a sense of obligation to the community and its members that is often, but not always, shared by the group members (e.g. in relation to product repairs or services that are more personal). On a sociological level, brand communities herald new forms of collectives emerging in contemporary society. Rather than communities creating symbols, they form around commercial symbols (Stratton and Northcote 2016). On a managerial level, brand communities are described as the perfect locus of value co-creation (Schau et al. 2009). Brand co-creation and consumer-generated branded content are among the most significant aspects of this value co-creation process.

A brand public is an organized media space kept together by a continuity of practices of mediation that are centered on a branded mediation device, such as a Twitter hashtag (Arvidsson and Caliandro 2015). Mediation is a dynamic, structured, interactive process where various parties assist other parties in building and sharing information and meanings using specialized communication techniques like SMS or Twitter shorthand. Brand publics then are made of structured aggregations of assorted meanings without the formation of collective values. In brand publics, participation is not structured by interaction but by private or collective affect. Brand publics differ from brand communities in three crucial ways (Arvidsson and Caliandro 2015):

1. Brand publics are sustained by mediation. People do not interact around the focal brand; instead mediation devices aggregate a multitude of individual perspectives on, or experiences of the brand, which are given publicity in the brand public.
2. Brand public participation is structured either by individual affects like desire for visibility or an urge to share a point of view or an experience, or by collective affects that drive waves of imitation; in either case there is no discussion of a shared passion.
3. Brand publics echo brand-related meanings and identities that come from the brand's marketing communications as well as from diverse meanings that people associate with brands in their everyday lives; but brand publics do not articulate a coherent collective identity around the focal brand as brand communities do.

Recent scholarship has focused on the diverse participants of some consumer tribes, brand communities or brand publics – and how such heterogeneity can work to increase cooperation and cohesion (Thomas et al. 2013). While past research has emphasized the homogeneity of co-consuming groups, privileging the shared experiences of community members over their differences, a new perspective claims that heterogeneity is often at play in consumer collectives. Heterogeneity is necessary for the development of strong and successful tribes, and heterogeneity often incites tensions and conflict that can be productive between community members and between members and companies such as in the case of brand extensions. Research has also investigated the existence of 'community brands' (Füller et al. 2013) like Geocaching or Bookcrossing, brands which are created by a community of consumers. In this way, communities use market mechanisms such as branding or marketing for their own projects, while liberating themselves successfully from the influences of corporations (see Case Study).

Box 4.4:   Critical Reflection

Critique of the concept of brand community

Zwick and Bradshaw (2016) argue that the central object at stake in CCT research, the consumer community, barely actually exists. According to these authors, the community concept therefore is employed by marketing experts as an ideological tool for maintaining social and behavioral commitment to brands and commercially mediated activities behind practices that hardly occur. They ponder why such ideologies are necessary, and what they allow marketers to do. Zwick and Bradshaw (2016) build on previous research to point out that from a sociological perspective user aggregations on the Internet are not to be understood as communities, at least not in anything that resembles the significance that that term has originally held in social theory.

Despite all the talk about communities – especially marketing scholars' and professionals' favorite version of commercial community, the brand community – Zwick and Bradshaw (2016) contend that they remain difficult to locate in traditional terms as understood in sociology, that is, as social formations characterized by dense webs of interpersonal interaction and durable attachments to a shared territory or identity. The non-enduring character of virtual communal engagement and social communication reduces engagement to pure participation and resembles an energetic but ultimately short-lived and meaningless flash mob rather than a collective of engaged subjects. In their vast majority, what people call online communities are rather brand publics than brand communities as they do not articulate a long-lasting collective identity around the focal brand as brand communities do.

CONCLUSION

In this chapter, we have offered many examples of how marketing managers can interact with and even enable marketplace cultures. However, the most practical application we can offer is to integrate these insights into the managerial mindset, as a way of thinking about marketing *per se*. Interacting with marketplace cultures will only make sound business sense for some brands and not others. Is your brand one of them? It means asking do we have tribes that use our brands and can we support their tribal practices? Or do we have a brand community or brand public? If so, how do we engage and support them? It means identifying the linking value that could be engineered into the pleasure proposition. It means conducting market research by really getting to know your consumers, learning from them, by actually hanging out with them, and sharing in community or tribal rituals.

Above all, it's all about connecting and collaborating.

Box 4.5:   Extended Case Study

Premium Cola

Afri-Cola Premium was a soft drink that had been present on the German market since 1931 and had a brand community of enthusiast consumers. Over the years, Afri-Cola Premium became a cult brand for its consumer population in Hamburg, North Germany.

(Continued)

(Continued)

The brand was purchased by Mineralbrunnen Überkingen-Teinach AG in 1999, who secretly changed the recipe and dropped 'Premium' from its name. A collective of brand enthusiasts ('Interessengruppe Premium') then ran a protest campaign lasting more than two years (1999–2001) opposing the changes to Afri-Cola's recipe. These protests raised public awareness, but remained unsuccessful, which is why in November 2001, the collective took the initiative of producing the original recipe cola (Huseman et al. 2015).

Baptized 'Premium Cola', the new product started as a small collective enterprise but quickly grew into a medium-sized entity that sought to link economics and ethics in a way that is unique yet logical to all its members. Premium Cola is only sold in selected outlets whose philosophy must be similar to that of the brand. Premium Cola is a local success that still continues today and since its creation has increased sales at an annual rate of around 100%. In 2012, Premium Cola sold more than 1,000,000 bottles with the declared mission of proving 'that morals and markets can go together'.

Premium Cola is entirely governed and managed by the community of consumers. The community's intention is to inspire change in the mainstream market through educational communication and provide a role model for both start-up and established market actors. Instead of expanding or selling at any price, the collective puts much thought into appropriate brand leadership and ethical economic behavior.

In parallel to this, Mineralbrunnen Überkingen-Teinach AG encountered some problems with Afri-Cola due to the unpopularity of the new recipe. The mixture was therefore changed again so that it tasted more like the original, with the caffeine content increasing in 2005 to around 200 mg/liter and listed again as an ingredient on the label. This new mixture also failed to spark great enthusiasm and on 1 April 2006 the firm changed back to the original recipe, with a caffeine content of 250 mg/liter. Since then, Afri-Cola has slightly regained market share.

Questions

1. What kinds of communities are attached to Afri-Cola and Premium Cola? Is this a brand community or a community brand?
2. What kind of brand mismanagement of the Afri-Cola brand community led to the creation of Premium Cola?
3. What are the connections between the feeling of community and the taste of the product?

RESEARCH DIRECTIONS

The study of marketplace cultures remains an integral part of CCT research. While much progress in understanding consumer tribes, brand communities, and brand publics has been made there is considerable scope for further research. Brand community research has understandably proved popular. However, in an increasingly global and interconnected world, how are the core values of a brand community sustained? Does a global brand have a brand community or instead, are its community values enacted differently around the world? Do different members of a brand community show different levels of moral responsibility towards each other and if so what does this mean for the core underpinning values of a brand community?

Concerning consumer tribes and brand communities that engage in entrepreneurial ventures, what happens to their supporting community values as they engage in or with the market, is an area of emerging interest. Do the original values of the tribe or brand community erode as it adopts the new role of 'traditional' market actor? If a brand attempts to leverage the common interests and passions of a consumer tribe, how do different members of the tribe respond to this?

More research is also required to understand how brand managers understand and interact with marketplace cultures. Connecting and collaborating with marketplace cultures is a different managerial mindset than the traditional command and control mindset adopted by brand managers; what are the organizational barriers to shifting managerial mindsets? Is there a need for a new professional figure named a Chief Culture Officer (CCO)? A Chief Culture Officer (see McCracken 2011) would monitor and master the culture outside the organization and especially the culture created by a community around the brand, its cultural meanings and social rules. When a company knows these meanings and rules, it is in a better position to anticipate and adapt the brand strategy to the community.

RECOMMENDED READING

Cova, B. (1997) 'Community and consumption: Towards a definition of the "linking value" of product or services', *European Journal of Marketing*, 31 (3/4): 297–316.

Cova, B., Kozinets, R.V., and Shankar, A. (eds) (2007) *Consumer Tribes*. Oxford: Butterworth–Heinemann.

Cova, B., Pace, S., and Skålén, P. (2015) 'Marketing with working consumers: The case of a carmaker and its brand community', *Organization*, 22 (5): 682–701.

Goulding, C., Shankar, A., and Canniford, R. (2013) 'Learning to be tribal: Facilitating the formation of consumer tribes', *European Journal of Marketing*, 47 (5/6): 813–32.

Maffesoli, M. (1995) *The Time of the Tribes: The Decline of Individualism in Mass Society*. London: Sage.

McCracken, G. (2011) *Chief Culture Officer: How to Create a Living Breathing Corporation*. New York: Basic Books.

Muniz, A.M. and O'Guinn, T.C. (2001) 'Brand community', *Journal of Consumer Research*, *27* (4): 412–32.

Schau, H.J., Muñiz Jr, A.M., and Arnould, E.J. (2009) 'How brand community practices create value', *Journal of Marketing*, 73 (5): 30–51.

Schouten, J.W. and McAlexander, J.H. (1995) 'Subcultures of consumption: An ethnography of the new bikers', *Journal of Consumer Research*, 22 (1): 43–61.

Thomas, T. C., Price, L. L., and Schau, H. J. (2013) 'When differences unite: Resource dependence in heterogeneous consumption communities'. *Journal of Consumer Research*, 39 (5): 1010–33.

REFERENCES

Antorini, Y.M., Muñiz Jr, A.M., and Askildsen, T. (2012) 'Collaborating with customer communities: Lessons from the LEGO Group', *MIT Sloan Management Review*, 53 (3): 73.

Arnould, E.J. and Thompson, C.J. (2005) 'Consumer culture theory (CCT): Twenty years of research', *Journal of Consumer Research*, 31 (4): 868–82.

Arvidsson, A. and Caliandro, A. (2015) 'Brand public', *Journal of Consumer Research, 42* (5): 727–48.

Brown, S. and Patterson, A. (2009) 'Harry Potter and the service-dominant logic of marketing: A cautionary tale', *Journal of Marketing Management, 25* (5–6): 519–33.

Cova, B. (1997) 'Community and consumption: Towards a definition of the "linking value" of product or services', *European Journal of Marketing, 31* (3/4): 297–316.

Cova, B. and Dalli, D. (2009) 'Working consumers: The next step in marketing theory?', *Marketing Theory, 9* (3): 315–39.

Cova, B. and Shankar, A. (2012) 'Tribal marketing', in L. Penaloza, N. Toulouse, and L.M. Visconti (eds), *Marketing Management: A Cultural Perspective*. London/New York: Routledge. pp. 178–93.

Cova, B., Kozinets, R.V., and Shankar, A. (eds) (2007) *Consumer Tribes*. Oxford: Butterworth–Heinemann.

Cova, B., Pace, S., and Skålén, P. (2015) 'Marketing with working consumers: The case of a carmaker and its brand community', *Organization, 22* (5): 682–701.

Füller, J., Schroll, R., and von Hippel, E. (2013) 'User generated brands and their contribution to the diffusion of user innovations', *Research Policy, 42* (6): 1197–209.

Goulding, C., Shankar, A., and Canniford, R. (2013) 'Learning to be tribal: Facilitating the formation of consumer tribes', *European Journal of Marketing, 47* (5/6): 813–32.

Goulding, C., Shankar, A., and Elliott, R. (2002) 'Working weeks, rave weekends: Identity fragmentation and the emergence of new communities', *Consumption Markets & Culture*, 5 (4): 261–84.

Goulding, C., Shankar, A., Elliott, R., and Canniford, R. (2009) 'The marketplace management of illicit pleasure', *Journal of Consumer Research*, 35 (5): 759–71.

Hatch, M.J. and Schultz, M. (2010) 'Toward a theory of brand co-creation with implications for brand governance', *Journal of Brand Management*, 17 (8): 590–604.

Husemann, K.C., Ladstaetter F., and Luedicke, M.K. (2015) 'Conflict culture and conflict management in consumption communities', *Psychology and Marketing*, 32 (3): 265–84.

Kozinets, R.V. (2002) 'Can consumers escape the market? Emancipatory illuminations from Burning Man', *Journal of Consumer Research*, 29 (1), 20–38.

Maffesoli, M. (1996) *The Time of the Tribes: The Decline of Individualism in Mass Society*. London: Sage.

Martin, Diane M., Schouten, John W., and McAlexander, James H. (2006) 'Claiming the throttle: Multiple femininities in a hyper-masculine subculture', *Consumption Markets & Culture*, 9 (3): 171–205.

McAlexander, J.H. and Schouten, J.W. (1998) 'Brandfests: Servicescapes for the cultivation of brand equity', in J.F. Sherry (ed.), *Servicescapes: The Concept of Place in Contemporary Markets*. Lincolnwood, IL: NTC Business Books. pp. 377–402.

McCracken, G. (2011) *Chief Culture Officer: How to Create a Living Breathing Corporation*. New York: Basic Books.

Muñiz, A.M. and O'Guinn, T.C. (2001) 'Brand community', *Journal of Consumer Research*, 27 (4): 412–32.

Pongsakornrungsilp, S. and Schroeder, J.E. (2011) 'Understanding value co-creation in a co-consuming brand community', *Marketing Theory*, 11 (3): 303–24.

Sandıkcı, Özlem and Ger, Güliz (2010) 'Veiling in style: How does a stigmatized practice become fashionable?', *Journal of Consumer Research*, 37 (June): 15–36.

Schau, H.J., Muñiz Jr, A.M., and Arnould, E.J. (2009) 'How brand community practices create value', *Journal of Marketing*, 73 (5): 30–51.

Schouten, J.W. and McAlexander, J.H. (1995) Subcultures of consumption: An ethnography of the new bikers', *Journal of Consumer Research*, 22 (1): 43–61.

Shankar, A., Cherrier, H., and Canniford, R. (2006) 'Consumer empowerment: A Foucauldian interpretation', *European Journal of Marketing*, 40 (9/10): 1013–30.

Stratton, G. and Northcote, J. (2016) 'When totems beget clans: The brand symbol as the defining marker of brand communities', *Journal of Consumer Culture*, 16 (2): 493–509.

Thomas, Tandy Chalmers, Price, Linda L., and Schau, Hope Jensen (2013) 'When differences unite: Resource dependence in heterogeneous consumption communities', *Journal of Consumer Research, 39* (5): 1010–33.

Turner V.W. (1969) *The Ritual Process: Structure and Anti-Structure*. Chicago, IL: Aldine.

Turner, V.W. (1974) 'Liminal to liminoid in play, flow and ritual: An essay in comparative symbology', *Rice University Studies, 60* (3): 53–92.

Zwick, D. and Bradshaw, A. (2016) 'Biopolitical marketing and social media brand communities', *Theory, Culture and Society, 33* (5): 91–115.

Zwick, D. and Cayla, J. (eds) (2011) *Inside Marketing: Practices, Ideologies, Devices*. Oxford: Oxford University Press.

5

CONSUMER-PRODUCED, EMERGENT, AND HYBRID MARKETS

Eminegül Karababa, Middle East Technical University
Daiane Scaraboto, Pontificia Universidad
Católica de Chile

CHAPTER OVERVIEW

- Emergent markets challenge established market structures and blur the distinction between producers and consumers.
- Consumer-produced markets emerge from consumer initiatives to oppose, complement, or substitute for mainstream markets.
- Most consumer-produced and emergent markets are hybrid economies, combining and merging different aspects of mainstream and alternative markets.
- Consumer-produced markets may promote social inclusion and changes in social and cultural norms.

INTRODUCTION

Consumer culture theory (CCT) research investigates the formation, operation, and transformation of contemporary markets, and also the modes of exchange and types of value (the perceived benefit of something – an object, a person, or an activity – to an individual or group [Karababa and Kjeldgaard 2014]), created or co-created in these markets (Schau et al. 2009). While investigating these market processes, CCT research challenges the assumptions of economic liberalism which dominate the current scholarly thought on markets in consumer research and marketing. In particular, CCT research demonstrates the role of consumers as an important market stakeholder. In everyday contexts, consumers are not only on the receiving side of the exchange process. They also contribute to the value creation process by performing various practices such as designing, producing, combining, and reusing products or making meanings for them.

By paying attention to consumers as important market stakeholders, CCT researchers have highlighted consumer-produced markets. These markets demonstrate a multiplicity of forms and co-existences in terms of actors, their relationships and roles, exchange mechanisms, and value types that are created, but all of them have consumers as key stakeholders. Most consumer-produced markets are hybrid economies that operate at the interstices between market and nonmarket economies (Scaraboto 2015: 153). This hybridity in consumer-produced markets arises from the co-existence of multiple logics of circulation, modes of exchange, modes of production, types of value, and the blurred roles of market actors. CCT researchers are interested in explaining hybridity in emerging and consumer-produced markets; the practices of consumers, marketers, producers, and other actors interacting in these markets; the rules that define the operation of these actors; dominances, resistances, and negotiations among actors; as well as the processes of market change throughout time.

THE CONTEMPORARY CONTEXT OF EMERGENT CONSUMER-PRODUCED MARKETS

Groups of consumers at the fringes of society frequently develop new practices or cultural products that challenge mainstream taste and norms. For example, a group of large-size women who felt marginalized from the fashion market congregated online and started blogging about fashion in ways that reflect their taste. Through developing a common identity – fatshionistas – these bloggers demonstrate how larger women can dress fashionably. Attentive companies will start serving the needs of these consumers by extending sizing or launching 'plus-sized' clothing lines and stores. Companies that listen closely to groups of consumers act as intermediaries, diffusing subcultural ideas and products into the mainstream market (Holt 2002). Yet, the emergence of markets based on consumer creation is not always the result of initiatives taken by companies. Occasionally, consumers engage in creative production to solve their own needs and make these solutions available to others through entrepreneurship or collective action (Thompson and Coskuner-Balli 2007). For example, fatshionista bloggers have jointly designed and launched clothing collections (e.g. premme.us), promoted plus-size fashion shows, and produced videos featuring large, fashionable women (e.g. https://vimeo.com/94364919). Similarly, members of a university-based football fandom group (ODTÜ'lü Kartallar) in Ankara, Turkey, collectively decide to produce fandom items, such as banners, posters, and t-shirts (Ay 2017). Some community members take the responsibility of designing the products and produce posters and banners. Others find manufacturers of t-shirts and jerseys. These fans then sell the items in the community and even those members who were active in the production process purchase the items as consumers.

As we approach 2020, consumers are better equipped than ever to collaborate with one another. The prevalence of Web 2.0 and social media offers opportunities for collaboration that are quantitatively (i.e., broader in scale, more frequent, faster) and qualitatively different (i.e., participatory, democratic, networked, personal) from those offered by traditional websites and traditional media. By collaborating online, consumers can develop ideas and cultural products that address their needs, and can also gather resources to produce, diffuse, and exchange those ideas and products independently from traditional market structures. In fact, these forms of collaboration among consumers facilitated by Web 2.0 and social media have allowed for the development of a new business model that has profoundly impacted consumer markets, worldwide: the platform company. Platform companies such as Airbnb (home rentals), Uber (transportation), Instacart (purchasing and deliveries), Fiverr and TaskRabbit (gigs and outsourcing of assorted tasks), operate by providing a way for consumers to connect one to another in solving their needs.

In what has been dubbed the emergence of platform capitalism, several businesses and entire markets have emerged by transforming how goods and services are produced and distributed. When compared to the hierarchical and centralized form of mainstream capitalist markets, platform capitalism seems more participatory and democratic, because consumers engage directly with each other to provide and consume offerings. This new model is extremely disruptive. Companies used to decide and control what was offered, when, to whom, and for how much. For example, heavily regulated taxi companies used to transport passengers in most cities. Then along came Uber, a platform company that connects individuals who act as drivers with others who need to take rides. Similarly, Snuuper, a Chilean-based platform business, has been transforming the local market research industry by crowdsourcing market information needs to individuals willing to undertake tasks such as checking retail prices, sharing photos of their experiences as consumers, or monitoring shelf stock in points of sale across the country.

Several platform businesses have become successful by facilitating collaboration among consumers. Toy Cycle (toy-cycle.org), for example, a platform for families to exchange toys, operates on a membership model. Parents pay a US$12 monthly fee to participate in the community, which grants them the right to post unlimited ads to give away or request toys. Another successful model is that of Food Assembly (thefoodassembly.com), a French-based collective aiming to reduce the number of intermediaries between consumers and food producers. There is no membership fee to participate, and the platform collects a fee from food producers, who still receive 80% for every product sold, compared to the 15–25% that most supermarkets offer them.

By facilitating consumer interaction and supporting the creation and distribution of value by consumers, these companies found a way to justify their existence in a market where consumers control how value is created and exchanged. In this scenario, companies need to rethink their approach to doing business, and consider how many-to-many, consumer-produced markets challenge traditional approaches to value creation and exchange by decentralizing, crowdsourcing, and opening all kinds of marketing tasks to negotiation among consumers.

Box 5.1:   Extended Case Study

Consumers assume market-changing roles: how fashion bloggers rule the fashion world

Several industries, including travel, photography, sports, and food, have seen changes promoted by the actions of consumers who engage in collaborative networks. Fashion lovers, for example, participate in discussion forums and on websites, and create and maintain their own blogs and social media accounts dedicated to style, fashion purchases, outfit sharing, fashion photography, and other related themes. But do contented consumers affect the markets they engage with? Dolbec and Fischer (2015) have studied how fashion lovers interact with one another online to examine how these consumers' actions shape the boundaries and the principles behind the fashion market – which are to design and produce artistic clothing that can be sold for a profit.

The authors identify three important consequences brought about by the participation of these consumers in the fashion market. First, consumers assume part of the work that maintains the fashion market and that professionals had previously monopolized. For example, consumers now engage in curating looks on outfit-sharing websites and also creating images that are similar to those produced by stylists and photographers. Moreover, the participation of consumers seeking images to post on their blogs and other platforms has broadened the very types of work carried out to sustain the fashion market. For example, fashion journalists, emulating consumer bloggers, now pay attention not only to the offerings of designers, but also to the garb sported by attendees at premiere fashion events such as Fashion Week.

Second, fashion bloggers emerged as a new category of actors who are gaining a unique status in the fashion market. Such bloggers are now seated in coveted positions at fashions shows, collaborating with fashion designers, and documenting fashion shows for widely read fashion magazines. This has led to contestation between traditional and emergent categories of actors. For example, some fashion critics and journalists make efforts to highlight the inferiority of the new categories of actors relative to traditional ones.

Third, these consumers have helped cement a new logic in fashion: the logic of accessibility. Logics 'define the content and meaning of institutions' such as the fashion market.

The logic of accessibility suggests that fashion should be accessible, that is, it should be relatively affordable and wearable. Dolbec and Fischer acknowledge that this logic did not emerge owing solely to consumers participating in the online fashion arena. However, consumers' embrace of the logic of accessibility appears to have helped to escalate its widespread recognition and adoption.

Websites such as Instagram and Tumblr, Twitter and Vine, lookbook.nu and chictopia, YouTube and Vimeo, are offering increasing opportunities for consumer interaction, content-creation, and sharing. As a result, consumers are increasingly participating in a wide range of markets. Dolbec and Fischer show that changes in markets should be expected, whether consumers are actively seeking them or not: the mere participation of connected consumers in these markets suffices to enact dramatic changes. Their activities challenge market dynamics in fields where engaged consumers are afforded easy opportunities to interact.

Questions

1. Other than contestation, what dynamics among actors in a market do you expect to see as consumers start making incursions into the domains of companies, media, and other professionals (e.g. photographers, models, designers)?
2. What differences do you expect to see in how traditional market actors and connected fashion consumers generate innovation in the fashion market?
3. Dolbec and Fischer propose four conditions that foster unintended market change propelled by contented consumers. These are: '(1) the existence of "places" (virtual or real) that afford opportunities for consumer interaction, (2) low costs for consumers to experiment with new behaviors, (3) the observability of experimental behaviors, and (4) existing product and technology infrastructures'. Can you think of another market, product category, or consumption activity in which these four conditions are met, and which would be a good candidate for consumer-propelled change?

THE HYBRID NATURE OF EMERGENT CONSUMER-PRODUCED MARKETS

Consumer-produced markets are projected to reach $335 billion by 2025, when they will account for half of the world's economy. Hence, it is important to understand how these markets emerge and operate. Consumer-produced markets are decentralized, largely unregulated, and more cooperative than competitive. Participants in consumer-produced markets frequently switch between the roles of producers and consumers. Even though they challenge the very foundations of traditional market forms, consumer-produced markets do not necessarily emerge out of attempts to resist capitalism or undermine its mainstream practices. For example, the Minimoto market studied by CCT scholars Martin and Schouten (2014) emerged from the actions of adult consumers who wanted to ride or race dirt bikes, but not on full-sized motorcycles. Rather, they took pleasure and excitement in riding minibikes which offered a nostalgic recall of their childhood and enabled them to attain the adrenaline rush of riding dirt bikes but with a greater sense of control and safety emanating from the smaller size of the machine. However, to engage in these activities, these adult riders had to make substantial modifications to these minibikes, which are designed for children.

At the beginning, several people collaborated to develop the first models of Minimotos, build tracks where they could practice and enjoy their bikes, and to organize and promote races. The market for Minimotos developed as some entrepreneurs among these consumers started businesses out of their dedication to the activity by, for instance, opening bike shops, or publishing magazines that focused on the hobby. Yet, because the hobby depended on collaboration and the voluntary work contributed by several individuals at its outset, these entrepreneurs are permanently bounded to the community, and need to care about its goals and values rather than simply go about developing their businesses as a mainstream start-up would. Hence the resulting Minimoto market follows the principles of the capitalist market, that is, profit-making and capital accumulation, but also communal values, including collaboration and the pursuit of common interests. To take community needs into account, these entrepreneurs in the Minimoto market cannot rely solely on profit-making, price-based exchanges to distribute products and services. They also distribute products and services through sharing, gift-giving, and lending.

This example also shows that other categorizations used by researchers and practitioners to make sense of conventional markets do not apply seamlessly to consumer-produced markets. Minimoto racers, for instance, cannot be easily described as a particular type of market actor, for they constantly switch among the roles of consumers, entrepreneurs, producers, distributors, and service providers. For instance, upon purchasing a regular children's bike on a conventional market, a Minimoto racer may work to customize the bike for adult use and for racing. This user may also resell, rent, or gift the customized bike, and offer customizing services to other racers, for free or for a charge. As it combines multiple possible motivations for participation (e.g. profit-making, generosity, or status-seeking), creates several types of value (e.g. profit, relationships, enjoyment), employs multiple modes of exchange (e.g. selling, sharing, gift-giving), and has actors that shift between several roles, the consumer-produced market for Minimotos can be considered a hybrid market.

Table 5.1 lists the key market features and examples of consumer-produced markets that combine multiples of those features, frequently giving rise to hybrid features, or hybrid markets. Often, hybrid markets differ from classical conceptions of markets in more than one market feature. By blurring several traditional features and developing new combinations of aspects that cut across dimensions, many hybrid markets defy categorization.

Table 5.1   Market features and hybrid market examples

MARKET features	PURE forms (non-exhaustive list)	HYBRID forms (non-exhaustive list)	EXAMPLES of markets with hybrid features
Actors	Designer Entrepreneur Manufacturer Consumer Distributor Regulator Service provider	*Prosumer*: Individuals whose roles as consumers and users are inextricably interwoven with those as producers and creators *Digital influencer*: a consumer who collaborates with brands to produce and share content on social media	*Threadless*: individuals act as designers, entrepreneurs, product qualifiers, and consumers *YouTube*: individuals act as content producers, distributors, critics, and consumers
Types of value	Economic Social Spiritual Emotional Hedonic	Combinations of pure types being aimed at and generated in one market	*Couchsurfing*: a collaborative consumer network whereby travelers can save money, make friends, have fun, and learn about different cultures by staying with local hosts
Modes of production	Hierarchical/vertical Centralized Networked Distributed Collaborative	*Crowdfunding*: a form of financing businesses and projects through raising monetary contributions from a large number of individuals	*Kickstarter*: A global community to back creative projects through crowdfunding
Modes of exchange	Selling Sharing Renting Bartering Gifting Lending	*Freemium*: the offering of the essential parts of a product or service for free, while charging for additional features *Spotify*	*Geocaching*: Basic access to Geocaching. com, created by a geocaching player/ entrepreneur, is free but additional features require paid membership
Underlying logics	Profit-making Reciprocity Sociality Discovery Hedonism	Combinations of pure types underlying the same market	*Airbnb*: Users generate income (or save money) through hospitality rentals, and experience destinations like locals
Spheres of interaction	Public/private Global/local Religious/secular Traditional/modern Online/offline Urban/rural	*Glocal*: a context in which both local and global discourses, cultural codes and conventions, practices, and values coexist (Featherstone and Lash 1995)	Electronic music markets (such as Dubstep, described in Hietanen, Rokka, and Roman's videography: https://vimeo. com/32192229)

Box 5.2:   Extended Case Study

The formation of a consumer-produced market

Beer pong started as a drinking game that requires players to throw ping-pong balls into a triangular formation of cups containing beer. Because excessive alcohol consumption and demeaning behaviors are encouraged within the game, beer pong has been banned at several United States' universities. After attending a beer pong competition in Las Vegas, the CCT researcher and co-founder of BPONG IRELAND, Stephen O'Sullivan, described the Beer Pong World Series as an experience filled with excitement juxtaposed with the seriousness of a sports tournament. Music, laughter, friendships, mockery, excessive consumption of alcohol, gambling, and debauchery coexist with passionate play by invested players who frequently cry or become aggressive upon elimination of the tournament.

Professional beer pong (https://bpong.com/) emerged in 2006 and currently generates millions of dollars every year for the entrepreneurs who organize it. As a formal organization, global BPONG manages the tournament, produces and commercializes merchandise associated with it, and earns profits from the events. However, consumers – those who originally envisioned this activity and made this market possible – feel entitled to guide beer pong in the directions they prefer. They contest marketers' efforts to tame the events by imposing certain guidelines.

In this case, the consumer entrepreneurs were three Irish university students (including O'Sullivan). They were first exposed to the game and practiced it as a sport on the Cork City University campus. After attending the Annual World Series of Beer Pong held in Las Vegas (you can watch several videos about this event on YouTube), the three friends decided to establish the Irish brand and bring the professionalism of the global brand to the Irish context. O'Sullivan (2010) reports on how these consumer entrepreneurs brought the global Beer Pong brand to Cork and made the experience relevant to the Irish consumers by adapting the experience to local expectations.

First, the entrepreneurs conceived competitions that people could enjoy – meetings where they could develop friendships and convert to this emerging community of BPONGers. At the beginning, rather than imposing the global standards and game rules, they left the scene to participants to create their own atmosphere and to shape the experience according to their preferences. The first 1,000 members enrolled on the Irish Beer Pong Facebook site in a short time. The Facebook page for BPONG IRELAND began to grow and community ties strengthened. Also, members maintained control over the gaming experience by sharing their experiences through posting comments, photos, and videos. Beer Pong followers in Cork mention that they enjoy attending the competitions every weekend, playing, mocking each other, establishing new friendships, and belonging to this local community. Because of the interaction among the consumers and consumer entrepreneurs, a community consciousness emerged, and linking value was co-created through these activities among the members (see Chapter 4 on consumer tribes).

Beer Pong members also started to demand BPONG merchandise with local flavor from the entrepreneurs, and started to design posters and jerseys for their own teams. While keeping the design of the global BPONG symbol, BPONG IRELAND introduced the local flavor by changing the original colors of the symbol from the American flag's colors to the Irish flag's green, white, and orange. They marketed beer pong tables and t-shirts with Irish colors and symbols like the Shamrock, the green three-leaf clover, while retaining the global table size. Through this combination of global and local symbolism beer pong consumers constitute and communicate their communal, team, and individual identities. To maintain and grow the community, members initiate newcomers to the community and teach them not only the game but also specificities of the Irish brand community such as the lingo used by the members.

In the case, three consumer entrepreneurs spread a focal brand in a manner that complements local meanings and practices. They operate like cultural gatekeepers. To maintain and grow the community, they create linking value for consumers by moving the experience from the campus to the city pubs and establishing an online social network. Their motivation is not only to accumulate economic capital from this business, but also to fulfill a desire to play the game locally at a professional level.

You can watch the videography in which O'Sullivan shows how consumer entrepreneurs developed the beer pong market: https://vimeo.com/sos12/sos.

Questions

Based on the beer pong case study, discuss the following questions:

1. Describe the consumer-produced beer pong market formation process in Ireland.
2. What are the market features and hybrid forms that you observe in the case (see Table 5.1)?
3. Consider any other examples of consumer entrepreneurs in everyday life and identify similarities and differences with the BPONG case.

VALUE CREATION IN CONSUMER-PRODUCED, EMERGENT, AND HYBRID MARKETS

Understanding how value is created is one of the most important topics for businesses researchers and practitioners because it is through creating, offering, and delivering value to customers that companies gain competitive advantage. But how is value created when consumers take the lead?

CCT research has looked at how consumers create value in consumer-produced markets that characterize the contemporary economy, looking at collaborative networks such as Couchsurfing and Hit Record. Take, for instance, the collaborative network of geocaching (www.geocaching.com), an outdoor treasure-hunting game facilitated by an online platform. Geocaching players use GPS coordinates to hide and seek containers, called 'geocaches', at specific locations all over the world. A typical cache is a small waterproof container containing a logbook and sometimes a pen. Upon finding the geocache, a player should date and sign the book to prove that it was found. Then, the cache should be placed back for the next player to find.

Geocaching is a global consumption phenomenon, with more than 15 million active players hunting for more than 2.7 million hidden treasures in all continents. In networks like this, consumers scattered across the world connect with one another to achieve common goals, which can be social (e.g. making friends, having fun) or economic (starting a business, networking with potential customers). Because these networks do not have a company behind them that designs and oversees the process of value creation, the many value-creating actions enacted by individual participants across the world must be somehow integrated so the entire network can reap the benefits of these actions (Figueiredo and Scaraboto 2016).

But how can individuals collaborate to create value in networks that are geographically dispersed? In geocaching, individual actions, such as a geocacher hiding or finding a geocache, are registered and stored in blog posts, photographs, comments, and reviews. These registrations accumulate and are accessed by participants who may see them years later or while living on other continents. Because registrations refer to beneficial actions performed by members, they yield value for the entire geocaching network. For example, when a geocacher reads stories about the adventures of objects moved from geocache to geocache by other players, she gains knowledge, a sense of adventure, and connection to other participants. Hence, collaborative networks store and redistribute the value outcomes of actions performed by their members.

Another relevant issue is to understand what types of value can be generated by consumer-produced markets. In the hospitality network of Couchsurfing (see Table 5.1), different types of value are generated. Everyday actions performed by users and registered in the Couchsurfing platform include those linked to non-economic value, such as the guests cooking a meal, or hosts giving insights into their home country. These actions create relationships, help participants develop and express their identities, learn new things, and live pleasurable experiences, thereby generating multiple types of benefits. Even when economic value is generated, it is not the only type. Consumers in the collaborative network of Airbnb, for instance, are not deriving only functional value from access to accommodation or profit from renting spare bedrooms. Participants in this network collaborate to create other types of value, including enjoyment, knowledge, and new social connections. These value outcomes are not produced by the company behind Airbnb, but by interconnected consumers whose value-creating actions build upon one another through the registrations that accumulate in the network.

Box 5.3:   Critical Reflection

The origins of alternative markets

Alternative markets have frequently been defined based on the desire of consumers or producers to escape and avoid capitalist markets. But could alternative markets also emerge as a response to economic crises, when impoverished consumers have restricted access to capitalist markets? CCT researchers have examined the case of Greece, a country strongly affected by the financial crisis and the subsequent development of austerity measures in 2008–2009. As Benmecheddal et al. (2017) note, the economic and financial crisis profoundly affected Greek citizens: during the recession, salaries and pensions were reduced, unemployment soared, thousands of stores and companies closed, taxes on housing and consumption goods were increased, and the circulation of money was severely restricted. Because of this, several bartering systems emerged in Greece following the crisis. In these systems, individuals would offer products or services, negotiating their equivalence and trading them directly one for another, without the use of money (or similar medium of exchange). Indeed, negotiating monetary equivalence between incommensurate things, apples and oranges for example, is the essence of a barter system.

Rather than necessarily being opposed to capitalism, the bartering systems that emerged in Greece complemented it: they were a temporary solution that disenfranchised consumers and producers found to continue to address their needs. Benmecheddal and his colleagues have called this type of solution 'constrained alternative markets': markets based on solidarity that develop in a particular political and economic context of crisis when people lack economic resources. In Greece, public policies were advanced to facilitate the development of bartering systems by, for instance, providing free space where consumers and producers could meet to barter.

The role of technologies in supporting systems of bartering is noteworthy: online platforms and virtual alternative currencies facilitate exchanges, allowing bartering systems to operate on a larger scale than face-to-face transactions would permit. These technological tools also operate as mechanisms of trust and reputation – offering participants additional incentives to engage in bartering.

Yet, for constrained alternative markets to develop and operate successfully under conditions of crisis, participants must engage in the bartering system with the aim of helping and supporting each other. Companies, for instance, should not aim to make a profit, but rather to provide products and services at minimal prices to avoid bankruptcy. Consumers must be willing to forgo market-based understandings of value and trade equally, bartering, for example, 'a one-hour guitar lesson for an hour of house cleaning' or 'an hour of a doctor's time for an hour of self-defense class' (Benmecheddal et al. 2017: 200).

TENSIONS IN CONSUMER-PRODUCED, EMERGENT, AND HYBRID MARKETS

When consumers engage in actions that lead to the emergence of a hybrid market, they often are not seeking to create a formal marketplace *per se*. Frequently, consumers are simply interacting one with another to achieve social-, identity-, meaning-, and status-related goals. Inevitably, when community-like collectives of consumers evolve into full-blown markets – which happens as one or more for-profit businesses begin to cater to this emergent customer base – tensions emerge at the boundaries between community and commerce. Take the case of online commerce platform Etsy. Etsy was launched in 2005 with the mission of enabling people to make a living from crafts, and to reconnect producers and buyers. Etsy was a pioneer among the online marketplaces created to commercialize arts and crafts, and followed the tradition of craft fairs, offering sellers individual stores where they present their goods for a fee. At the outset, Etsy allowed sellers to commercialize only items they had produced themselves or vintage items (objects older than 20 years).

At its origin, Etsy provided an example of a platform company supporting a community where producers and consumers collaborated to create value though complex interactions between commercial and social interests. A significant shift in the Etsy ecosystem occurred, however, in 2013, when Etsy revised its policies to allow approved sellers to use production assistance to make their goods, going against their ethos of exclusively commercializing handmade and unique products, to keep businesses at a small and personal scale. Although Etsy has attempted to ensure producers partner in ways that are aligned with the values and policies of the marketplace, some sellers have expressed concern that Etsy's handmade ethos is now nothing more than a marketing gimmick. And even as some Etsy vendors embrace the chance to scale up and meet demand by outsourcing production, others have abandoned Etsy, complaining it has 'alienated its crafters and lost its soul' (Dobush 2015). These recent developments have resulted in disruptions to the hybrid nature of this consumer-produced market, and raise questions regarding what types of value should participants pursue in such markets.

THE POTENTIAL OF CONSUMER-PRODUCED, EMERGENT, AND HYBRID MARKETS

CCT researchers aim to uncover the potential of consumer-produced and hybrid markets. For instance, Scaraboto and Figueiredo (2017) studied the circulation of religious statues among Catholic households, a consumer-produced, hybrid market that combines several underlying logics and modes of production to generate different types of value. In what is known as the Small Chapels Movement (SCM), a well-organized hierarchy of priests and lay volunteers coordinates the transferring of thousands of small wooden chapels from neighbor to neighbor, with the goal of spreading the church's message among Catholic households.

For participating communities, the moving chapels create an alternative economy, one based not on traditional capitalist values but on participation, community, and faith. Money does, of course, play some role. Households make monetary donations to the Catholic church for the honor of hosting a chapel. This activity generates economic value for the church, but that is not they only type of value generated in this hybrid economy. For lay volunteers, social status is enhanced: working as a neighborhood's representative of the church is a prestigious role. Likewise, for the families, parishes, and communities interconnected by the regular visitation of these small chapels, there is spiritual value, too. For Catholics, Mary, as the mother of Jesus Christ, is one of the most powerful holy figures, and recipients of the small chapels that house her feel blessed by their access to divinity, support, and good luck. Finally, the small chapels often become a favored local symbol of the family group, transcending their religious significance to be, quite simply, beloved and familiar objects.

This research has found that the entanglement of various types of value and various market logics in the SCM, much like the entanglement of roots in a forest, makes this hybrid market very resistant to external threats, such as a potential overtaking by the capitalist market. When multiple logics of value creation and exchange are combined in the same market, participants find it difficult to disentangle economic value from the various other types of value outcomes created. This blurring minimizes perceived tension between the alternative economy and the mainstream market, and placates external criticism over the generation of economic value in an alternative economy that is led by a religious institution. For instance, the redirecting of money collected through donations to the formation of young priests makes it difficult for one to judge the church as profit-seeker even though it generates more than half a million dollars per year from the work of volunteers and donations from participants.

Given that it generates various types of value, the hybrid market of SCM accommodates the goals of diverse participants. Hence, participants will often rely on this system of value creation to access multiple resources and address several needs. Consequently, participants would lose much should this plural resource stream be threatened, and make efforts to assure the continuity of this consumer-produced market, such as volunteering time and making monetary donations when the movement needs support. Participants who depend on a consumer-produced market to provide them with multiple types of value outcomes are likely to concur with its guidelines and loosely implemented governing mechanisms, which explains how consumer-produced markets can be successful despite the absence of centralized control and well-established hierarchical structures in them.

Consumer-produced markets also have the potential to include consumers who are marginalized, stigmatized, or neglected by traditional mainstream markets. For instance, consumers who want to extend the life of their household goods by repairing them may not be able to rely on the mainstream market for replacement parts, information, or assistance. Companies will derive more profit from selling these consumers a new product, hence repairing is not incentivized. As consumer-produced markets tend to create several types of value simultaneously, they are less likely to exclude certain consumers or consumer needs solely based on their profit-generating potential. Because consumer-produced markets favor addressing consumer needs over generating profit, they tend to develop innovative and economical solutions to consumer problems. For example, The Repairers Club (www.facebook.com/ClubDeReparadores/) is a consumer-produced market created in Argentina that seeks to promote repair as a strategy for responsible, sustainable, and practical consumption. The Repairers Club organizes itinerant, voluntary, and collaborative repair meetings where people of all ages and occupations exchange knowledge and tools to extend the useful life of objects, preventing them from becoming waste.

Initiatives like this are particularly relevant in developing countries, where the tensions, limitations, negotiations, and politics related to citizenship through mainstream market consumption are most markedly evident. In Brazil, for instance, shopping malls became a site of class and racial-based conflict when groups of mostly dark-skinned and working-class youths in Sao Paulo organized on Facebook to meet and hang out at malls. Thousands showed up, and occupied the halls, singing, flirting, and parading their style. Mall operators reacted by banning further *rolezinhos*, Brazilian Portuguese slang for 'little outings'. Police abuse and racial profiling followed, leading to a proliferation of politicized *rolezinhos* around the country, as well as protests targeting malls, legally considered a public space, for being exclusively accessible by Brazil's white elite.

In contexts often marked by extreme disparities in wealth, consumers disenfranchised from the mainstream market tend to develop makeshift solutions to address their consumer needs. In Brazil, making do with one's own resources is so common that Brazilians have a term for it: *gambiarra*. *Gambiarra* allows disenfranchised consumers to produce objects that, through their form, aesthetics, or functionality, replace market-ready solutions. For instance, consumers may create a barbecue grill out of an old shopping cart, or connect an electric kettle to a tap to have hot water in the bathroom where central heating is not available.

Consumers who engage in *gambiarra* frequently do so because they have limited access to mainstream markets. This is due in part to limited financial resources, that is, they lack money because they are unemployed, or because the little money they make is only sufficient to address their basic subsistence needs. It may also be due to geographic isolation, which is not uncommon in many countries in Africa and South America. Many consumers live in remote and sparsely populated areas of Brazil or areas poorly served by transport networks. In Brazil or the Democratic Republic of the Congo, for example, the vast river systems and equatorial climates have hampered the development of roads and railways. Or mainstream companies may not be interested in serving lower-income consumers, as is the case for most mainstream fashion brands. Through resorting to the resources they have at hand and developing creative solutions to their needs, these consumers may participate in consumer culture to a certain extent, and may inspire entrepreneurship that can extend these solutions to other disenfranchised consumers.

Finally, consider recent controversies around companies like Uber, Airbnb, and Airtasker questioning the profit-making orientation of these companies, which are at the center of the so-called sharing economy. Nevertheless, when understanding these companies as part of consumer-produced markets, it is evident that these platform-businesses create value types other than the economic. On Airbnb, users exchange accommodation for money, but often undertake other actions that do not create immediate economic benefit: meeting guests, giving gifts, or providing travel advice. These are the collaborative and often peripheral actions that help the system move. Nevertheless, although Airbnb has member reviews, it is up to users whether they mention other forms of value. To capture additional value, the company should create additional ways for participants to register these other value-creating actions. What amazing stories have you discovered from talking to your Uber driver? Have you brought a gift for your Airbnb host? What have you learned from your Airtasker helper? Questions like these would allow these networks to accumulate other types of value, which not only enrich the network, but encourage other participants to engage in similar actions. Hence, for consumer-produced markets to reach their full potential to promote economies that are more egalitarian, inclusive, fair, and sustainable, it is important to identify, understand, and foster the peculiar aspects that make these markets less market-like.

Box 5.4:   Critical Reflection

Consumer-produced markets interact and challenge social hierarchies

Consumer-produced markets, like any other market, interact with institutional structures, sometimes being shaped by them and sometimes transforming them. CCT research demonstrates how performances in the marketplace not only reproduce social structures or dominant gender hierarchies (see Chapters 7, 8, or 9) but also potentially challenge them. In their research investigating the women's flat track roller derby marketplace (https://wftda.com/), Thompson and Üstüner (2015) ask if it is possible for derby grrrls to challenge the dominant gender hierarchies through marketplace performances. If so, how do they manage to do so without losing their legitimacy in society?

(Continued)

(Continued)

Roller derby as an institution has its own rules, league requirements, and media representations that define its cultural form. At the global level, in metropolitan cities, expectations of this cultural form and gender performativities – the social expression of gender which is regulated by the gender norms – of roller derby players are defined. For example, in the global roller derby marketplace context, showing physical aggression is a gender performativity. However, in general, physical aggression in global derby marketplace is blended with playful eroticism. Although these performativities spread globally through the media, adaptations are needed in local small town contexts for local derby grrrls to maintain their social status in the town while challenging taken-for-granted gender norms. That is, two institutional structures, the global and local, are confronted in reshaping the social expressions of gender.

In the local context, derby grrrls adapt gender performativities by engaging in two different processes: glocalization and institutional commitment. Glocalization helps these women to negotiate the global performativities with local norms and tastes. For example, in the local context derby grrrls may reduce their use of the coarse language that is acceptable to more cosmopolitan audiences. In this way, a school teacher who plays roller derby, for instance, may accommodate her occupational identity and maintain her social status in front of audiences that include her students and their parents, with whom she interacts on a daily basis.

Institutional commitment contains two stages. In the first stage, when women are introduced to the field of roller derby, they find this experience shocking and unnatural, as it challenges their gender socialization. For example, the unapologetic physicality expected in roller derby is contrary to the conventional roles of mother or wife. In the second stage, conventional gender orientations of the members are opposed to their new positions in the roller derby community. By becoming a team captain and building a persona, a derby grrrl who has spent her life being a housewife and a mother gains a formal leadership role, and attains social recognition that is absent in her everyday gender role. In the institutional commitment process, becoming a member of the community and getting a social position in the community allow these women to adopt previously unacceptable gender expressions.

In addition, through performing these scripts, derby grrrls attain a reflexive awareness of their femininity through two processes: cultivating embodied cultural capital and negotiating embodied discontinuities across social fields. New skills, such as mastering and coordinating multiple athletic abilities, challenge conventional norms of femininity and create reflective awareness of women since embodiment results in internalization of the new cultural capital. This embodied reflexivity can further create a disparity between the derby grrrl persona and the everyday persona when a derby grrrl travels across two social fields with opposing norms.

This example shows that a consumer-produced market is not limited to simple economic exchange process. Consumer-produced markets exist in a society and interact with the institutional structures of the society. This interaction is dialectical; while social structures are shaping the marketplace actors, a novel institutional structure of the consumer-produced market may challenge the dominant hierarchies of the society.

CONCLUSION

This chapter has shown how contemporary emergent consumer-produced market forms differ from conventional capitalist market forms. By paying attention to how emergent, consumer-produced markets differ from mainstream markets, researchers can explore how the new market forms shape (and are being shaped by) culture and transform the ways in which we see ourselves and the world we inhabit.

RESEARCH DIRECTIONS

1. Understand value creation processes in consumer-produced markets by focusing, for instance, on the practices of value creation. Try to identify, in a specific market, the types of recurrent actions enacted by consumers that create value for themselves and for others.
2. Develop critical approaches to consumer-produced markets. Explore, for instance, how these market-producing agents challenge power dynamics at the societal and institutional levels. That is, as consumers become more agentic, do they necessarily become more powerful? Are any other market actors (e.g. companies, industry representatives, regulators) seeing their power and agency reduced?
3. How does hybridity unfold for different market features? This can be studied by examining, for example, markets that cut across spheres of interaction or in which different logics are combined.
4. To examine how consumer experience unfolds in consumer-produced markets, where experiences are shaped by interactions with many other participants and do not follow a script created by the marketer, as in conventional settings.
5. Consider the tensions consumers experience when their involvement in consumer-produced markets becomes 'work-like' – and hence potentially less pleasurable for them. How can consumers deal with such tensions? Is it possible that they will revert to a mainstream market to reduce the effort required to address their needs?

RECOMMENDED READING

Chase, Robin (2015) *Peers Inc: How People and Platforms Are Inventing the Collaborative Economy and Reinventing Capitalism*. New York, NY: Public Affairs.

Humphreys, Ashlee and Grayson, Kent (2008) 'The intersecting roles of consumer and producer: A critical perspective on co-production, co-creation and presumption', *Sociology Compass, 2* (3): 963–80.

Karababa, Eminegül and Kjeldgaard, Dannie (2014) 'Value in marketing: Toward sociocultural perspectives', *Marketing Theory, 14* (1): 119–27.

Scaraboto, Daiane (2015) 'Selling, sharing, and everything in between: The hybrid economies of collaborative networks', *Journal of Consumer Research, 42* (1): 152–76.

Sundararajan, Arun (2016) *The Sharing Economy: The End of Employment and the Rise of Crowd-Based Capitalism.* Cambridge, MA: MIT Press.

REFERENCES

Ay, Utku (2017) *Design, Making and Consumption of Football Fandom Products by a University-Based Football Fandom Group*, Unpublished Masters Thesis, Industrial Design Department, Graduate of Natural and Applied Sciences, Ankara, Turkey.

Benmecheddal, Ahmed, Gorge, Hélene, and Özçağlar-Toulouse, Nil (2017) 'Rethinking alternative markets in the context of economic crisis and austerity in Greece', *Journal of Macromarketing, 37* (2): 193–205.

Dobush, Grace (2015) 'How Etsy alienated its crafters and lost its soul', *Wired*. 19 February. Available at www.wired.com/2015/02/etsy-not-good-for-crafters/.

Dolbec, Pierre-Yann and Fischer, Eileen (2015) 'Refashioning a field? Connected consumers and institutional dynamics in markets', *Journal of Consumer Research, 41* (6): 1447–68.

Featherstone, Mike and Lash, Scott (1995) 'Globalization, modernity and the spatialization of social theory', in Mike Featherstone, Scott Lash, and Roland Robertson (eds), *Global Modernities*. London: Sage.

Figueiredo, Bernardo and Scaraboto, Daiane (2016) 'The systemic creation of value in collaborative consumer networks', *Journal of Consumer Research, 43* (4): 509–33.

Holt, Doug B. (2002) 'Why do brands cause trouble? A dialectical theory of consumer culture and branding', *Journal of Consumer Research, 29* (1): 70–90.

Karababa, Eminegül and Kjeldgaard, Dannie (2014) 'Value in marketing: Toward sociocultural perspectives', *Marketing Theory, 14* (1): 119–27.

Martin, Diane M. and Schouten, John W. (2014) 'Consumption-driven market emergence', *Journal of Consumer Research, 40* (5): 855–70.

O'Sullivan, Stephen (2010) 'And in the beginning there was a brand: The BPONG IRELAND brand community'. https://marketing.conference-services.net/resources/327/2342/pdf/AM2011_0370.pdf.

Scaraboto, Daiane (2015) 'Selling, sharing, and everything in between: The hybrid economies of collaborative networks', *Journal of Consumer Research, 42* (1): 152–76.

Scaraboto, Daiane and Figueiredo, Bernardo (2017) 'Holy Mary goes round: Using object circulation to promote hybrid value regimes in alternative economies', *Journal of Macromarketing, 37* (2): 1–13.

Schau, Hope J., Muñiz Jr, Albert M., and Arnould, Eric J. (2009) 'How brand community practices create value', *Journal of Marketing, 73* (5): 30–51.

Thompson, Craig. J. and Coskuner-Balli, Gokcen (2007) 'Countervailing market responses to corporate co-optation and the ideological recruitment of consumption communities', *Journal of Consumer Research*, *34* (2): 135–52.

Thompson, Craig. J. and Üstüner, Tuba (2015) 'Women skating on the edge: Marketplace performances as ideological edgework', *Journal of Consumer Research*, *42* (2): 235–65.

6

GLOCALIZATION OF MARKETPLACE CULTURES

Gokcen Coskuner-Balli, Chapman University
Burçak Ertimur, Fairleigh Dickinson University

CHAPTER OVERVIEW

- Today, it is impossible to examine and understand marketplace cultures without considering global cultural forces and realities.
- Global consumer culture is characterized by multidirectional flows of people, technology, financial capital, mediated images, and ideas.
- Historically, the debates on the impact of globalization on consumer culture have featured two opposing trends: a culturally uniform, homogenized versus a culturally plural, heterogenized consumer culture.
- The term glocalization captures the simultaneous presence of these predicted trends and regards cultural homogenization and heterogenization as interrelated processes that co-shape one another.
- Glocalization is manifested via processes such as re-appropriation, reterritorialization, and hybridization, all of which are outcomes of multidirectional global flows.
- Hybrid cultural products synthesize global and local influences and can produce tensions in the marketplace that require marketers to manage their legitimacy in the eyes of consumers.
- As cultural forms that help us interpret and organize the world, brands play an important role in constructing glocal marketplace cultures.

INTRODUCTION

Imagine how consumers around the world go about their daily lives today. In the United States, Darcy stops by at Starbucks to get Ethiopian fair trade coffee. In Japan, Yasu visits a comic book store to pick up *Bat-Manga!: The Secret History of Batman in Japan*, the superhero comic book his friend had recommended. In Turkey, Burcu takes a sip from a can of Cola-Turka while listening to her favorite Turkish rock band on her iPod. In Greenland, Aqqaluk signs on to the Internet to chat with his peers in Thailand. In Jordan, Diana settles in front of the TV to watch her favorite Turkish soap opera. As evident in these examples, consumer practices and experiences are increasingly transcending national and geographic boundaries, and reflecting global interconnections (Castells 1998; Ritzer 2004).

Daily transactions such as buying a cup of coffee at Starbucks occur locally around the world. Yet, the webs of interconnectedness become apparent when one reflects on the network of coffee growers in Ethiopia, the packagers, advertisers and marketers in the United States, and the worldwide consumers of coffee. Furthermore, the increased connectivity creates cultural conditions that encourage consumers to consider global referents in building their identities (Cayla and Arnould 2008). Consider how a teenager in Greenland makes connections with other young people through the Internet and compares his/her life and consumption practices to those who live in the United States, Thailand, or Argentina. Or how Turkish soap operas have become popular throughout the Arab world, offering symbolic referents particularly to Arab women through depictions of 'secular lifestyles interweaved with Islamic values' (Gurmen 2016). Along with processes such as increased worldwide communication and migration, the mixing and fusing of cultures has also intensified (Kraidy 2005; Tomlinson 1999). As a result, we see the creation of new products that are hybrids of different cultures such as Bat-Manga (Japanese manga adaptation of Batman) and Turkish Rock music along with localized versions of mass-produced global products like Cola-Turka.

In summary, it is impossible to examine and understand marketplace cultures today without considering global cultural forces. What is globalization and what are its consequences? Do global forces lead to a homogenized consumer culture where multinational chains such as McDonald's take over markets around the world? Or can we talk about a more heterogeneous distribution and creation of consumer culture? As the increased flows of people, ideas, and brands define the daily lives of consumers all around the world, how do the forces of homogenization and heterogenization manifest themselves? What is glocalization and what are its social, cultural, and managerial implications? Finally, what role do brands play in construction of global consumer culture? This chapter provides answers to these questions and presents cases for readers' further engagement with theoretical discussions surrounding glocalization of marketplace cultures.

GLOBAL CONSUMER CULTURE

Globalization refers to the rapidly increasing worldwide integration and interdependence of societies and cultures. It involves worldwide diffusion of practices, relations, and forms of social organizations (Ritzer 2004). The famous anthropologist Appadurai proposes that globalization can be conceptualized as a series of resource flows that are organized by five dimensions or 'scapes': ethnoscapes, mediascapes, technoscapes, financescapes, and ideoscapes. These scapes can be thought of as pathways that traverse the globe and enable certain kinds of resources to travel and intermingle with other kinds of resources.

Appadurai further elaborates on these terms in the following way. *Ethnoscape* refers to the shifting terrains of people that constitute the world in which we live: tourists, immigrants, and refugees to cite a few. *Technoscape* refers to the global systems and networks of technology, ranging from the Internet to transport systems. *Financescapes* refers to the increasingly unpredictable flows of finance that rebound around the world. *Mediascapes* refers to the increasing importance of global media, from television, the Internet, magazines, to the flow of audio. *Ideoscapes* refers to the increasing importance of global flows of ideas and ideologies, concepts that are generated in one locality but then become available to audiences around the world and take on extraordinary global significance (Appadurai 1990).

In its 2016 report, the McKinsey Global Institute provides an outlook on the scope and complexity of global flows. By 2012, the combined value of trade in goods and services plus financial flows had reached $26 trillion, or 36 percent of global GDP, from just $5 trillion, or 23 percent of the world GDP, in 1990. In 2014, the combined trade had totaled to $30 trillion, or 39 percent of the global GDP. Whereas flow of goods and finance has declined, flows of data and information have increased. Trade was once dominated by tangible goods and was largely confined to advanced economies and their large multinational companies. Today, global data flows are surging and digital platforms allow more countries and smaller enterprises to participate in the global economy.

Considering globalization in terms of intensified flows of people, goods, money, information, images, and technology, and identifying the changing trends in these global flows provide a useful lens to examine global consumer culture. However, we also need to build on this image of flows to conceptualize the social, cultural, and political implications of globalization. As posed at the beginning of the chapter, do global forces lead to a homogenized consumer culture where multinational chains such as McDonald's take over markets around the world? Or can we talk about a more heterogeneous distribution and creation of consumer culture? We now turn to discussing these debates on the impact of globalization on consumer culture.

Globalization and Cultural Homogeneity

One critical perspective on the impact of globalization on consumer culture predicts homogenization of cultural experiences. This view considers the Western world as the dominant center of globalization where goods and ideas flow primarily from the Western to the Eastern world. It is fair to characterize this perspective as pessimistic in the sense that the power of Western culture over other cultures is thought to threaten and eventually lead to destruction of local identities and cultures. One theory that speaks to this homogenization of culture is the McDonaldization theory. Ritzer's (2004) McDonaldization theory suggests that as companies aim to see their profit grow through unilateral homogenization, they produce standardized social forms that are centrally conceived and controlled such as McDonald's hamburger. Standardized products such as McDonald's have become so widespread because of the dominance of rationalization and the principles of the fast-food restaurant such as efficiency, predictability, calculability, and control in the United States and in the rest of the world.

Some other trends that lend support to the cultural homogenization thesis include: proliferation of transnational firms, globalized capitalism, globalized consumerism, and global consumption homogenization (Ger and Belk 1996). Transnational corporations with revenues at times surpassing GNPs of countries have great influence on consumers' lives across the world. Biggest online platforms such as Facebook, YouTube, WhatsApp, and Instagram have user bases that surpass populations of many countries. The McKinsey Global Institute's Connectedness Index, which measures the extent to which countries around the world are integrated into the global network of flows, reveals only a small set of countries that dominate the inflows and outflows of goods, services, finance, people, and data. Singapore tops the latest rankings, followed by the Netherlands, the United States, and Germany. Figure 6.1 depicts the large gaps between leading countries and the rest of the world in terms of connectedness.

Another trend that contributes to the homogeneity of global consumer culture is the dominance of capitalism and the neoliberal market logic as its underlying market system (see Chapter 11 for a detailed history of neoliberalism). Scholars note that globalization intensified with the neoliberal deregulation of markets in the late 1980s. As the political ideology of neoliberalism gained increasing acceptance in the late 1970s and beginning 1980s, many countries including the United Kingdom, United States, Canada, and Germany adopted this market policy. As a result, neoliberalism, which requires minimum government intervention in markets and valorizes individual competition, responsibility, and opportunity seeking, has become the dominant economic system in global consumer culture.

Global consumer culture is also characterized as homogenous in terms of the overarching consumer ethos and experiences. Across the world, the norm has become to associate one's wellbeing and success with gaining access to consumer goods and services (Ger and Belk 1996). This standard has also taken hold in countries that historically had a communist regime such as Romania as well as those in less affluent parts of the world, such as Turkey. Consumers have become similar not only in their desires for consumer goods, but also in terms of their experiences of the commercial marketplace. Across the world, they have access to the same experiences and consume the same fashion, entertainment, food, and brands (Belk 1995). Today it is possible for consumers in

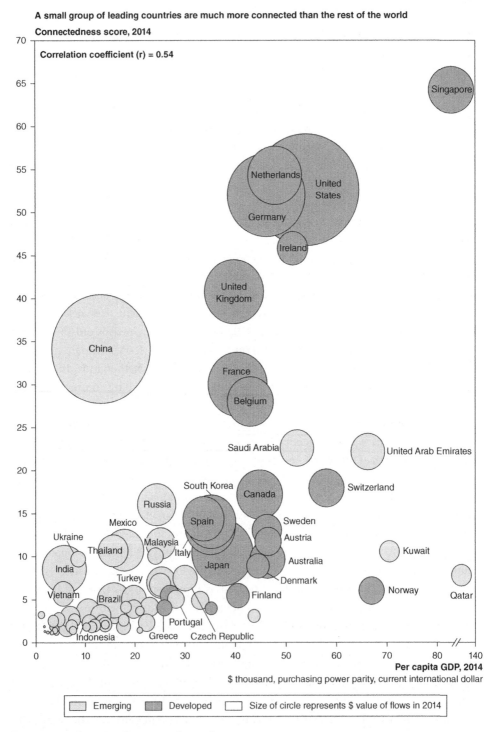

A small group of leading countries are much more connected than the rest of the world

Connectedness score, 2014

Correlation coefficient (r) = 0.54

Per capita GDP, 2014

$ thousand, purchasing power parity, current international dollar

Emerging   Developed   Size of circle represents $ value of flows in 2014

Figure 6.1 Country Connectedness Score

Source: IMF; McKinsey Global Institute analysis

two remote geographical locales of the world to start their day with coffee at Starbucks, have lunch at McDonald's, check their Facebook account in the afternoon, and watch *Game of Thrones* in the evening.

Globalization and Cultural Heterogeneity

It is better to conceive global culture as a field in which many cultural forms are announced, accumulate, and collide. (Featherstone 2006: 390)

As mentioned above, one view of globalization holds that flow of cultural practices has predominantly resulted in McDonaldization and Americanization of the world. While there is a good deal of evidence for this, the flow of goods, ideas, and technology is not unidirectional. Consider the popularity of Eastern origin practices such as karate, yoga, and Tai chi in the West. The influence of globalization processes on consumer identities, experiences and practices is much more multifaceted than predicted by the cultural homogenization thesis.

Illustrating the complex local interpretations of globalization, Ger and Belk (1996) identify four types of reactions globalization can bring about in local contexts: return to local roots, consumer resistance, local appropriation, and creolization. Fueled by marketization of global goods by multinational firms and the global media, local effects of globalization in the Less Affluent World (LAW) include increased ethnic and religious movements and geographic nationalism. While these reactions can lead to fundamentalism and polarization among local communities, they can also indicate return to roots and revival of local traditions. Globalization can also result in consumer resistance in local contexts. Rejection of global brands can emanate from nationalist ideologies. In India, for example, there is an anticonsumption movement against Coca-Cola impelled by the nationalist ideology of Swadeshi (Varman and Belk 2009). Being a key marker in India's nationalist identity throughout the colonial and postcolonial phases, the swadeshi ideology entails a search for the pure and authentic Indian culture, one that is not inflicted by Western and especially British as well as global and neoliberal influences. The nationalistic ideology underlies the anti-coke movement and culls from images of economic exploitation as well as invokes tradition, patriotism and alternate local identity challenging the authenticity of Coca-Cola in the local market. Rejection of global products and brands can also be linked to environmental concerns. The local food movement in the United States, for example, calls for opting for local alternatives to address concerns such as sustaining biodiversity, reducing environmental footprint, contributing to local economies. One growing market system supporting local production and consumption is the community supported agriculture (CSA) model of farming. This model of direct marketing between farmers and consumers encourages locally grown food consumption

MN grown

as an alternative to the global food supply chain managed by transnational corporations (Thompson and Coskuner-Balli 2007).

Another reaction to global consumer culture is appropriation of global consumer goods and reconfiguration of their meaning in their local contexts. Consider how global brands such as Avon, Amway, and Herbalife that rely on consumer distribution networks offer opportunities for women in countries such as China, India, and Africa to become micro-entrepreneurs. One study investigating women's participation in direct selling of Avon cosmetics reports that Avon networks help South African women increase their income, build self-esteem and autonomy, and overall serve as a mechanism for empowerment (Dolan and Scott 2009).

Last, globalization can lead to creolization, that is, 'the meeting and mingling of meanings and meaningful forms from disparate sources' (Ger and Belk 1996: 290). Consider the popularity of fusion cuisine across the world. In the United States one example of fusion food style is Tex-Mex, which combines Southern United States and Mexican cuisines. California-style pizza, which was popularized by chain restaurants such as California Pizza Kitchen and Wolfgang Puck, is the product of creolization of Italian style thin crust with fresh and local toppings such as avocado and artichokes.

GLOCALIZATION

The multiple processes that connect and integrate different aspects of cultural products to the local cultures go beyond accounts of global homogenization and local appropriation. Robertson (2001) uses the term glocalization to capture the simultaneous presence of universalizing and localizing tendencies. For example, what it means to be a young Danish, American or Turkish teenager is always contextualized locally and always shaped by the global ideas of youth and youth consumption practices. However, the interpretations of the local and the global do not necessarily occur in a symmetrical fashion. Wilk's (1995) thesis of global structure of common difference notes that transnational companies have the power to organize and promote cultural differences along specific dimensions. For example, the global structures of common difference that emanate from Starbucks' market dominance correspond to the emergence of the 'third place', which is a neutral ground between home and office where people can gather and interact (Thompson and Arsel 2004). The global structure of common difference also operates to form the global youth segment (Kjeldgaard and Askegaard 2006). The global youth culture is mediated through the market, meaning that the representation of products, images, and identity scripts portrayed via markets 'provide resources for articulating local versions of youth culture' (2006: 235). Teenagers use the global youth culture as a referent to express their identities. The local youth projects in

Denmark, Turkey or in the United States are determined by global structures of common difference, yet, their articulations at the local level depend on the sociocultural and historical context. For example, due to the lack of consumption opportunities, Greenlandic teenagers stress similarities and inclusion rather than difference within a global youth cultural lifestyle. Accordingly they favor new Greenlandic rock music that reflects their everyday experiences of being young, as opposed to the more traditional Greenlandic rock imbued with nationalistic stories of colonial repression of their parents' generations. They also use the Internet to connect with their peers worldwide and to look for similarities. As they observe and assure themselves of the commonalities they have in relation to the global youth culture, Greenlandic teenagers are able to cope with the deprivation of consumer goods.

Glocalization is also evident in the re-appropriation of cultural practices in their places of origin (Askegaard and Eckhardt 2012). Cultural appropriation is the use of a culture's symbols, artifacts, genres, rituals, or technologies by members of another culture (Rogers 2006). Re-appropriation refers to making these symbols, artifacts or technologies one's own 'in their places of origin after a process of sanctioning in (most often) the western hotbed of consumer culture production' (Askegaard and Eckhardt 2012: 46). Consider the regained popularity of yoga in India. Yoga practice spread to the West more than a century ago, and during the course of its diffusion, it became associated with New Age spirituality (in comparison to Hinduism) and gained a renewed focus on health and fitness (Campbell 2007; Ertimur and Coskuner-Balli 2015). These new associations and modifications made the practice re-appealing for the Indian consumers. Yoga has now been re-appropriated in India as a stress-relieving technique in multinational corporations and is offered for weight control, muscle toning and flexibility (Askegaard and Eckhardt 2012).

HYBRIDITY

The encounters of local and global influences also lead to hybrid cultural products. The anthropologist Néstor García Canclini, famous for his theorization of hybridization, describes this process as 'socio-cultural processes in which discrete structures or practices, previously existing in separate form, are combined to generate new structures, objects and practices' (Canclini 1995: xxv). Hybridization encapsulates a process of deterritorialization and reterritorialization. Specifically, deterritorialization refers to 'an appropriation process, a cultural pattern that is taken from its social context and applied to a new one in a different physical space. Reterritorialization denotes the making of this cultural pattern one's own, by producing a local form in this new society and geography' (Yazicioglu 2010: 240). An example of a hybrid cultural product is Turkish

Rock music. As rock music spread to Turkey starting in the 1960s, it was first deterritorialized and appropriated to the Turkish culture with infusions from folk tunes. In the decades to follow, a local rock sound with Turkish lyrics emerged and rock music was reterritorialized. Today, Turkish rock music resembles its global counterparts with its shared myths and values, but consumers reinterpret global symbols to establish local meanings exemplified in the genre *Türkçe* Rock. The Real World Scenario in Box 6.1 discusses the appeal of another recent hybrid cultural product, Korean popular music (K-Pop), mixing Western teen group conventions with particularly Korean values and aesthetic preferences, particularly among Asian consumers.

Box 6.1:   Real World Scenario

The 'Korean Wave'

Released in 2012, Psy's 'Gangnam Style' remained as the most watched video on YouTube for four and a half years (Figure 6.3 portrays Psy performing in South Korea). While Psy (real name Park Jae-sang) is the first Korean solo artist to have a top-selling US single, the South Korean popular culture has been on the rise globally since 1990s. *Hallyu* (or the 'Korean Wave') is the umbrella term that refers to the popularity of South Korean popular culture in Asia, including products such as Korean popular (K-pop) music, TV dramas, film, and fashion.

In an interview with Jens Erik Gould of *TIME* magazine, Psy reflects on whether language can be a barrier to adoption, a key concern of marketers that promote cultural products to global markets: 'When I signed with Scooter Braun and I decided to go overseas to promote my song, the only concern was how should I communicate with the public and the audience with my language. Scooter and I talked a lot about that: should we translate or not? Finally we didn't, and I think that was a really good decision. Music is already a huge language and for this song even if you don't have any idea what I'm talking about, you can still figure out that there's fun and there's energy'(Gould 2012).

K-pop is yet to conquer the mainstream of American pop culture, although 'Gangnam Style' will remain the first video ever to top over 1 billion views on YouTube. One explanation for the sweeping popularity of K-pop in Asia resides in the ongoing act of cultural hybridization that occurs as local consumers engage with and negotiate global forms to construct their own identities and cultural spaces. From this viewpoint, the South Korean cultural industry's interpretation of Western popular culture has successfully aligned with Asian audiences. Such a fit would have been harder to achieve if Western popular culture were to be directly imported. Through collaborations with Western artists and emulating Western cultural production technology and aesthetics, the South Koreanized version of Western popular culture created a direct, readily acceptable affinity with Asian consumers.

Reterritorialization of cultural products in new cultural spaces can lead to tensions in the marketplace. Consider the discussions surrounding whether yoga is a religious practice (i.e., identity tension); whether it is owned by Hindus (i.e., ownership tension); and whether it is should be practiced in its original form (i.e., authenticity tension). The Real World Scenario in Box 6.2 showcases issues around ownership of glocal cultural practices in detail within the context of yoga.

Box 6.2:   Real World Scenario

Ownership of glocal cultural practices

In a globalized word, cultural practices cross and re-cross national borders, and are shaped by multidirectional flows of people, technology, financial capital, mediated images, and ideas. These flows can create ownership tensions, that is, disagreements over who owns and accrues commercial gain from global cultural practices. Consider the practice of yoga, a 2,500-year-old discipline with its origins in Sanskritic culture and roots in Indian religious traditions. Today, yoga has become part of the global landscape, practiced by consumers worldwide and constituting a multibillion-dollar market. Syman (2010: 9) argues that yoga 'is the one of the first and most successful products of globalization'.

We illustrate from our research on how glocal yoga resulted in an ownership tension that was negotiated through its re-appropriation in India as a sign of unique cultural and national identity. Appointed into the office in 2014, the Indian Prime Minister Narendra Modi took several actions to (re)claim yoga as India's cultural property upon its global popularity and spread. First, he initiated the national Make in India campaign, a nation-building initiative that includes yoga as part of its focus. Second, he appointed a Minister of Yoga, Mr Naik, to promote recognition for the practice. In an interview about his role, Mr Naik said, 'There is little doubt about yoga being an Indian art form ... We're trying to establish to the world that it's ours ... [Yoga] is our system and it has not received enough prominence. We will take it to the masses' (Minister Naik quoted in *The Week*, 2015). In fact, government is seeking a geographical protection for yoga, similar to how Cognac is a protected geographic indicator of French brandy (World Intellectual Property Organization 2004). Finally, in 2014, Prime Minister Modi proposed an International Yoga Day to the United Nations (UN) General Assembly, characterizing the practice as 'an invaluable gift of India's ancient tradition' (Modi 2014).

New Delhi Television (NDTV) ran a segment prior to the first International Yoga Day on 21 June 2015 asking what this day is truly about – spirituality, physical fitness or an international push for the government's cultural agenda. Sumbit Patra, the spokesperson of Bharatiya Janata Party (the Indian People's Party) argued, 'Tomorrow is a day of celebration. It is a day of celebration because ... yoga is something which originated from the

(Continued)

(Continued)

great land of India. And tomorrow, yes, the whole world knew about it, but tomorrow it is getting stamped. Well yes, the stamp from the United Nations that India as the country which gave birth to yoga. And now co-sponsors from across the world would be celebrating yoga towards a better life and that's what our Prime Minister wanted. Now the Prime Minister wanted something that is good for mankind, something that is good for humanity, something which originated from India, why should it not be going to an international platform? And we have successfully done it ... yoga has been practiced across the world over decades, but the most essential part is the recognition ... and yes it [yoga] is a property of mankind, but definitely it is a pride of India ... the country from which yoga has originated is India and the country which should propagate yoga across the world is India, which it has successfully done.' One hundred and ninety-two countries participated on the first International Yoga Day and Delhi hosted the world's largest yoga session, with over 35,000 participants (Singh 2015).

Similar ownership tensions emanating from global flows occur in a variety of different contexts. Take the controversial history of baklava, the flaky, phyllo dough with chopped nuts in between, covered with honey. Several cultures, including Turks, Greeks, and Armenians, claim to have created this popular confection. When the European Union presented baklava as the national dessert of Greek Cyprus in promotional posters in 2006, Turkish baklava makers were not happy. A few years later, the then US President Barack Obama's praise for baklava served during a White House dinner in honor of Greek Independence Day prompted Turkish foodmakers to start an international patent process for other national food items, like the *simit* (a bagel-like bread with sesame seeds) (Schleifer 2012). Another example of ownership tensions arising from global flows is the Polynesian dance Ka Mate haka, traditionally performed by New Zealand's international rugby team, the All Blacks. In 2009, the New Zealand government decided to seek intellectual property rights for the dance after the Italian car company Fiat used the dance in its commercials (Healy and Glowczewski 2014).

One recent study explored the emergence of American Yoga as a hybrid cultural practice that came into being as yoga was reconfigured through dialectical exchanges between India and the West and acquired new forms and meanings in the geographical and cultural sphere of the United States (Coskuner-Balli and Ertimur 2017). The researchers identified an array of reterritorialization strategies which helped the hybrid cultural product of yoga gain legitimacy in this new local culture (see Figure 6.2). Specifically, American Yoga brands aligned desired outcomes with American social issues and values to legitimize yoga. For example, the famous yoga brand Jivamukti offers kirtan chanting in its classes as a way to deal with the stresses of modern American lifestyle 'relieving it [the mind] from its usual chatter — grocery lists, money worries, petty arguments' (Eckel 2009: E6). Other American yogis brought yoga into schools while leaving out religious elements like Sanskrit words, chanting, and prayer poses. Brands such as KarmaKids, Little Flower Yoga, and Bent on

Learning are among the many that are offered to children at private and public schools. The Extended Case Study on American Yoga at the end of this chapter further details the process of hybridization and divulges the challenges facing hybrid brands.

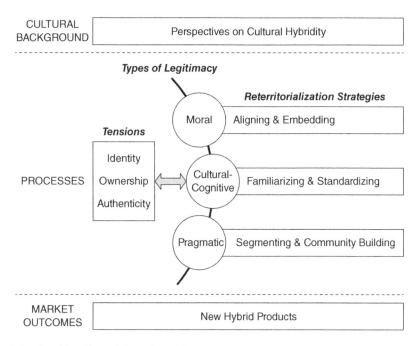

Figure 6.2   Legitimation of American Yoga

Figure 6.3   Psy at Seoil College in Seoul, South Korea

(*Source*: Wikimedia Commons)

INFLUENCE OF BRANDS IN A GLOCAL WORLD

Askegaard (2006: 84) suggests that brands are significant ideoscapes in the globalization process: brand is 'a central metaphor for understanding marketplace actors and practices in the modern game of identity formation'. Likewise, Cayla and Arnould (2008) propose to think of brands as similar to songs, folktales, movies, and theatre as cultural forms. They are a way of interpreting and organizing the world: 'To talk of brands as cultural forms is to acknowledge that branding is a specific form of communication, which tells stories in the context of products and services, addresses people as consumers, and promises to fulfill unmet desires and needs. In other words, branding is a specific symbolic form, a particular way of talking about and seeing the world' (Cayla and Arnould 2008: 86).

In their analysis of advertising during China's social transition from communism to consumerism, Zhao and Belk (2008a) find that Western brands appropriate the dominant anticonsumerist political ideology in their ads to promote consumption within China's political and social transition. For example, one strategy they adopt is to use socialist landmarks in their ads. As seen in Figure 6.4, the watch brand Citizen is pictured in front of Tiananmen Square, 'the sacred birthplace of the socialist nation'. The ad also showcases the Memorial Hall of Chairman Mao, the Monument to the Heroes of the People, and the Great Hall of the People. The placement of the Citizen logo is strategically done as it is presented above the square replacing the red star that symbolizes the Chinese Communist Party. In addition to China's more contemporary transition, the researchers also document advertising and brands' role in spreading consumerist values in the context of global brands that help legitimize Western lifestyle in 1930s (Zhao and Belk 2008b). Analyzing Chinese advertising posters the authors find that global marketers appropriate local symbols to construct culturally desirable meanings around initially foreign elements. For example, advertisers use Confucian images and heroic Chinese figures to market modern and Western products.

Brands also help forge new ways for consumers to think beyond the nation they live in as an imagined community. They contribute to building transnational identities and connections by operating along the three key dimensions of time, space, and culture. Studying the role of brands in constructing glocal cultures in Asia, Cayla and Eckhardt (2008) find that regional brands downplay their national origin and attempt to appear global and Asian. For example, the Singaporean beer brand Tiger stays away from depicting any national landmarks or places in its advertising, hence, positioning itself as Asian rather than Singaporean. Brands also adopt a multicultural brand engineering strategy that involves drawing from multiple cultural referents to build brands. The Singapore-based bank, Overseas Chinese Banking Corporation (OCBC), for instance, added green to its colors to complement the Chinese red in the hopes of becoming a major presence

Figure 6.4 Advertising for Citizen watch in China (Zhao and Belk 2008a: 139)

in Asian financial services as it expanded into Muslim markets such as Malaysia and Indonesia.

Another study showcases how global and local brands are interconnected and occupy positions that are in symbolically oppositional to one another in a brandscape. Akin to Appadurai's notion of scapes, brandscape refers to consumers' active constructions of personal meanings and lifestyle orientations from the symbolic resources provided by an array of brands (Sherry 1998: 122). Within the brandscape one dominant/hegemonic, typically market driving and experiential brand (e.g. Starbucks) and other brands (e.g. local coffee shops in towns and cities around the world) are linked together in competitive relationships. This 'hegemonic brandscape' then creates a cultural system that 'shapes consumer lifestyles and identities by functioning as a cultural model by which consumers act, think and feel' (Thompson and Arsel 2004: 632). In contrast to the common belief regarding local brands becoming extinct in the face of competition from global brands, the authors find that in the United States, local coffee shops were not destroyed. On the contrary, they rode on oppositional meanings fostered *vis-à-vis* Starbucks. Local coffee shops offer aesthetic, social and political alternatives to Starbucks. In this way, local coffee managers were able to create servicescapes that provide a symbolic salve 'for the feelings of cynicism, alienation, disenchantment, and disempowerment that could result from the increasingly ubiquitous presence of corporate influence in everyday life' (p. 639). To get an overview of the factors that allow local brands to compete with global brands, refer to the Critical Reflection in Box 6.3.

The oppositional meanings of global and local can get more complicated when religious ideologies are also in play in the marketplace. Consider how Muslim consumers in Turkey view global brands as tyrants who seek to oppress those of the Muslim faith. In Izberk-Bilgin's (2012) study on the influence of Islamism on low-income Turkish consumers' constructions of brand meanings, participants report a strong belief that multinational corporations financially support the Iraq war and Israel's interests in the Middle East. Interestingly, they boycott multinational corporations as well as national companies who do not share their Islamist views. Refer to the Critical Reflection in Box 6.4 for more details on consumers' ideological commitments that fuel movements with an antiglobal ethos.

Box 6.3: Critical Reflection

How can local brands compete with global brands?

If global brands are desirable in all societies, is there room and chance of success for local brands? There are several factors to consider in addressing this question. First, while the success of global brands may be an indication of (worldwide) consumer interest and fascination, it is important to recognize that consumers view global brands in diverse ways. Especially in developing countries and emerging markets, global brands may be associated with high status and quality, while at the same time regarded as inauthentic, homogenic, colonizing, and unfamiliar. Second, consumers often use global brands in ways that incorporate local practices and meanings. Consider the common coupling of a BigMac with ayran (a traditional, yogurt-based, salty drink) in Turkey or the popularity of American sushi like Philadelphia rolls (sushi with cream cheese) in the United States. These examples illustrate the appeal of (hybrid) brands and products that combine the modern and the traditional, and the local and the global. Third, consumers seek difference and diversity to express their identities; a project/desire that is further fueled by exposure to global flows, yet, proves to be difficult with increasing number of standardized global brands that dominate the marketplace.

Some global brands choose a glocal strategy that combines global standardization and local adaptation as a solution to address the above issues. Even in such cases, there is still room for local brands to successfully compete with powerful transnational brands that penetrate their home and foreign markets. Ger (1999) highlights key factors that allow local brands to successfully compete with powerful transnational brands that penetrate their home and foreign markets. First, local brands can build upon their cultural competencies and resources to deliver unique perceived value and gain a competitive advantage. While they may be constrained with regards to economic resources in comparison to transnational brands, their knowledge of culturally valued consumption patterns can allow them to imbue their products with symbolism of authenticity. Consider Selamlique Turkish Coffee that praises itself in protecting the age-old, authentic rituals of Turkish coffee consumption. With the Turkish marketplace becoming increasingly populated with alternative coffees and brands, Selamlique positions itself as a sophisticated Turkish coffee brand that blends the traditional and the innovative with its capsule coffee machine and fortune telling application (Aksoy 2017).

Second, local brands must identify and target those segments of consumers whose preferences align with their niches. Such segments may include global consumers motivated to find alternative products and experiences, local consumers driven by the desire to return to their roots and/or underprivileged global consumers who are underserved by transnational brands. For instance, Green Mama is one of Russia's top manufacturers of cosmetics, with headquarters in France and production facilities in Russia. The company draws on its French connection to create perceptions of a quality producer and leverages its Russian origin by using native Russian plants as ingredients for its products. The success of Green Mama came at a time in mid-1990s when Russian consumers were confronted with an influx of foreign products as their country transitioned from a socialist to a market economy. With its homegrown ingredients and foreign quality standards, the brand appealed particularly to those consumers who were critical of and felt impoverished by the market economy and exhibited locally oriented consumption patterns (Ger et al. 2012).

Third, local brands must position themselves on localness not just in their home markets, but also in foreign markets. It is crucial for local brands to aim for global presence (as much as their economic resources allow) to construct positive symbolism specifically to overcome common associations around local products as exotic or low quality. For example, the Filipino brand Jollibee fast food outsells McDonald's and Kentucky Fried Chicken and leads with more than 50 percent market share in its home market. The company takes pride in its family-oriented approach to management and spotlights the importance of family values in its marketing communications as well (www.jollibee.com.ph/about-us/). Jollibee has also been expanding internationally, and currently, 30 percent of its sales come from its international stores (Wu and Daga 2017). When opening stores in the US, the company made a point of not using a franchise model, and instead, kept its stores company owned (Burton 2017). Jollibee firmly bridges the local and the global with emphasis on its Filipino heritage and values, and growing global locations and following. In summary, local brands can succeed by 'out-localizing' transnational brands rather than trying to imitate them.

Box 6.4: Critical Reflection

Antiglobalization movement

The pessimistic view of the impact of globalization holds that globalization leads to a loss of cultural diversity by promoting a uniform, Westernized consumer culture. Economic and political global policies such as free trade agreements, environmental regulations, and intellectual property rights favor wealthy industrialized countries and powerful multinational corporations, hampering development of poor countries and contributing to growing inequality in the world. Such interpretations of globalization as processes of homogenization and promoting cultural superiority of Western nations, as in Coca-colonization and McDonaldization, have created antiglobalization critics (Witkowski 2005). For example, the International Forum on Globalization (IFG) was formed in 1994 with an antiglobal political agenda critiquing the negative cultural, social, political as well as environmental impacts of globalization (http://ifg.org). What became known as the antiglobalization movement can be traced back to the series of protests that took place a few years later in 1999 against the global trade negotiations that were under consideration during the World Trade Organization Ministerial Conference in Seattle. The demonstrations led by unions, environmentalists, consumer protection groups, labor rights groups, and leftist consumers contested issues such as unfair competition from cheap foreign labor, relocation of polluting manufacturing facilities to third-world cities, and an ever-expanding capitalist system as consequences of globalization.

The antiglobalization movement reflects how consumers' political and ideological commitments influence their choices and behaviors in the marketplace. There is no doubt that antiglobal thinking poses challenges to marketing. For instance, critics claim that marketing of products, ideas, and lifestyles from rich countries like the United States displaces local cultural products from developing countries. Viewing marketing as promoting unsustainable consumption, antiglobal activists emphasize the need to reduce levels of consumption due to environmental concerns and material inequity at a global level (Cherrier 2009; Iyer and Muncy 2009; Witkowski 2005). Nevertheless, it is important to recognize that antiglobalization advocacy comes in different forms and not all types of antiglobal sentiments are resistant to marketing practices (Cayla and Arnould 2008). A great example is the concept of *politically motivated brand rejection*, a form of anticonsumption behavior that involves refusal to consume a brand because of its perceived associations with a political ideology. Within the context of the Turkish marketplace, Sandıkcı and Ekici (2009) find that some consumers refrain from drinking Coca-Cola because the brand represents an imperialistic form of globalization in their view. However, these consumers' rejection of Coca-Cola does not extend to other brands like Starbucks, McDonald's or Walt Disney Movies that also represent economic dominance of American brands. Similarly, the successes of local versions of Coca-Cola like Cola Turka in Turkey and Zamzam Cola in Iran showcase how brands can capitalize on antiglobal sentiments and implement market strategies that allow them to pursue antiglobal positions in the marketplace.

CONCLUSION

In this chapter we have discussed globalization with respect to its implications for consumer culture. First, we introduced the concept of flows to think about the movement of ideas, media, people, finance, and technology. We then presented the two common views on the implications of globalization: cultural homogeneity and cultural heterogeneity. Whereas the cultural homogeneity discussions highlight that flow of cultural practices has predominately resulted in McDonaldization and Americanization of the world, research on cultural heterogeneity highlights the multifaceted nature of global flows for consumer identities, experiences, and practices. The cultural homogeneity discourse and globalization critiques (presented in the Critical Reflection boxes) reflect how consumers' political and ideological commitments influence their choices and behaviors in the marketplace.

It is also important to note, however, the complex local interpretations and outcomes of globalization. Cultural heterogeneity is manifested via processes such as reappropriation, reterritorialization, and hybridization. Hybrid products can come into being as a synthesis of local and glocal influences and produce tensions in the marketplace. We used the Real World Scenarios of K-pop to illustrate the prominence of hybrid products and of American Yoga to showcase the tensions hybrid products can produce in the marketplace and strategies marketers can adopt to manage legitimacy in the eyes of consumers. These examples, and also the case study in Box 6.5, illustrate the most important and interesting role brands play in constructing glocal marketplace cultures.

Box 6.5:   Extended Case Study

American Yoga

The Indian monk Swami Vivekananda, who toured the country in 1890s speaking about yoga and Hinduism, is often credited with officially introducing yoga to the United States. Yet, there are vast differences between the way yoga is practiced in America today and the yoga Vivekananda preached about more than a century ago. A CBS News segment on the differences between Indian versus American yoga features an interview with Nicole Lastova, a north Virginian instructor who teaches yoga at the American Embassy in New Delhi: 'There's no yoga fashion. I felt a bit self-conscious when I go to a class here [in New Delhi, India]. There's definitely a strictness. You listen to your teacher, whereas at my studio in America it was just a lot of more love when the teacher touched you, a lot more warmth.' She goes on to argue that the biggest difference between the

(Continued)

(Continued)

way yoga is practiced in America is the 'freedom of expression in each pose', where as in India 'there is one way to do it and you do it the right way' (www.youtube.com/watch?v=I58C9PopnVU).

A more satirical viewpoint is showcased in a video called 'If Gandhi Took a Yoga Class' created by CollegeHumor. In this tongue-in-cheek video, the famous Indian nationalist leader Mahatma Gandhi visits a yoga class in the United States. He is taken aback by the ambiance of the studio, filled with the cinnamon stick aroma of Yankee candles and music by Coldplay, and warmed up to a high temperature. During class, the instructor corrects Gandhi's terminology of the pose urdhva mukha svanasana as up dog, advises him to pick up the pace to burn carbohydrates, and recommends wearing a lycra top while Gandhi tries to explain his traditional attire of dhoti (a long white strip of cotton wrapped around the body). During the break, Gandhi overhears students chatting enthusiastically about new classes like yogalates (fusion of yoga and pilates). The video gets at the heart of American Yoga, a hybrid cultural product that fuses ancient physical yoga poses and spiritual aspects of the practice from its Indian origins with the Western physical exercise culture, popular music, and English script.

American Yoga emerged as a result of the dialectical exchanges between India and the Western world. That is, yoga was transformed as it spread and gained new meanings and forms in the United States. Yet, its practice also changed within India itself, as modern interpretations of yoga were imported back to its place of origin (i.e., re-appropriated), the Indian marketplace. According to the 2016 Yoga in America Study, over 36 million Americans practice yoga today, representing about a 50 percent growth in the number of practitioners just within the last four years. They spend more than 16 billion dollars on yoga classes, equipment, clothes, and accessories. In accordance with its popularity, there is a wide variety of American Yoga brands, including Power Yoga, Jivamukti Yoga, CorePower just to name a few. While yoga is traditionally aimed at spiritual transformation and achieving union with the divine, American Yoga is athletic as well as meditative, and embodies secular meanings that accommodate religious diversity of Americans. Its identity is entrepreneurial, syncretic, and health and fitness focused.

Consider the YogaFit brand, which is a user friendly, fitness-oriented yoga practice for American consumers that uses English names (instead of Sanskrit) for the poses and removes elements like Om'ing and chanting. Its founder Beth Shaw is proud of her innovative brand: 'I pioneered a lot of fitness trends, like Yoga Butt with the core ball, Yoga Core with the core ball, Yoga Strength with the weights ... We're doing a program where it's been in our kids' program. We have a Yoga Fit Seniors ...'. She also licensed the YogaFit name for a fitness franchise company to open up studios and created one of the earliest yoga teacher training programs in the United States. Another big player among the American Yoga brands is CorePower Yoga (Figure 6.5). As of August 2016, CorePower had opened more than 150 studios in 19 states, offering a variety of classes like Hot Fusion (combination of Hot Yoga with Power Yoga for detoxification and strength building),

Yoga Ryder (combination of yoga and spinning), and Yoga Sculpt (yoga and weight train-ing). The founder, Trevor Tice, likens the brand to Starbucks in creating a yoga culture similar to the ways in which Starbucks created a coffee culture in America.

Figure 6.5   Advertising for CorePower Yoga class

A key challenge for hybrid cultural brands is to appear legitimate in the eye of their target consumers. Achieving such social fitness so that their actions are deemed proper, desirable, and appropriate within the system of norms, values, and beliefs that govern society is not a simple task. As discussed in the chapter, hybrid products can be critiqued on the basis of their origins (i.e., is the hybrid brand authentic?), identity (i.e., to what extent does the identity of the hybrid brand conforms to its original identity?) and claims to own-ership (i.e., who owns the hybrid brand, the founders of its original version or its new, hybridized version?).

The success of CorePower Yoga can be traced to its specific strategies that were aimed at legitimizing the brand. For example, the brand's efforts to make yoga accessible to all types of consumers through offering a variety of styles, class levels (e.g. beginner friendly, yoga experience required), and class times along with their own teacher training programs helped standardize the brand and its experiences. Such types of standardiza-tion help with achieving cultural cognitive legitimacy by which a practice becomes known and understood by consumers. CorePower Yoga also responded to consumers' unique tastes and expectations to meet their substantive needs, and in turn, attain pragmatic legitimacy. Specifically, the brand mixes yoga poses, class scripts, and material aspects of yoga studies in a selective fashion. For example, CorePower Yoga combines fitness and spiritual goals in its classes by offering hot yoga classes that incorporate weight training and spinning as well as spiritual practices such as the ritualistic closure of the class with the salutation 'namaste'. CorePower Yoga instructors are also careful to adapt scripts to respond to the demands of different consumer segments that prefer to attend classes at a regular gym versus a specialized yoga studio.

(Continued)

(Continued)

Questions

1. In the spirit of the idea that the process of hybridization breeds innovation, identify other examples of innovative American Yoga styles and classes.
2. Locate other examples of hybrid cultural products. Explain the local and global influences that underlie these hybrid cultural products. In another words, what were the cultural elements that were mixed and fused to create these hybrid cultural products?
3. Identify two brands within a hybrid product category (you may use one of the categories identified in your response to the prior question):
    a. Explain how these brands are positioned in the marketplace.
    b. Evaluate the legitimacy and authenticity of these brands from your point of view. Are their legitimacy and originality ever questioned in the marketplace? If so, by whom? What kinds of responses do the proponents of these brands express in return?

RESEARCH DIRECTIONS

We encourage future research that examines the impact of digital technologies on global flows. Digitization is transforming global flows by enabling creation of purely digital products and services, facilitating greater cross-border exchanges, and adding value through digital capabilities such as digital tracking of goods (McKinsey Global Institute 2016). These changes are likely to boost formation of hybrid cultural products, allow local brands greater chance of success in competing with transnational companies, and broaden consumer participation in global flows. Will consumers' experiences with hybrid products and services become increasingly ordinary? Does increased hybridization ease potential cultural tensions? Or does it produce new types of tensions in addition to identity, ownership, and authenticity related concerns? How can marketers grapple with these tensions and manage brand meanings for different product categories? Also, how do the structures of glocal marketplace cultures evolve? As local brands proliferate with more power, do antiglobal sentiments targeting American brands subside? While governments, multinational corporations, and powerful financial institutions historically drove globalization, consumers are now assuming much more active and influential roles in glocalization of marketplace cultures. Do new modes of connectivity mobilize more antiglobalization movements enabled by diasporic global communications? How do global consumer communities contribute to creation of new cultural forms and counter tendencies to Americanization?

RECOMMENDED READING

Appadurai, A. (1990) 'Disjuncture and difference in the global cultural economy', *Theory, Culture, and Society*, 7: 295–311.

Askegaard, S. and Eckhardt, G.M. (2012) 'Glocal yoga: Re-appropriation in the Indian consumptionscape', *Marketing Theory*, 1 (16): 1–15.

Belk, R.W. (1995) 'Hyperreality and globalization: Culture in the age of Ronald McDonald', *Journal of International Consumer Marketing*, 8 (3/4): 23–37.

Cayla, J and Eckhardt G.M. (2008) 'Asian brands and the shaping of a transnational imagined community', *Journal of Consumer Research*, 35 (August): 216–30.

Chen, S. (2016) 'Cultural technology: A framework for marketing cultural exports – analysis of hallyu (the Korean Wave)', *Cultural Technology*, 33 (1): 25–50.

Coskuner-Balli, G. and Ertimur, B. (2017) 'Legitimation of hybrid cultural products: The case of American Yoga', *Marketing Theory*, 17 (2): 127–47.

Ger, G. (1999) 'Localizing in the global village: Local firms competing in global markets', *California Management Review*, 41 (4): 64–83.

Ger, G., Kravets, O., and Sandıkcı, Ö. (2012) 'International marketing at the interface of the alluring global and the comforting local', in L. Peñaloza, N. Toulouse, and L.M. Visconti (eds), *Marketing Management: A Cultural Perspective*. London: Routledge. pp. 30–42.

Gurmen, E. (2017) 'How Turkish soap operas took over the world', www.thefader.com, March 1.

Robertson, R. (1992) *Globalization: Social Theory and Global Culture*. London: Sage.

Thompson, C.J. and Arsel, Z. (2004) 'The Starbucks brandscape and consumers' (anti-corporate) experiences of glocalization', *Journal of Consumer Research*, 31 (December): 631–42.

Yazicioglu, T.E. (2010) 'Contesting the global consumption ethos: Reterritorialization of rock in Turkey', *Journal of Macromarketing*, 30 (3): 238–53.

REFERENCES

Aksoy, C. (2017) 'Istanbul is our inspiration', www.skylife.com/en/2017-09-business/istanbul-is-our-inspiration.

Appadurai, A. (1990) 'Disjuncture and difference in the global cultural economy', *Theory, Culture, and Society*, 7: 295–311.

Askegaard, S. (2006) 'Brands as global ideoscape', in J.E. Schroeder, M. Salzer Morling, and S. Askegaard (eds), *Brand Culture*. New York: Taylor and Francis.

Askegaard, S. and Eckhardt, G.M. (2012) 'Glocal yoga: Re-appropriation in the Indian consumptionscape', *Marketing Theory*, 1 (16): 1–15.

Belk, R.W. (1995) 'Hyperreality and globalization: Culture in the age of Ronald McDonald', *Journal of International Consumer Marketing, 8* (3/4): 23–37.

Burton, M. (2017) 'Filipino cult favorite Jollibee plans global expansion'. www.eater. com/2017/9/25/16360552/jollibee-global-expansion-pret-a-manger.

Campbell, C. (2007) *The Easternization of the West.* Boulder, CO: Paradigm.

Canclini, N.G. (1995) *Hybrid Cultures: Strategies for Entering and Leaving Modernity.* Minneapolis, MN: University of Minnesota Press.

Castells, M. (1998) *End of Millennium.* Oxford: Blackwell.

Cayla, J. and Arnould, E. (2008) 'A cultural approach to branding in the global market-place', *Journal of International Marketing, 16* (4): 86–112.

Cayla, J. and Eckhardt, G.M. (2008) 'Asian brands and the shaping of a transnational imagined community', *Journal of Consumer Research, 35* (August): 216–30.

Cherrier, H. (2009) 'Anti-consumption discourses and consumer-resistant identities', *Journal of Business Research, 62* (2): 181–90.

Coskuner-Balli, G. and Ertimur, B. (2017) 'Legitimation of hybrid cultural products: the case of American Yoga', *Marketing Theory, 17* (2): 127–47.

Dolan, C. and Scott L. (2009) 'Lipstick evangelism: Avon trading circles and gender empowerment in South Africa', *Gender and Development, 17* (2): 203–16.

Eckel, S. (2009) 'Yoga enthusiasts hear the call of kirtan', *The New York Times,* 5 March.

Ertimur, B. and Coskuner-Balli, G. (2015) 'Navigating the institutional logics of markets: implications for strategic brand management', *Journal of Marketing, 79* (2): 40–61.

Featherstone, M. (2006) 'Genealogies of the global', *Theory, Culture and Society, 23* (2–3): 387–419.

Ger, G. (1999) 'Localizing in the global village: Local firms competing in global markets', *California Management Review, 41* (4): 64–83.

Ger, G. and Belk, R.W. (1996) '"I'd like to buy the world a coke": Consumptionscapes of the less affluent world', *Journal of Consumer Policy, 19* (3): 271–304.

Ger, G., Kravets, O., and Sandıkcı, Ö. (2012) 'International marketing at the interface of the alluring global and the comforting local', in L. Peñaloza, N. Toulouse, and L.M. Visconti (eds), *Marketing Management: A Cultural Perspective.* London: Routledge. pp. 30–42.

Gould, J.E. (2012) 'Psy talks "Gangnam Style" and newfound fame', *TIME,* 28 September. http://entertainment.time.com/2012/09/28/psy-talks-gangnam-style-and-new-found-fame/.

Gurmen, E. (2017) 'How Turkish soap operas took over the world,' www.thefader.com, 1 March.

Healy, J.D.L. and Glowczewski, B. (20014) 'Indigenous and transnational values in Oceania: heritage reappropriation, from museums to the World Wide Web', *Etropic, 13* (2): 44–55.

Iyer, R. and Muncy, J.A. (2009) 'Purpose and object of anti-consumption', *Journal of Business Research, 62* (2): 160–8.

Izberk-Bilgin, E. (2012) 'Infidel brands: Unveiling alternative meanings of global brands at the nexus of globalization, consumer culture, and Islamism', *Journal of Consumer Research, 39* (4): 663–87.

Kjeldgaard, D. and Askegaard, S. (2006) 'The glocalization of youth culture: The global youth segment as structures of common difference', *Journal of Consumer Research, 33* (2): 231–47.

Kraidy, M.M. (2005) *Hybridity, or the Cultural Logic of Globalization*. Philadelphia, PA: Temple University Press.

McKinsey Global Institute (2016) 'Digital globalization: The new era of global flows', March.

Modi, N. (2014) 'PM addresses the United Nations General Assembly)', 27 September. www.narendramodi.in/pm-at-un-general-assembly-6666.

Ritzer, G. (2004) *The McDonaldization of Society*. Thousand Oaks, CA: Pine Forge Press.

Robertson, R. (1992) *Globalization: Social Theory and Global Culture*. London: Sage.

Robertson, R. (2001) 'Globalization theory 2000+: Major problematics', in G. Ritzer and B. Smart (eds), *Handbook of Social Theory*. London: Sage. pp. 458–71.

Rogers, R.A. (2006), 'From cultural exchange to transculturation: A review and reconceptualization of cultural appropriation', *Communication Theory, 16*: 474–503.

Sandıkcı, Ö. and Ekici, A. (2009) 'Politically motivated brand rejection', *Journal of Business Research, 62* (2): 208–17.

Schleifer, Y. (2012) 'The White House dessert that sparked a minor Turkish-Greek conflict', *The Atlantic*, 4 April. www.theatlantic.com/international/archive/2012/04/the-white-house-dessert-that-sparked-a-minor-turkish-greek-conflict/255439/.

Sherry, J.F. (1998) 'The soul of the company store: Nike Town Chicago and the emplaced brandscape', in John F. Sherry (ed.), *ServiceScapes: The Concept of Place in Contemporary Markets*. Chicago, IL: NTC Business Books. pp. 109–46.

Singh, R. (2015) 'International Yoga Day and what it means for India', www.forbes.com/sites/ranisingh/2015/06/29/international-yoga-day-and-what-it-means-for-india/.

Syman, S. (2010) *The Story of Yoga in America: The Subtle Body*. New York: Farrar, Straus and Giroux.

The Week (2015) 'Does Yoga belong to India', 7 February. http://theweek.com/articles/537675/does-yoga-belong-india.

Thompson, C.J. and Arsel, Z. (2004) 'The Starbucks brandscape and consumers' (anti-corporate) experiences of glocalization', *Journal of Consumer Research, 31* (December): 631–42.

Thompson, C.J. and Coskuner-Balli, G. (2007) 'Countervailing market responses to corporate co-optation and the ideological recruitment of consumption communities', *Journal of Consumer Research, 35* (August): 135–52.

Tomlinson, J. (1999) *Globalization and Culture*. Chicago, IL: University of Chicago Press.

Varman, R. and Belk, Russell W. (2009) 'Nationalism and ideology in an anticonsumption movement', *Journal of Consumer Research, 36* (June): 686–700.

Wilk, R. (1995) 'Learning to be local in Belize: Global systems of common difference', in Daniel Miller (ed.), *Worlds Apart: Modernity Through the Prism of the Local*. London: Routledge. pp. 110–31.

Witkowski, T.H. (2005) 'Antiglobal challenges to marketing in developing countries: Exploring the ideological divide', *Journal of Public Policy and Marketing, 24* (1): 7–23.

World Intellectual Property Organization (2004) *WIPO Intellectual Property Handbook*. WIPO Publication No. 489 (E).

Wu, K. and Daga, A. D. (2017) 'Exclusive: Filipino fast food group Jollibee eyes bid for UK's Pret A Manger – sources'. www.reuters.com/article/us-pret-m-a-jollibee-exclusive/exclusive-filipino-fast-food-group-jollibee-eyes-bid-for-uks-pret-a-manger-sources-idUSKCN1BT12F.

Yazicioglu, T.E. (2010) 'Contesting the global consumption ethos: reterritorialization of rock in Turkey', *Journal of Macromarketing, 30* (3): 238–53.

Zhao, X. and Belk, R.W. (2008a) 'Politicizing consumer culture: Advertising's appropriation of political ideology in China's social transition', *Journal of Consumer Research, 35* (August): 231–44.

Zhao, X. and Belk, R.W. (2008b) 'Advertising consumer culture in 1930s Shanghai: Globalization and localization in Yuepenfai', *Journal of Advertising, 37* (2): 45–56.

PART THREE

The Socio-Historic Patterning of Consumption

7
SOCIAL CLASS

Paul Henry and Marylouise Caldwell,
University of Sydney Business School

CHAPTER OVERVIEW

- Social class influences the distribution of socio-economic opportunities, and quality of life.
- Socialization in your social class group shapes your sense of self, where you feel or 'at home' or 'out of place' and how you think about the world.
- A class group exhibits distinctive consumer tastes and consumption patterns.
- These patterns of taste preferences reflect different combinations of economic, social, and cultural resources.
- Class-based preferences are more emotional and habituated and less rational and calculative.
- Social class distinctions are expressed as matters of taste and reproduce the symbolic boundaries between more and less well resourced groups.

INTRODUCTION

In an age of great change that features increased geographic mobility, technological advances in production and consumption, faster fashion cycles, disruption to old industry and occupational types, more diverse lifestyle options, and breakdown of old left–right political allegiances, social roles, categories, and hierarchies can be disrupted, fragmented, and re-organized. For example, the forces of globalization, industrial automation, and corporate downsizing have radically transformed the nature of working-class and middle-class identities. However, these structural influences of social class remain firmly in place and continue to position people into hierarchies of distinctive class groups. Yet, we do acknowledge that the turbulence of change often disguises the underlying role of class in modern societies. In this chapter, we seek to illuminate the continuing relevance of social class.

HOW CLASS SETS PEOPLE APART

Systemic economic inequality sits at the heart of social class. Casual observation in daily life where we see people who are obviously either better off or worse off than ourselves, provides evidence of economic disparity. If you look at any major city you will find pockets of (dis)advantage where statistics reveal layer upon layer of inequality that ranges from family income, education, occupation, unemployment, and interestingly a large range of inequitable health outcomes. In particular, health statistics point to very different patterns of physical activity and dietary consumptions. They also point to different levels and types of stress experiences and ultimately differences in quality of life between advantaged and disadvantaged groups. Inequality results in different lived experiences. News stories detailing an increasing gap between incomes of the rich and poor appear regularly in mass media. The disparity in life chances is usually attributed to income and wealth – and clearly this is a part of it.

However, sociologists have long argued that structural conditions of advantage and disadvantage – that is, those that endure across generations – are normalized through social class. In other words, socialization in one's social class leads individuals to believe that the conditions that lead to their experiences of relative advantage or disadvantage reflect their own personal preferences, choices, and tastes. For example, Allen (2002) studied the choice processes that lead working-class young adults to choose proprietary schools of commerce whose degrees offer little market value while their students also assumed considerable debt, via student loans, to pay tuition. Allen takes up Bourdieu's metaphor of 'feel for the game' in describing the secure experience of everyday life within one's class conditions. Allen shows that these students gravitate to these institutions because they feel exceedingly comfortable in these settings. The schools specifically cater to their desires for a homey, friendly environment. On the other hand, conventional college and university settings trigger their anxieties about feeling inferior to more academically advanced students and feeling intimidated by teachers and other authority figures. Allen describes these institutions as offering working-class students a seductive facsimile of higher education. They promise 'an economical, quick, applied clerical training in a cordial, homey, and familial educational environment' (Allen 2002: 523). They cater to the students' class-based predispositions. Parsing these terms, 'economical' and 'quick' caters to a taste for necessity and the pragmatic goal of gaining educational credentials as quickly as possible in order to move on to the 'real world' of paid work. 'Applied' knowledge implies the mastery of practical, hands-on skills whose consequences can be immediately seen and appreciated, rather than playing with abstract concepts (an intellectual skill found to be one of the more intimidating aspects of conventional academic settings). And 'cordial' promises an accepting, non-judgmental setting which contrasts to these students' prior feelings of being unable to measure up to the middle-class 'teachers' pets' in their high school classes. Hence, the reproduction of these working-class students' class disadvantage did not require any coercive acts on the part of more powerful societal actors. Rather, it is built into their socialization, their internalized (and naturalized) limits on their perceived horizons of possibility, and their collectively shared taste and preferences for certain kinds of educational experiences.

The shared meanings and stories that members of a society use to make sense of their life situations and experiences can also contribute to the reproduction of social class and its array of structural inequities. One class of cultural stories – ideologies – serve to normalize socio-economic hierarchies by framing them as a natural order of things or providing explanations that mask the underlying structural forces. For example, in Western cultures, it is common to believe that those who have attained a higher level of social status have done so through a combination of hard work and talent. This ideological narrative also encourages the attribution that those who remain on the lower rungs of the status hierarchy lack these success-conferring qualities; hence, their relative failings are deemed to reflect personal flaws and inadequacies rather than structural barriers.

While hard work and ability are important factors to achievement, one's starting point in the social class hierarchy is functionally equivalent to starting a race with a head-start or a handicap; if the gap is sufficient, the objectively faster runner will not be able to win the proverbial race no matter how much effort he/she invests. To further illustrate, consider these two hypothetical ideal types. Jean is born into a family environment where educational achievement is an unspoken normative expectation and she grows up in a middle-class social milieu constituted by affluent neighborhoods, high caliber schools; abundant opportunities for personal development (via travel); no anxieties about economic shortfalls that might negatively impact her life and she is surrounded by peers who hail from similar backgrounds and readily envision themselves pursuing exciting professional careers. In contrast, Jim is born into an impoverished family whose limited resources are devoted to 'making ends meet'; where school systems are often underfunded and understaffed; where his peer group has few expectations of going to college and perhaps harbor a sense of hostility and defiance toward those who are pursuing such a path, such that rebelling against the academic game becomes a badge of honor; and where the middle-class professional world so familiar to Jean is both foreign and intimidating.

Both of our hypothetical individuals might 'work hard'. For example, Jean might, like her peers, invest considerable time and energy (and experience considerable stress) in seeking to attain admission to an elite university whereas Jim might labor in a physically demanding, after-school job to provide additional income to the family. Their respective fields of investment, however, promise very different returns for their efforts in terms of social class pay-off. Even if Jim seeks to invest his personal resources in the academic game, he remains disadvantaged to Jean whose upbringing had been oriented around cultivating the intellectual skills needed for educational achievement. This is not to say that someone, like Jim, cannot overcome these limitations and attain some degree of academic success and upward mobility. However, Jim's path to middle-class status would have to negotiate a series of structural obstacles that are completely absent in Jean's world. Furthermore, these naturalized differences in life experiences – and the key factor of whether their lives are marked by a sense of necessity or a contrasting sense that life is a series of endless opportunities – are often reflected in their consumption taste and experiences; ranging from the brands that constitute their personal ensemble of goods to the different types of vacation and travel experiences (an excursion through historic sites in Rome versus a trip to Disneyland); to one's relative comfort in formal restaurants and high-end retailers.

Ideological narratives suggesting that personal success – in the specific sense of attaining a higher position in the socio-economic hierarchy – is exclusively due to personal (and moralized) attributes such as hard work, determination, or 'character' direct attention from the underlying structural influences that reproduce social class and its stratified distribution of resources and life opportunities, lifestyle orientations, and consumption tastes. These influences involve distinctive socialization experiences within groups, where people experience similar mixes of resources and habituated lifestyles. Common experiences generate similar expectations, (consumption) preferences and worldviews. In daily life, we notice different taste preferences when we enter into social class settings that are different to our own. Cues may include different styles of clothing, haircuts, cosmetic use, food choices, and mannerisms, styles of interacting, topics of conversation and moral codes. For example, think about the differences between upmarket and downmarket pubs and bars. Where do you best fit? Where do you feel most comfortable? Or are you a person who feels at home in either or neither? How might these feelings relate to your social background and past experiences? This introduction raises several sub-questions that we address in this chapter. What types of resources (dis)advantage consumers? How are these resources systematically distributed? How do they shape lifestyle and consumption preferences (tastes)?

Box 7.1: Critical Reflection

The classification problem

If class exerts such a powerful influence on social organization then why is it often viewed as an ill-defined concept where marketing researchers often reduce social class to demographic categories (proxies) such as education, income and/or occupation – ability to buy? This approach is fine, just so long as these proxy variables classify people into groups that reflect the particular conceptualization of social class that the researcher intends. For example, in our Bourdieusian conceptualization discussed further on, the proxy variables seek to capture groupings of people who exhibit a similar mix of capitals, lifestyle preferences, and consumption motivations (c.f. position in the social space). In operationalizing Bourdieu's conceptualization, Holt (1998) employs education and occupation, together with father's education and occupation as classification measures. The reason for capturing information about the father is that father's education affects rearing conditions during formative years where habitus is formed. The key point here is that it is important from the outset to conceptually specify precisely what you want to measure before selecting an appropriate classification scheme. However, too often the goal of theoretically-informed classification is lost and class ends up being reduced to groups of people with similar economic capacity.

The classification problem is compounded by the fact that many different classification schemes have been proposed. One reason for multiple classifications is that they are based on distinct theoretical orientations that are used to understand and analyze class structures. For example, John Goldthorpe employs an occupational classification to capture a Weberian conceptualization of class that considers a mix of endowments of economic, status, and power resources. Eric Olin Wright employs a different occupational classification to capture a Marxist spirit that emphasizes economic power and shared political interests. Still other classifications focus solely on using occupational levels as proxies for social status. In doing so, these status-oriented schemes emphasize social capital at the expense of the other capitals. Each of these alternatives uses different classification schemes. This is because the conceptualizations they seek to capture differ. Consequently, it is critical to appreciate that the proxy variables used to classify are just that – proxies. The take-away from this is that it is important to think carefully about the particular conceptualization of social class that you wish to capture and ensure that the classification scheme that you use is appropriate for the intended job.

A (QUICK) CLASS HISTORY

Karl Marx's (1867) canonical writings on the socio-economic differences and conflicts among the proletariat (working class) and bourgeoisie (a multifaceted group that includes the managers and owners of enterprises) are a theoretical touchstone for sociological analyses of social class. For Marx, class groupings hinge upon one's position in the system of production. Do you sell your labor to those who own the means of production (i.e., are you a member of the proletariat?) or do you profit from exploiting the labor of others (i.e., are you a member of the bourgeoisie)? Marx's theory highlighted that class segments have different degrees of control over their lives and that class advantages often translate into having power over others. Max Weber (1922) built on this conceptualization by highlighting the role of social status as a resource that influences perceptions of self and others. Weber argued that social groups were distinguished by their respective combination of resources types – wealth (economic capital), prestige (i.e., social status), and power (i.e., political influence or ability to exert influence over others, such as an owner might have over an employee). Weber further argued that these status groups were characterized by distinctive processes of socialization and lifestyles. These ideas were further developed by Lloyd Warner (1949) in his community studies in the United States, where he compared the lifestyles of middle- and working-class Americans. Warner found that socialization into a particular class group inculcates distinctive 'worldviews' about self and place in the social order. His findings were subsequently applied in consumer research and advertising communications throughout the 1950–60s (see Holt 1997).

Of all theories of social class, Pierre Bourdieu's book *Distinction* (1984) has exerted a profound influence on the CCT researcher's conceptualization and analyses of social class. As the title implies, social status sits at the heart of Bourdieu's theory of social practice. However, it will be seen that Bourdieu's theory presents more parsimonious answers to the three key questions we seek to address, and in particular, provides a more explicit account of taste formation that drives distinctive consumption preferences. We present here a summary of his pertinent ideas.

BOURDIEU AND (SOCIAL) DISTINCTION

Bourdieu conceptualizes the social class hierarchy as a multidimensional social space within which social groups are positioned in relation to each other and where the boundaries between groups are defined by the volume and forms of capital they possess. Bourdieu posits three types of capitals (i.e., resources that are deployed in competitions for social status) – economic, social, and cultural. The first two forms of capital resemble Weber's wealth and prestige dimensions. In contrast to prestige, however, Bourdieu's notion of social capital places greater emphasis on the capacity of social networks to provide its members with social connections and means of influence to facilitate access to economic opportunities. Examples of such social connections include alumni groups of elite private schools and top universities, whose networks open up business and political opportunities for their graduating students.

Cultural capital refers to knowledge and skills that are acquired though one's primary socialization as a child and young adult – via family, educational institutions, peer groups, and media – and secondary socialization through latter life experiences and personal pursuits. In Bourdieusian terms, cultural capital encompasses everything from one's internalized sense of manners (i.e., table etiquette) to more formal kinds of knowledge and skills (knowing how to play a piano, being able to solve mathematical equations, or analyze a poem).

Bourdieu (1986) further proposes that cultural capital is materialized in three ways. The first is embodied cultural capital, which refers to enduring dispositions of the mind and body. As a simple example, learning to ride a bicycle or dance ballet or play an instrument all build embodied cultural capital as do educational processes that train one to think in an analytic manner. These forms of cultural capital are skill-based and shape how one acts and improvises in any given social situation. Cultural capital can also take an objectified form (such as objects that signal one's taste or possess certain knowledge or cultivated skill). For example, if you are visiting someone's home that is decorated with mid-20th century furniture and art, the likely assumption is that the owner has both a taste for this aesthetic and knowledge about this genre of art and design. We can go further to assume if the visitor shares these taste and knowledge, that a bonding type conversation would likely be precipitated by these objectified forms of cultural capital. Finally, institutional-ized forms of cultural capital include things like certificates and degrees that demonstrate one's educational and professional credentials and also allow for ready inferences about the quality of one's cultural capital (i.e., a degree from Harvard tends to carry more pres-tige and credibility that one from a junior college and so forth).

Bourdieu highlights that these different forms of capital are convertible. Most com-monly, consumers spend economic capital to gain cultural capital – such as the tuition paid for college – and presume that the resulting degree and its qualifications can then be con-verted into better employment prospects (and hence economic capital). Similarly, cultural capital can be converted into social capital, such as when one using their knowledge about a given domain – be it sports, entertainment, or politics – to strike up conversations and build affinities with those sharing similar interests (see Chapter 4 on brand communities).

In shaping consumer taste (generally in ways that consumers experience as being intuitive or a gut reaction), one's stock of cultural capital directs them to act in ways that align with the norms and values that characterize their social class group and to affiliate with individuals sharing similar social backgrounds. For example, what kind of neighborhood people prefer to live in: in inner city pockets where residents routinely sip ethically produced coffee or suburbs with double brick homes and large backyards with easy access to large chain supermarkets? In this sense, Bourdieu's concept of cul-tural capital helps to explain Lloyd Warner's finding that class groups are characterized by distinctive worldviews.

Bourdieu's theorization further highlights the role of consumption taste and pref-erences in marking social distinctions and creating feelings of collective affinities or indifference among consumers. For example, we tend to feel a stronger sense of common-ality with those who share our tastes than those who don't and these taste-affinities tend to reinforce the sense that one belongs or does not belong in particular class groups (see Chapter 12 on taste). For example, those who possess higher levels of cultural capital tend to have taste for more abstract and intellectualizing consumer practices – such as pon-dering the meaning and form of abstract art, watching avant-garde films, or listening to musical genres that are distinct from mainstream commercial fare – and those who share these experiences have a common frame-of-reference that they find interesting and that affords a sense of personal compatibility. Conversely, lower cultural capital consumers who gravitate toward more readily accessible and easily enjoyed entertainment offerings like monster truck rallies would likely feel little commonality with a higher cultural capital enthusiast of obscure foreign films and perhaps experience some sense of antipathy or intimidation during such an encounter.

These responses are not just cognitive evaluations. They also have a significant emotional component, which often kicks in before we can rationalize the reasons for such feelings. For example, a HCC (higher cultural capital) person may react with disdain at the prospect of buying fashionable clothing at Walmart, Monoprix (France) or H&M (Europe) and they may scoff at the suggestion of picking up a burger from McDonalds or Hessburger (Finland) or Jolibee (Philippines) on the shopping trip. The negative reaction is visceral. On the other hand, a LCC (lower cultural capital) person may be positively stimulated by the chain store (Walmart for example) experience, proud that they picked up some really nice bargains to wear and topped an enjoyable experience with a cheeseburger. This is a simple (albeit stereotypical) example, but illustrates how the same situation is experienced differently depending on habituated dispositions.

Bourdieu's theory further posits that all forms of capital are not equally valued across social fields. For example, the cultural knowledge that might gain recognition and respect in a professional class setting could be deemed as pretentious or useless in a working-class setting. Whereas having gotten front row seats to the Broadway play *Hamilton* might be a status marker in a HCC setting, such a seeming 'bragging right' might be greeted with a disinterested 'so?' by a LCC consumer who has a taste for mixed martial arts fights or rugby but little interest in Broadway musicals. For Bourdieu, any form of capital that is recognized as legitimate and conveys status in a given field constitutes symbolic capital or what is more conventionally characterized as status.

Putting these ideas all together, one's position in the social space is determined by the level and type of resources he or she possesses. Bourdieu further highlights that different factions exist within the same general level of the status hierarchy. For example, in a given middle-class neighborhood, we might find one household that has relatively high levels of economic capital but only moderate levels of cultural capital – for example, imagine someone who runs a successful family business – living in close proximity to a literature or philosophy professor who has considerable cultural capital (i.e., educational credentials, knowledge of high culture) but only moderate levels of economic capital. In each of these settings, the forms of capital that function as sources of symbolic capital (status in that particular social field) would also vary. By providing a lens for understanding how social distinctions are constituted and reproduced through taste, Bourdieu's framework allows the analyst to tease out the differences in consumer lifestyles among not only class-stratified social groups (e.g. professional versus working class) but also among more proximate class factions who would, from more general demographic and psychographic measures, be classified and indiscriminately aggregated as say middle-class consumers (see Holt 1997).

Furthermore, Bourdieu's theory suggests that not only does the overall quantity of capitals determine one's class position but also the specific mix of capital types plays a role. For example, a professor or professional artist may accrue high cultural capital but far less economic capital due to relatively lower incomes. In contrast, small-medium business owners may achieve substantial economic capital but little social and cultural capital due to the time needed to build and maintain their businesses. In addition to total quantity and specific mix of capital types, Bourdieu advises that the length of time that capitals have been held contributes to position in the social space – and relative distinction. Specific position is also associated with distinctive lifestyles and the consumption objects and practices necessary to enact the lifestyle in question.

CULTURAL CAPITAL AND HABITUS

As discussed in the preceding section, some forms of cultural capital can be embodied as skills, aptitudes, and naturalized taste that engender potent emotional responses to objects and experience that are either compatible or incompatible to one's socialized preferences. Embodied cultural capital is a component of an internalized structure that Bourdieu terms the habitus and which he defines as:

> A system of lasting, transposable dispositions which, integrating past experiences, functions at every moment as a matrix of perceptions, appreciations, and actions and makes possible the achievement of infinitely diversified tasks, thanks to analogical transfers of schemes permitting the solution of similarly shaped problems. (Bourdieu 1977: 95)

To restate this complex definition in more accessible terms, the habitus is related to the idea of habit – that is routines that are formed over time, through repetition, and operate in almost automatic or non-conscious fashion. Thus, the habitus is a nexus of routinized behavioral tendencies that emerge from the internalization of (external) social structures through primary socialization. Thus, the habitus is the embodied (and cognitive) outcome of one's socialization in a particular combination of gender, class, religious, ethnic, regional, etc. orientations. These different external influences create enduring tendencies and predispositions that shape one's capacity for action and the ways in which they respond and improvise to the demands of a given social situation. While the habitus can be transformed through practice and repetition, such changes are effortful because they require that one learn a new array of embodied habits, emotional orientations, and interpretive tendencies (c.f. Thompson and Üstüner 2015). The concept of habitus suggests that we experience the world holistically in ways that are shaped by our history of socialization and the co-existing cognitive and emotional orientations that are formed through socialization.

Given the complexity of the habitus, consumer researchers have often sought to focus on certain structural influences that have become internalized (and hence embodied), with class and gender being the most commonly studied structural influences on consumers' habitus. In this chapter, we will focus on the class influence (for discussions of the gendered habitus and consumption practices see Chapter 8 and Coskuner-Balli and Thompson 2013; Martin et al. 2006; Moisio et al. 2013).

Bourdieu proposes that class shapes the formation of the habitus through three broad structural influences: (1) the degree of economic necessity and material deprivation that one confronts in his/her everyday life; (2) the extent to which one's upbringing empha-sizes the value of practical knowledge – such as becoming a tradesman or knowing how to fix things – or more intellectualized and aestheticized forms of knowledge – such as would be valued for example in an elite liberal arts college; (3) the extent to which one's goals in life focus on 'making do' and acquiring a reasonable level of material comfort or involve a more existential quest for self-enrichment and personal growth. In general, these three dimensions tend to co-occur, those who are socialized under conditions of economic anx-iety and relative material deprivation tend to value practical know-how, and their life aim is to acquire a comfortable life that is insulated from economic uncertainty. In contrast, those who are socialized in more affluent settings – where material comfort is a taken-for-granted given – are more likely to adopt a more intellectualizing and aestheticizing orientation and to gain satisfaction from cosmopolitan experiences that broaden their horizons and present new life challenges (Bourdieu and Wacquant 1992). Across these three dimensions, there can also be variations – that is, degree of economic abundance or necessity; degrees to which practical or intellectual knowledge is valued, and so forth.

For example, lower-middle-class households tend to not be that far removed from conditions of necessity. While they emphasize the importance of education and academic achievement, they typically do so for instrumental reasons, such as viewing a degree from a good school as a means to attain a well-paying job. In contrast, children born into more affluent households may view education as an end in itself that makes a person more interesting, more well-rounded, more creative. In the end, affluent students who acquire these aestheticized forms of cultural capital will most likely be able to convert them into valuable forms of social capital (such as marrying someone from an even more affluent family) and economic capital in the professional job market. However, these instrumental goals do not need to be as salient (and motivating) for those who are born into a higher social status as they are for middle-class strivers (Holt 1998).

To further illustrate these differences, we can consider a comparative test that Bourdieu used to demonstrate the differences in the habitus of those hailing from working-class backgrounds and more elite, professional-class ones. In this test, individuals see a black and white photo of the time-worn and misshapen hands of an elderly woman and give their reactions. Bourdieu reports that the professional-class people offer elaborate interpretations in which they interpret the image as a symbol of some higher-order mean-ing (the passage of time; the wisdom and experience acquired over the course of life) while also commenting on the aesthetic value of the image, drawing comparisons to other artistic referents such as Gustave Flaubert's portrait of an elderly servant woman. In contrast, working-class respondents focus more on the material characteristics of the image and the concrete outcomes it suggests (i.e., her hands look arthritic; arthritic hands would hurt; it would be hard to do my job with hands in such bad shape; I feel bad for someone with such deformed hands).

A characteristic of sociological theory is that it is concerned with the general tendencies that define social groups, recognizing that there will always be individual level differences (or what might be characterized as variance around the statistical mean). Bourdieu's theo-rization is consistent with this sociological orientation and, hence, it seeks to explain the 80% whose habitus reproduces the internalized norms of their class group, rather than the 20% whose tendencies diverge. Building on this idea (and the previously noted point that the three structural influences on the habitus tend to be correlated), consumer researchers have adopted the analytic terms of higher cultural capital (HCC consumers) and lower cultural capital (LCC consumers) to describe differences between the habitus of consumers who have been socialized under conditions of affluence (and tend to exhibit a more intellectualizing and self-edifying orientation) and those who have been socialized under conditions of relative economic necessity (and tend to exhibit a more pragmatic and security-seeking orientation). In making these classifications, consumer researchers create a measurement scale that assesses the level of education and job status of a con-sumer's parents and the consumer's own educational history among other factors (see Holt 1998; Üstüner and Holt 2010).

While these measures of HCC and LCC orientations are a bit coarse, they have proven to be remarkably robust in predicting differences in consumers' taste and the ways in which they understand their consumption practices. For example, compared to HCC consum-ers, LCC spend proportionately less of their discretionary income on books, newspapers, magazines, art objects, music, and live performances. In these ways, the higher-level dis-position (abstract thinking) feeds into specific consumption practices and builds a stock of tangible cultural capital. Bourdieu referred to the outcome of greater abstraction as the aesthetic sense, being 'one manifestation of the system of dispositions produced by the social conditioning associated with a particular class of conditions of existence ... it unites all those who are products of similar conditions while distinguishing them from all others' (1984: 56). Thus, taste fosters 'like' attracting 'like'. Distaste on the other hand repels and fosters others' disgust and intolerance. We hasten to say that one of the most interesting characteristics of embodied dispositions is their taken-for-granted nature. They are enacted with little conscious awareness. They also attract little reaction from the actions of others; unless they violate preferred modes of being and doing.

Box 7.2:   Critical Reflection

The intersection with other characteristics

The effect of other major determinants of social organization – gender, ethnicity, race, and lifecycle position – often obscure the role of social class. These other characteristics combine with class to shape socio-historical experience and habitus. We leave these topics for other contributors to this text (see Chapters 8, 9, and 10). However, we note the struggle that stems from tensions between 'being a family carer' and 'professional achievement' motivations faced by the mother featured in Box 7.3. Our point in raising these issues is not to disparage the continuing significance of class. Rather, to sensitize the reader to nuances that need to be incorporated into a sociological analysis of consumption. For example, Henry addressed some of these points of intersectionality in his study of social class in Australia by controlling for some of these other major influences. For example, his study confined the sample by gender (to males), life stage (25–30 years, no children vs. 50+, with children), class (manual working vs. professional occupations using Goldthorpe's classification). These screening criteria yielded a two-dimensional sampling for males classified by class and life stage. Of course, there are many other sampling strategies that seek to control for some of the other major social variables. However, it is important to note that the main class-distinctive tendencies usually emerge when the researcher is sensitized to the possible mix of influences that shape social life. The use of the word 'tendencies' highlights that while class plays a (sometimes) influential role in shaping social behaviors, it is in no way determinant, and dispositions can be translated into many different patterns of consumption behavior.

TASTE AND LIFESTYLE

Bourdieu (1984: 173) specifies the relationship between taste and lifestyle thus:

> Taste, the propensity and capacity to appropriate (materially or symbolically) a given class of classified, classifying objects or practices, is the generative formula of lifestyle, a unitary set of distinctive preferences which express the same intention in the specific logic of each of the symbolic sub-spaces, furniture clothing language, or body hexis.

Here, Bourdieu is stating that our consumption choices are made in relation to the tacit influences of our socialization and our choice of them helps define our social position. Through their repetitions, these choices and preferences form enduring patterns that define consumer lifestyles. These patterns are reflected in our bodies and mannerisms. A certain thematic consistency is evident across choices for consumer goods that differ in kind.

Holt (1998) brought Bourdieu's theory of taste to the fore among consumer research-ers and his delineation of six (interrelated) dispositional dimensions remains the most accessible and complete set that can be found in the CCT literature today. Prior to Holt's work, considerable debate existed as to whether Bourdieu's theory was relevant to a different time and place (i.e., France in the 1960s compared to the United States in the 1990s). Crucially, Holt argued that the focal analysis should be on the continu-ing relevance of embodied taste dispositions and not on comparison of the array of class-distinctive material goods and consumption interests because the class-associa-tions of particular goods and patterns of consumption will vary across time and place. Accordingly, Holt proposed that class position is revealed not so much by what consum-ers consumes (ballet versus *Star Wars* films) but *how* consumers consume; that is, the ways in which they experience and interpret their consumer experiences as well as the goals they pursue through these actions.

Holt (1998) identified six dimensions that tended to distinguish the consumption styles of higher and lower cultural capital consumers: The first is material versus formal aesthetics. That is, do consumers take a utilitarian stance toward their possessions – emphasizing properties such as comfort, functionality, durability, and ease of care – or do they put aesthetic and self-expressive considerations to the forefront, even if it might mean compromising on some degree of functionality or other utilitarian benefits. The second dimension is critical versus referential reception of media. Here, the difference is that HCC consumers view media – such as movies and television shows – as an impe-tus for interpretation, seeing them as a means to understand artistic genres or expose them to edifying ideas. In contrast, LCC consumers tend to assess such cultural forms in terms of its relevance to their lives and the emotional responses it engenders. Their orientation is realistic in the sense that they prefer stories (even in the context of fan-tasy and science fiction) that they can personally identify with. The third dimension is materialism versus idealism. The taste of LCC consumers – who have been socialized under conditions of necessity – tend to value comfort, material abundance, and are hence prone to ostentatious displays. In contrast, HCC consumers are motivated by ideals of refinement, understatement, and aesthetic pleasure. For example, whereas an ideal meal for an LCC consumers might be an all-you-can-eat buffet, an HCC consumer would more likely prefer nouvelle cuisine in which small portions are to be savoured for their complex flavor profiles, cooking techniques, and pleasing presentation. Here, we note that the consumption practices of HCC are no less signals of status (by displaying cultural capital) than LCCs' ostentatious displays (signaling economic capital); they are merely more subtle.

The fourth dimension is local versus cosmopolitan. LCC consumers to define their horizons in relation to their immediate social surroundings and their tastes tend toward the parochial and familiar. In contrast, HCC consumers see themselves as citizens of the world and have cosmopolitan taste for new, horizon-expanding experiences (i.e., world music, foreign films, fusion cuisines, travel to non-touristic locales). Holt's fifth dimension is communal versus individualistic forms of consumer subjectivity. LCC consumers use consumption as a means to fit into their social group and gain experiences of communal connection and belonging. In contrast, HCCs' orientation is a bit more paradoxical. They too wish to be accepted by their HCC peers; however, the terms of this social display hinge on appropriate displays of authenticity (an ideal of being true to oneself and not following the crowd) and expressing eclectic taste in ways that mark one's taste as being relatively unique. For HCCs, the identity model is akin to being an artist where consumption is their means of self-expression. To be accepted in the community of 'consumer artists', one therefore has to display an authentic style and creative spark. Holt's final dimension is autotelic versus self-actualizing leisure. Holt argues that LCC consumers view their leisure activities as sources of relaxation and enjoyment. In contrast, HCCs are more likely to view their leisure experiences as opportunities for self-enrichment, personal development, or optimization of their wellbeing or potential (as in the case of taking a yoga class or engaging in challenging tasks such as marathon running or competing in obstacle racing). Holt notes that LCC interviewees also like to learn. However, they emphasize the intrinsic enjoyment that results from the (repeated) application of the same skills and place far less importance on experiences of variety, change and challenge (for more on taste see Chapter 12).

Though separated by nearly 30 years and cultural context (the United States versus France), Holt's six dimensions are remarkably similar to the taste dispositions that Bourdieu identified in his analysis of French consumers during the 1960s. [The English version of his *Distinction* was published in 1984, Bourdieu's original fieldwork was conducted much earlier.] For example, the differing HCC versus LCC consumer reactions to the photograph of the old woman's hands that Bourdieu reported is quite similar to the referential versus critical orientations that Holt found were respectively invoked by his LCC (referential) and HCC (critical) consumers. (For more on taste see Chapter 12.)

SELF-PERCEPTIONS AND EXPECTATIONS

Figure 7.1 highlights class differences in how people think about themselves and how these self-perceptions affect expectations about the future and reactions to unexpected events (Henry 2005). Henry asked respondents from either manual (working-class) or professional (upper-middle-class) occupational groups (males aged in their 20s) to describe themselves. In the first vignette, a young accountant who exudes self-confidence and an elevated capacity for long-term planning and achievement-oriented goal striving, offers this self-portrayal:

I am fairly well determined. I plan things ahead. I'm pretty well goal-oriented. Try and set a goal whether it's personal or business. I can multi-task, but I tend to become heavily involved when I strive for something. I focus on doing the job well … I'm not pretentious at all, but I do think that I am highly intelligent. I see myself as the classic maths-trained guy. I like to see myself as down-to-earth, but I've had the comment that people say I'm arrogant. Well I'm not, that's just people misinterpreting I suppose because I try to achieve things and that in itself being status. It just comes down to me being eight years younger than anyone else in the job. They see me as a threat, but I'm not out to get anyone. I just have very much a limitless vision of what I can be. (p. 769)

In the manual working-class group, far different self-concepts are evident, as these consumers described themselves in ways that exhibit more pervasive self-doubts, less confidence in their capacity to succeed and a more pessimistic outlook on life:

I'm a perfectionist and therefore never get anything done. I start thinking about how I can build the [electronic amplifier] box. You finally get round to doing something about it, and it ends up not turning out very well anyway, so you shove it in the corner. So you end up hardly ever doing anything … there is nothing that makes me stand out, except the fact that I'm always dreaming about something, thinking about something. Unfortunately, that makes me recede more than stand out. Because you just sit over there and think about something, and they [others] go – what are you looking so grumpy about? That's a common response. (p. 771)

Henry (2005) suggests that his working-class respondents' circumspect orientation led them to be risk-averse, preferring options that seem safe and familiar versus those that would require them to venture into unfamiliar or discomforting domains. In contrast, his middle- and upper-middle-class respondents embraced new opportunities and regarded risk taking as a necessary component of pursuing their ambitious goals.

Henry (2005) went on to examine how these differing self-perceptions impacted financial planning and everyday budgeting. Upper-class people tend to incorporate the accumulation of financial capital into everyday life. They also believe they can grow their financial wealth. Hence, they tend to take a longer-term view in planning their financial futures. This orientation results in more elaborate budget planning that incorporates present needs with future goals. The same applies to the use of more elaborate investing strategies that extends past that of property and financial instruments into investment in additional formal education and personal appearance (healthy body, grooming, clothing etc.). Hence, higher classes are more likely to selectively invest across a greater range investment types. On the other hand, working-class people engage in less careful budgeting and cast a more limited eye towards the future. Note that in the Henry (2005) study the informants were all in their 20s where income differences between working and professional informants are actually small. This is because working-class informants' incomes peak earlier in life, but young professional incomes are just starting the financial climb.

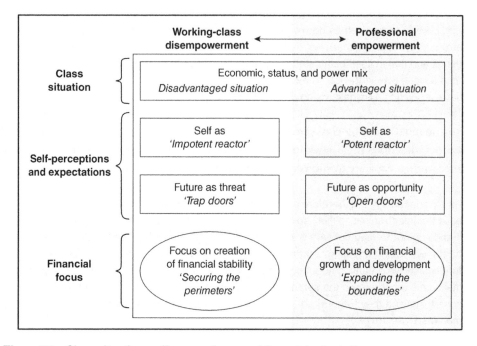

Figure 7.1   Class situation, self-perceptions, and financial orientations

In a study of US-born middle-class (HCC) and working-class (LCC) 'emerging' adults (ages 22 to 33), Weinberger et al. (2017) report that their HCC respondents were characterized by a predilection for longer-term planning, an openness to change, and confidence that their choices would inevitably lead to a successful life outcome. These class-shaped traits in turn lead to a greater capacity to imagine their (prosperous) future self and a related proclivity to seek out novel consumption experiences with cultural capital-enhancing potential. Through this focus on exploratory consumption experiences, these HCC consumers aim to build a diversified portfolio of life experiences before settling down into a more stable and presumably less adventurous married life with children. In contrast, their LCC working-class consumers displayed a working class 'desire for the familiar, a fear of the unknown, and longing for stability' (Weinberger et al. 2017: 332). Accordingly, these consumers proceed with caution and no small degree of trepidation, and generally engage in unfamiliar experiences for instrumental reasons (such as joining the military to learn a trade).

From all appearances, the consumers in Weinberger et al.'s study seem to be doing nothing more than following their own taste and preferences. However, their study demonstrates that consumption subtly forges distinctions between higher and lower cultural capital consumers and hence reproduces inequities in their respective stocks of cultural capital. These emerging adult HCC consumers have some awareness of the cultural capital gains afforded by their exploratory experience consumption. However, they attribute little importance to the longer-term economic benefits that may accrue from their inquisitive, cosmopolitan orientation. Instead, they portray their voracious pursuit of novel, edifying experiences merely as a quest for self-enrichment and personal development, much like Holt's adult HCC consumers.

Box 7.3:   Real World Scenario

Recovery from a socio-economically displaced lifestyle

The lifestyle that a person is socialized into becomes naturalized and taken for granted. However, the ability to enact that preferred lifestyle can change dramatically. Such changes highlight the power of habituated preferences that span preferred activities and patterns of behavior, material objects, aesthetic tastes, and desired social networks. Such a circumstance can be triggered by a loss of economic capital which results in downward economic mobility, whether due to illness, job loss, natural disaster, or family breakup. For example, family breakup and divorce can be seen as a disruption in social capital endowment. It often results in assets splits and income declines. Woman with children are particularly impacted. Old lifestyles are turned upside down and this brings the interconnectedness between economic, social, and cultural capital into sharp relief.

We illustrate using a case from our research. After more than 20 years of marriage and shared affluent living, Agnes has endured an emotionally stressful divorce. Of the changes that she has had to negotiate, however, none stands out more to Agnes than the sense that she is now time constrained and unable to pursue her own personal interests. In pre-divorce life, Agnes was a full-time homemaker. While that role has many well-documented demands, Agnes did not have to punch a proverbial clock and felt that she had a relatively high degree of control over her time, once her children were off to school, with opportunities to socialize with friends, take exercise courses, and enjoy leisure-oriented shopping.

Now she works a full-time job outside the home. Owing to these twin demands of raising her children as a single parent and her time-demanding job, Agnes reports grappling with a pervasive sense of exhaustion and a nagging frustration over having to forgo so many of the activities which had once been sources of pleasure as well as valued aspects of her identity (such as the feeling of well-being that accrues from regular exercise).

(Continued)

(Continued)

Agnes took great pride and satisfaction in hosting groups of people at her old home. She enjoyed cooking big meals for large groups of guests. She no longer entertains with dinners, barbeques, and afternoons by the pool. She no longer has the time for her daily gym workouts and coffee with friends. Even though she owns an exercise machine, at the end of the day she lacks the energy to use it. She experiences this change viscerally as bodily discomfort. In addition, time constraints mean that she does less home cooking in the evening and buys a lot more takeaway food. She worries about the consequences of less healthy eating will have on her family.

Agnes has had to give up the old home that she had lovingly designed and decorated herself. She described this as her 'dream home'. She misses the pool, the well-appointed entertaining areas, and in particular the large well-organised kitchen that enabled her to pursue her passion for cooking. She also misses the big garden that she carefully nurtured and had provided a wonderful source of therapy. Agnes hates her new rented home. Even though it could be considered relatively large in comparison to other homes in the area, she has had to downsize. She complains about not being comfortable having friends over. Agnes also claims it is less convenient to entertain. She states that she can't find things because of cramped storage facilities. Old furniture is too large to fit in the new house. Consequently, she has stored much of the furniture and equipment in the garage. Overall, Agnes states that it does not feel like a home.

Though she earns a good income, Agnes is now much more careful with her finances. The ex-husband previously managed the finances. Given the demanding job, she discusses new routines such as having to be much more organized in preparation for a quick start in the mornings. The increased effort in logistical and financial planning adds to the stressed lifestyle.

Agnes yearns for the lifestyle that is lost. Her sense of loss extends far beyond a diminishment of her financial standing. Rather, her lifestyle displacement has fostered a loss of identity as she can no longer participate in the activities that had once structured her sense of self. Agnes has also experienced a loss of social capital as she has become disconnected from her previous social networks and now lacks time and energy to build new ones. Though Agnes is still relatively well off, her lifestyle displacement is still acutely felt, both physically and emotionally.

SOCIAL REPRODUCTION AND MOBILITY

Consistent with the predictions of Bourdieu's theory of social class reproduction, numerous studies have shown that the social class into which one is born exerts a significant influence on the social class one attains in adulthood (Blanden 2013). In the US context, for example, intergenerational elasticity is estimated to be 0.41. This index measures the extent to which income levels are able to change across generations.

To illustrate, let's imagine that someone is born into an American family that earns $10,000 less income than the average income for a US household. An index of 0.41 means that 41% per cent of that difference (or $4,100) is passed on to the children of that household when they become income earning adults. [The estimate of this generationally aggregated index involves complex statistical and econometric procedures that are beyond the scope of this chapter to explain. Interested readers can consult Corak (2001) for further details on these measurements and scaling procedures.] In effect, these enduring, intergenerational differences equate to the structural handicap (or staggered start) that consumers face in the grand race for economic opportunity. However, the other and more positive side of this statistic, is that while being born into a lower-income household poses, on average, enduring disadvantages relative to those born into more affluent circumstances, a reasonable proportion of this handicap is overcome, as children – across the developed economies – tend to have more relatively prosperous lifestyles than their parents.

This positive movement across generations with respect to some combination of income levels, educational attainment, and occupation state is referred to as upward intergenerational mobility. Upward generational mobility is positively correlated to economic growth and rising standards of education. For example, government programs that improve access to educational resources for lower-income families exert a significant positive effect on upward generational mobility, Not surprisingly, Scandinavian nations – which provide their citizens with universal access to higher education – have the highest rates of upward intergenerational mobility in the Western world (Blanden 2013).

Consumers can also have to cope with lifestyle disruptions caused by downward mobility. In the intergenerational case, downward mobility would imply that children, as adults, attain a lower rung in the socio-economic hierarchy than their parents. For example, some analysts warn that millennials could be the first generation in US history to experience widespread downward mobility owing to the diminishment of job security, the neoliberal dismantling of the social safety net, the rise of outsourcing, automation, privatization, and other transformation factors which are creating an increasingly precarious economic environment (Standing 2014).

Downward mobility can also strike in a more immediate fashion when households suffer a significant loss in resources due to job loss and illness that incapacitates, natural disaster that destroys homes and property, poor financial investment decisions, or dispersal of financial resources due to divorce. The negative consequences of downward mobility are not just a diminishment of economic capital and financial vulnerability (as troubling as those changes can be). In the face of dominant neoliberal ideologies of individualism and personal responsibility, downward mobility is often interpreted as personal failure, which adds an additional layer of emotional trauma to these losses. As the case of

Agnes in Box 7.3 illustrates, it also leads to an inability to enact one's habituated lifestyle patterns and tastes, which can in turn lead to a profound sense of identity loss and a host of negative emotions.

Consumers who have more stocks of cultural and social capital have more resources to leverage in their efforts to cope with the unwanted consequences of financial downward mobility. For example, a failed business person may use the experience and social network to rebuild a new and stronger business. Similarly, a laid off professional may apply his/her generalized problem-solving skills in an entrepreneurial start-up. However, as Box 7.4 illustrates, loss of remaining capitals for those already living on the edge makes recovery far more difficult. These conditions of exacerbated deprivation can engender particularly traumatic experiences of hopelessness and helplessness.

Saatcioglu and Ozanne (2013) examine inhabitants of a US working-class trailer park (caravan park) and compare residents with different class origins; for example people who have experienced downward mobility from lower-middle-class lifestyles to those who have been conditioned into life as working poor. They found that these two groups are distinguished by their distinctive moral outlooks, and lifestyle orientations, even though they live in very similar circumstances with comparable current income levels. The downwardly mobile residents see their situation as being short term and look to a future living elsewhere. Consequently, they seek to minimize their expenditures on their current living quarters – spending money only on necessary maintenance and very little on decoration and aesthetic improvements – so that they can pool their savings for their envisioned returned to a more economically advantaged life in the future. While they retain their established consumption preferences, expenditures for such goods and services are also placed on hold in order to again build their stock of economic capital for a life beyond their current downwardly mobile state and, hence, anticipate returning to their previous consumption patterns. Saatcioglu and Ozanne (2013) also describe mobilization of embodied cultural capital to assist recovery, noting the application of a 'hardworking and disciplined' self-concept. Examples of this orientation include setting up a home business, attending community college to upskill, and online stock trading. This future-oriented outlook contrasts with long-term working poor residents who exhibit a fatalistic outlook, a strong desire to feel comfortable in their immediate surrounds, and a diminished sense of autonomy, feeling resigned to their life struggles with little chance of altering their precarious circumstance. Where the downwardly mobile (but optimistic) segment focused on building economic capital through savings and hard work, this latter group, who have been conditioned to a life of impoverishment, seek to build their social capital so they can have help in the face of crisis moments and feel they are part of a supportive community of people who have to make do as best they can.

Box 7.4:   Real World Scenario

Below the poverty line

We enter a run-down public housing estate to meet Celeste, a single mother of four. Some of the apartments are empty and boarded up. We pass two neighbors arguing. Celeste later confirms that such disturbances are common. Consequently, she does not let her kids play outside at all. Her flat is constituted by a lounge area, a small kitchen, and three cramped bedrooms – one for the two girls, one for the two boys, and one for Celeste. Her apartment has no heating or cooling (though far from ideal, this situation is manageable given Sydney, Australia's fairly temperate climate). Nonetheless, on a hot day, the air feels stale and oppressive. Celeste further explains that her apartment can be unpleasantly cold in the winter, which necessitates that she and her children remain heavily dressed when indoors.

The lounge area is dominated by a dilapidated and oversized couch and living room table. Piles of household items such as kids' shoes clutter the room. This leads into a small poorly equipped kitchen that is dominated by a large dining table and fridge that also seems too large for the diminutive scale of the kitchen. Celeste has little storage space so objects are strewn about which further contributes to the disorganized and cluttered feel of Celeste's living space.

One reason that so many items seem to not fit, in the most literal sense, Celeste's apartment is that she bought them second-hand, via E-bay, Gumtree, and Recycle. In making these purchases, her primary choice criterion was affordability rather than the item's spatial compatibility or aesthetic appeal. Her provisioning (i.e., groceries and household needs) requires lengthy travel on public transport. Consequently, she does one big shop each week for which she draws up a detailed shopping list following a check of the supermarket specials catalogue. Processed and packaged foods dominate, with little space for fruit and vegetables. She makes the point that fresh products can spoil, which means wasted money.

Celeste had previously worked as shop assistant but is not currently employed. She currently relies on public assistance. Her weekly budget is largely consumed by her housing costs of about $350 per week and meeting the basic needs of her four children. One of her major goals is to find part-time work that would pay enough that she could move to a better neighborhood. However, she faces many structural obstacles in attaining this objective. Owing to her childcare responsibilities, she can only work limited hours. A second barrier is that she does not own a car and her living area is poorly serviced by public transport, making it quite difficult for her to commute to areas where employment opportunities lie. All this makes her reliant on public assistance. Compounding her dilemmas, Celeste is socially isolated and struggles with a pervasive sense of being on her own.

(Continued)

(Continued)

Comparing Celeste to our other single mother, Agnes (Box 7.3), both have divorced yet their lifestyles are marked by a stark gap in resources. Agnes lost substantial economic capital in the divorce, but not all. She also drew on previous professional career experience, habituated competencies, and her social capital to gain a well-paid managerial position. This comparison illustrates the buffer that accrued forms of capital provide to more socio-economic advantaged individuals; even when they in some sense slide down the status hierarchy, their fall is cushioned and they have a greater capacity to recover their status position (though as Agnes' case also illustrates, not without having to make some unwanted tradeoffs). In contrast, low-resourced individuals, such as Celeste, face much bleaker prospects when their lifestyles become disrupted by an economic downturn, as their more limited stocks of cultural and social capital cannot be as readily converted into new forms of economic capital. Hence, their capacity to recover is more limited and locks them into perilous conditions that, in turn, dampen their confidence and hope for a better life, creating a rather self-fulfilling prophecy.

APPLICATIONS AND CONCLUSION

In sum, people from distinct class groups react differently to the same marketing stimulus or consumption situation. Distinctive embodied taste preferences act as emotional triggers that stimulate various degrees of acceptance or rejection of products or consumption experiences. Marketers seeking to communicate with specific class groups, or to design products, services and experiences where consumer reactions are likely to vary by class, must take on board the ideas developed in this chapter. Furthermore, class-based taste distinctions are often subtle. They can apply to objects, environments, ideas, and other people. For example, a person from one class group may be sympathetically moved by a dramatic performance, whereas one from another class may react with bemused irritation. One person may feel exhilarated by new marketplace technologies, another may feel threatened and insecure when facing technological changes. One person may react with feelings of distaste in a downmarket restaurant, whereas another may feel comforted and welcome. One person may experience delight when served a particular meal, whereas another may experience disgust. Bourdieu (1984) refers to the feeling of comfort in the fit between habituated preferences and the environment, or discomfort when habituated preferences are contravened. However, these examples indicate that the (dis)comfort can potentially encompass the full range of emotions – sympathy, irritation, exhilaration, threat, distaste, warmth, delight, and disgust.

Each of these class-conditioned emotions can potentially drive consumption choices. They can also be employed in persuasive advertising where the nuances of style, look, and feel can make or break perceived authenticity and message acceptance. For example, in promotion of craft and hobby-related products messaging around challenge and continuous learning may be appropriate for HCCs, whereas ease of mastery may resonate more strongly with LCCs.

Distinctive motivations can also be used to understand barriers to consumption among particular class groups. For example, a present time orientation among LCCs may result in a general disregard for goods and practices that promise future pay-offs, such as financial investments or preventative health care practices (i.e., regular exercise and healthy eating). Conversely, HCCs may feel little need to display luxury brands (even though they have superior spending capacity) because they already feel confident and empowered. Consequently, a nuanced understanding of class-distinctive motivations can provide a mirror onto consumer reactions across a range of circumstances.

Box 7.5:   Extended Case Study

Military recruiting campaigns

Militaries around the Western world face particular difficulties in recruiting personnel. Recruitment quotas are especially difficult to meet during times of economic upturn and high employment. Consequently, modern militaries spend considerable amounts of money on recruitment advertising. The problem is not so acute for officer pathway entry. These recruits are typically more highly educated and motivated by longer-term goals to develop leadership careers. Consequently, those applying for officer entry are typically drawn from HCC backgrounds. These HCC recruits have higher expectations and feel more confident in their capacities to achieve. However, filling the bulk of positions – the rank and file enlisted soldiers – is always more challenging. It has been said that enlisting at entry level in the army is the last stop when you can't get a job in a fast food burger outlet. These kinds of perceptions don't help in recruiting. Those applying for rank and file entry are typically drawn from LCC backgrounds. Consequently, the rank and file enlistees tend to have lower educational credentials and sign up with the short-term goal of gaining a secure job. Longer-term opportunity is of less immediate importance for LCCs. Indeed, pathways to progression in the military are typically more restricted for rank and file recruits. However, such limitations tend to affect lower-class people across the entire spectrum of life. These experiences constrain self-potential. The differing motivations between better and less well-educated (HCC vs. LCC) recruits suggest the need for distinctive recruitment strategies that vary by social class.

The question for recruiters is just which motivational appeals will work best to achieve their targets. In the 1990s, the United States Army employed the slogan 'Be all you can be'. This implied high aspiration and desire for personal growth. It is not hard to see that messaging appeals involving stretching personal capacities fell on deaf ears for people

(Continued)

(Continued)

who lack the confidence to reach out of their comfort zone. This approach produced disillusionment among active personnel (Shyles and Hocking 1990) and the US military adopted new themes that promote the idea of belonging to the world's mightiest force. The current US advertising highlights the pride in position and that of acceptance among military peers that recruits can expect to feel. Hence, security is now emphasized over challenge. In 2016, the British military also faced shortfalls in recruiting enlisted personnel. At that time, their promotional messaging focused on highlighting the skills that soldiers can learn. However, this appeal was not translating into enquiries. In 2017, they launched a new advertising campaign using the slogan 'This is belonging', that highlighted the unique and lasting bonds of friendship that are built in the service. The idea of camaraderie is a more focused idea than that of the US 'fitting in' and 'secure place' approach. Rather, the British approach is much more directly related to the personal bonds that will accrue from military service. Interestingly, unlike the US approach that features more tailored messaging aimed at enlisted recruits, the British are aiming their campaign across all ranks. Meanwhile back in Australia, the military recruiting communications implore the audience to 'Challenge Yourself'. This slogan seems out of step with US and British approaches. However, the recruitment problem for Australia is different in that filling officer entry and skilled technical positions presents the greater challenge.

There are clearly other types of motivations at play when a person considers a military option. For example, excitement and escape from the mundane and of course, patriotism. In these areas there does appear to be some recognition of national cultural differences. The US communications tend to embed notions of patriotism powerfully in the background of all their campaign materials, whereas this appears less so with British military communications. The Australian communications tends to foreground emotional experience, excitement, and adventure, whereas the current British ads actually employ the irony of gruelling marches through inclement weather in their 'This is belonging'.

All three of these nations' militaries appear to recognize similar social class-based differences in the motivations that distinguish recruits. Those from advantaged social classes are looking for challenge, change, and future advancement. They are looking more towards the longer term. Whereas, recruits from less advantaged social classes are looking more narrowly to immediate job placement, recognition with relative security, and engage in less thought as to where the job may lead in the future. These class-based distinctive ways of viewing the world appear to hold across (Western) national cultures.

Questions

1. Type 'military recruiting campaigns' into Google search and you should find an array of material from different countries. Select a campaign and evaluate it through the social class lens of differing worldviews between HCC and LCC recruits.
2. Thinking about military recruiting in your own country, suggest ways you would recommend refining persuasive messaging to selected class groups.
3. Consider how this recommendation may vary by class and gender.

RESEARCH DIRECTIONS

We suggest several areas for future research. The first is to undertake studies that provide a more integrated consideration of the influences that economic, social, and cultural capital exert on the relationships between social class and consumption. To date, consumer researchers have emphasized cultural capital. This analytic tendency reflects that cultural capital is most directly linked with taste and lifestyle preferences. However, less is known about how the different mixes of capitals influence consumption. For example, cases where two people exhibit similar cultural capitals, yet quite different amounts of economic and social capitals. How do the people with capital imbalances manage? Further, these imbalances may be sparked by imposed downward mobility (such as that due to job loss or divorce), or alternatively due to differences in career trajectories where financial and social opportunities diverge. A related area involves further examination of interaction between social class and other dimensions of social identity (e.g. gender, ethnicity, life cycle etc.). For example, how do intersections among social class, ethnicity, and gender influence how consumers' preferences and lifestyle orientations evolve over the life course? Relatedly, to what extent can the habitus be transformed through secondary socialization and consumers' volitational efforts to transform their habituated tendencies and preferences? Are some forms of primary socialization more malleable than others?

In this regard, we could also more fully evaluate the extent to which consumers' feelings and cognitive evaluations are bound by their habitus. In other words, can consumers transcend the limits and tendencies that are set by their socialization? Much of contemporary democratic discourse and political institutions is premised on the assumption that citizens can and will put aside their own particular interests in the interest of the greater societal good. Bourdieu's theory suggests that such a dis-interested orientation may be, in reality, quite difficult to attain. What kind of social processes and strategies could be utilized to enable citizen-consumers to evaluate societal issues in ways that do not implicitly privilege their parochial interests?

RECOMMENDED READING

Arsel, Zeynep and Thompson, Craig (2011) 'Demythologizing consumption practices: How consumers protect their field-dependent capital from devaluing marketplace myths', *Journal of Consumer Research*, 37 (February): 791–806.

Bernthal, Matthew, Crockett, David, and Rose, Randall L. (2005) 'Credit cards as lifestyle facilitators', *Journal of Consumer Research*, 32 (1) 130–45.

Bettany, Shona M., Kerrane, Ben, and Hogg, Margaret K. (2014) 'The material-semiotics of fatherhood: The co-emergence of technology and contemporary fatherhood', *Journal of Business Research*, 67 (7): 1544–51.

Carfagna, Lindsey B., Dubois, Emilie A., Fitzmaurice, Connor, Ouimette, Monique Y., Schor, Juliet B., Willis, Margaret, and Laidley, Thomas (2104) 'An emerging eco-habitus: The reconfiguration of high cultural capital practices among ethical consumers', *Journal of Consumer Culture, 14* (2): 158–78.

Cronin, James M., McCarthy, Mary B., and Collins, Alan M. (2014) 'Covert distinction: How hipsters practice food-based resistance strategies in the production of identity', *Consumption Markets & Culture, 17* (1): 2–28.

Henry, Paul and Caldwell, Marylouise (2008) 'Spinning the proverbial wheel: Social class and marketing', *Marketing Theory, 8* (December), 387–406.

Kravets, Olga, and Sandıkcı, Özlem (2014) 'Competently ordinary: New middle class consumers in the emerging markets', *Journal of Marketing, 78* (4): 125–40.

Lamont, Michèle (1992) *Money, Morals, and Manners: The Culture of the French and the American Upper-Middle Class.* Chicago, IL: University of Chicago Press.

Martineau, Pierre (1958) 'Social classes and spending behavior', *Journal of Marketing, 23* (2): 121–30.

Marx, Karl (1867) *Das Kapital: Kritik der politischen Oekonomie*, 1st edition. Hamburg: Verlag von Otto Meissner.

Savage, Mike (2015) *Social Class in the 21st Century.* London: Penguin Random House.

Shyles, Leonard and Hocking, John E. (1990) 'The army's "Be All You Can Be" campaign', *Armed Forces and Society, 16* (3): 369–83.

Standing, Guy (2014) *The Precariat: The New Dangerous Class.* New York: Bloomsbury.

Turner, Bryan S. and Edmunds, June (2002) 'The distaste of taste: Bourdieu, cultural capital and the Australian postwar elite', *Journal of Consumer Culture, 2* (2): 219–40.

Wright, David (2005) 'Commodifying respectability: Distinctions at work in the book shop', *Journal of Consumer Culture, 5* (November): 295–314.

REFERENCES

Allen, Douglas (2002) 'Towards a theory of consumer choice as sociohistorically shaped practical experience: The Fits-Like-a-Glove (FLAG) framework', *Journal of Consumer Research, 28* (March): 515–32.

Blanden, Jo (2013) 'Cross-country rankings in intergenerational mobility: A comparison of approaches from economics and sociology', *Journal of Economic Surveys, 27* (1): 38–73.

Bourdieu, Pierre (1977) *Outline of a Theory of Practice.* New York, NY: Cambridge University Press.

Bourdieu, Pierre (1984) *Distinction: A Social Critique of the Judgement of Taste.* Cambridge, MA: Harvard University Press.

Bourdieu, Pierre (1986) 'Forms of capital', in *Handbook of Theory and Research for the Sociology of Education* (ed. John Richardson, trans. Richard Nice). New York: Greenwood.

pp. 241–58. [Originally published as 'Ökonomisches Kapital, Kulturelles Kapital, Soziales Kapital' (1983) *in Soziale Ungleichheiten* (ed. Reinhard Kreckel). Goettingen: Otto Schartz & Co. pp. 183–98.]

Bourdieu, Pierre and Wacquant, Loic (1992) *An Invitation to Reflexive Sociology*. Chicago, IL: University of Chicago Press. pp. 1–59.

Corak, Miles Raymond (2001) *'Are the Kids All Right?: Intergenerational Mobility and Child Well-being, in Canada'*. Statistics Canada, Analytical Studies Branch, 2001. Accessible at www.statcan.gc.ca/pub/11f0019m/11f0019m2001171-eng.pdf.

Coskuner-Balli, Gokcen and Thompson, Craig J. (2013) 'The status costs of subordinate cultural capital: At-home fathers' collective pursuit of cultural legitimacy through capitalizing consumption practices', *Journal of Consumer Research*, *40* (1): 19–41.

Henry, Paul (2005) 'Social class, market situation, and consumers' metaphors of (dis)empowerment', *Journal of Consumer Research*, *31* (March): 766–78.

Holt, Douglas B. (1997) 'Poststructuralist lifestyle analysis: Conceptualizing the social patterning of consumption', *Journal of Consumer Research*, *23* (March): 326–50.

Holt, Douglas B. (1998) 'Does cultural capital structure American consumption?', *Journal of Consumer Research*, *25* (June): 1–26.

Martin, Diane M., Schouten, John W., and McAlexander, James H. (2006) 'Claiming the throttle: Multiple femininities in a hyper-masculine subculture', *Consumption Markets & Culture*, *9* (3): 171–205.

Marx, Karl (1867) *Das Kapital: Kritik der politischen Oekonomie*, first edition. Hamburg: Verlag von Otto Meissner.

Moisio, Risto, Arnould, Eric J., and Gentry, James W. (2013) 'Productive consumption in the class-mediated construction of domestic masculinity: Do-It-Yourself (DIY) home improvement in men's identity work', *Journal of Consumer Research*, *40* (2): 298–316.

Saatcioglu, Bige and Ozanne, Julie (2013) 'Moral habitus and status negotiation in a marginalized working-class neighbourhood', *Journal of Consumer Research*, *40* (December): 692–710.

Shyles, Leonard and Hocking, John E. (1990) 'The army's "Be All You Can Be" campaign', *Armed Forces and Society*, *16* (3): 369–83.

Standing, Guy (2014) *The Precariat: The New Dangerous Class*. New York: Bloomsbury.

Thompson, Craig J. and Üstüner, Tuba (2015) 'Women skating on the edge: Marketplace performances as ideological edgework', *Journal of Consumer Research*, *42* (2): 266–83.

Üstüner, Tuba and Holt, Douglas B. (2010) 'Toward a theory of status consumption in less industrialized countries', *Journal of Consumer Research*, *37* (June): 37–56.

Warner, W. Lloyd (1949) *Social Class in America: The Evaluation of Status*. New York: Harper.

Weber, Max (1922) *Wirtschaft und Gesellschaft: Grundriss der verstehenden Soziologie*. Tübingen.

Weinberger, Michelle, Zavisca, Jane and Silva, Jennifer (2017) 'Consuming for an imagined future: Middle-class consumer lifestyle and exploratory experiences in the transition to adulthood', *Journal of Consumer Research*, *44* (2): 332–60.

8
GENDER(S), CONSUMPTION, AND MARKETS

Luca M. Visconti, Università della Svizzera italiana, Lugano, and ESCP Europe, Paris
Pauline Maclaran, Royal Holloway, University of London
Shona Bettany, Liverpool Business School

CHAPTER OVERVIEW

- Gender identity refers to a person's sense of being male, female, or any other combinations of these.
- Gender roles describe masculine or feminine behaviors in accordance with societal norms.
- Sex, the biological distinction male/female, does not coincide with gender identity/role, yet grounds them.
- LGBTQ refers to sexual orientation (i.e., to whom a person is attracted).
- CCT research on gender assumes that sex *per se* does not account for the meanings a person attributes to his/her consumption. Gender instead does.
- Advertising, branding, positioning, and segmentation are all highly affected by considerations about femininity, masculinity, and sexual orientation.

INTRODUCTION

Why is gender important and how do we research it? This chapter hopes to address both these questions by looking at consumer culture theory (CCT) research on the topic and summarizing existing bodies of thought with gender as their central focus. Understanding of gender, its making, deconstruction, and effects is crucial to any marketing manager. For example, the way men and women are represented in advertising is relevant in defining their social roles. Box 8.1 provides a brief review of how women have been portrayed in commercial communication over time, and the extent to which the transformation of these representations has accompanied their socio-political empowerment. As a result of positioning strategies, products can also be gendered. Meat is said to be masculine (Rozin et al. 2012); fairytales as well as dolls and toys set standards of femininity/masculinity from infancy onwards. Think of two opposite but both iconic American dolls: Barbie (www.barbie.com) and the American Girl (www.americangirl.com). These brands convey radically different models of femininity, with Barbie establishing aspirational standards of beauty, professional, and social fulfillment and the American Girl supporting instead a more heroic model of womanhood emphasizing triumph over adversity, perseverance, resourcefulness, and kindness toward others (Diamond et al. 2009).

Distinctions between men/women and masculinity/femininity is also often used to segment a market (refer to Box 8.2 for further details). A gender-based segmentation of markets has been largely accepted in domains as varied as the automotive (think of Jeep and 4 x 4 cars), cosmetics, fashion or epilation (e.g. Gillette) markets, but has sometimes backfired on marketers when translated to other industries (Box 8.3 describes Bic's attempt at gendering pens). Brands can also have strong gender connotations, as per Harley–Davidson (Schouten and McAlexander 1995) or Porsche (Avery 2012). The effects of altering brands' and products' long-established gendered meanings is unpredictable, with both examples of success (think of the current 'agender' trend, which we describe in the case study that closes this chapter) or failure (e.g. Mercedes' 2008 launch of its SUV GLK for women). Last, gender can also account for marketers' lower interest in women's production, as illustrated by the case of artworks created by female and male artists. Cameron, Goetzmann, and Nozari (2017) show that female graduates from the Yale School of Art are less likely than their male counterparts to achieve auction sales. This means that marketers act as gatekeepers preventing female artists from accessing the most prestigious sale channel (i.e., auctions), which negatively impacts their market quotations. Notably, the few female artists reaching auctions outperform male artists, which proves that female artists are not less creative than men.

Foundational theories of gender are discussed in the chapter's main sections, whereas applications to marketing practice feature in the boxes and cases. Before discussing further, we introduce the reader to various 'loaded' terms that recur in gender research and are valuable to understand. The first is the word *gender* itself, a term that people often confuse with *sex*. So, when we speak of gender differences, we often mean sex differences. Gender research makes a distinction between the two: gender being associated with the activities, behaviors, and roles that a given society deems appropriate for men and women and sex understood as the biological categories of male/female. Second, *gender identity* refers to a person's sense of being male, female, or combinations of these, as well as being androgynous or transgender (i.e., a person whose sense of personal identity and gender does not correspond with the sex assigned them at birth). Third, *gender roles* describe masculine or feminine behaviors in accordance with societal norms, which can be quite variable. Finally, *sexual orientation* refers to whom a person is attracted to, and may be lesbian, gay, straight, bisexual, asexual, or queer – the latter being a term for sexual orientation that defies definition along binary gender divisions.

Ignoring these distinctions, marketing, and consumer researchers have long conflated gender with biological sex. In the 1990s, gender research in CCT took a turn toward a more sociologically and anthropologically informed orientation. Accordingly, CCT research on gender has taken a critical perspective on the conventional male/female binaries and developed more nuanced conceptions of the relations among consumption, gender and sexuality. For the rest of this chapter we focus on the three key streams that comprise this CCT research, namely: (1) feminist critiques; (2) studies on masculinity; and (3) LGBTQ studies.

GENDER IN CONSUMPTION AND ACROSS MARKETS

Femininity and the Feminist Critique

The feminist movement dates back to the early suffragettes of the 1800s and their campaigns for women's right to vote and own property. Since that time, there have been several iterations of feminism, often referred to as 'waves', the suffragettes being the first wave. The *second wave* (1960–1980s) was most concerned with women's role in the family, her unpaid labor in the family, as well as seeking better access to the male-dominated workplace. Heavily influenced by Betty Friedan's *The Feminine Mystique* (1974), feminists at this time accused marketers of reinforcing (and even creating) many negative stereotypes of women, particularly through passive and decorative portrayals of women in advertisements (see Box 8.1). In contrast, their *third wave* sisters (1990 onwards) had a certain rapprochement with the market, concerning themselves with the micro-politics of gender identities often facilitated by marketers. For example, the 'pink pound' is a term used in the UK to describe the spending power of the gay community. Now, over the last five years, a *fourth wave* has emerged as young activists use social media to inspire a new collective and technologically driven feminism. How markets and marketing activities intertwine with this wave is yet to be fully determined.

Over its history, feminism has developed many diverse theoretical perspectives. They range from the *liberal feminism* that dominated initially (subsequently critiqued for being too white and too middle class), to *intersectional feminism*, which instead recognizes how women's condition varies at the intersection of other dimensions of oppression (class, race, sexuality, etc.) and has its roots in the black feminist movement of the 1990s (for a more comprehensive guide to these movements see Hearn and Hine 2015; Maclaran and Kravets 2018). However, key principles that underpin all feminist thinking include: (1) society should treat men and women as equals, and currently this is not the case;

(2) the male domination of all social institutions (otherwise known as *patriarchy*) is to blame for gender inequality; and, (3) a commitment to a feminist epistemology, meaning the study of the gendered nature of knowledge.

Box 8.1:   Real World Scenario

The evolution of advertising on women (1950–2010) in one box

The representation of women in advertising is a key area of critique for gender scholars. From the late 1960s onwards feminists pointed to stereotypical role portrayals that were continually being reinforced through advertising imagery (see, for example, the top 10 sexist ads of the 1950s and 60s: www.youtube.com/watch?v=ibugG89odt0). Typically, these images emphasized women's domestic duties and caring responsibilities, portraying them in much more limited ways than their male counterparts. For example, Courtney and Whipple's (1983) study of advertising revealed that women were more likely to be depicted in non-professional roles, whereas men were usually portrayed as professionals. In addition to being shown as wives, mothers, or sex objects (and sometimes all three), they were often represented as dependent on men and associated with more frivolous concerns than men. Famous American sociologist Erving Goffman (1976) undertook an extensive study of gendered advertising portrayals in his book *Gender Advertisements*, exposing the many ways that representations reinforced male superiority. Among the many subtle differences in male and female advertising representations, Goffman's study highlighted that men were characterized as confident and in charge of social situations, whereas women were shown as vulnerable and submissive.

Responding to these critiques, as well as the need to keep pace with the spending power of women, advertisers began to move away from such stereotypical framings in the 1980s. Images of female empowerment began to proliferate as advertising sought to win the pocketbooks of professional women. There was also a concomitant development of increasingly image-conscious male markets (e.g. male beauty products and brands) that required more nuanced portrayals of masculinities as, for example, the 'metrosexual', a heterosexual male who likes fashion and shopping (Mort 1996). Today, billboards, magazines, and social media abound with so many messages of female empowerment that we might be forgiven for daring to think we have really reached a postfeminist era.

Not so, however, and studies continue to show that despite the lip-service paid to female empowerment, many problems still remain. Often empowerment is equated with a sexual license – the infamous television series *Sex and the City* typifies this position – that continues to put the emphasis on women's bodies. The 'carnal feminine' is a recurrent motif in advertising that portrays women as being at the mercy of their bodies' appetites, unable to resist the lures of consumption, especially guilty pleasures like chocolate (see Stevens and Maclaran 2008).

The first feminist voices to emerge in the 1990s from within consumer research are good examples of these principles in action. They critically re-analyzed many of the major propositions and assumptions about consumers that were canonized in the marketing literature and revealed their underlying masculinist biases (Costa 1991; Fischer and Bristor 1994; Hirschman 1993). These scholars exposed the patriarchal assumptions embedded in consumer research and in conceptions of marketer/consumer relationships. They unveiled how marketing relied upon masculinist discourses. A discourse is a body of text meant to communicate specific data, information, and knowledge. All discourse is partial in its point of view, and is in this sense biased. Further, because discourse is biased in this way, all discourse implies certain power relationships. Production, associated with masculinity and the public domain, was accorded superior value to consumption, associated with femininity and the private sphere. For example, marketing strategies presented the customer in a *feminized position* – being seduced, targeted, or penetrated (in the case of market expansion). And consumer research adopted a *machine metaphor*, to convey how consumers processed information during purchase decision-making. This model – based on input (information)/output (final choice) – privileged reason over emotions and mind over body (Joy and Venkatesh 1994).

To understand why reason and the mind are considered superior to emotions and the body, we need to explore how discourse reflects and reproduces masculine power via implicit meanings. A feminist analysis reveals how binary oppositions (masculinity/femininity, mind/body, reason/emotion, culture/nature, active/passive, etc.) rely on each other for their meaning – so being masculine depends on not being feminine; to appear rational you should not be emotional, and so forth. Historically, masculine attributes are privileged over feminine ones. Hence, stereotypical masculinity is usually associated with the mind, reason, culture, and activity, whereas femininity is usually associated with the body, emotion, nature, and passivity. These gender biases are often encoded in consumer culture representations and practices. For example, Holt and Thompson (2004) illustrate how brands like Apple, Harley–Davidson, and Nike embody masculine ideals that enable men to feel like 'men-of-action heroes' when their identity is otherwise under threat. Likewise, the American Girl brand draws from ideals of traditional femininity that emphasize female bonding and caring for others (Diamond et al. 2009). Sometimes too, these dichotomies are not straightforward, as in the case of the recurrent man-in-nature theme that associates nature with being a character-building challenge (i.e., white water rafting or mountain climbing). However, this is often about mastery of nature, as in Belk and Costa's (1998) mountain man study where participants reenact 19th-century fur trade rendez-vous and celebrate a trapper existence that was ultimately about killing animals for their hides.

Feminist scholars in CCT seek to reveal that *gender boundaries are fluid* with many resultant masculinities and femininities that challenge the male and female stereotyping we have just seen in the preceding examples, as well as many of the taken-for-granted norms in a heteronormative society, that is, a society that categorizes people as female or male with expectations of how each sex should behave. In this respect, Judith Butler has proved a useful theorist with her concept of *gender performativity*, which highlights the fluid nature of gender and sexuality. Butler (1990, 1993) argues that gender is continuously recreated through our actions and words, and these acts construct and perform gender identities. If we adhere to society's gender norms (i.e., masculine behaviors for men, feminine behaviors for women, and opposite sex desire) we reinforce the status quo, but if we challenge the repetition of these norms in some way (female aggression, male caring, lesbian/gay desire, etc.) then change to these norms may eventually come about. Compliance or inversion of said gender norms can occur at both the consumer and the marketer level. Through their decisions, marketers can also contribute to challenge gender norms. Dove's *Real Beauty* campaign, for example, challenged cultural expectations that women should continuously strive to be sexually desirable for men. In the early 2000s, Jean Paul Gaultier less successfully attempted to push a make-up line for men that rebelled against established models of masculinity. A decade later, the agender revolution has revamped the same issue with a much stronger impact on consumer preferences. CCT researchers have also used Butler in studying new masculinities (Brownlie and Hewer 2007; Schroeder and Zwick 2004) and alternative femininities (Martin et al. 2006; Stevens et al. 2015; Tuncay Zayer et al. 2012). Following Butler, Üstüner and Thompson (2015) explored how women used the discourses and practices of roller derby to perform a mode of femininity that challenged traditional norms and expectations. They showed how performing this derby grrrl identity helped women to transform attitudes and predisposition that had been formed through their upbringing as children. These derby grrrls used their public performances of an alternative gender identity to subtly challenge constraining gender norms and expectations that held sway in their communities, through a process the authors characterized as ideological edgework (an analogy with the edgework undertaken by skydivers who push the boundaries of their skills without crossing into the sphere of uncontrollable risk).

Ecofeminism is another fruitful theoretical perspective in relation to environmental issues and also in challenging binary ways of thinking that devalue the feminine. Ecofeminism focuses on the connections between women, the body, and nature. Ecofeminism shows that the devaluation of the feminine is also manifest in the belief that mankind has dominion over nature (Gaard 1993; Plumwood 1993). This perceived superiority legitimizes a human-centered worldview that sees the environment as a free resource to be destroyed in the service of industry. Ecofeminism seeks to change this human-centered outlook and instead proposes an ecocentric framework that views humans and nature as intimately connected and interdependent. Stevens, Kearney, and Maclaran (2013) took an ecofeminist lens to critique marketing communications that attribute human characteristics to animals, usually in a playful or humorous way. Looking specifically at dairy industry advertisements featuring cows, they explore how cow images are often endowed with human properties such as feminized facial expressions and the ability to speak or dance (for great examples of this see The Laughing Cow's most famous cheese commercials: www.youtube.com/watch?v=EaHhnvZbkgs). Although such advertising is highly amusing and engaging, it also reinforces a narrative of human superiority and a mastery of nature, which masks the animals' often inhumane treatment by the dairy industry.

Contrary to feminist perspectives that are used to critique marketing activities, Linda Scott (2005) and colleagues (Scott et al. 2015) demonstrate how the market can be used for feminist objectives, specifically women's empowerment in poor rural communities in Africa and Bangladesh. [Linda's blog at www.doublexeconomy.com more thoroughly illustrates her view of how consumption can be used to create a global network of women that supports economic development in underdeveloped areas. For example, she discusses in detail how poor women in South Africa lifted themselves out of poverty by becoming Avon representatives.]

Masculinity

As per femininity, consumer researchers' definitions of masculinity are often discordant. We discuss three contrasting theoretical positions on masculinity: (1) essentialism, (2) role congruency theory, and (3) CCT. Essentialism and role congruency theory are both keen to define masculinity as a system of culturally shared beliefs about what it means to be a man and how a man should act, feel, think (Easthope 1990; McKelley 2011),

---

Box 8.2: Critical Reflection

Gendered marketing segmentation

Blue is for boys, pink is for girls is pretty much a given in Western countries. Yet, this gendered color coding only became pronounced from the 1950s onwards, mainly on account of marketers' seeking new market opportunities. Indeed, a century ago, pink was often associated with boys. According to the advice of American *Earnshaw's* trade magazine for children's wear in 1918: 'The generally accepted rule is pink for the boys, and blue for the girls. The reason is that pink, being a more decided and stronger color, is more suitable for the boy, while blue, which is more delicate and dainty, is prettier for the girl' (Paoletti 2012).

Associations with masculinity and femininity – and, therefore, what it means to be masculine or feminine – change across cultures as well as over distinct historical periods. Consider how 16th-century fashion for noblemen in Britain would appear completely ridiculous today with frilly accessories such as ruffs worn under the neck, decorative brooches in their hats with upturned brims and knee-length puffy trousers.

As our brief examples indicate, marketers have long treated gender as a key demographic variable to segment markets and have often been accused of contributing to gender stereotyping by emphasizing (or even constructing) gender differences rather than similarities. Much early (pre-1990s) consumer research scholarship was based on comparative studies between men and women to elaborate variations in purchasing behaviors or product usage. Primarily influenced by psychology, researchers typically explored how sex role norms impacted both family and individual decision-making (i.e., Meyers-Levy 1988) or developed scales based on Bem's (1974) sex-role inventory (used to assess the extent a person identifies with masculine and feminine characteristics and gender roles) to better understand gender identity and its effect on choice of particular products and their associated routines. Still in evidence today and often stereotyping masculine and feminine traits, this research remains at a superficial level, silent on the reasons for perceived variances between the sexes and, indeed, often contributing to them as in the above example.

and – we add – consume. *Essentialism* states that men's behavioral specificities depend on men's and women's biological differences (Cohen 2009). In doing so, scholars from this tradition identify different sets of functional (e.g. 'breadwinner' role), physical (e.g. athleticism and force), and sexual (e.g. aggression) traits that distinguish men from women (McKelly 2011). Critics of essentialism, however, charge that it conflates gender roles and biological sex, and ultimately generates a body of knowledge that Fischer (2015) labels as 'sex difference research'. Essentialist consumer researchers have theorized about the effects of high levels of the testosterone hormone, a typical male trait, on a variety of market behaviors. For example, Nepomuceno and colleagues (2016) showed how testosterone affects romantic gift-giving choices. The same biology-is-destiny, hormonal explanations are also applied to women, such as studies that women's ovulation cycle affects their market behaviors and purchase preferences (Durante et al. 2011; Wang and Griskevicius 2014).

Role congruency theory (Eagly and Karau 2002) relies upon sociology instead of biology, and argues that social approval is granted when gender roles are coupled with other social roles. For example, the masculine role is usually associated with the position of being the 'leader', a social role seen as opposite to femininity. If role congruency theory acknowledges the social construction of gender roles, it nonetheless remains normative since established gender roles are not to be questioned if a man/woman wants to receive social approval. The notion of 'hegemonic masculinity' – the 'most honored way of being a man' (Connell and Messerschmidt 2005: 832) – clearly illustrates the point. Hegemonic masculinity is the set of behaviors and practices that grant social dominance to men. The more a man deviates from said behaviors, the less he is likely to maintain social power. Prescribed behaviors also include specific consumption patterns that we expect from men who want to dominate the social order (i.e., being in line with hegemonic masculine standards). Consumer scholars have extensively documented the effects of hegemonic masculinity on consumption showing that social expectations about masculinity affect consumers' advertising response (e.g. men's response to male body representations in advertisements; Elliott and Elliott 2005); disposal of consumer goods (e.g. frequency of clothing disposal; Lang et al. 2013); interest in products (e.g. a metaphoric link between meat and masculinity; Rozin et al. 2012); consumer experiences (e.g. multisensory gendered interactions; Krishna et al. 2010); shopping behaviors (Otnes and McGrath 2001); and even brand preferences.

For example, Avery (2012) showed how gender roles, and transgressions of their normative expectations, could create fragmentation and dissension within a community of brand owners. She focused on the tension between male owners of Porsche sports cars and the new faction of women consumers who entered the brand community after the launch of its first SUV, the Porsche Cayenne. The backdrop to this tension is that the Porsche brand had historically catered to men and was culturally coded as a highly masculine brand. After the introduction of the Cayenne, male owners of Porsche sports cars defined themselves as the ingroup and cast women owners as the outgroup. To explain, ingroup/outgroup identities relate to the representations of people belonging/external to a given community that members of that community hold. In the case of Porsche, male owners took it as a cultural given that they had an exclusive (gendered) right to drive and own Porsches, whereas outgroup female were only granted a legitimate role in the community as passengers (but not as drivers or owners). In light of these established social expectations, role congruency theory provides explanations for Porsche's challenge in launching its Cayenne SUV, its first model overtly targeting the female market (the so-called 'soccer moms'). For these male owners, this Cayenne launch was seen as a transgression of the dominant gender and social roles within the Porsche community or, from a marketing perspective, as a breach of the Porsche's masculine brand image.

In line with role congruity theory, CCT research acknowledges that masculinity is socially constructed, and thus exposed to constant transformations. CCT research thus rejects essentialist interpretations of masculinity, and of gender more broadly. As such, masculinity is never natural and always cultural. In contrast to role congruity theory, however, CCT challenges the idea of hegemonic masculinity in various ways. First, CCT researchers highlight that masculinity and gender roles are time- and space-specific. It means that various hegemonic masculinities may exist and differ across eras and cultures

(McKelley 2011). If we think of the social acceptance of men wearing skirts, this fashion norm can shift over time – think of ancient soldiers' military apparel – and locale, as the Scottish tradition of kilts clearly illuminates. Second, CCT research also shows that men, either individually or collectively, can proactively resist hegemonic norms and instigate changes in gender roles. For example, men have actively challenged models of parenting that frame childcare and domestic tasks, like preparing family meals, as women's work, giving rise to new categories such as at-home dads (Coskuner-Balli and Thompson 2013; Gregory and Milner 2011). For all these reasons, CCT research emphasizes the concept of *masculinities*, rather than the singular masculinity, to acknowledge the plurality of gender role models that men can use as reference points in their gender performances.

To this point, we have discussed how masculinity has been conceptualized from the perspectives of essentialism and role congruity theory and then clarified how CCT research on masculinity differs from these two perspectives. Now, we will discuss this CCT research stream in more detail. The first and perhaps most well established research stream addresses *gender identity projects and masculinity/ies*. For example, Holt and Thompson (2004) discussed how American men experienced emasculation through historically rapid socio-economic marginalization. Metaphorically, emasculation relates to any conditions that make a man feel diminished in his masculinity ('less man', so to say). The socio-economic marginalization Holt and Thompson refer to arises from men's loss of their breadwinner role, an identity threat that they try to compensate by using specific products to perform the role of 'man-of-action hero'. This role is built on tensions between the two opposite US male myths of the 'breadwinner' and the 'rebel'. Also focused on identity threats, Lai, Lim, and Higgins' (2015) worked on singleness in Britain. They demonstrated that singleness is always culturally pathologized, meaning that the state of being unmarried is often seen as a cultural deviance from a dominant cultural norm (i.e., a married heterosexual couple with children). However, the social construction of masculinity in the UK still renders male singleness as less negative (imagine the 'carefree bachelor') than women's singleness, which is constructed as abject and forlorn (imagine the 'Bridget Jones' character, for instance). This research stream has further shown that social class standing influences the ways in which men interpret and use brands and consumption practices in constructing their masculine identities. For example, upper-class versus working-class men interpret Do-It-Yourself (DIY) work differently, and respectively either as a therapy to intellectual work or as a duty to accomplish their masculine 'family steward' role (Moisio et al. 2013). Similarly, working-class men tend to fully embrace the machismo images conveyed by Harley–Davidson motorcycles – incorporating it into their collectively shared idea of legitimate masculinity – whereas professional-class Harley bikers tend to deploy these macho meanings in a more ironic fashion that signals the playful and escapist nature of their weekend warrior persona (Schouten and McAlexander 1995).

A second stream of studies analyzes *the construction and performance of masculinity within specific consumption and/or life domains*. On the one hand, we find works focusing on 'typical' masculine consumption domains, as per DIY house maintenance (Moisio et al. 2013) or the commercial fur trapping activity and trade, which reached their peak during the first half of the 19th century in the Rocky Mountain American West. Though this historical era is long past, the myth of the 'mountain man' (Belk and Costa 1998) survives through recurrent gatherings that re-enact an idealized version of this lifestyle and its portrayal of an authentic, rugged masculinity. In this regard, the mountain man myth also represents a masculine archetype, built upon a willingness to confront dangers, isolation, and the character-building challenges of life in the wilderness. This archetype enjoys considerable cultural and commercial resonance as illustrated by the iconic brand figure of the Marlboro man, or Leonardo DiCaprio's academy award winning portrayal of the 19th-century frontiersman Hugh Glass in *The Revenant* (2015).

On the other hand, some of this research also investigates how men negotiate new gender roles by undertaking consumption practices culturally coded as 'feminine'. In this regard, men doing domestic foodwork (i.e., activities related to the preparation of food for family members) has attracted substantial attention (Newcombe et al. 2012). Preparing and serving food in a domestic/familial context is a caring practice (think of the anthropological meaning of breast feeding), and thus associated with femininity. Klasson and Ulver (2015) show that men actively involved in domestic foodwork may thus feel their masculinity at risk. Sometimes they react by seeking to masculinize these practices. Whereas women's act of cooking is associated with caring and providing sustenance to family members, men instead undertake cooking to express technical mastery (i.e., cooking is a quasi-scientific task), to display performative and creative skills (i.e., cooking becomes a spectacle), and even athletic control (i.e., cooking is a physically challenging task). Indeed, this masculinized image of cooking aligns with the communication strategies advertisers use to represent men in food commercials, when targeting a male market segment. In some cases, however, men may consciously reject stereotypical associations between foodwork and femininity (i.e., cooking is '*not* women's stuff') as a way to enact an alternative masculinity that disavows patriarchal stereotypes.

Fashion consumption and discourses have also attracted interest among CCT researchers. Men's interest in fashion and consumption of fashion products has reached new cultural heights in recent decades, with the 1990s being a key inflection point driven by the twin forces of changing gender norms and aggressive marketing of men's fashion and grooming products. However, a calculated fashionability has long been a defining trait among certain factions of upper-class men (e.g. aristocrats, dandies). Beyond elites, men's attention to fashion has long been associated with homosexuality. In fact, the word *metrosexual* was created in the mid-1990s to highlight a social transformation that saw an increasing number of heterosexual men overtly engage in personal grooming, body enhancement, and fashion-addiction (Rinallo 2007).

A third stream of CCT research deals with *gender inequalities and the strategies that can be put in place to ameliorate them* (Fischer 2015). As per whiteness in ethnic research, consumer researchers have generally assumed that masculinity occupies the dominant position in most social arrangements (see Chapters 6, 7, and 9 on global culture, class, and race and ethnicity, respectively). As such, scholars interested in gender inequalities have usually focused more on the plight of women/femininity than on men/masculinity. Nevertheless, masculinity can also be at socio-cultural risk. First, sociological research has recurrently discussed men's 'emasculation': that is, a symbolic loss of patriarchal power and once taken-for-granted masculine privileges that have accompanied trends toward greater gender-based equity and, most particularly, women gaining a foothold in professions that had once been almost exclusive male domains. These social changes are often interpreted as having led to the 'femininization' of contemporary culture (Douglas 1977). Second, non-heterosexual orientations can also threaten hegemonic masculinity, as research on gay men has shown (Visconti 2008). The documented coexistence of 'typically masculine' and 'typically feminine' behaviors in some gay men – what Kates defines as 'gender (in)flexibility (2002) – helps increase the porosity across established gender roles. The fact that (homosexual) men may combine masculine and feminine traits in fact challenges patriarchal representations of masculinity. Third, research has analyzed the ambivalence and identity tensions that arise when men participate in consumption/life domains that have been generally regarded as feminine spheres (as in the previously noted examples of fashion, foodwork, or parenting). When entering such feminized domains, men perform 'gender tourism' (Thompson and Holt 2004), an expression used to identify men's exploration of formerly feminine consumption and life spheres. 'Femininization' of contemporary culture, gender (in)flexibility, and gender tourism all destabilize the normative foundations of hegemonic masculinity and its restrictive definitions of what it means to be a real man. Companies can benefit from both providing men with symbolic resources that help them to play at being manly (think of razors, distinctively targeting men, separate from women) or to instead expand men's legitimate gendered behaviors (think of brands such as Nivea providing men with grooming products and self-care meanings formerly reserved for women).

LGBTQ

The majority of consumer research on sexuality focuses on non-heterosexual consumers, a phenomenon of note, particularly in terms of the framing of LGBTQ (i.e., lesbian, gay, bisexual, transgender, and queer) consumers as other-than-the-norm. Much of the research within that framing has investigated (white, middle-class) gay men and less so, lesbian women. This pattern mirrors LGBTQ portrayals in advertising and marketing that largely promotes *heteronormativity* (the assumption that sex between men and women is the only norm) and *homonormativity* (the assumption that the norm for non-heterosexual relationships is between gay white men, often middle class, often in a stable monogamous relationship) through portrayals of what has been called 'domesticized gayness' (Nölke 2018). That is, a version of being LGBTQ that does not unsettle the mainstream audience, or cause negative reactions. The dominance of a particular portrayal of non-heterosexuality subtly makes other types of non-heterosexuality invisible, and perhaps more stigmatized.

LGBTQ research, as it relates to marketing, consumer research, and CCT, has four main themes (Ginder and Byun 2015; Heejung and Olson 2014). The first (and most extensively researched) theme addresses *gay/lesbian/hetero consumer responses to advertising representations of gay and lesbian lifestyles*. These studies encompass such work as: analyses of gay/lesbian ads (Um 2012); the ways in which advertisers invoke multiple gender meanings and symbols in advertisements that target both LGBTQ and straight consumers (Dotson et al. 2009); gay and lesbian responses to gay-oriented ads (Oakenfull 2007, 2013a); how heterosexual consumers respond to gay-targeted ads (Angelini and Bradley 2010; Borgerson et al. 2006); and, advertising strategies for gay/lesbian consumers (Oakenfull and Greenlee 2004; Oakenfull et al. 2008).

Second, research has examined *consumer behavior and attitudes of gay and lesbian consumers* (Reilly and Rudd 2016) in regard to purchasing decisions of lesbian households (Wilkes and Laverie 2007); gay/lesbian evaluations of corporations (Oakenfull 2013b); and, the viability of the gay/lesbian market segment (Fugate 1993).

Third, research explores *linkages between gay identity and consumption* (Clarke and Smith 2015) including studies on gay community brand relationships (Kates 2000, 2004); gay consumption subcultures (Haslop et al. 1998; Kates 2004; Rudd 1996; Visconti 2008); gay fashion consciousness (Clarke and Smith 2015; Sha et al. 2007); gay shopping behavior and influence factors (Cotner and Burkley 2013; Peñaloza 1996; Reilly and Rudd 2006); and, the gay market (Branchik 2002; Keating and McLoughlin 2005).

The fourth theme relates to *commercial landscapes where LGBTQ consumers are the primary customer group* and the ones who establish and control the ambiance (e.g. LGBTQ bars and clubs); gay scene service encounters (Haslop et al. 1998; Bettany and Rowe 2015); LGBTQ tourism (Coon 2012; Hughes 2002; Melián-Gonzáles et al. 2011); and, analyses of Pride events (Ammaturo 2016; Kates 2003; Kates and Belk 2001). Other studies in this stream have investigated the contrasting case where gay/lesbian consumers confront marketplace discrimination (Heejung and Olson 2014; Walsh 2009; Walters and Moore 2002).

We may note three contemporary developments within the debates around LGBTQ consumers and CCT. The first relates to what has been characterized as the *'dream market'* of LGBTQ consumers (Peñaloza 1996; Oakenfull 2007). Marketers have been quick to develop new market opportunities in response to growing acceptance, and often glamorizing of LGBTQ consumers. Some within the LGBTQ community, however, feel that such strategic actions are exploitative, and that LGBTQ politics has been hijacked for corporate profits. The burgeoning cultural acceptance of homosexuality, including developments such as the legalization of same-sex marriage (Walters and Moore 2002) has also inspired consumer research on reframing of the gay market by corporate America (Ragusa 2005) and the mainstreaming of homosexual identities, stereotypes, and aesthetics (Clarke and Smith 2015; Clarke and Turner 2007), through film and popular media representations (Kates 2002).

This mainstreaming (or 'gaystreaming') focuses on white, middle-class gay men creates an interesting situation for marketers, as the stigma of being LGBTQ reduces for this highly sought after group, then that part of a person's identity may become less relevant to the consumer choices they make (Oakenfull 2013a). This thereby reduces marketers' ability to define and target them as a segment of consumers. However, thinking about this situation in the context of the argument above, that LGBTQ portrayals are largely homonormative, makes an interesting context for marketers trying to attract consumers across the whole gamut of LGBTQ identities. Do they target smaller and finer segments based on different LGBTQ categories or do they continue to largely target the stereotypical white, affluent, gay male segment?

The second area CCT scholars consider relates to the *binary model of gender and sexuality*. In other words the assumption that there are two genders, male and female, and that non-heterosexual activity or relationships are either between two men or between two women (Clarke et al. 2012). This dominant idea about who does LGBTQ sex with whom means LGBTQ identities not fitting this binary assumption (such as bisexual and transgender/transsexual) are rendered largely invisible. CCT researchers have argued that this contributes to new consumer discrimination and vulnerabilities (Bettany and Rowe 2015; Oakenfull 2013a). The recent emergence of new understandings of fluid (i.e., not fixed as male or female) gender and of non-monosexuality (i.e., people who identify as attracted to more than one or all genders) further complicates the picture of non-heterosexuality for the marketer and consumer researcher. For example, without showing or alluding to sexual activity directly, how might marketers communicate that a person in a visual advertisement is bisexual?

A third area of interest in LGBTQ research concerns the *structures through which sexuality is understood, researched, and theorized*. In other words, how do we think about LGBTQ consumers as a socio-cultural group? Researchers have tended to talk about groups of LGBTQ consumers as a type of 'subculture' (Haslop et al. 1998; Kates 2004; Rudd 1996; Visconti 2008) or an LGBTQ 'community' (Haslop et al. 1998). Although this research has undoubtedly been valuable in helping understand LGBTQ consumers, in contemporary consumer culture thinking about LGBTQ consumers as a subculture or community may overlook the diversity among LGBTQ consumers. For example, the subcultural frame implies that LGBTQ consumers' cultural aesthetics, tastes, and identity practices are relatively

homogeneous (Brewis and Jack 2010). This presumed uniformity has already been challenged by consumer researchers, as outlined in the previous two sections. So how might
consumer researchers think about LGBTQ consumers as a cultural or social group? CCT
provides different theories of how and why groups form that could be used to address
this question. For example, social movement theory provides insights into how disparate
individuals organize temporarily around a particular cause or event. This framework could
be used to understand LGBTQ Pride events (Ammaturo 2016), where people who identify
broadly as non-heterosexual or as 'allies' (people who are not LGBTQ themselves but support LGBTQ politics) join together to celebrate alternative identities, politics, and activities.

CONCLUSION

Our discussion illustrates the general point that at any stage in human history sex-related
traits (i.e., man/woman and male/female) have been loaded with socio-cultural meanings
that shape how we understand our gender identity and frame expectations about appropriate gender behaviors (i.e., gender roles). This condition holds true for global consumer
culture as in other cultures and historical periods and places. We have documented the
transient nature of gender categories, suggesting that they constantly if slowly change
under the conjunction of individual performance (Butler 1990) and macro level forces,
including the way marketers strategically use gender. Historically, some groups have been
more vulnerable to gender-based discrimination and institutional biases than others,
such as women and LGBTQ people today. However, as research on vulnerable masculinities has shown, all social groups including heterosexual men, can be disadvantaged by
dominant gender norms (e.g. Robert 2009; Thompson and Holt 2004; Molander et al.
forthcoming). Former discussion on gender tourism (Thompson and Holt 2004) clearly
highlights the point. On the other hand, socially marginalized gender groups can still
wield collective power, as the feminist and LGBTQ movements demonstrate (Catterall
et al. 2000; Peñaloza 1996). Pride parades have historically claimed LGBTQ rights and par-
ity in social life. Political battles that have resulted in women gaining the right to vote or
homosexual couples to legally marry or adopt children also testify to dominated gender
groups' active role and power.

Consumption and markets – or, in an embodied phrasing, consumers, marketers, and
their institutions – largely collaborate in the making of gender, for good and for bad. They
can reinforce privileged positions and heighten social injustice or conversely ameliorate
inequality and empower marginal gender groups (Fischer 2015). Sometimes, these effects
are ambivalent. For example, a gay club can make LGBTQ people feel secure, provide
them with 'market citizenship' (i.e., the right to exist in the market), and thus support
their social acceptance (Kates 2003). Yet, a gay club can also increase ghettoization (i.e.,
spatial and social segregation) and thus stigmatization (i.e., shame). In sum, this chapter

proves that marketing decisions invoking, mobilizing or targeting gender always entail social and political effects, thus making gender a particularly sensitive terrain of market action. While more research is still needed (see below), it is fundamental to ask who gains and who loses from marketing decisions that affect gender structures (see Box 8.3), and how those consequences can be better balanced.

Box 8.3: Critical Reflection

To whom are gender distinctions useful?

Classifying is not only inevitable but potentially useful. As Bowker and Star show (2000: 319), 'classifications are powerful technologies' that help organize world complexity, advance knowledge, and orient action. At the same time, classifications imply approximation, are socially constructed, and need to change over time. Remember that gender classifications imply a combination of cultural, ethical, moral, political, and sometimes legal traits, which historical analysis best allows to unravel. When used normatively, gender classifications inevitably lead to personal/social costs. For example, the classification of women has impacted their representation in advertising (see Box 8.1) and constrained their market roles. Among other discriminations, banks and credit card companies are known for having pursued discriminatory lending practices for women (Kendig 1973). Likewise, men have been privileged in various market and social domains, but almost marginalized in others (e.g. fashion, food-work, and parenting). Homosexuality has long been classified as a disease – only in 1973 the American Psychiatric Association and in 1990 the World Health Organization removed homosexuality from the list of mental disorders. In 2017, more than 70 countries still have anti-LGBTQ laws.

Who benefits from gender categorizations, though? Recipients are countless. First, the groups that hold dominant social positions have a vested interest in maintaining established categorizations to defend their privileges. Paraphrasing Lipsitz's (2006) theory on interethnic dynamics, in the gender context, men are ideologically predisposed to defend their 'possessive investment in maleness' that has long granted privilege over women. Second, the group that is dominated may also benefit from using existing categorizations to signal a problem and contest orthodox categorizations. Think of LGBTQ Pride parades. By making LGBTQ gender identity salient, these people become visible to ask for fairer life and market conditions (Peñaloza 1996; Visconti 2008). Third, companies also benefit from gender categorizations. Although so-called big data analysis of consumer preferences and purchase patterns now facilitates segmentation strategies that are based on individual and household's measurable behaviors, marketers continue to heavily rely upon market segments that are based on rather coarse gender categories. This archaic circumstance testifies to marketers' will to maintain long-established gender roles to segment the market instead of questioning them. Additionally, companies can

(Continued)

(Continued)

develop gendered versions ('his' and 'hers' varieties) of their products to serve pre-sumed differences in men's and women's consumer needs, and thus multiply their market opportunities. Yet, this attempt can backfire on brands, as recently occurred to Bic with the disastrous launch of the new 'Bic for her' (see Ellen DeGeneres' hilarious reaction: www.youtube.com/watch?v=eCyw3prlWhc). That being said, companies can also benefit from the abolishment of gender categories, as the recent 'agender' move-ment illustrates (see Box 8.4).

Box 8.4: Extended Case Study

The agender consumer in fashion

The fashion industry is clearly organized on the basis of socio-demographic (typically, income, geography, and gender) and psychographic (i.e., lifestyles) criteria. To date, gen-der boundaries have played a particularly strong role, with fashion lines and fashion shows clearly distinguished between men and women. While maintaining these categorical dis-tinctions, the fashion industry has relentlessly contributed to the transformation of the cultural standards of masculinity and femininity. Over time men's representation in fashion has included the refined gentlemen of the 1950s, the hippy pacifist rebel of the 1960s, the macho of the 1980s, the minimalist adolescent male of the 1990s, and then the metro-sexual of the 2000s (now evolved into what has been labeled 'the spornosexual', a man with higher body self-consciousness).

Since 2014, we are potentially witnessing a major turnaround in the industry – maybe even in society? Only time will tell. Prada, the Italian fashion brand, heralded the so-called 'agender' transformation, which posits that the evolution of gender roles may lead to the absence of any gender identity at all. Being agender thus means being genderless. The revolutionary aspects are clear: the agender movement is not only modifying extant cultural meanings of being man/woman (i.e., ideas of masculinity/femininity) but radically dismantling them. With its traditional snobbish intellectual-ism, Prada subtly insinuated the ambiguity during the 2015 Spring/Summer menswear fashion show (see Blanks 2015). The show was focused on the reinterpretation of denim – a fabric they chose specifically for its gender-neutral connotations – with the goal of highlighting that what fits a man may also fit a woman, and vice versa. Men and women were walking the catwalk dressed alike; the soundtrack was from *Psychic TV*, an English band whose creative duo has spent years undergoing cosmetic surgery to become gender-neutral humans.

Following this example, many other fashion brands have joined the agender move-ment. In February 2015, Selfridges – the UK high-end department store – launched its first agender assortment (see www.selfridges.com/GB/en/features/articles/content/agender-the-conceptspace). Tellingly, the retailer brand subverted traditional category management logics by bringing garments of various fashion brands – originally separated in male/female lines – within the same agender department. In doing so, Selfridges asserted power over these distributed fashion brands (given the manipulation of the original gendered connotations) and explored 'the interplay' found in between the masculine and the feminine. The same year, Alessandro Michele became Creative Director at Gucci and started subverting male aesthetic codes. From its inception, his design for men has been regarded as a 'gender fluid' interpretation of male fashion. Bows, chiffon, embroidered shirts and silk night-gowns were literally diverted from the female wardrobe to enter that of his man. As a result of its double-digit growth, Michele's cultural revolution translated into commercial success. Masstige brands (i.e., brands positioned between luxury and mass-market) also joined the conversation. In 2015, the masstige brands Diesel launched the 'Gender Neutral' campaign and Abercrombie announced the adoption of gender-neutral fitting rooms in some of its stores (Columbus, Ohio, and Hong Kong, China). Subsequently, fast-fashion brands also went agendered, with Zara's 'Ungendered' line (2016) and H&M's 'Denim United' line (2017) respectively. Lastly, the South African modelling agency *My Friend Nad* (www.myfriendned.co.za/) has started representing agender models.

From a branding perspective, the 'agender turn' in fashion helps imbue a sense of uniqueness and cutting edge cultural relevance to a brand; it can stimulate brand advocacy in online and offline settings, and ultimately build brand preference. This branding strategy also provides significant economic advantages. From a producer perspective, integrating male and female fashion shows can dramatically cut costs (since a company can invest in one show instead of two) and – by bringing together men's and women's fashion – helps focus fashion commenters' attention on menswear, which typically receives less attention than womenswear. From a retailer perspective, the coming of an agender era would not only allow customers to buy from both male/female assortments, thereby favoring cross-selling, but also cut category management costs.

Questions

1. Should you advise a fashion brand on the agender movement, which opportunities and risks do you see for a brand? Under which conditions do you think that the agender movement may be more than a fad and thus justify a long-term marketing strategy?
2. How would your answer change should you compare Asian versus Western markets?
3. Now consider the depilation industry (in particular, razors). Do you think that there is also potential for an agender shift in this industry? Why or why not?

RESEARCH DIRECTIONS

There are many areas at the intersection of marketing and gender that invite further research. It is fair to say that extant work in CCT has focused most on issues of representation but there is much research on the role of consumption and markets in alleviating or contributing to gender injustice and global poverty. Feminist perspectives are also missing, as Hearn and Hein (2015) have highlighted, such as intersectional feminism that emphasizes how class, race and able-bodiedness intersect with gender. This research has the potential to further reinvigorate theorizations around gender and consumption.

In comparison to women/femininity, consumer research on men/masculinity is rarer. We thus invite further research on the domains where men are potentially more vulnerable. From a marketing perspective, this specifically refers to consumption domains that men are less likely to access due to socially established standards of masculinity. For example, in many countries, men remain quite hesitant to dye their hair for fear that such a practice will be perceived as vain (with its feminine connotations). Thus, men's internalized norms often contradict their desire to look younger or feel better. In seeking to develop the market for men's hair-coloring products and services, companies have struggled to overcome this cultural, gender-based barrier.

Research at the intersection of femininity and masculinity to explore contexts and forms of male/female collaboration that redress gender injustices is welcome. In conclusion and in line with our discussion, we encourage research on the suppression of gender-normative distinctions in language, behavior, and marketing practice, paying particular attention to the role that consumers and marketers can play in this regard.

There are many fruitful areas presenting themselves to researchers interested in LGBTQ and CCT. The first relates to the hyper-fragmentation (i.e., the high number) of identity categories around LGBTQ and gender. This pluralism poses unique problematics to researchers concerned with the link between identity and consumption, particularly where they make claims for their research to represent 'the LGBTQ community'. How this fragmentation interfaces with the politics of LGBTQ regarding the market is also of concern, particularly in the context of the growing legitimization and appropriation of (certain forms of) LGBTQ identity, by legal, market, and organizational structures. The differently experienced discriminations and vulnerabilities that emerge from marketers' construction of LGBTQ identities is also certainly worthy of examination and critique. Lastly, more research on characterizations of LGBTQ consumers as groups would be of value. Saying that LGBTQ consumers are part of a 'community' built on sexual orientation is misleading, since their inner heterogeneity undermines the very idea of community. New social theories could more effectively highlight the social links among LGBTQ consumers (such as assemblage, flat ontology, or social movement theories). To date, marketers have mostly represented the LGBTQ market as a community, yet other forms of representations could be more appropriate. Thus, this type of research would be of considerable benefit in helping marketers to improve their segmentation and targeting strategies. For example, a social movement perspective would suggest that what bonds LGBTQ consumers is not sharing a similar lifestyle (more consistent with a community-based perspective) but pursuing a common political agenda. Among others, Absolute Vodka has successfully adopted a social movement framework to target the LGBTQ market. Instead of positioning itself on a given lifestyle, Absolute Vodka has instead consistently supported equal rights and defended the value of diversity.

RECOMMENDED READING

Baker, Brian (2013) *Contemporary Masculinities in Film, Fiction and Television: Mobility, Trauma, Nation*. London: Bloomsbury Academics.

Catterall, Miriam, Maclaran, Pauline, and Stevens, Lorna (2000) *Marketing and Feminism: Current Issues and Research*. London: Routledge.

Ginder, Whitney, and Byun, Sang-Eun (2015) 'Past, present, and future of gay and lesbian consumer research: critical review of the quest for the queer dollar', *Psychology and Marketing, 32* (8): 821–41.

Hearn, Jeff and Hein, Wendy (2015) 'Reframing gender and feminist knowledge construction in marketing and consumer research: Missing feminisms and the case of men and masculinities', *Journal of Marketing Management, 31* (15–16): 1–55.

hooks, bell (2004) *The Will to Change: Men, Masculinity, and Love*. New York: Simon and Schuster.

REFERENCES

Ammaturo, F. R. (2016) 'Spaces of pride: A visual ethnography of gay pride parades in Italy and the United Kingdom', *Social Movement Studies, 15* (1): 19–40.

Angelini, J. R. and Bradley, S. D. (2010) 'Homosexual imagery in print advertisements: Attended, remembered, but disliked', *Journal of Homosexuality, 57* (4): 485–502.

Avery, J. (2012) 'Defending the markers of masculinity: Consumer resistance to brand gender-bending', *International Journal of Research in Marketing, 29* (4): 322–36.

Belk, R. W. and Costa, J. A. (1998) 'The Mountain Man myth: A contemporary consuming fantasy', *Journal of Consumer Research, 25* (3): 218–40.

Bem, S. L. (1974) 'The measurement of psychological androgyny', *Journal of Consulting and Clinical Psychology, 42* (2): 155–62.

Bettany, S. M. and Rowe, D. S. (2015) *The Politics of In/Appropriate/d Others: Moving Beyond the Vulnerable Consumer in the LGBT Market/Movement.* Chicago, IL: Macromarketing Conference.

Blanks, T. (2015) Spring 2015 Menswear – Prada. *Vogue* [online], 22 June. www.vogue.com/fashion-shows/spring-2015-menswear/prada.

Borgerson, J. L., Schroeder, J. E., Blomberg, B. B., and Thorssén, E. (2006) 'The gay family in the ad: Consumer responses to non-traditional families in marketing communications', *Journal of Marketing Management, 22* (9–10): 955–78.

Bowker, G. C. and Star, S. L. (2000) *Sorting Things Out: Classification and Its Consequences.* Boston, MA: MIT Press.

Branchik, B. J. (2002) 'Out in the market: A history of the gay market segment in the United States', *Journal of Macromarketing, 22* (1): 86–97.

Brewis, J. and Jack, G. (2010) 'Consuming chavs: The ambiguous politics of gay chauvinism', *Sociology, 44* (2): 251–68.

Brownlie, D. and Hewer, P. (2007) 'Prime beef cuts: Culinary images for thinking "men"', *Consumption Markets & Culture, 10* (3): 229–50.

Butler, J. (1990) *Gender Trouble: Feminism and the Subversion of Identity.* New York, NY: Routledge.

Butler, J. (1993) *Bodies That Matter: On the Discursive Limits of 'Sex'.* New York, NY: Routledge.

Cameron, L., Goetzmann, W. N., and Nozari, M. (2017) 'Art and gender: Market bias or selection bias?'. Yale Working Paper. Available at https://papers.ssrn.com/sol3/papers.cfm?abstract_id=3025923.

Catterall, M., Maclaran, P., and Stevens, L. (eds) (2000) *Marketing and Feminism: Current Issues and Research.* London: Routledge.

Clarke, V., Hayfield, N., and Huxley, C. (2012) 'Lesbian, gay, bisexual and trans appearance and embodiment: a critical review of the psychological literature', *Psychology of Sexualities Review, 3* (1): 51–70.

Clarke, V. and Smith, M. (2015) 'Not hiding, not shouting, just me': Gay men negotiate their visual identities', *Journal of Homosexuality, 62* (1): 4–32.

Clarke, V. and Turner, K. (2007) 'Clothes maketh the queer? Dress, appearance and the construction of lesbian, gay and bisexual identities', *Feminism and Psychology, 17* (2): 267–76.

Cohen, D. S. (2009) 'No boy left behind? Single-sex education and the essentialist myth of masculinity', *Indiana Law Journal, 84* (1): 135–88.

Connell, R. W. and Messerschmidt, J. W. (2005) 'Hegemonic masculinity: rethinking the concept', *Gender and Society, 19* (6): 829–59.

Coon, D. R. (2012) 'Sun, sand, and citizenship: The marketing of gay tourism', *Journal of Homosexuality, 59* (4): 511–34.

Coskuner-Balli, G. and Thompson, C. J. (2013) 'The status costs of subordinate cultural capital: At-home fathers' collective pursuit of cultural legitimacy through capitalizing consumption practices', *Journal of Consumer Research, 40* (1): 19–41.

Costa, J. A. (ed.) (1991) *Proceedings of the First Conference on Gender, Marketing and Consumer Behaviour*. Salt Lake City, UT: University of Utah Printing Service.

Cotner, C. and Burkley, M. (2013) 'Queer eye for the straight guy: Sexual orientation and stereotype lift effects on performance in the fashion domain', *Journal of Homosexuality*, *60* (9): 1336–48.

Courtney, A.E. and Whipple, T.W. (1983) *Sex Stereotyping in Advertising*. Lexington, MA: Lexington Books.

Diamond, N., Sherry Jr, J. F., Muñiz Jr, A. M., McGrath, M. A., Dotson, R. V., Hyatt, E.M., and Petty Thompson, L. (2009) 'Sexual orientation and gender effects of exposure to gay- and lesbian-themed fashion advertisements', *Journal of Fashion Marketing and Management: An International Journal*, *13* (3): 431–47.

Dotson, Michael J., Eva M. Hyatt, and Lisa Petty Thompson (2009) 'Sexual Orientation and Gender Effects of Exposure to Gay-and Lesbian-themed Fashion Advertisements', *Journal of Fashion Marketing and Management: An International Journal*, 13 (3): 431–447.

Douglas, A. (1977) *The Feminization of American Culture*. New York: Farrar, Straus and Giroux.

Durante, K.M., Griskevicius, V., Hill, S.E., Perilloux, C., and Li, N.P. (2011) 'Ovulation, female competition, and product choice: Hormonal influences on consumer behavior', *Journal of Consumer Research*, *37* (6): 921–34.

Eagly, A.H. and Karau, S.J. (2002) 'Role congruity theory of prejudice toward female leaders', *Psychological Review*, *109* (3): 573–98.

Easthope, A. (1990) *What a Man's Gotta Do: The Masculine Myth in Popular Culture*. New York and London: Routledge.

Elliott, R. and Elliott, C. (2005) 'Idealized images of the male body in advertising: A reader-response exploration', *Journal of Marketing Communications*, *11* (1): 3–19.

Fischer, E. (2015) 'Towards more marketing research on gender inequality', *Journal of Marketing Management*, *31* (15–16): 1718–22.

Fischer, E. and Bristor, J. (1994) 'A feminist poststructuralist analysis of the rhetoric of marketing relationships', *International Journal of Research in Marketing*, *11* (4): 317–31.

Friedan, B. (1963) *The Feminine Mystique*. New York, NY: W.W. Norton and Co.

Fugate, D.L. (1993) 'Evaluating the U.S. male homosexual and lesbian population as a viable target market segment: A review with implications', *Journal of Consumer Marketing*, *10* (4): 46–57.

Gaard, G. (1993) 'Living interconnections with animals and nature', in *Ecofeminism: Women, Animals, Nature*, Philadelphia, PA: Temple University Press. pp. 1–12.

Ginder, W. and Byun, S.E. (2015) 'Past, present, and future of gay and lesbian consumer research: Critical review of the quest for the queer dollar', *Psychology and Marketing*, *32* (8): 821–41.

Goffman, E. (1976) *Gender Advertisements*. Cambridge, MA: Harvard University Press.

Gregory, A. and Milner, S. (2011) 'What is 'new' about fatherhood? The social construction of fatherhood in France and the UK', *Men and Masculinities*, *14* (5): 588–606.

Haslop, C., Hill, H., and Schmidt, R.A. (1998) 'The gay lifestyle – spaces for a subculture of consumption', *Marketing Intelligence and Planning, 16* (5): 318–26.

Hearn, J. and Hein, W. (2015) 'Reframing gender and feminist knowledge construction in marketing and consumer research: Missing feminisms and the case of men and masculinities', *Journal of Marketing Management, 31* (15–16): 1–55.

Heejung, R.H. and Olson, E.D. (2014) 'The effects of social justice and stigma–consciousness on gay customers' service recovery evaluation', *Journal of Business Research, 67* (6): 1162–9.

Hirschman, E.C. (1993) 'Ideology in consumer research 1980 and 1990: A Marxist and feminist critique', *Journal of Consumer Research, 19* (4): 537–55.

Holt, D. B. and Thompson, C. J. (2004) 'Man-of-action heroes: The pursuit of heroic masculinity in everyday consumption', *Journal of Consumer Research, 31* (2): 425–40.

Hughes, H. (2002) 'Gay men's holiday destination choice: A case of risk and avoidance'. *International Journal of Tourism Research, 4* (4): 299–312.

Joy, A. and Venkatesh, A. (1994) 'Postmodernism, feminism, and the body: The visible and the invisible in consumer research', *International Journal of Research in Marketing, 11* (4): 333–57.

Kates, S.M. (2000) 'Out of the closet and out on the street!: Gay men and their brand relationships', *Psychology and Marketing, 17* (6): 493–513.

Kates, S.M. (2002) 'The protean quality of subcultural consumption: An ethnographic account of gay consumers', *Journal of Consumer Research, 29* (3): 383–400.

Kates, S.M. (2003) 'Producing and consuming gendered representations: An interpretation of the Sydney gay and lesbian Mardi Gras', *Consumption Markets & Culture, 6* (1): 5–22.

Kates, S.M. (2004) 'The Dynamics of brand legitimacy: An interpretive study in the gay men's community', *Journal of Consumer Research, 31* (2): 455–64.

Kates, S.M. and Belk, R.W. (2001) 'The meanings of lesbian and gay pride day resistance through consumption and resistance to consumption', *Journal of Contemporary Ethnography, 30* (4): 392–429.

Keating, A. and McLoughlin, D. (2005) 'Understanding the emergence of markets: A social constructionist perspective on gay economy', *Consumption Markets & Culture, 8* (2): 131–52.

Kendig, D. (1973) 'Discrimination against women in home mortgage financing', *Yale Review of Law and Social Action, 3* (2): 166–80.

Klasson, M. and Ulver, S. (2015) 'Masculinising domesticity: An investigation of men's domestic foodwork', *Journal of Marketing Management, 31* (15–16): 1652–75.

Krishna, A., Elder, R., and Caldara C. (2010) 'Feminine to smell but masculine to touch? Multisensory congruence and its effect on the aesthetic experience', *Journal of Consumer Psychology, 20* (4): 410–18.

Lai, A.L., Lim, M., and Higgins, M. (2015) 'The abject single: Exploring the gendered experience of singleness in Britain', *Journal of Marketing Management, 31* (15–16): 1559–82.

Lang, C., Armstrong, C.M., and Brannon, L.A. (2013) 'Drivers of clothing disposal in the US: An exploration of the role of personal attributes and behaviours in frequent disposal', *International Journal of Consumer Studies*, 37 (6): 706–14.

Lipsitz, G. (2006) *The Possessive Investment in Whiteness. How White People Profit from Identity Politics*. Philadelphia, PA: Temple University Press.

Lynch, J. and Schuler, D. (1994) 'The matchup effect of spokesperson and product congruency: A schema theory interpretation',' *Psychology and Marketing*, 11 (5): 417–45.

Maclaran, P. and Kravets, O. (2018) 'Feminist perspectives in marketing: Past, present and future', in M. Tadajewski, M. Higgins, N. Dhlokia, J. Denigri-Knott, and R. Varman (eds), *The Routledge Companion to Critical Marketing*. London: Routledge.

Martin, D.M., Schouten, J.W., and McAlexander, J.H. (2006) 'Claiming the throttle: Multiple femininities in a hyper-masculine subculture', *Consumption Markets & Culture*, 9 (3): 171–205.

McKelley, R. (2011) 'Masculinity, social construction of', in *Encyclopedia of Women in Today's World*. Vol. 2., edited by M.Z. Stange, C.K. Oyster, and J.E. Sloan. Los Angeles, CA: Sage. pp. 904–6.

Melián-González, A., Moreno-Gil, S., and Araña, J.E. (2011) 'Gay tourism in a sun and beach destination', *Tourism Management*, 32 (5): 1027–37.

Meyers-Levy, J. (1988) 'The influence of sex roles on judgement', *Journal of Consumer Research*, 14 (4): 522–30.

Moisio, R., Arnould, E.J., and Gentry, J.W. (2013) 'Productive consumption in the class-mediated construction of domestic masculinity: Do-It-Yourself (DIY) home improvement in men's identity work', *Journal of Consumer Research*, 40 (2): 298–316.

Molander, S., Kleppe, I.A., and Östberg, J. (forthcoming) 'Hero shots: Involved fathers conquering new territory', *Consumption Markets & Culture*.

Mort, F. (1996) *Cultures of Consumption: Masculinities and Social Space in Late Twentieth Century Britain*. London: Routledge.

Nepomuceno, M.V., Saad, G., Stenstrom, E., Mendenhall, Z., and Iglesias, F. (2016) 'Testosterone at your fingertips: Digit ratios (2D: 4D and rel2) as predictors of courtship-related consumption intended to acquire and retain mates', *Journal of Consumer Psychology*, 26 (2): 231–44.

Newcombe, M.A., McCarthy, M.B., Cronin, J.M., and McCarthy, S.N. (2012) '"Eat like a man": A social constructionist analysis of the role of food in men's lives', *Appetite*, 59 (2): 391–8.

Nölke, A. (2018) 'Making diversity conform? An intersectional, longitudinal analysis of lgbt-specific mainstream media advertisements', *Journal of Homosexuality*, 65 (2): 224–55.

Oakenfull, G. (2007) 'Effects of gay identity, gender and explicitness of advertising imagery on gay responses to advertising', *Journal of Homosexuality*, 53 (4): 49–69.

Oakenfull, G. (2013a) 'Unraveling the movement from the marketplace: Lesbian responses to gay-oriented advertising', *Journal of Marketing Development and Competitiveness*, 7 (2): 57–71.

Oakenfull, G.W. (2013b) 'What matters: Factors influencing gay consumers' evaluations of "gay-friendly" corporate activities', *Journal of Public Policy and Marketing*, 32 (special issue): 79–89.

Oakenfull, G. and Greenlee, T. (2004) 'The three rules of crossing over from gay media to mainstream media advertising: Lesbians, lesbians, lesbians',' *Journal of Business Research*, 57 (11): 1276–85.

Oakenfull, G.K., MacCarthy, M.S., and Greenlee, T.B. (2008) 'Targeting a minority without alienating the majority: Advertising to gays and lesbians in mainstream media', *Journal of Advertising Research*, 48 (2): 191–8.

Otnes, C. and McGrath, M.A. (2001) 'Perceptions and realities of male shopping behavior', *Journal of Retailing*, 77 (1): 111–37.

Paoletti, J. (2012) *Pink and Blue: Telling the Boys from the Girls in America*. Indiana, IN: Indiana University Press.

Peñaloza, L. (1996) We're here, we're queer, and we're shopping! A critical perspective on the accommodation of gays and lesbians in the U.S. marketplace', *Journal of Homosexuality*, 31 (1/2): 9–41.

Plumwood, V. (1993) *Feminism and the Mastery of Nature*. London: Routledge.

Ragusa, A.T. (2005) 'Social change and the corporate construction of gay markets in the New York Times' Advertising Business News', *Media, Culture and Society*, 27 (5): 653–76.

Reilly, A. and Rudd, N.A. (2006) 'Is internalized homonegativity related to body image?', *Family and Consumer Sciences Research Journal*, 35 (1): 58–73.

Rinallo, D. (2007) 'Metro/fashion/tribes of men: Negotiating the boundaries of men's legitimate consumption', in B. Cova, R. Kozinets, and A. Shankar (eds), *Consumer Tribes: Theory, Practice, and Prospects*. Oxford: Elsevier. pp. 76–92.

Robert, William (2009) 'Masculinities and vulnerability: The solitary discourses and practices of African-Caribbean and white working-class fathers', *Men and Masculinities*, 11 (4): 441–61.

Rozin, P., Hormes, J.M., Faith M.S., and Wansink, B. (2012) 'Is meat male? A quantitative multimethod framework to establish metaphoric relationships', *Journal of Consumer Research*, 39 (3): 629–43.

Rudd, N.A. (1996) 'Appearance and self–presentation research in gay consumer cultures: Issues and impact', *Journal of Homosexuality*, 31 (1/2): 109–34.

Schouten, J.W. and McAlexander, J.H. (1995) 'Subcultures of consumption: An ethnography of the new bikers', *Journal of Consumer Research*, 22 (1): 43–61.

Schroeder, J.E. and Zwick, D. (2004) 'Mirrors of masculinity: Representation and identity in advertising images', *Consumption Markets & Culture*, 7 (1): 21–52.

Scott, L. (2005) *Fresh Lipstick: Redressing Fashion and Feminism*. New York, NY: Palgrave.

Scott, L., Dolan, C., and Steinfield, L. (2015) *Women's Empowerment through Access to Markets*. Case Study, University of Oxford. www.sbs.ox.ac.uk/sites/default/files/Research_Areas/Strategy_And_Innovation/Docs/mwedo–casestudy–final–may2015.pdf.

Sha, O., Aung, M., Londerville, J., and Raleston, C.E. (2007) 'Understanding gay consumers' clothing involvement and fashion consciousness', *International Journal of Consumer Studies, 31* (5): 453–9.

Stevens, L. and Maclaran, P. (2008) 'The carnal feminine: Women, advertising and consumption', in S. Borghini, M.A. McGrath, and C. Otnes (eds), *European Advances in Consumer Research*, Vol. 8. Duluth, MN: Association for Consumer Research. pp. 169–74.

Stevens, L., Cappellini, B., and Smith, G. (2015) 'Nigellissima: A study of glamour, performativity, and embodiment', *Journal of Marketing Management, 31* (5–6): 1–22.

Stevens, L., Kearney, M., and Maclaran, P. (2013) 'Uddering the other: Androcentrism, ecofeminism and the dark side of anthropomorphic marketing', *Journal of Marketing Management, 29* (1–2): 158–74.

Thompson, C. J. and Holt, D. B. (2004) 'How do men grab the phallus? Gender tourism in everyday consumption', *Journal of Consumer Culture, 4* (3): 313–38.

Tuncay Zayer, L., Sredl, K., Parmentier, M.-A., and Coleman, C. (2012) 'Consumption and gender identity in popular media: Discourses of domesticity, authenticity, and sexuality', *Consumption Markets & Culture, 15* (4): 333–57.

Um, N.H. (2012) 'Seeking the Holy Grail through gay and lesbian consumers: An exploratory content analysis of ads with gay/lesbian–specific content', *Journal of Marketing Communications, 18* (2): 133–49.

Üstüner, T. and Thompson, C.J. (2015) 'Women skating on the edge: Marketplace performances as ideological edgework', *Journal of Consumer Research, 42* (2): 235–65.

Visconti, L.M. (2008) 'Gays' market and social behaviors in (de)constructing symbolic boundaries', *Consumption Markets & Culture, 11* (2): 113–35.

Walsh, G. (2009) 'Disadvantaged consumers' experiences of marketplace discrimination in customer services', *Journal of Marketing Management, 25* (1/2): 143–69.

Walters, A.S. and Moore, L.J. (2002) 'Attention all shoppers, queer customers in aisle two: Investigating lesbian and gay discrimination in the marketplace', *Consumption Markets & Culture, 5* (4): 285–303.

Wang, Y. and Griskevicius, V. (2014) 'Conspicuous consumption, relationships, and rivals: Women's luxury products as signals to other women', *Journal of Consumer Research, 40* (5): 834–54.

Wilkes, R. E. and. Laverie, D. A. (2007) 'Purchasing decisions in non-traditional households: The case of lesbian couples,' *Journal of Consumer Behaviour, 6* (1): 60–73.

9
RACE AND ETHNICITY

Kevin D. Thomas, University of Texas at Austin
Samantha N.N. Cross, Iowa State University
Robert L. Harrison III, Western Michigan University

CHAPTER OVERVIEW

- Race and ethnicity are embedded within the broader construct of culture.
- Race and ethnicity are socially constructed with overlapping and distinctive qualities.
- In Western societies, the role of power helps distinguish race from ethnicity.
- Issues like colorism highlight the heterogeneity found in racial and ethnic categories.
- The relationship between race and market practices is understudied, particularly among white consumers.
- Intersectionality enables a more nuanced understanding of race and ethnicity to emerge.

INTRODUCTION

In popular press and even in dictionary definitions, the terms culture, race, and ethnicity are often used interchangeably, or as synonyms. Yet, while they all refer to socially constructed differentiating characteristics of a particular group or society, the motivations and implications behind these social constructions differ in markedly distinct ways. In particular, the construct of race focuses heavily on the visible, also called phenotypical characteristics of particular groups of people, as a way to identify, rank, differentiate, group and include/exclude. Ironically, while race, as a construct, has been shown to be the most superficial and least differentiating of the three social constructions mentioned, it is unarguably the most visible and historically, one of the most divisive marketplace discriminators. Yet, academic researchers who study consumer experiences, consumption behaviors, and consumer culture have delved deeply into both ethnicity and culture as influencers on consumption, while seemingly either discounting race or embracing it as a facet of ethnicity.

In this chapter, we tease race out from under the umbrella of ethnicity. We argue that, as a construct, race *does* function differently. Why? The notion of race had a different socio-historical purpose; creating hierarchy both in society and in the marketplace – all of which affect consumer culture. In fact, one can argue that race has historically been the construct most linked to the marketplace, since race as a hierarchical differentiator started there, with the need to economically and morally justify the trading of fellow human bodies; a market-driven motivation later rationalized by a social construction based on superficial but highly visible markers.

We also argue that the consumer researchers who have most attempted to expand our knowledge of the impact of race in the marketplace have primarily been those who focus on understanding consumer culture and consumer culture theory. Hence, this chapter focuses on the work of those researchers, researchers who have persevered over the past 50 years in studying race as a marketplace construct, tied to, but distinct from, that of ethnicity.

POSITIONING RACE AND ETHNICITY WITHIN THE BROADER CULTURAL LANDSCAPE

The concepts of race and ethnicity are overlapping, but distinct (Cross and Cross 2007). More specifically, we position culture as an overarching term that encompasses an array of interconnected involuntary and chosen social identities, such as race, ethnicity, gender, nationality, social class, and sexual orientation. Thus, in discussing issues of social identity development and market dynamics, it is essential to recognize that there are meaningful similarities and differences between racial, ethnic, and cultural identities.

Race

There exist two major ways of understanding the phenomenon of race: biological and socially constructed (Goldberg 1990; James 2012). The former positions race as an articulation of genetic and/or phenotypic, that is, visual, differences. Characteristics such as hair texture, skin color, eye shape, and bone structure are used to divide humans into distinct racial categories. While this perspective is not inherently hierarchical, historically this concept of race has supported a racialized social hierarchy placing whites at the top and blacks on the bottom of the metaphorical pyramid (Goldberg 1990). Research conducted since the late 20th century has greatly discredited the 'race as biology' theory. For instance, Witherspoon et al. (2007) demonstrates there is as much, if not more, genetic difference within racial categories as between them. Additionally, recent attempts to replicate the finding of Giles and Elliot's (1962) landmark skeletal remains study, wherein they were able to correctly identify 85% of the sample's racial background simply by examining differences in cranial configurations have been woefully unsuccessful. In four retest attempts the average identification rate dropped to 33% – the same as random chance given that the original study only included three racial categories.

As a consequence of these new realities, in 1998 the American Anthropological Association issued a statement refuting race as a biological construct, asserting:

> With the vast expansion of scientific knowledge in this century it has become clear that human populations are not unambiguous, clearly demarcated, biologically distinct groups ... we conclude that present-day inequalities between so-called 'racial' groups are not consequences of their biological inheritance but products of historical and con-temporary social, economic, educational, and political circumstances.

In essence, the American Anthropological Association's statement on race and the bio-genetic research upon which it emerged serves to reposition our understanding of race from a biological truth into a socially constructed reality.

The socially constructed approach characterizes race as a concept born of social institutions and practices (Graves 2002). Like other socially constructed concepts (e.g. gender, class, and sexuality), race is perceived as inherently slippery and political. Although it is represented as fixed and objectively real, the experience of race is fluid and context-specific. It is what Hall (Jhally 1997) termed a floating signifier. In other words, the concept of race is constantly subject to redefinition depending on the historical moment and the cultural context, and means different things to different people.

Biology is not absent from the socially constructed understanding of race. The body is still used to discern racial identity. Specifically, visible physical differences in skin tone, hair texture, and facial features act as the language from which the boundaries of racial categories are understood (Jhally 1997). However, the meaning placed upon visible physical differences and the racial boundaries they create are neither static nor universal. For instance, an African-decent individual with light-brown skin tone, wavy hair texture, and traditionally characterized 'fine' facial features could be racially categorized as black, colored, or multiracial across differing temporal and geographic contexts.

It is important to recognize that noting physical differences does not necessitate adherence to a hierarchical structure – difference can be perceived without privileging certain distinctions over others. However, the way value and meaning has historically been assigned to differing physical attributes has maintained a social hierarchy that favors individuals with particular characteristics, such as lighter skin, straighter hair, and finer facial features (James 2012). As such, a shared definition of race surfaces across both understandings of the concept. Regardless of the approach, race can be defined as a system of power and classification. Yet, unlike the largely debunked 'race as biology' theory, which renders inequities as unavoidable byproducts of biological composition, the more prevalent socially constructed theory, which situates inequities as consequences of socio-political conditions, provides the possibility for enacting compensatory change.

Ethnicity

The term ethnicity is often used to refer to people who share the same race but also share a set of traditions and customs that distinguish their ethnic groups from other ethnic groups within their racial group (Benet-Martínez 2012). Ethnicity is often determined by sharing a specific geographic location, religious identity, language, speech, and dress styles (Sanchez et al. 2014). For example, Chinese and Taiwanese are both categorized racially as Asian, but they practice different customs and languages and have distinct geographic origins that set the boundaries for identification with separate and distinguishable ethnic groups (Sanchez et al. 2009). Both ethnic and racial identities are connected to unique sets of customs, beliefs, practices, traditions, historical narratives, and cognitive styles that create the culture surrounding race/ethnic identities (Sanchez et al. 2014). These traditions represent the 'network of knowledge' passed down over generations of people and come to represent the meaning and self-understanding of ethnic cultural identities (Benet-Martínez 2012).

Within Western countries, the concept of race supports and produces hierarchical social/economic/cultural power relations, while ethnicity is predominantly a matter of choice and convenience (Cornell and Hartmann 2007). For example, marginalized individuals have had little choice about their racial or ethnic identification. While research suggests that in contemporary society, individuals have more choices regarding how to racially self-identify, e.g. as multiracial, black, or white (Rockquemore and Brunsma 2002), if an individual does not possess the phenotypic traits associated with their chosen racial identification, society is not likely to accept their choice of racial identification as true/authentic. However, historically, white individuals can view ethnicity as a 'symbolic identity' that can change through individual choice, with minimal social significance for their lives (Waters 1990).

Culture

Culture is typically viewed as a homogenous system of collectively shared meanings, ways of life, and unifying values shared by members of society. Consumer culture theory (CCT) researchers explore 'the heterogeneous distribution of meanings and the multiplicity of overlapping cultural groupings that exist within the broader socio-historic frame of globalization and market capitalism' (Arnould and Thompson 2005: 869). Thus, from a CCT perspective, culture can also be understood as a result of symbolic communication, with a group's skills, knowledge, attitudes, values, and motives all serving as key symbolic aspects of both in-group and out-group communication. The meanings of symbols are learned and deliberately perpetuated in a society through its institutions and artifacts. The essential core of culture consists of normalized ideas and the values attached to them. A given cultural system's beliefs and values will create a particular set of expected, taken-for-granted behaviors. Collectively, these habitual ways of behaving serve to distinguish the members of one cultural group from another. Existing (and presumed) racial and ethnic differences are two ways in which cultural distinctions are realized. Conversely, cultural differences are generally present within a given ethnic or racial classification. Figure 9.1 provides a visual representation of key sites of identity and related cultural attributes.

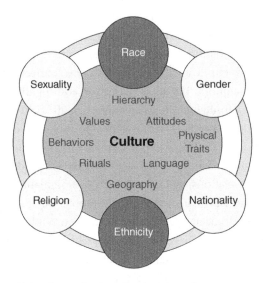

Figure 9.1   Key sites of identity and related cultural attributes

THE ROLE OF POWER

The system of power brought about through race possesses unique qualities in relation to the classification system of ethnicity, particularly when viewed in the context of Western societies. Cornell and Hartmann (2007) provide five distinguishing qualities associated with race. First, generally persons or entities external to the groups who are racially designated impose racial identification. Thus, in South Africa's apartheid system between 1948 and 1991 the government classified people as white, black, and mixed race/colored, for instance. Second, race is a fairly new form of human classification, its origin coinciding with the rise of European colonialism in regions of the world inhabited by people possessing markedly different phenotypic traits from those of Europeans. The construction of race worked to justify the spread of colonialism and imperialism (Smedley 1999), such as the development of the plantation economy in the new world with the labor needed to sustain it. In South Africa, the European population reclassified all of the preexisting tribal ethnicities like Tsonga, Zulu, Basotho, Swazi, and Ndebele into the black racial category. Third, race typically involves forms of institutionalized power, such as the government's ability to regulate racial categories via the census data or its history of depriving specific racial groups while privileging others of social, economic, and political status. In South Africa, racial classification determined education, employment, and residential options. Apartheid divided the races. Fourth, racial identities are situated within a tiered system, wherein certain races are perceived as superior to others. In South Africa, white Europeans were at the top, coloreds in the middle and blacks on the bottom of the apartheid-era social hierarchy. Fifth, within official policy and popular understanding race is constructed as an innate quality of the groups distinguished by observable physical traits (Cornell and Hartmann 2007: 26–30). Given its naturalized existence and unique relationship to dominant social structures and institutions, race may provide a more nuanced understanding of consumption markets, unavailable through the lens of culture and ethnicity.

That is not to say the classification systems of race, ethnicity, and culture, and their relationships to power are mutually exclusive. At their essence, race, ethnicity, and culture are respectively constructed by how people look (race), think and feel (ethnicity), and behave (culture) (Dalal 2002). However, these terms are often conflated and require simultaneous inquiry to obtain understanding. For instance, in the United States the phrase 'black culture' describes social practices considered distinct to individuals racialized as black (Cashmore 1997). This practice blurs the line between race and culture, as it creates a perception that the social practices associated with black culture are innate, and thereby a product of race, as opposed to practices learned and connected to culture within black society. The term African American is often used synonymously with the racial identifier black (Bailey 2006; Bristor et al. 1995). However, the two are not equivalent. As an identifier of a specific ethnic group (descendants of enslaved Africans born and raised in the United States), the term African American does not capture the lived experience of black individuals living in, or with ancestry from, places beyond the borders of the United States. Conversely, black as a racial category does not effectively communicate the cultural variance that exists between bodies that are phenotypically read as black in the US context (e.g. African American and Afro-Caribbean).

Previous research indicates the lived experience of race is not monolithic (Bonilla-Silva 2017; Rockquemore and Brunsma 2002). Differences produced by the interaction of racial make-up, socioeconomic status, gender, sexual orientation, with other identity sectors beget a heterogeneous racial population. That said, race continues to serve as a strong predictor of one's social position. For instance, within the United States the racial categories of black and white have the greatest social distance and the most spatial separation, in large part due to wealth disparities experienced across generations. These categories also share the strongest historically rooted taboos against interracial marriage and miscegenation (Rockquemore and Brunsma 2002; Smedley 1999). Furthermore, a socio-historical perspective demonstrates that whiteness typifies a position of social and economic privilege, while blackness represents a position of socio-economic marginalization (Bone et al. 2014).

Thus, the study of racial identity (as opposed to ethnic or cultural identity) in many instances may better enable an understanding of existing power differentials between social groups. In sum, while racial identity may be viewed as a component of culture, it is still important to acknowledge differences in lived experiences between race and other elements of culture, such as ethnicity, given its distinctive historical roots and socio-political implications.

A HISTORY OF RACE AND ETHNICITY CONSUMER RESEARCH

Consumer ethnicity research began in 1932 with the publishing of 'The Southern Urban Negro as a Consumer' (Edwards 1932). The faculty and students at Fisk University carried out this study based on qualitative research data. They analyzed the buying power and consumer habits of southern city-dwelling African Americans in order to design targeted advertising appeals. A review of recent literature highlights three eras of research that focus on: (1) consumption patterns among ethnic and/or racial minorities (1981 to 1988);

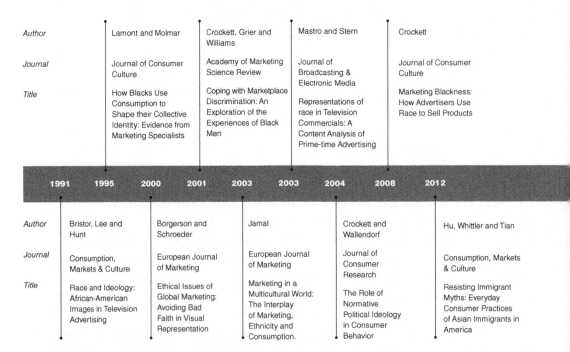

Figure 9.2 Themes in CCT race-related research, 1991–2018

(2) the adaptation strategies that migrants undergo to accommodate a new (market) culture (1989 to 2006); and (3) the role of institutional forces in the (de)construction of ethnicity and/or race (2007 to present) (Visconti et al. 2014). Another review of the content of consumer ethnicity research revealed three overarching trajectories: acculturation studies, consumer ethnocentrism studies, and ethnic marketing studies (Jafari and Visconti 2015). Acculturation studies examine how border crossing influences consumers' interactions with one another, with the market, and also with different political, ideological, and socio-cultural institutions (Jafari and Visconti 2015) (see Luedicke 2011, for a review and Chapter 10 of this book). Consumer ethnocentrism studies examine how ethnicity influences individual and organizational preferences for certain market offerings (e.g. brands, products, and services) in cross-cultural contexts (see Grier et al. 2006). Ethnic marketing studies examine how marketing can serve certain ethnic market segments (see Burton 2000).

One may argue that since race is an artificial construction, it may have less impact than imagined, or that since racial difference is often closely associated with ethnic difference, studies on ethnically different consumers inevitably include racially different consumers. However, over the years, a growing subset of researchers have maintained that racial differences have a separate impact on the consumer experience and have tried to understand the scope and depth of this impact.

The timeline in Figure 9.2, while not exhaustive, portrays the path and themes of race-related research by CCT scholars.

COMPLICATING RACE AND ETHNICITY: THE CASE OF COLORISM

'Colorism is the allocation of privilege and disadvantage according to the lightness or darkness of one's skin' (Burke and Embrich 2008: 17). Practices of colorism tend to favor lighter skin over darker skin as indicated by a person's appearance as proximal to a white phenotype (Hall 2005). Perhaps surprisingly, hair texture, eye color, and facial features, education and income also affect perceptions of who is considered dark or light skinned (Hunter 2007). Colorism beliefs and practices operate both within and across racial and ethnic groups (Bonilla-Silva 2017). Intra-group colorism represents one form of internalized oppression, while inter-group colorism makes manifest the internalized superiority of one group towards another. Internalized oppression occurs when people believe and make part of their self-image (see Chapter 1) the myths and misinformation that society communicates to them about their group.

Colorism is a persistent problem for people of color regardless of gender or social class. The effects of colorism are global in reach, impacting developed and developing regions of the world. Colorism privileges light-skinned people of color over dark in access to income, and in terms of consumption, such as education, housing, and potential marriage partners. Colorism is related to, but not synonymous with the larger system of racism. The practice of colorism pre-dates colonialism; however, the promotion of Western standards of beauty that accompanied imperialist and colonial expansion by European powers, such as Great Britain and France, helped make colorism a global phenomenon. The contemporary globalization of colorism is in part a byproduct of the proliferation of Westernized beauty standards disseminated through media images. One lingering echo of the age of European imperialism is the international beauty pageant that invariably favors lighter-skinned contestants over darker-skinned ones.

The impact of colorism is considerably broad in scope. Behavioral scientists have conducted numerous studies globally that show individuals are more favorably disposed toward people with lighter skin, rating them smarter, wealthier, and even happier. One such study showed participants 60 photos, including some pictures of the same person that were altered to make their skin look darker. Study participants gave lower scores on intelligence to people with darker skin. Research suggests that employers prefer light-skinned black males to dark-skinned males with superior qualifications and experience (Banerji 2006). Previous research also indicates that immigrants with light skin earn on average 8–15% more than similarly qualified immigrants with dark skin (Hersch 2008). Across the globe, darker-skinned people are more likely than lighter-skinned people to face discrimination. In Latin and South America, people see light skin as more attractive. In Mexico and in Brazil, light skin represents power.

Box 9.1:   Real World Scenario

Skin-lightening products in Ghana

In August of 2016, the West African nation of Ghana began implementing a new ban on hydroquinone, the primary chemical in many skin-bleaching products. The ban highlights a wider backlash against skin-bleaching. Similar bans have already taken place in the European Union, Japan, Australia, and the United States. Ghana's Food and Drugs Authority (FDA) has positioned the ban as a matter of public safety. Hydroquinone is linked to serious health complications including skin discoloration, blistering, and cancer. However, consumer demand for skin-lightening creams is largely associated with racial bias – specifically, colorism. A form of discrimination that privileges lighter skin over darker skin. While the decision to ban hydroquinone is a step in a positive direction, basing the ban solely on the product's health-related issues may be a fatal flaw in the campaign to end its use. In essence, the ban attempts to restrict access to skin-lightening products without addressing the deeper roots of their popularity among consumers.

Much of the prominence of colorism can be traced to European colonization. During colonization a race-based social class system was established in Ghana (and other colonized African countries) which placed white Europeans at the top of the social order, with mixed-race and indigenous Africans following in descending order. Under this social system, access to resources and opportunities became directly tied to the lightness of one's skin. Although Ghana gained its political independence in 1957, the social structure that accompanied colonialism remains embedded in Ghana's broader culture. Present-day Ghanaian media reflects and reinforces the tenets of colorism. The vast majority of advertisements (beauty-related and otherwise) utilize light-skin models. On the rare occasion when dark-skin models are featured, they are typically depicted in disparaging ways. While most users of skin-lightening products in Ghana are well aware of its potentially life-threatening side effects, they are willing to put their health at risk for the opportunity to better their stigmatized social status. Given the socio-historical context of its usage, policies banning hydroquinone without addressing the cultural and structural issues that accompany colorism are likely to be ineffectual.

Box 9.2:   Critical Reflection

Neglecting race

The overall dearth of race-related consumer research may be in part an outcome of scholars not wanting to reify it as a biological construct. As discussed in the introduction of this chapter, the modern concept of race largely emerged from a market need – to

(Continued)

(Continued)

justify the mass marketing of Africans into chattel slavery. Through slave markets, one's human worth became directly associated with one's phenotypic traits. During colonialism, race, supported by racial science, created a biologically based hierarchy of human beings, wherein, white bodies and black bodies were positioned as counter forces. The white 'race' embodied aspirational qualities, such as intelligence, nobility, and refinement. While the black 'race' came to represent that which is deemed unfavorable – simple-mindedness, savagery, and ineptitude. The science community has since refuted the findings of racial biology as false and the consequence of pseudoscience. Thus, the lack of broader engagement with race among consumer researchers may be due to a belief that to do so would be to support a concept not only rooted in discrimination, but also invalidated by modern science. Scholars often choose instead to engage with terms like ethnicity and culture that developed in the social sciences, and as such, researchers may view these constructs as socially (rather than biologically) constructed.

In some cases, consumer researchers choose to practice color-blind politics, which asserts that focusing on race and/or ethnicity propagates discriminatory behavior, and therefore such factors should not be considered when evaluating life conditions. For instance, in a perceived effort to treat all of its citizens equally under the law, the French government has banned the collection of racial and ethnic demographic data since 1978, choosing instead to address market-based social inequalities through policies connected to geography and social class. However, prominent sociologists (Bonilla-Silva 2017) have argued that color-blindness may actually enable discrimination to persist. As discriminatory practices shift from blatant to subtle, turning a blind eye to systems and institutional practices embedded with racial and ethnic inequities facilitates the ongoing presence of race and/or ethnicity-based discrimination both in and outside marketplaces.

Explicitly highlighting race and ethnicity as determining factors in one's lived experience can be problematic too. This is particularly the case for scholarly work that neglects to incorporate the socio-historical context of race and ethnicity into research. Under such conditions race and/or ethnicity can be positioned (or read) as natural or biological, rather than political and contextual. Once a racial and/or ethnic group is divorced from the social conditions from which they are defined, their racial or ethnic identification becomes their defining characteristic. For instance, African Americans are often positioned as conspicuous shoppers, preferring to spend a greater portion of their income on highly visible status brands than comparable white consumers. While empirical data do suggest higher levels of conspicuous consumption exist within select conspicuous consumption product categories and demographic segments for African Americans, when the buying behavior of all African Americans is examined across all conspicuous consumption product categories, African American consumers actually spend the same or less than comparable white consumers (Charron-Chénier et al. 2017). Furthermore, in categories where African Americans outspend white consumers, systemic issues, such as discriminatory pricing tactics (e.g. redlining) may have a greater impact than personal preferences shared along racial lines. When investigating the impact of race on consumer behavior, researchers must be cognizant of the heterogeneity that exist within racial categories as well as the socio-historical context and socio-political implications that shape them.

A growing body of consumer research is using the concept of intersectionality to illustrate the diversity of market-based experiences that exist within racial and ethnic categories. Intersectionality proposes that all aspects of one's identity stemming from race, class, gender, education, and so on, should be examined as interacting with each other and affecting one's privilege and perception in society. Further, intersectionality proposes that these facets of identity simply cannot be analyzed separately. An intersectional perspective is not simply a view of personal identity, but rather an overarching analysis of power hierarchies present within identities (Cooper 2015). For instance, investigating how race and class combine to influence consumption practices, Crockett (2017) was able to provide a far more nuanced understanding of how middle-class blacks in the United States perceive and manage racial stigma.

Box 9.3:   Critical Reflection

Reconceptualizing race

The limited consumer research related to race and/or ethnicity primarily focuses on black (predominantly African American) consumers. Although there is a growing body of research that highlights marketplace experiences of Hispanic/Latino and Asian consumers, the racialized marketplace experience of white consumers remains woefully understudied. Rather than deconstructing the socially constructed racial identity of white consumers, marketing researchers typically position them as 'average' and 'raceless'. For example, samples that contain predominately white consumers are repeatedly classified as 'general market'. When describing such sample groups researchers often provide distinguishing gender and social class data, but neglect to discuss racial dynamics. As such, the concept of race becomes exclusively associated with non-white consumers, and by extension the focus of race-related consumer research typically becomes an investigation of oppressive behaviors and forces present in markets, while the opposing side of market-based discriminatory practices, privilege, is largely overlooked. Inequity inherently has two sides – those receiving less than their fair share and those receiving more. Therefore, to understand (and hopefully alleviate) marketplace inequities, both oppression and privilege need to be acknowledged and tended to. Focusing solely on the oppression aspect of the equation can have the unintended effect of normalizing positions of privilege, which can shift the perception of compensatory market-based actions and policies into acts of (reverse) discrimination. Much like gender-related consumer research endeavors to problematize maleness and male privilege, consumer research related to race must venture to unsettle whiteness and white privilege.

(Continued)

(Continued)

While race is generally linked to phenotypic traits, such as skin color, hair texture, and facial features, it should be noted that these physical qualities are not the only ways in which race is understood. For instance, ethnicity can become racialized. A racialized ethnicity is one wherein the cultural practices and other social qualities of a defined ethnic group are divorced from their socio-political circumstances and linked to a biological origin. The social qualities associated with the ethnic group are positioned as deviating from the norm, often in a deleterious or extraordinary fashion. Given the ways in which their cultural practices are affixed to their biological makeup, Hispanic/Latino consumers are often regarded as a racialized ethnic group. Similarly, religious practices can be racialized. This is frequently how Muslim populations are looked upon in marketplaces. The substantive cultural practices that undergird the Islamic faith give way to sweeping (derogatory) generalizations that then may incite discriminatory beliefs and practices such as islamophobia.

CONCLUSION

The concepts of race and ethnicity exist under the wider notion of culture. Although race was once considered a biological trait, today it is predominantly conceptualized as a socially constructed phenomenon, much like ethnicity. Sadly many still subscribe to a biological view. Ordinary people, marketers, and public policy-makers use both race and ethnicity to categorize and distinguish one group of individuals from another. However, race came into existence with the explicit intent to create a hierarchical social order among groups of people. Given its socio-historical context and socio-political implications, studying the relationship between race and consumer culture may provide insights unattainable through the lens of ethnicity. While there is a growing body of consumer research, particularly among consumer culture theory scholars, that examines race and its socio-political ramifications, far more research has been conducted around ethnic identities.

Rather than regarding race and ethnicity as distinct concepts, scholars have often applied the two interchangeably or positioned race as a subset of ethnicity. Such positioning can lead to a discounting of power dynamics, and a shifting in the understanding of race and ethnicity from social and contextual constructions to innate and biological traits. The preponderance of race and ethnicity consumer research relates to non-white populations. As a result, the impact of race and ethnicity among white consumers remains markedly understudied. However, it should be noted that CCT scholars, such as Zeynap Arsel and her work related to hipster culture, are beginning to shift the tide. While race is most often associated with phenotypic traits, other sites of identity, such as ethnicity and religion, can be used to demarcate racial distinctions.

Box 9.4:   Extended Case Study

The rise of multiracial consumers

In 1993, *TIME* magazine featured a computerized morphed image of a multiracial woman in its special issue 'The Changing Face of America'. Twenty years later, *National Geographic* also featured a series of facial images of multiracial individuals in America in a special 125th anniversary issue. Both magazines highlighted the increasing complexity and fluidity of racial and ethnic classifications, challenging our assumptions of ethnic and racial categorizations and identity.

However, the growth of mixed race consumers (i.e., consumers who are assigned to two or more racial groups) in the marketplace is not just a US phenomenon, but a global one. In the United States and Japan, the birth rate of mixed race children has been explosive, increasing 50% to 4.2 million in the United States since 2000 (2010 US census); and 200% in Japan between 1987 and 2012 (Quigley 2013). In Canada, the mixed race population increased by 25% between 2001 and 2006 (Thompson 2012), and in the United Kingdom, 10% of British children are being raised in interracial households (John 2002). Similar trends are expected in France, Germany, Sweden, Switzerland, Italy, Turkey, and Australia (Euromonitor International 2015).

Yet, portrayals of mixed race individuals, families, and social groups in film, television, and advertising still remain narrow, resulting in limited perceptions of the multiracial experience, presenting challenges for filmmakers, television directors, advertisers, actors/actresses, and their audiences. Mixed race consumers simultaneously embrace the increase in multiracial representations, as they can relate to other mixed race actors and representatives, while expressing frustration at the restricted representations in many of the portrayals. Advertisements featuring mixed race individuals depict narrow and stereotypical social roles, with limited phenotypic markers: 'not too light not too dark' skin tones. While these portrayals may be seen as non-alienating, with across-the-board appeal, at one level, at the other, it excludes the wide range of phenotypic attributes of mixed race individuals, so vividly encapsulated in the *National Geographic* special issue (Harrison et al. 2015, 2017).

At the family level, mixed race bodies are often portrayed in isolation, or shown as stemming from other multiracial bodies, rather than from the union of different racial bodies. When advertisers and filmmakers step forward to give a more nuanced representation of the mixed race family, some consumers see these portrayals as progressive and representative of our changing societies, but others do not, resulting in backlash stemming from recent historical taboos on race mixing (miscegenation) and from dominant racial groups fearing dilution of the race. One example includes the passionate, sometimes virulent, reactions to General Mills' 2013 Cheerios advertisement 'Just Checking', featuring a mixed race family (https://www.youtube.com/watch?v=yOmXfX7Lxow). Yet, influential global advertisers and brands, like General Mills, Benetton and Coca-Cola,

(Continued)

(Continued)

continue to portray racial diversity in their ads. Filmmakers across the globe, in particular, persist, and have persisted through the decades to portray both the positives and negatives of mixed race families and partnerships, and the resultant challenges. Memorable films such as *Guess Who's Coming to Dinner, Sayonara, Unbowed*, and *Bend it Like Beckham*, and including more recent additions, such as *Loving, Belle, Get Out*, and *A United Kingdom*; TV shows such as the classic *I Love Lucy* to the more recent *Scandal*, challenge societal norms on interracial romantic attraction. Yet, these portrayals of different racial partners often reinvigorate old racial taboos, and raise resistance from consumer audiences.

The population of mixed race individuals and families is growing and so are their representations in the media. As marketers, advertisers, directors and filmmakers continue to struggle with the challenge of representing that growth, it is important to remember that the mixed race experience need not be confined to the individual, or even the family, but also portrayed within groups, and within wider bodies or series of work.

Questions

1. In what ways might the mixed race consumer experience differ from that of the mono-racial consumer experience?
2. What role do marketers, advertisers, filmmakers and television directors play in ensuring that portrayals of mixed race individuals and families are fairly and proportionately represented?
3. Some have argued that multiracial portrayals need to move beyond black and white and embrace the full spectrum of mixed race combinations. Can you name examples of brands, movies, and shows that attempt to capture the full spectrum?
4. The Disney Princess movies increasingly portray a range of ethnically different princesses, who challenge gender roles. Do you think this series of movies also challenges social norms on race? Why or why not? Can you name other series (movie or television) that challenge racial norms?

RESEARCH DIRECTIONS

As regions and nations become increasingly diverse both racially and ethnically, researchers and practitioners of consumer behavior will need to further integrate the study of race and ethnicity along with a broader conceptualization of discrimination that examines oppression and privilege into their work. This reconceptualization will require deeper consideration of the racial identity of white consumers and a shift to intersectionality so that the heterogeneity present within racial and ethnic groups can be more effectively investigated and serviced in the marketplace. We offer the following as guiding questions:

1. How does incorporating both privileged and marginalized perspectives of race change the way consumer research is done?
2. What steps need to be taken to ensure that race-related consumer research does not advance a biological (e.g. innate) understanding of race?
3. How do contextual factors, such as geographic location, impact how race and ethnicity influence consumer behavior?
4. What self-reflection should researchers do concerning their race and ethnicity (and other aspects of their identity) when conducting consumer research?

RECOMMENDED READING

Bone, Sterling A., Christensen, Glenn L., and Williams, Jerome D. (2014) 'Rejected, shackled, and alone: The impact of systemic restricted choice on minority consumers' construction of self', *Journal of Consumer Research, 41* (2): 451–74.

Burton, Dawn (2009) 'Non-white readings of whiteness', *Consumption Markets & Culture, 12* (4): 349–72.

Crockett, David (2017) 'Paths to respectability: Consumption and stigma management in the contemporary black middle class', *Journal of Consumer Research,* 44: 3.

Cui, Geng (2001) 'Marketing to ethnic minority Consumers: a historical journey (1932–1997)', *Journal of Macromarketing, 21* (1): 23–31.

Gopaldas, Ahir and DeRoy, Glenna (2015) 'An intersectional approach to diversity research', *Consumption Markets & Culture, 18* (4): 333–64.

Harrison, Robert, Thomas, Kevin D., and Cross, Samantha N.N. (2017) 'Restricted visions of multiracial identity in advertising', *Journal of Advertising, 46* (6), 503–20.

Henderson, Geraldine R., Hakstian, Ann-Marie, and Williams, Jerome D. (2016) *Consumer Equality: Race and the American Marketplace*. Santa Barbara, CA: ABC-CLIO, LLC.

Johnson, Guillaume D., Thomas, Kevin D., and Grier, Sonya A. (2017) 'When the burger becomes halal: A critical discourse analysis of privilege and marketplace inclusion', *Consumption Markets & Culture,* 1–26.

Visconti, Luca M., Jafari, Aliakbar, Batat, Wided, Broeckerhoff, Aurelie, Dedeoglu, Ayla Özhan, Demangeot, Catherine, Kipnis, Eva, et al. (2014) 'Consumer ethnicity three decades after: A TCR agenda', *Journal of Marketing Management, 30* (17–18): 1882–922.

REFERENCES

American Anthropological Association (1998) AAA Statement on Race. www.americananthro.org/ConnectWithAAA/Content.aspx?ItemNumber=2583.

Arnould, Eric J. and Thompson, Craig J. (2005) 'Consumer culture theory (CCT): twenty years of research', *Journal of Consumer Research*, *31* (4): 868–82.

Bailey, Ainsworth A. (2006) 'A year in the life of the African-American male in advertising: A content analysis', *Journal of Advertising*, *35*: 83–104.

Banerji, Shilpa (2006) 'Study: Darker-skinned black job applications hit more obstacles'. Available at http://diverseeducation.com/article/6306/.

Benet-Martínez, Verónica (2012) 'Multiculturalism: Cultural, social, and personality processes', in Kay Deaux and Mark Snyder (eds), *The Oxford Handbook of Personality and Social Psychology*. Oxford: Oxford University Press. pp. 623–48.

Bone, Sterling A., Christensen, Glenn L., and Williams, Jerome D. (2014) 'Rejected, shackled, and alone: The impact of systemic restricted choice on minority consumers' construction of self', *Journal of Consumer Research*, *41* (2): 451–74.

Bonilla-Silva, Eduardo (2017) *Racism without Racists: Color-blind Racism and the Persistence of Racial Inequality in America*, 5th edn. Lanham, MD: Rowman & Littlefield.

Bristor, Julia M., Lee, Renee Gravois, and Hunt, Michelle R. (1995) 'Race and ideology: African-American images in television advertising', *Journal of Public Policy and Marketing*, *14* (1): 48–59.

Burke, Meghan and Embrich, David G. (2008) 'Colorism', *International Encyclopedia of the Social Sciences*, (2): 17–18.

Burton, Dawn (2000) 'Ethnicity, identity and marketing: A critical review', *Journal of Marketing Management*, *16* (8): 853–87.

Cashmore, Ernest (1997) *The Black Culture Industry*. London: Routledge.

Charron-Chénier, Raphaël, Fink, Joshua J., and Keister, Lisa A. (2017) 'Race and consumption: Black and white disparities in household spending', *Sociology of Race and Ethnicity*, *3* (1): 50–67.

Cornell, Stephen E. and Hartmann, Douglas (2007) *Ethnicity and Race: Making Identities in a Changing World*, 2nd edn. Thousand Oaks, CA: Pine Forge Press.

Cooper, Brittany (2015) 'Intersectionality', in Lisa Disch and Mary Hawkesworth (eds), *The Oxford Handbook of Feminist Theory*. Oxford: Oxford University Press.

Crockett, David (2017) 'Paths to respectability: Consumption and stigma management in the contemporary black middle class', *Journal of Consumer Research*, *44*: 3.

Cross, William E. and Binta Cross, T. (2007) 'Theory, research, and models', in Stephen M. Quintana and Clark McKown (eds), *Handbook of Race, Racism and the Developing Child*. New York, NY: Wiley. pp. 94–114.

Dalal, Farhad (2002) *Race, Colour and the Process of Racialization: New Perspectives from Group Analysis, Psychoanalysis, and Sociology*. New York: Routledge.

Edwards, Paul K. (1932) *The Southern Urban Negro as a Consumer*. New York: Prentice Hall.

Euromonitor International (2015) *Cultural Diversity and Its Impact on Global Consumer Markets*. London: Euromonitor International.

Giles, Eugene and Orville Elliot (1962) 'Race identification from cranial measurements', *Journal of Forensic Sciences*, 7 (2): 147–57.

Goldberg, David (1990) *Anatomy of Racism*. Minneapolis, MN: University of Minnesota Press.

Graves, Joseph L. (2002) 'What a tangled web he weaves: Race, reproductive strategies and Rushton's life history theory', *Anthropological Theory*, 2 (2): 131–54.

Grier, Sonya A., Brumbaugh, Anne M., and Thornton, Corliss G. (2006) 'Crossover dreams: Consumer responses to ethnic-oriented products', *Journal of Marketing*, 70 (2): 35–51.

Hall, Ronald E. (2005) 'From the psychology of race to the issue of skin color for people of African descent', *Journal of Applied Social Psychology*, 35 (9): 1958–67.

Harrison, Robert L., Thomas, Kevin D., and Cross, Samantha N.N. (2015) 'Negotiating cultural ambiguity: The role of markets and consumption in multiracial identity development', *Consumption Markets & Culture*, 18 (4): 301–32.

Harrison, Robert, Thomas, Kevin D., and Cross, Samantha N.N. (2017) 'Restricted visions of multiracial identity in advertising', *Journal of Advertising*, 46 (6), 503–20.

Hersch, Joni (2008) 'Profiling the new immigrant worker: The effects of skin color and height', *Journal of Labor Economics*, 26, (2): 345–86.

Hunter, Margaret (2007) 'The persistent problem of colorism: Skin tone, status, and inequality', *Sociology Compass*, 1 (1): 237–54.

Jafari, Aliakbar and Visconti, Luca M. (2015) 'New directions in researching ethnicity in marketing and consumer behaviour: A well-being agenda', *Marketing Theory*, 15 (2): 265–70.

James, Michael (2012) 'Race', *The Stanford Encyclopedia of Philosophy* (Winter 2012 Edition) (ed. Edward N. Zalta). Web. 10 September 2014.

Jhally, Sut (ed.) (1997) *Race: The Floating Signifier*. Northampton, MA: Media Education Foundation.

John, Cindi (2002) 'Changing face of Britain: Britain's blurring ethnic mix'. http://news.bbc.co.uk/hi/english/static/in_depth/uk/2002/race/changing_face_of_britain.stm.

Luedicke, Marius K. (2011) 'Consumer acculturation theory: (Crossing) conceptual boundaries', *Consumption Markets & Culture*, 14 (3): 223–44.

Quigley, J.T. (2013) 'In Japan, will hafu ever be considered whole? Mixed-race individuals and their families seek acceptance in a homogeneous Japan', *The Diplomat*, http://thediplomat.com/2013/10/in-japan-will-hafu-ever-be-considered-whole/.

Rockquemore, Kerry A. and Brunsma, David L. (2002) 'Socially embedded identities: Theories, typologies, and processes of racial identity among black/white biracials', *The Sociological Quarterly*, 43 (3): 335–56.

Sanchez, Diana T., Shih, Margaret J., and Garcia, Julie A. (2009) 'Juggling multiple racial identities: Malleable racial identification and psychological well-being', *Cultural Diversity and Ethnic Minority Psychology*, 15 (3): 243–54.

Sanchez, Diana T., Shih, Margaret J., and Wilton, Leigh S. (2014) 'Exploring the Identity Autonomy Perspective (IAP): An integrative theoretical approach to multicultural and multiracial identity', in Verónica Benet-Martínez and Ying-yi Hong (eds), *The Handbook of Multicultural Identity: Basic and Applied Psychological Perspectives*. Oxford: Oxford University Press. pp. 139–59.

Smedley, Audrey (1999) *Race in North America: Origin and Evolution of a Worldview*. New York: Basic Civitas Books.

Thompson, Debra (2012) 'Making (mixed-) race: Census politics and the emergence of multiracial multiculturalism in the United States, Great Britain and Canada', *Ethnic and Racial Studies*, 35 (8): 1409–18.

Visconti, Luca M., Jafari, Aliakbar, Batat, Wided, Broeckerhoff, Aurelie, Dedeoglu, Ayla Özhan, Demangeot, Catherine, Kipnis, Eva, et al. (2014) 'Consumer ethnicity three decades after: A TCR agenda', *Journal of Marketing Management*, 30 (17–18): 1882–922.

Waters, Mary C. (1990) *Ethnic Options: Choosing Identities in America*. Berkeley, CA: University of California Press.

Witherspoon, David J., Wooding, Stephen, Rogers, Alan R., Marchani, Elizabeth E.W., Watkins, Scott, Batzer, Mark A., and Jorde, Lynn B. (2007) 'Genetic similarities within and between human populations', *Genetics*, 176 (1): 351–9.

10
GLOBAL MOBILITIES

Fleura Bardhi, City, University of London
Marius K. Luedicke, City, University London
Zahra Sharifonnasabi, Queen Mary,
University of London

CHAPTER OVERVIEW

This chapter discusses:

- how technological transformations and global politico-economic interdependences have led to the rise of global mobilities;
- how global mobilities can take different forms from economic and political migration to global nomadism to expatriatism;
- how for consumers, global mobility can be a source of capital accumulation, potential social mobility, as well as consumer empowerment;
- how global mobilities can also be challenging and may result in feelings of homelessness, ontological insecurity, and social isolation.

INTRODUCTION

This chapter examines the phenomenon of global mobilities from a consumer culture theory perspective, focusing specifically on the cross-border movements of people. Human global mobilities take many forms, from economic and political migration, through professional and educational sojourning and expatriation, short-term business and leisure international travel, to global nomadism. A growing social, economic, political, and cultural interconnectedness of people, institutions, and nations across the globe has contributed to an unprecedented level of people crossing national borders. Today, over 247 million individuals live permanently outside of their countries of birth. International travel, currently accounts for one-twelfth of world trade (World Bank 2016).

Global mobilities not only affect consumers who emigrate or travel to foreign countries, but also affect consumers at home, particularly under current cultural condition known as 'liquid modernity' (Bauman 2000). In liquid modernity, social structures, institutions, and traditions are constantly changing, and doing so more rapidly than ever before (Bauman 2000, 2007). Consumers are thus compelled also constantly to adjust their identity projects and consumption practices (Bardhi and Eckhardt 2017). As permanent and stable lives increasingly confer limited competitive advantage both in the labor market and markets for distinction and prestige, consumers must become more flexible and adaptable, ready and willing to change their life goals, strategies, loyalties and commitments depending on the situation. That is, they must become more mobile in their own culture (Bauman 2000). Liquid modernity is argued to be an 'epoch of nomads', because nomads, through their flexible and highly malleable life strategies, are ideally suited for adapting to unpredictable, liquid conditions (Bardhi et al. 2012; Bauman 2000). Thus, engaging in global mobility has become an important consumer and professional strategy.

Consumer culture theory (CCT) researchers have already developed a broad range of important insights on these types of global mobilities, using a diverse set of theoretical perspectives. Specifically, CCT scholars have examined mobile consumers' identities and lifestyles through the lens of acculturation theory; explored the global consumer cultures that produced such identities through the lens of globalization theory; and investigated how different types of mobilities shape local consumption practices and produce intra-culturally diverse consumer cultures. From such studies, we garner useful insights on the impacts that global mobilities have on consumers' relationship to material possessions (Bardhi et al. 2012) on consumers' selfhood and identity positions (Askegaard 2005) on the symbolic meaning of objects in consumers' lives (Mehta and Belk 1991) and on consumers' cultural experimentation practices (Gaviria and Emontspool 2015). Peñaloza (1994), who conceptualized Mexican migrants to the United States as a 'consumer subculture'; Thompson and Tambyah (1999), who investigated the identity implications that follow from consumers' experiences of temporary, serial, resettlements; and Bardhi et al. (2012), who studied consumer nomadic lifestyle, exemplify such cultural analyses.

In this chapter, we summarize the main theoretical perspective on global mobilities in CCT research, specifically those of cultural flows, hybridity, creolization, and deterritorialization. We then discuss the research that examines the implications of global mobilities for consumer identity and lifestyles, where we summarize the research on consumer migration and acculturation, mobile consumer lifestyles, mobile families and remittances, and conclude with the conflicts produced by global mobility.

THEORIES OF GLOBALIZATION IN CONSUMER CULTURE RESEARCH

In order to make sense of globalization forces, and how these forces affect consumer culture, consumer identities, and consumption practices, we first need a vocabulary to understand globalization. CCT researchers challenge the conventional homogenization–heterogeneous dichotomy that dominates theories of globalization in international marketing and consumer behavior literatures (cf. Levitt 1983). They argue that globalization cannot be seen as a process of cultural homogenization, where the ubiquity of American and global brands, products, ideas, and cultures erases localized cultural differences; nor can globalization be seen as simply producing more cultural and market diversity through the merging of global and local cultural forms (see Wilk 1995). Instead, CCT scholars consider globalization of consumer culture a much more complex process, and draw on anthropological and sociological theories to study it. To convey an idea on how CCT scholars make sense of globalization, we next review theories on global flows, creolization, hybridity, and deterritorialization.

Global Flows

The work of anthropologist Arjun Appadurai (1990), who argues that globalization should be understood as a complex, overlapping, and disjunctive order of the economy, culture and politics, has been very influential to CCT scholars. For Appadurai, globalization is a decentralized process of integration through a combination of five global flows: Ethnoscape, Financescape, Ideoscape, Mediascape, and Technoscape. The suffix 'scape' emphasizes like geographic landscapes, the irregular, overlapping form of these global flows.

The ethnoscape notion captures the movement of people, such as immigrants, refugees, exiles, tourists, guest workers, expatriates, etc. and their shifting landscapes. Financescape captures the global movement of capital and money as well as national and global financial institutions and markets (e.g. tax havens, stock exchanges, currency markets, commodity speculation, etc.). Ideoscape consists of series of interconnected images political, cultural, and historical in nature. In late 1980s to early 1990s when Appadurai developed this theory, he noted that global ideoscapes are dominated by ideas such as democracy, individual freedom, human rights, welfare, or sovereignty that are all anchored in the Enlightenment worldview. More recently, scholars have argued that ideas around consumer society – for example consumer rights, consumer freedom of choice, the equation of happiness with consumption – have become equally prominent in the global ideoscape. Mediascape refers to distribution of the electronic capability to produce and disseminate information (e.g. newspapers, magazines, TV stations, film production studios) as well as images created by media (e.g. documentary or entertainment content). Technoscape captures the fast-moving and ever-changing technology and information hardware and software as well as their fluid global configurations.

Appadurai's global flow perspective highlights global and cross-border movements and their implications. The result of these five global flows is a decentralized global marketplace that disperses production across the globe, circulates consumer products globally, and in which a wide range of cultural values, not just the ones symbolizing modernity and Western ways of life, influence local consumer tastes (Faist 2000). This flows perspective also rejects the idea of culture as national and essentially territorial, expressed through ethnicity, language, and religion. Instead, it promotes the idea of cultures as mutually co-constructed by local, ethnic particularities, and global consumer cultures (Appadurai 1990; Hannerz 1996). For example, contemporary consumer cultures in India result from myriad cultural interactions and exchanges with other nations, and manifests in particular local foods, entertainment styles, and consumer products (Appadurai and Breckenridge 1988).

Appadurai's theory also recognizes the ideas of *global spaces* and *global consumer culture*, where a power hierarchy is established between global cities with their urban, highly networked areas, and rural zones with low network accessibility (cf. Bardhi and Eckhardt 2017). Human global mobilities are at the center of formation of such global spaces, such as the global city (Sassen 2012). Sassen (2012) argues that the cultural fluidity of big cities can perform as an empowering platform, giving individuals space to present themselves through consumption (see also Gaviria and Emontspool 2015). The emergence of the networked, global city signals the advent of new groups of consumers, who center their identities on mobility, and become distinctive markets for a variety of services.

Creolization, Hybridity, and Deterritorialization of Cultures

How do local cultures respond to global flows and pressures of globalization? CCT researchers tend to agree that globalization is a set of processes through which local cultures and the globalization forces we have defined interpenetrate and co-construct each other (see also Robertson 1995). CCT research challenges the outdated concept of a 'pure, core culture', arguing that national borders today only partially map cultural boundaries, if at all.

Based on this theoretical view of globalization, scholars have examined a variety of practices where the local and the global interact, and explored various processes of local and global market development (Vikas et al. 2015), product creolization (Eckhardt and Mahi 2004), and Easternization of consumer culture (Askegaard and Eckhardt 2012; Thompson and Troester 2002). Overall, CCT research has highlighted three related processes, i.e., hybridization, creolization, and deterritorialization of culture, to which we turn next.

Hybridization represents the fusion of two of more elements from different cultures resulting in new cultural forms (Craig and Douglas 2006: 330; Pieterse 2003 [1995]).

Thompson and Troester (2002), for example, illustrate hybridization in their study of cultural influences of Eastern healing practices on the Western healthcare system. They show how a combination of two distinct health approaches – one based on the scientific method and another based on holistic concepts such as integrity of the body or its relationship with the outer world – co-exist in the Western healthcare market. As a result of such cultural hybridization local practices are not entirely lost, and the meanings of the adopted practices are not fully distorted either. Hybridization can thus entail a notable transformation of existing product meanings and practices, but does not necessarily fully distort or dismantle previous meanings. Cova, Pace, and Park's (2007) study on brand communities in different geographical locations, for example, confirms that while local communities are formed around localized meanings (e.g., the Warhammer game revolves around history and strategy in France, and imaginary violence in the United States), these communities also ascribe to globally shared attributes and rituals. In another context of high-school proms in the United Kingdom, Tinson and Nuttall (2010) discuss them as a hybrid consumption tradition where students engage in co-creating a practice that incorporates American prom traditions with existing local celebrations.

Conceptually, studies addressing the hybridization of consumer culture are based on assumptions that do not call attention to power hierarchies between cultures. In contrast, *creolization* is an anthropological term to capture the new cultural formations that result from local appropriations of foreign or global cultural forms. Through creolization, 'the peripheral culture absorbs the influx of meanings and symbolic forms from the center [and] transforms them to make them in some considerable degree their own' (Hannerz 1990: 127). In consumer research, cultural creolization – or the outcome of locals' interpretations of meanings and symbols from other cultures (Hannerz 1990: 127) – is used to describe the globally informed, yet localized nature of culture. Importantly, in the processes of creolization, consumers are not seen as passive or disempowered, but as agents in transforming and appropriating global brands, products, ideas, and images (Eckhardt and Mahi 2012).

Deterritorialization is another, distinct outcome of global mobilities. It results when culture becomes detached from specific physical locations and disembedded from local social networks (Bardhi et al. 2012; Cayla and Eckhardt 2008). Scholars employing the analytic lens of deterritorialization view culture as multi-centered and dynamic, and not necessarily bounded by national borders. Therefore, they study disconnections between cultures and particular physical places (Faist 2000: 13). Cayla and Eckhardt (2008), for example, show how Asian brands, through their regional branding, and advertising communication and imagery, which are not anchored in a shared history of the region, are nevertheless constituting a regional identity and cultural form of being 'Asian'. This imagined regional community provides regional consumers with a sense of belonging and pride in the global marketplace.

Similarly, world music can be considered deterritorialized because it is neither Western popular music, nor globally available music, but a combination of ethnic music, folk music, and foreign music that is disassociated from any single place of origin, but connected to many (Connell and Gibson 2004). The commercialization and the global spread of the Halloween ritual is another example for deterritorialization of cultural rituals. This Irish-origin festivity has been transformed into a global consumption ritual that now incorporates elements from a range of different customs and rituals (McKechnie and Tynan 2008). Whereas the local origin of the Halloween ritual has been lost, it is now celebrated as a global consumption ritual whose scripts and performances are co-produced by local culture and global media and branding.

CCT research has also shown how the deterritorialization of culture has contributed to the legitimization of stigmatized practices and the normalization of niche markets. As such, deterritorialization enhances consumers' experiences of empowerment. The emergence of global markets for Muslim women's veils, for example, empowered women by reframing a practice that has previously been stigmatized as a symbol of subordination and lack of agency as fashionable and liberatory (Sandıkcı and Ger 2010, see also Ger 2013). Similarly, the global consumption of Bollywood movies has contributed to the creation of transnational Sikh communities that remind foreign-born young Sikhs of Sikh rituals and thus empower members of such marginalized groups (Takhar et al. 2012).

IMPLICATIONS OF GLOBAL MOBILITIES FOR CONSUMER IDENTITIES AND LIFESTYLES

How do these global flows and the resulting dynamics of hybridization, creolization, and deterritorialization affect individuals and their choices of brands and consumption practices? How do these forces affect the ways in which consumers make sense of themselves as individuals (i.e., their identity) and as actors positioned in larger social structures (i.e., social status)? Which kinds of consumer lifestyles do these global mobilities give rise to, and which problems might they cause?

As one might expect, consumers' opportunities for identity construction vary dramatically depending on who and what is moving from where to where, and to which extent consumers have control over these movements. We first take a look at those consumers who cross national borders in search of a safer, or more affluent life (i.e., migration and acculturation). Then, we shed light on consumers who choose mobile lifestyles (i.e., global nomadic consumers and cosmopolitans). Finally, we discuss how consumers who stay in their home context experience the influx of immigrant consumers at their proverbial doorstep (i.e., indigenes' acculturation).

Consumer Migration and Acculturation

Not only goods, money, technologies, spiritual practices, music, and ideas move across national borders, but people move as well, fleeing from war, persecution, and inhumane or hopeless living conditions. Historically, people most typically emigrate from less affluent and more conflicted regions, to more affluent and less conflicted ones seeking protection, respect, social security, employment, and better consumption opportunities for themselves and their families. Although some migrants eventually return to their home countries, migration most often results in a linear, permanent relocation.

The challenges that migrants face when trying to settle in a foreign country are manifold. They not only need to adapt to a new natural environment, but also to different 'economic (income, status), biological (food, health), physical (urbanization), social (family, friendships, discrimination), and cultural (clothing, religion, language) conditions' (Luedicke 2011: 221). Unsurprisingly, this adaptation process often produces psychological stress, particularly when migrants feel nostalgic, isolated, alienated or stigmatized and excluded in the country of settlement (Jafari and Goulding 2008; Peñaloza 1994).

Researchers and policy-makers commonly refer to this intricate process of adaptation as 'acculturation' (Ward 1974). Research on acculturation now offers a multitude of models that conceptualize the range of acculturation strategies, address what facilitates the success of each strategy, and explain which strategies lead to more favorable outcomes for migrants. Despite a wealth of studies in this area, however, we still do not know for sure whether migrants that 'integrate' experience less stress than those who 'separate' themselves from a foreign culture and society, fully 'assimilate' to it, or experience a 'marginalizing' loss of cultural identity (Rudmin 2007). In fact, whether acculturation causes mostly stress, or is rather a positive experience, is contingent upon a complex range of socio-cultural and individual factors, both in and outside of a migrant's control (Berry 2001)

For migrants, one important part of the acculturation process is adapting to the consumption demands, practices, and symbolic meanings that exist in a foreign country. Inevitably, migrants not only learn where to buy things, but also the meanings and status signals that particular brands and products convey in their new context, and how established consumers wear, eat, drive, or share specific brands, goods, and services (Peñaloza 1989).

Consumer researchers have identified a range of 'consumer acculturation' strategies that migrants tend to choose from when acculturating into a foreign consumer culture (Luedicke 2011). In one of the first consumer acculturation studies, Wallendorf and Reilly (1983) compared the food intake of Mexican immigrants with the intake of American consumers. They found, among other things, that, at the time, some Mexican-American immigrants tended to 'over-assimilate' to US consumer culture by consuming larger amounts of red meats, eggs, white breads, and convenience foods than Anglo-Americans. Interestingly, these immigrants seemed to assimilate to an internalized idea of Anglo-American food consumption that had, in fact, already changed (1983: 300).

Two decades later, consumer acculturation research has moved from the idea of gradual assimilation to understand the process as more complex, allowing for resistance and moving between adaptation strategies. Askegaard, Arnould, and Kjeldgaard (2005), for example, revealed how migrants mix and match the best elements of the both cultures, or oscillate between different cultural identities.

Often, consumers migrate with the desire to integrate or assimilate to a new culture, but fail because they lack the economic and cultural capital required to perform the new consumer lifestyle (Üstüner and Holt 2007). Migrant consumers may also face a host culture inhospitable to divergent migrant lifestyles (Jafari and Goulding 2008; Luedicke 2011). Such 'shattered identity projects' (Üstüner and Holt 2007) can spark conflicts between migrants and locals who are unwilling to embrace unwanted globalization on their front steps, so to speak.

In their study of Turkish migrant women that migrated from rural Turkey to a major Turkish city with its Westernized lifestyles and consumer culture, Üstüner and Holt (2007) show how migrants end up isolated from mainstream consumer society rather than integrated. Consequently, they see their optimistic acculturation projects 'shattered' owing to an intractable paucity of economic, social, and cultural resources (Üstüner and Holt 2007: 51).

Choosing suitable brands and consumption practices plays a key role for consumers in their acculturation process. Through consumption, migrants can better cope with feelings of culture shock and homesickness, but can also signal to indigenous consumers which acculturation strategy they are pursuing, and protect themselves against local hostilities.

Culture shock is the feeling of disorientation experienced when someone is subjected to an unfamiliar culture, way of life, or set of attitudes. Homesickness is a feeling of longing for one's home during a period of prolonged absence. Migrants may experience both culture shock and homesickness when living abroad. In such cases, some possessions from their country of origin become sacred, which is to say are carefully preserved and venerated, as carriers of ethnic identity (Mehta and Belk 1991). Migrants use these sacred possessions to display their cultural heritage, to create a sense of belonging and community with fellow migrants (Mehta and Belk 1991), and to create a sense of home abroad.

For migrants dealing with culture shock or homesickness, special possessions, but also brands and foods from the home country, can become important sources of comfort (Bardhi et al., 2010). For an illustration, consider the following quote from an interview with a Canadian accountant who along with his wife and their two kids permanently relocated to the United Arab Emirates (UAE). He explains how even after 15 years in the country, consumer products from Canada help them to connect to home and feel more at home abroad.

> One of the things we never find here is a brand called Kraft. As a kid, I was raised on Kraft peanut butter. So, you are kinda like whatever mom gets. Now, we actually bring a lot of stuff with us. When we visit home, once every 2–3 years almost, we go to a place called Costco and buy jars of peanut butter and put them in the luggage and bring them over here. Sometimes we bring coffee with us because the coffee here doesn't taste the same. There is no proper granulated sugar here and since we do a lot of baking, we buy bags of sugar and put them in the container and ship them over here along with all kinds of things that we don't get here.

This interview excerpt nicely illustrates how migrants' sense of home is tied to favorite brands and shopping sites from the past, and particularly to 'childhood friendship' (Fournier 1998: 362) brands like Kraft peanut butter. Noting the unavailability of these brands in the foreign country, and regularly performing the practice of going back home and importing them, allows consumers to connect with, and thus keep their home consumer identity alive, despite the distance. Through understanding which things they 'never find here', consumers also refine their understanding of the foreign consumer culture and forge their own, hybrid consumer identity position within it (Üstüner and Holt 2007).

For migrants whose children grow up in a foreign consumer culture, seeing their ties to home eroding in the next generation can create identity tensions. Consumption can help migrants to attenuate such a loss. As Sutton-Brady et al. (2010) illustrate, Korean migrants to Australia sometimes borrow Korean-made DVDs to familiarize their Australian-born children with their Korean heritage.

Lastly, consumption helps migrant consumers to avoid local hostility. Particularly in contexts where right-wing political parties have publicly positioned immigrants as scapegoats for their country's socio-economic problems, migrants can feel constrained in their consumption choices. Jafari and Goulding (2008), for example, illustrate how Muslim women migrants to the United Kingdom often feel pressured to remove their headscarves in public to avoid being overtly discriminated against. Similarly, Hu, Whittler, and Tian (2013) show that Asian immigrants to the United States feel pressured to adopt specific consumption strategies to counteract negative stereotypes that American consumers hold against them.

In summary, consumer acculturation research helps us to better understand the role that consumption plays for migrants when adjusting to a foreign culture. To date, this literature has shown how choosing or avoiding certain brands and consumption practices can help migrants to cope with culture shock, culture loss, homesickness, discrimination, and other intricacies of acculturation, but it also suggests that consumption cannot entirely solve these problems.

Mobile Consumer Lifestyles

Migration is one form of human global mobility and the most studied among consumer researchers. More recently, however, scholars have also begun to pay attention to global mobile lifestyles that contemporary globalization processes have produced, specifically global nomadism and cosmopolitanism. In contrast to migration, these mobile lifestyles are voluntarily mobile rather than imposed upon consumers by economic and political conditions. Additionally, the pattern of mobility is not linear and does not necessarily lead to permanent relocation to a host country. The main focus of this research has been to understand these types of consumer lifestyles and consumer identities, their ideological moorings, and how they shape consumer behavior.

Global nomadism. Global nomadism describes the lifestyle of people who are voluntarily unmoored from physical location or territory and engaged in both frequent relocation and short-term international travel (Bardhi et al. 2012; D'Andrea 2009). Like traditional pastoral nomadic tribes or the Roma gypsy, global nomads frequently relocate from country to country. This does not necessarily have to happen with a kin collective or family. Contemporary global nomads engage frequently in individual mobility. They are often born in countries different from their nationalities, travel frequently, and while living in one place are routinely involved in work and holidays to other locales. Two groups of global nomads have been identified, 1) those that engage in global mobility because of professional reasons, and 2) those that embrace mobility as part of a new age lifestyle, such as practitioners of New Age yoga and surfing (e.g. D'Andrea 1999). Global professional nomads typically work in a variety of areas, including academia, sports, real estate, consultancy, travel and tourism, healthcare, or volunteer for international NGOs. Professional and entrepreneurial global nomads have become an important target group for the global hotel and travel industry, global media, global banking and financial services, etc. For example, Pullman Hotels have re-positioned their marketing to target the professional global nomad in their global city locations as illustrated in this commercialmaterial:http://www.pullmanhotels.com/gb/discovering-pullman-hotel/pullman-commercial-2015/index.shtml.

This ad portrays the global nomad as a peripatetic male, multiethnic, business professional living out of an unidentified and fairly standardized global hotel and in a global city. He most likely holds a managerial or consultancy position. His culture and country of origin seems irrelevant as he is portrayed as being at home in any destination, thanks to the standardized service and brandscapes of global hotel chains like Pullman. This identity project is positioned within the high cultural capital, elite social classes, and the gender position of male ideology of competition (Thompson and Tambyah 1999). It is also a highly individualized identity project as the ad portrays the professional nomad as a 'lone wolf', socializing mainly in global hotel's social events or professional setting.

Travel is a mode of self-development. The ad also emphasizes the flexibility and adaptability of global nomadic skills sets required in contemporary global economy. His lifestyle and values are part of a new global business elite of globally mobile professionals deterritorialized from a country of origin or destination.

CCT research reveals a range of ways in which global nomadism impacts consumer behavior. Bardhi, Eckhardt and Arnould (2012), for example, show that global nomads relate to their possessions differently. For example, the global nomads have minimized their possessions and strive to own only a bare minimum of necessities. They tend to rely on rented or leased apartments and transport, access to hotels, and carry very few possessions as they relocate to another country. They tend to value most things that are immaterial, such as digital services and photos, as well as portable, such as their portable technology. These things facilitate their mobility, while possessions that are bulky or carry an identity value are seen as inhibiting their mobility.

Bardhi et al. (2012) further reveal that in global nomadism consumers value possessions in their particular context, but dispose of them when they move to the next location. These consumers are mainly drawn to things that perform a functional/instrumental role in their nomadic lives. In other words, in global nomadism, possessions are not valued because they display a sense of identity or help these consumers maintain a connection to a homeland or family left behind, for example, but because of their functionality in enabling mobility. Bardhi et al. (2012) conclude that nomadic consumers have developed an ephemeral and instrumental attachment to possessions, which they call liquid, as a way to manage their fragmented, nomadic lifestyle (cf. Bardhi and Eckhardt 2017).

Bardhi et al. (2012) extrapolate from these findings that this liquid form of attachment may also translate to how global nomads relate to places. Nomadism challenges the traditional notion of home as anchored to either a homeland (country of origin) or a particular house/place where one lives. As illustrated by the Pullman ad, global nomads identify themselves as 'citizens of the world' and do not anchor their identity to a particular national territory or place. They feel equally or even more comfortable living in a new country; they characterize their present residency as 'home base' but they are not emotionally attached to it.

Global nomads have designed a set of consumption practices that help them feel at home in each locality. For example, Bardhi et al. (2012) find that global nomads have established routines of traveling, relocating, as well as daily practices, such as those related to running, yoga, cooking, music listening, etc., that they deploy in each destination. Jason, one of their informants, testified to investing time and effort in building a knowledge of the new country he relocates to by starting to learn the language, cook its food, listen to its music, and read about its history before moving there. These homemaking practices provide a temporary sense of rootedness and orientation for a particular period of time, ranging from weeks to several months.

For a profile of the global nomad as a consumer see Box 10.1.

Box 10.1:   Real World Scenario

Who is the global nomadic consumer?

Meet Luca, an Italian IT consultant, who works for a large multinational corporation for a project in Vietnam. He loves travel and living in different countries and he sees traveling as a source of self-development and discovery. Luca does not remember a time when he was not traveling and moving for work, studies or leisure. He was born in Saudi Arabia where his parents were expatriates working in the oil industry. Growing up, he often travelled with his parents to visit his family in Italy or take vacations in other countries. He returned to Italy and finished his high school and university degrees, during which time he continued to travel around Europe. After finishing his high school, he took a year off to travel around the world. After graduation, Luca actively pursued a career abroad and started to work on a project in Denmark. Since then he has worked and lived in 12 countries during the past nine years, including the UK, United States, Botswana, Papua New Guinea, Russia, Australia, etc.

Luca does not own an apartment or a house; rather, he lives in rental apartments provided by his employer or client. He does not have a permanent home address, but does have a personal email account. In fact, he testifies not to own many possessions and relocates from place to place with one carry-on bag. He does not own a car, but relies on public transport or sharing economy services, such as renting a car by the hour from the *BMW Drive Now* program, the *Zipcar* car clubs, or Uber services. While he is not very picky about his living conditions, he tries to live next to a major airport for easy access to weekly trips to and from the airport, or in the city center as a convenient location to quickly form social connections and create a sense of home.

Luca is a member of a frequent flyer club and has a very established routine of preparing for travels. He feels at home in his airline's frequent flyer club, and relaxes when he hears the soundscape of his airline. Similarly, he remains loyal to his favorite hotels in each of the locations that he has lived or visited. He requests to stay in the same room if possible and expects to find the room arranged and prepared in a particular way that is consistent across destinations. He is very ritualistic when it comes to his exercise routines. He tries to have a frictionless experience of movement during his travels. From our research, we show that these are attempts to establish a sense of security and stability when life includes a constant change of environment.

Luca testifies that his most valuable possession is his mobile phone and laptop. However, he is very much aware that he needs to replace these possessions regularly. At times, he may not be able to use them in some of the locations he travels to because of the lack of digital infrastructure or potential legal regulations. Over time, he has developed a tendency to 'travel light' and not get attached to possessions, people, and places. For him, possessions serve a useful role within a given locality and are often disposed of when Luca is relocating to another place. He also has learned to live in the present and live life to the fullest in each locality. This orientation sometimes gets him into trouble with his family when he forgets birthdays or holiday celebrations while his parents are in Italy and he is abroad. Luca extensively uses digital communication services for his work to stay in touch with friends around the world, to pay his bills and manage his apartment while traveling.

Luca has developed an omnivorous and cosmopolitan taste for foods, music, arts, and culture. Different from the stereotypical Italian expat or migrant who nostalgically consumes pizza and spaghetti, Luca prefers to eat the local foods as much as possible to explore the local culture and cuisine. In his fridge, he stores foods from all his past 'homes', such as HP sauce from his time in London, pickled herring from his time in Scandinavia, as well as the ingredients for fresh homemade pasta. This omnivorous eclecticism extends to his reading and musical taste.

Luca does not define himself by any nationality, including his country of origin; he has three citizenships and sees passports as a necessity for fluid mobility. Home is wherever he is – a base of operations. Socially, he spends time with his local colleagues, while he also relies on expat or other transnational communities in a locality (e.g. Internations – www.internations.org/ or Hash House Harriers). Social media platforms enable Luca to keep up with events and to join groups and clubs, such as running, hiking, and dining. Luca loves traveling and living in different countries and does not plan to retire or settle down any time soon.

As shown, global nomads, like Luca, display distinct consumption profiles across food, music, home ownership, and material possessions, which distinguish them from other mobile consumers. Understanding global nomad consumers is specifically important for global and international sectors such as hospitality, healthcare, finance, education, etc.

Cosmopolitan lifestyles. CCT research has also documented how global mobilities shape consumers' taste, specifically enhancing their cosmopolitanism, resulting in a higher cultural capital taste orientation. Cosmopolitanism is a taste structure defined as an 'intellectual and aesthetic stance of openness towards divergent cultural experiences' (Hannerz 1990: 239). Cosmopolitan consumers are oriented outside their immediate locality with broad international outlooks, willing to engage with other cultures, and curious about places, people, cultures, and their historical contexts. Typically, cosmopolitans are portrayed as people who are comfortable living and working in foreign countries, engage in international travel, and are fluent in foreign languages (Hannerz 1996). Concepts that stand in opposition to cosmopolitanism are nationalism, ethnocentrism, parochialism, and patriotism. Prior research has established that cosmopolitanism is an important orientation of mobile consumers, and that global nomads are cosmopolitans. Additionally, people tend to become more cosmopolitan when they engage with a greater variety of foreign products and cultural symbols (Cannon and Yaprak 2002), which can be seen as a form of virtual travel (Emontspool and Georgi 2016).

Two key CCT studies have examined cosmopolitan tastes and consumption behaviors. The first study is that of Holt (1997), who studied cosmopolitan lifestyles within affluent middle-class consumers in the United States. He conceptualized cosmopolitanism as a lifestyle or value orientation of the elite social classes that anchor themselves outside their localities, in urban socialities, and lifestyles of metropolitan areas. Cosmopolitans represent the upper tier of the middle class, a highly educated urban class with high cultural capital (HCC) taste. Holt finds that cosmopolitan consumers travel regularly on holidays or to metropolitan areas to attend to their networks, and participate in national rather than local organizations. While both cosmopolitans and locals have a preference for variety in their consumption patterns, they differ with regard to what constitutes variety (Holt 1997: 13), i.e., what is exotic for the local is mundane for the cosmopolitan. Further, locals find comfort in the familiar and tend to avoid foreignness, while cosmopolitans seek out and desire exotic consumption objects, products, and experiences.

The second key CCT study is authored by Thompson and Tambyah (1999) and examines cosmopolitanism among the transnational expatriate elite. Thompson and Tambyah show that the cosmopolitan identity project is constructed on the basis of the ideology of cosmopolitanism, situated and produced within the 'institutional matrix of global cultural tourism' (1999: 216) that organizes the global flows of objects, people, and resources in a global system of 'sending societies', 'destination societies', and an 'extensive network of tourist-support and service businesses' (1999: 219). The cosmopolitan identity project is positioned within the high, elite social classes and gender position of male ideology. Cosmopolitan identity is shifting; cosmopolitans are positioned to participate in many worlds without becoming part of them (cf. Hannerz 1990).

Commercial travel has been always an important part of cosmopolitan narratives, and Thompson and Tambyah (1999) show that cosmopolitan expatriates think of travel as means of self-development and self-enhancement. Their connection with local cultures remains important and they consume actively cultural differences in a reflexive, intellectualizing manner (1999: 216) by incorporating diversity into their identities and adapting their consumption patterns, tastes, and material possessions to local cultures. Additionally, cosmopolitan ideals of freedom, mobility, and detachment coexist with consumer desires for personal connections, stability, and attachments. Their data show that cosmopolitan expatriates embody practices that resist their own ideals of cultural flexibility such as periodically longing for cultural ambiences and environmental qualities of their home countries. They reinforce emotional ties to family and home by making regular visits to their home countries and phoning regularly to friends and family. They also travel with home possessions to help them create a sense of home while mobile. Similar to migrants, expatriates often experience feelings of being out of place and they long for community and social connection. In response, they strive to create a sense of community through transient relations with other expatriates. They participate in expatriate social clubs and communities, like the online global community of InterNations (www.internations.org) to experience a sense of sociality through common consumption practices and activities.

We have so far discussed the research on a variety of types of human global mobility and implications for consumption. However, this discussion has mainly focused on individual mobility. We turn next to families and global mobility.

Mobile Families and Economic Remittances

Remittances are economic resources sent back to the home country by people living abroad. These remittances are either in the form of official investment and bank transfers or in the forms of unofficial and informal flows, such as gift giving. The cultural, economic, and political significance of remittances are profound, with the worldwide remittance in 2015 exceeding $601 billion, of which developing countries received about $441 billion, nearly three times the amount of official development assistance (World Bank 2016). Although the true size of remittances, including unofficial and informal flows, is significantly larger, the official records show economic remittances sent by migrant and expat communities to be as high as 42% of the GDP in some developing countries, such as Tajikistan, Kyrgyz Republic, and Nepal.

In CCT, theories of transnationalism and transnational families have been used to explore the relationship between economic remittances, family-making practices, and consumption (see Peñaloza and Arroyo 2010). Of particular note is the concept of the *transnational social field*, which is defined as 'combinations of social and symbolic ties, positions in networks and organizations, and networks of organizations that can be found in at least two geographically and internationally distinct places' (Faist 1998: 216). Transnational families inhibit transnational social spaces that are formed of different institutions (e.g. family, organizations, markets) and connect different localities and cultures through monetary exchanges, flows of objects, and personal connections.

In transnational spaces, consumption continues to be a driving force that holds transnational families together. For example, monetary remittances are used to compensate for the absence of family members by providing financial resources for necessary family expenditures, such as healthcare, food, education, rent, and paying back loans (Peñaloza and Arroyo 2010). Remittances and the objects that are sent back home by migrants as gifts, impact the type of consumption that transnational families can afford, and function as an acculturative agent for members of the families who stayed behind and never left their home countries (Hughes and Askegaard 2008). In the context of transnational families, the economic capital earned by migrants abroad is transferred to economic, social and, at times, cultural capital (such as gaining educational credentials) of family members in the home country. Monetary remittances and objects sent back home are used by members of the family to negotiate their social relations and social status, for example, when children are seen with branded clothes and toys in their village. The case of transnational remittances illustrates the local cultural and social embeddedness of transnational consumption.

Living in a transnational family structure and relying on income earned in another country is not limited to migrants, as Peñaloza and Arroyo (2010) have shown in the case of Mexican migrants in the United States with families in Mexico. The phenomenon of transnational family structures is on the rise due to the requirements of the contemporary global economy. International work assignments, where individuals work in one country and live in another (Lau et al. 2012) and 'dual-career commuter couples' who choose to live in separate geographic locations with frequent visits (Rhodes 2002) are some other examples of transnational families. In this case, multiple countries and localities impact consumption at a point in time. These families are well educated and professional, with an average age of mid- to late thirties, ranging between 25 to 65 years old, with 40% to 50% having children, and more than half married for at least nine years (Anderson and Spruill 1993; Rhodes 2002). For transnational families, remittances, in the form of cash flow or flows of objects as gifts, hold families together and perform as an acculturative agent when individuals are physically far from the host culture (Askegaard et al. 2005).

Human Global Mobilities and Conflict

Global nomads, cosmopolitan consumers, and economic migrants typically choose a mobile lifestyle, whereas political refugees normally have no choice but to flee from war and persecution in order to survive. For indigenous consumers, in turn, who are expected to welcome these nomads, cosmopolites, and migrants to their home country, or even their neighborhood, and acculturate to their lifestyles, choices are relatively limited as well.

Berry (2001) makes the important point that immigration psychology encompasses the attitudes and orientations of immigrant groups (the traditional focus of research) and those of the indigenous population that constitutes the dominant society. While indigenous consumers have received less attention, their cultural experiences are fundamentally affected by immigration and their reactions to these population influxes can influence the kinds of experiences and acculturation strategies of immigrant groups. Berry (2001: 681) identifies four strategies that indigenous consumers adopt when responding to an influx of, and a co-existence with, mobile consumers. These strategies are multiculturalism, segregation, melting pot, and exclusion. In multiculturalism, the cultural diversity offered by immigrants is valued and encouraged. This pluralistic orientation, however, might be limited to certain classes of immigrants and certain types of culture – food and music for example – but not extended to other domains such as religion. The multiculturalism tends to be fragile. Socio-economic or political turmoil where members of the dominant society see immigrants as a social threat or drain on societal resources can easily displace multiculturalism. In segregation, the larger society is willing to tolerate immigrants so long as they remain in designated socio-cultural enclaves and participate in mainstream fields under specific contractual conditions – such as performing service work. This orientation tends to incent immigrants to avoid forming relationships with the host culture. The melting pot strategy demands immigrants assimilate to the dominant culture and embrace its language, norms, and taste. This, in turn, pushes immigrants toward a process of assimilation. Assimilation attenuates obvious expressions of cultural difference. Finally, exclusion manifests an extreme version of segregation in which immigrants are never accepted as having a legitimate place in the dominant society. The plight of Romani (pejoratively known as gypsies), a nomadic ethnic group who face significant discrimination throughout Europe, exemplifies this condition.

This relatively abstract level of 'strategies', however, is not fine-grained enough to understand why the influx of global consumers can cause conflict in destination countries. A potentially better way of exploring the sources of conflict in migration settings is to analyze the relationships that indigenous and immigrant consumers wish to form with each other, and compare these expectations to those relationships that they think they actually have. As Luedicke's (2015) CCT study on indigenous consumer acculturation shows, Alan Page Fiske's (1991) theory of the four fundamental relational models is useful for this purpose.

In this study, Luedicke explores how indigenes who have lived in a small Western Austrian village for generations envision their authority, community, equality, and market-based relationships with first, second, and third-generation immigrants from Turkey. The study shows why these indigenes struggle with the Turkish migrant consumers. The Austrians see their political and cultural dominance slowly eroding. They believe that immigrants garner too many financial and cultural benefits relative to what they contribute. They also believe that homeowners in their community, and even once-iconic local brands, are selling out their heritage to immigrant consumers. Locals resent that immigrants have gained sufficient resources to take ownership of 'their' local resources and consumer culture. As a consequence, indigenes may well try to be humanistic Europeans who welcome migrant consumers to their village and respect their alternative ways of being, but despite such cognitive efforts, locals still end up discriminating quite drastically against these immigrants (Luedicke 2015). This discriminatory behavior is sometimes termed nativism.

Box 10.2 illustrates how migrant consumers perceive the situation in the Austrian village and how they try to cope with the negative feelings produced by discrimination.

Box 10.2:   Critical Reflection

How indigenes disillusion their immigrants

How does Özkan, a 28-year-old metal welder who was born in rural Austria into a first-generation immigrant family from rural Turkey, experience life in an Austrian village? How does he perceive and interact with local, indigenous Austrian citizens? What are his workplace experiences? How does he feel treated in local market settings? For most local consumers in such a village, from workers to high cultural capital intellectuals, the acculturation experiences of a second-generation immigrant are difficult to imagine. So, let us share some empirical insight from our research in such a setting.

Özkan was born in 1989 to Turkish immigrant parents in a small, Western Austrian town. He is an Austrian citizen, went through school, completed his apprenticeship as a metal welder at the second attempt, and married a Turkish woman with whom he has a daughter. His father immigrated to Vienna in 1976 and spent his entire life working for Austrian construction companies. His father married a Turkish woman, bought a house, and raised three sons. His mother worked most of her life for a cleaning company.

Özkan speaks the local dialect like a local, pursues his job like a local, and pays taxes like a local. He works all day and most weekends, does not drink alcohol, and does not commit crimes, except for speeding and the occasional road race. He is as religious as most locals, but attends service in a mosque, not a church. Özkan is also a resourceful consumer. He buys cars in Germany, drives to Italy to buy cleaning products for family and friends, and saves most of his income eventually to buy a house. He is well connected to other Turkish immigrant families in the town and beyond. He prefers his daughter growing up in the small town rather than in the neighboring city, because 'in the village people watch out for each other'. Some of his local work colleagues have become friends. On all of these dimensions, he seems firmly integrated into the Austrian society and lives both, Turkish and Austrian culture. However, because he has inherited Turkish complexion and hair color from his parents, locals tend to treat him like a '*Zuag'reister*' (foreigner) not an '*Einheimischer*' (local).

However, Özkan is also an angry man. Throughout his life he has so many frustrating experiences with locals discriminating and taking advantage of him that he maintains a mental 'black list' of people that he will exact revenge on, if fortune ever turns. His former landlord is on this list, because he agreed the lease with a handclasp, but then never repaired anything and also forced Özkan to replace an expensive wooden floor that he did not damage. A police officer who stopped Özkan in his car is on his list, asking 'Why you drive so fast?' imitating a Turkish immigrant voice. He continued using this way of speaking ('I you ask, why you drive so fast') after Özkan responded to him in local dialect, and fined him, while letting the Austrian driver that raced against him leave straight away. And he is also not on good terms with his Austrian neighbors, who regularly complain and once even called the police when Özkan had friends over on a Saturday evening and the children were running through the flat.

Özkan feels like he is treated as a guilty party whatever he does. He sees working-class Austrians living on welfare, drinking, exploiting the state, and complaining against the 'fucking Turks', while he and the other immigrant families are working hard, saving money, and doing all the dirty work. To him, the injustice of discrimination and being treated like a nuisance, rather than an honest, valuable taxpayer, is almost unbearable. He summarizes: '*What do I have to prove? Do I really have to act like they think a Turk should act? Smash someone's face? Run around with a knife and stuff? Do I really have to act like that to be accepted as Turk as a normal citizen? I don't understand it. What do they want? This situation is very difficult for me.*'

How do Özkan and fellow first-, second-, and third-generation immigrants cope with this situation? He appreciates that many locals actually reach out to the Turkish community and nurture individual relationships with co-workers, beginning to understand and respect their fellow villagers more. He also sees that his own immigrant community, in turn, is gradually eroding and, with increasing wealth, replaces mutual support with more individual lives and consumption practices (see Luedicke 2015 for the locals' side). But nevertheless, Özkan is angry: '*Theoretically, I have the right to tell the locals to fuck off, grab their throat, and ask them "where is the letting contract" when renting a place. But I don't do that. I could also go on a killing spree and then go to prison. Then my family and I would be taken care of. But I always calm myself. I don't do anything illegal … The time will come when I can take revenge, when I am the landlord and tell them that they broke something, and then the attorney is a Turk, too. What will they do then?*'

From our research, we know that many local villagers understand that they are discriminating against immigrants and do not pay them respect. They justify their behavior, in part, as attempts at rebalancing skewed authority, equality, and community relationships between Turks and Austrians (Luedicke 2015). The complex and troubled relationship with the Turks seems to animate local fears that the immigrants will eventually take over and take revenge, dominating locals like they have been dominated before. Some locals even said that they 'did not have a slave revolt yet'.

In a larger historical perspective, hopes are that the two cultures will eventually blend and Turkish names and cultural ways will become commonplace in the village. It remains for consumer behavior researchers to explore ways to speed up the process of acculturation via fostering a more positive acculturation culture and providing immigrant consumers with equal access to wealth and respect.

Immigrants are easy to spot and easy to condemn in political campaigns whereas the more intangible global flows of (neoliberal) ideologies (see Chapter 11), hyperindividualistic lifestyles, fundamentalist religions, or ecological and technological risks are more difficult to address. This co-mingling of global mobilities seems to create fertile grounds for discriminatory and protectionist regimes to gain power. Existing CCT studies on consumer acculturation sadly indicate that immigrants are easy targets for discriminatory practice by indigenous consumers who themselves experience massive cultural transitions due to global flows of all sorts.

CONCLUSION

Global mobility has become an integral part of consumers' daily professional or leisure lives. It constitutes an important area of research for CCT scholars. Mobile lifestyles affect consumer wellbeing, sense of security, and empowerment in complex ways. CCT scholars have shown that consumers may benefit from mobilities via, for example, increased access to consumer products and markets. Embracing mobile lifestyles can be a path to upward mobility, experiencing new ways of life, accumulating cultural and economic capital, in turn leading to empowerment, and the acquisition of new resources to perform and negotiate one's identity (see Chapter 1). However, for many, global mobility is an experience of alienation, cultural shock, and often ethnic and racial discrimination. Lacking the necessary cosmopolitan cultural or economic capital inhibits the chances of successful consumer acculturation.

Box 10.3:   Extended Case Study

Globalization, food cultures, and travel[1]

Food cultures have become increasingly transnational in character, facilitating encounters and consumption of the cultural Other. Growth in migrant communities as well as travels abroad have resulted in inclusion of foreign cuisines in our daily diets. For example, Mexican and Chinese food have become integral parts of the American food culture, as has the Döner kebab version of Turkish food in Northern Europe. Food becomes the locus of innovative cultural boundary crossing and enables us selectively and temporarily to incorporate the Other into the self. Hybridizing food cultures also problematizes the neat organization of domestic food into categories of what is local and what is foreign. Exotic food categories, such as Coca-Cola, sushi, pizza, curry, burgers, Lo Mein, etc. for example, become commonplace in many cuisines and part of many urban consumers' daily diet. Consequently, they are disembedded from their culture of origin.

Shifting our focus to international travel, let us consider how food consumption changes during travel. Millions of people cross borders every day for leisure or business. Travel is more and more commonplace, yet, stories of cultural shock and alienation continue to emerge. How do travelers manage negative experiences of cultural shock and alienation? How does travel change their relationship to domestic and foreign food? These are some of the questions we raise based on findings from a qualitative study of 28 American

---

[1]This case study is based on a study published in the following two articles: Bardhi, F., Ostberg, J., and Bengtsson, A. (2010) 'Negotiating cultural boundaries: Food, travel and consumer identities', *Consumption Markets & Culture, 13* (2), 133–57; Bengtsson, A., Bardhi, F., and Venkatraman, M. (2010) 'How global brands travel with consumers: An examination of the relationship between brand consistency and meaning across national boundaries', *International Marketing Review, 27* (5): 519–40.

middle-class travelers from a large, East coast US city during a 10-day leisure and edu-cational trip to China. As part of their MBA program, these middle-aged executives were asked to participate in a study about their consumption before, during, and after their visit to China. While this was their first visit to China, they did not expect to face any challenges with Chinese cuisine or Chinese culture during their visit. The participants testified to consuming Chinese food routinely, especially through visits to the so-called 'China town' in their home city. In fact, American food culture is multicultural and for many American consumers, Chinese cuisine is part of daily consumption.

Typically, travel abroad is considered as a search for difference, variety seeking, pleas-ure, and play with the exotic cultural Other. During the first couple of days, these travelers enjoyed experimenting with various Chinese foods. They enjoyed the local beers, cheap fresh fruit, vegetarian dishes, Chinese deserts, and etc.

> 'The fruits in China were awesome. The grapefruit juice in China is really fresh; it's like a taste that I didn't notice anywhere not even here [US]. Here you can just taste the bitterness; over there you can taste the natural, so I had that every morning. I also liked the desserts. They make little cakes, Chinese cakes, which are really good ...' (Melissa)

However, after several days in China, informants wanted a break from local Chinese food and began to experience local food more negatively, full of anxiety and alienation. As Daniel puts it:

> 'Soon we had all realized how sick of Chinese food we got to be and if there would be our choice of where to dine, we would go for Western food.'

This negative stance escalated over time as the informants perceived the Chinese food to be monotonous; or they lacked the knowledge to make sense of it:

> 'Sometimes food came out and we didn't know what it was ... Slowly we reached with our chopsticks and tasted something: is it chicken, pork, duck, veal, lamb? We knew it is meat but we didn't know what meat it was.' (Greg)

Negative attitudes towards Chinese food experiences extended to include serving style, as the use of chopsticks turned the mealtimes into chores:

> 'I was not really comfortable with the dishes and way of eating. It was my first time and I felt forced to use chopsticks. If I go here at our [Chinese] restaurants, you will always have a fork. So, there it was pretty hard to handle them and I was like eating rice with chopsticks and it took me forever ... We did like the food, but around the third or fourth day, it was like I need a break.' (Gracie)

(Continued)

(Continued)

The national origin of the food was one way informants classified their inter-cultural experiences. In the following quote, Pauline made sense of her dining experience by using social class (informants ate at restaurants that catered to upper-middle classes locally) and ethnicity (us versus them, the Chinese) to interpret the servicescape. By categorizing the servicescape, informants classified themselves as different. As Pauline stated, she imagined herself part of a 'normal', 'average-looking' global middle-class community.

> 'The customers look pretty normal, in the sense that they looked like us, other than that they were Chinese. There weren't bums there, but there weren't people in furs there either, they were just kind of average looking people and not a lot of Westerners in the sense like there were a lot of Chinese customers. We were a little out of place because we were Westerners. Didn't feel uncomfortable but it wasn't like the whole place was full of Americans or Westerners, it was like the place was very much part of the culture.' (Pauline)

Culture shock experienced through consumption in China created a situation where consuming non-Chinese food became symbolic of searching for and finding 'home' abroad. Consuming non-Chinese food provided a sense of familiarity and confidence for our informants. These risk-free and predictable foods provided comfort.

> 'The pizza itself was like thin crust, it reminded me of pizza that I could just find like at a food shop at home so it was very familiar in look. I couldn't recall the taste of Chinese pizza versus American pizza, but the texture of it, the look, it just had that aura of I can just be eating this somewhere like in the States and be okay with it ... So every time we saw Chinese food, I was unsure what the taste would be or what it actually was, beef, pork, or chicken. With the pizza it was a comfort in knowing that it is just bread and dough and sauce and cheese. The comfort of eating the pizza, knowing what to anticipate, reminded me of home.' (Sabrina)

Globalization processes have created a standardized socio-cultural environment that enables travelers to find 'home' abroad as illustrated in the quote by Melissa below. By turning to foods protoypical of American culture, travelers can restore their sense of control and affirm their cultural identity. Note how Melissa engaged in extensive effort to find familiar food.

> 'It was like 9 pm and I don't know where to find pizza place here. I go for pizza and I don't care if I have to walk or pick a cab. So, I ask these people in the hotel where to get some pizza and it was like pizza, it's kind of far from here ... I see a pizza place, oh my god pizza like now I feel like calm. So I bought a Hawaiian pizza that I like, but the cheese is not real cheese that you have here [US], like really oily kind like it just hangs, it's more like kind of stays, more like thick; but it's not like that all that dripping thing;

it was really good pizza and it had pineapple which is good and fresh so that was a non-Chinese experiment. When I had it I was like: now this is home, because I [was] just getting tired of the [Chinese] food.' (Melissa)

Food and brands not preferred in the domestic setting by dint of familiarity and non-Chinese became desirable in the foreign cultural context. Familiarity and relative scarcity fuels positive evaluation in a culturally different context. In other words, global fast food chains such as McDonald's, KFC, Pizza Hut, Starbucks became symbols of home, and helped travelers cope with culture shock. Note also that the association with home infused consumption of the humble McDonald's hamburger in China with positive emotion.

'The food is much, much different than everything I ever had, so it was kind of interesting that whole McDonald's thing [...] I was excited to find the McDonald's because I knew they have a hamburger and something that was familiar for me to eat. So, from that perspective I ate more McDonald's in China than I have the last 10 years in the US, so it was kind of an exciting event in that regard.' (Daniel)

Questions

1. Have the findings of this study and behavior of these travelers surprised you? Why did they experience cultural shock and alienation?
2. Discuss how prior exposure to Chinese food back in the United States shapes their experience with Chinese food and culture during this trip?
3. Can you think of other types of travelers that may not experience such cultural alienation from this trip, but embrace the cultural diversity and experimentation? How would they experience this trip?
4. What can you conclude about how travel changes our consumption and relation to brands? What is the role that global brands play in this case? What can be some implications for the likes of McDonald's and Starbucks, for example?

RESEARCH DIRECTIONS

We suggest some areas for future research. The first is further exploring the dark sides of global mobilities and their impacts on consumers' wellbeing and feelings of (dis)empowerment. By this we mean exploring the challenges and consequences of fragmented and decentralized mobile lifestyles, including psychological wellbeing and social security and the role of consumption in managing these challenges. Consumer culture scholars have highlighted the central role of material objects, especially those symbolizing the country of origin, in managing homesickness when migrants live far from their country of birth. Global nomads, on the other hand, develop dematerialized consumption patterns and a liquid relationship to possessions to manage their unstable nomadic lives, where the absence of locality is dominant. Further examinations of the challenges and difficulties of mobile lifestyles and the role of consumption in restoring stability while maintaining fluidity is required. For example, how can consumption facilitate transnational family structures and maintain a sense of collectivity when members of the family live for extended periods in separate geographical locations? What consumption forms and rituals emerge in response to transnational family settings? How can brands better cater to geographically dispersed families?

The second area that demands further exploration is the prospect of global mobilities in light of the recent global political changes. The rise of antiglobalization narratives in Western countries and the United Kingdom's departure from the European Union (Brexit) are two important dynamics in our contemporary global political landscape that could impact the future of global mobilities, disrupt transnational family arrangements, and limit access to crucial services such as healthcare and education. More studies on the origins of these global political changes and their implications for the future of human mobilities and consumption are required. Specific questions for further research may include:

1. How do specific instances of populist political discrimination – such as a US travel ban targeting citizens of seven nations, a vote against European migrants to the United Kingdom, or a right-wing anti-immigrant election victory in Austria – affect the relationships between, and consumption choices of, immigrant and indigenous consumers in the discriminating and discriminated countries? For, example, how do such decisions affect the perception and consumption of brands from the countries initiating discrimination?
2. When physical border crossings are inhibited, what other forms of mobilities emerge and how can consumption facilitate the new forms? Consider here the migrant camps that have formed on a number of international borders.
3. How do shifts in acculturation culture – e.g. the spirit of a multicultural, cosmopolitan nation being replaced with a spirit of anxious nativism – affect the consumption and workplace decisions of global mobile consumers, and what happens to employers, leisure destinations, and shopping meccas in case the class of global mobile professionals and consumers stay away?

RECOMMENDED READING

Bardhi, F., Eckhardt, G.M., and Arnould, E.J. (2012) 'Liquid relationship to possessions', *Journal of Consumer Research*, *39* (3): 510–29.

Bardhi, F., Ostberg, J., and Bengtsson, A. (2010) 'Negotiating cultural boundaries: Food, travel and consumer identities', *Consumption Markets & Culture*, *13* (2): 133–57.

Luedicke, M.K. (2015) 'Indigenes' responses to immigrants' consumer acculturation: A relational configuration analysis', *Journal of Consumer Research*, *42* (1): 109–29.

Vikas, R.M., Varman, R., and Belk, R.W. (2015) 'Status, caste, and market in a changing Indian village', *Journal of Consumer Research, 42* (3): 472–98.

REFERENCES

Anderson, E.A. and Spruill, J.W. (1993) 'The dual-career commuter family: A lifestyle on the move', *Marriage and Family Review, 19* (1–2): 131–47.

Appadurai, A. (1990) 'Disjuncture and difference in the global cultural economy', *Theory, Culture and Society, 7* (2): 295–310.

Appadurai, A. and Breckenridge, C.A. (1988) 'Why public culture?', *Public Culture, 1* (1): 5–9.

Askegaard, S., Arnould, E.J., and Kjeldgaard, D. (2005) 'Postassimilationist ethnic consumer research: Qualifications and extensions', *Journal of Consumer Research, 32* (1): 160–70.

Askegaard, S. and Eckhardt, G.M. (2012) 'Glocal yoga: Re-appropriation in the Indian consumptionscape', *Marketing Theory, 12* (1): 45–60.

Bardhi, F. and Eckhardt, G.M. (2017) 'Liquid consumption', *Journal of Consumer Research, 44* (3): 582–97.

Bardhi, F., Eckhardt, G.M., and Arnould, E.J. (2012) 'Liquid relationship to possessions', *Journal of Consumer Research, 39* (3): 510–29.

Bardhi, F., Ostberg, J., and Bengtsson, A. (2010) 'Negotiating cultural boundaries: Food, travel and consumer identities', *Consumption Markets & Culture, 13* (2): 133–57.

Bauman, Z. (2000) *Liquid Modernity*. Cambridge: Polity.

Bauman, Z. (2007) *Liquid Times: Living in an Age of Uncertainty*. Cambridge: Polity.

Berry, J.W. (2001) 'A psychology of immigration', *Journal of Social Issues, 57* (3): 615–31.

Cannon, H.M. and Yaprak, A. (2002) 'Will the real-world citizen please stand up! The many faces of cosmopolitan consumer behavior', *Journal of International Marketing, 10* (4): 30–52.

Cayla, J. and Arnould, E.J. (2008) 'A cultural approach to branding in the global marketplace', *Journal of International Marketing, 16* (4): 86–112.

Cayla, J. and Giana M. Eckhardt (2008) 'Asian Brands and the Shaping of a Transnational Imagined Community', *Journal of Consumer Research*, 35 (2): 216–230.

Connell, J. and Gibson, C. (2004) 'World music: Deterritorializing place and identity', *Progress in Human Geography, 28* (3): 342–61.

Cova, B., Pace, S., and Park, D.J. (2007) 'Global brand communities across borders: The Warhammer case', *International Marketing Review, 24* (3): 313–29.

Craig, S.C. and Douglas, S.P. (2006) 'Beyond national culture: Implications of cultural dynamics for consumer research', *International Marketing Review, 23* (3): 322–42.

D'Andrea, A. (2009) *Global Nomads: Techno and New Age as Transnational Countercultures in Ibiza and Goa*. London: Routledge.

Eckhardt, G.M. and Mahi, H. (2004) 'The role of consumer agency in the globalization process in emerging markets', *Journal of Macromarketing, 24* (2): 136–46.

Emontspool, J. and Georgi, C. (2016) 'A cosmopolitan return to nature: How combining aesthetization and moralization processes expresses distinction in food consumption', *Consumption Markets & Culture*, 1–23.

Faist, T. (1998) 'Transnational social spaces out of international migration: Evolution, significance and future prospects', *European Journal of Sociology, 39*: 213–47.

Faist, T. (2000) 'Transnationalization in international migration: Implications for the study of citizenship and culture', *Ethnic and Racial Studies, 23* (2): 189–222.

Fiske, A.P. (1991) *Structures of Social Life: The Four Elementary Forms of Human Relations: Communal Sharing, Authority Ranking, Equality Matching, Market Pricing*. Glencoe, IL: Free Press.

Fournier, S. (1998) 'Consumers and their brands: Developing relationship theory in consumer research', *Journal of Consumer Research, 24* (4): 343–73.

Gaviria, P.R. and Emontspool, J. (2015) 'Global cities and cultural experimentation: Cosmopolitan–local connections', *International Marketing Review, 32* (2): 181–99.

Ger, G. (2013) 'Islamic marketing at the nexus of global markets–religions–politics and implications for research', *Marketing Theory, 13* (4): 1470593113499702.

Hannerz, U. (1990) 'Scenarios for peripheral cultures', in A.D. King (ed.), *Culture, Globalization and the World System*. Basingstoke: Macmillan. pp. 107–28.

Hannerz, U. (1996) *Transnational Connections: Culture, People, Places*. London: Routledge.

Holt, D.B. (1997) 'Poststructuralist lifestyle analysis: Conceptualizing the social patterning of consumption in postmodernity', *Journal of Consumer Research, 23* (4): 326–50.

Hu, J., Whittler, T.E., and Tian, K. (2013) 'Resisting immigrant myths: Everyday consumer practices of Asian immigrants in America', *Consumption Markets & Culture, 16* (2): 169–95.

Hughes, M.U. and Askegaard, S. (2008) 'Capital build-up and transfer: The case of Turco-Danish transmigrants', *Advances in Consumer Research, 35*: 164–5.

Jafari, A. and Goulding, C. (2008) '"We are not terrorists!" UK-based Iranians, consumption practices and the "torn self"', *Consumption Markets & Culture, 11* (2): 73–91.

Lau, Y.K., Ma, J.L., Chan, Y.K., and He, L. (2012) 'Risk and protective factors of marital adjustment to cross-border work arrangement of Hong Kong residents: The perspective of stationary spouses', *Journal of Comparative Family Studies*, 715–30.

Levitt, T. (1983) 'The globalization of markets', *Harvard Business Review, 61* (3): 92–102.

Luedicke, M.K. (2011) 'Consumer acculturation theory: (Crossing) conceptual boundaries', *Consumption Markets & Culture, 14* (3): 223–44.

Luedicke, M.K. (2015) 'Indigenes' responses to immigrants' consumer acculturation: A relational configuration analysis', *Journal of Consumer Research, 42* (1): 109–29.

McKechnie, S. and Tynan, C. (2008) 'Halloween in a material world: Trick or treat?', *Journal of Marketing Management*, 24 (9–10): 1011–23.

Mehta, R. and Belk, R.W. (1991) 'Artifacts, identity, and transition: Favorite possessions of Indians and Indian immigrants to the United States', *Journal of Consumer Research*, 398–411.

Peñaloza, L. (1989) 'Immigrant consumer acculturation', in T.K. Srull (ed.), *Advances in Consumer Research*, vol. 16. Association for Consumer Research. pp. 110–18.

Peñaloza, L. (1994) 'Atravesando fronteras/border crossings: A critical ethnographic exploration of the consumer acculturation of Mexican immigrants', *Journal of Consumer Research*, 21 (1): 32–54.

Peñaloza, L. and Arroyo, J. (2010) 'Here, there, and beyond: Remittances in transnational family consumption', *Theoria y Praxis*, 10: 131–61.

Pieterse, J.N. (2003 [1995]) 'Globalization as hybridization', in R. Robertson and K.E. White (eds), *Globalization: Analytical Perspectives*. London: Taylor and Francis. pp. 265–90.

Rhodes, A.R. (2002) 'Long-distance relationships in dual-career commuter couples: A review of counseling issues', *The Family Journal*, 10 (4): 398–404.

Robertson, R. (1995) 'Glocalization: Time–space and homogeneity–heterogeneity,' in M. Featherstone, S. Lash, and R. Robertson (eds), *Global Modernities*. London: Sage.

Rudmin, F.W. (2007) 'Acculturation alchemy: How miscitations make biculturalism appear beneficial', *Psykologisk Tidsskrift*, 2: 4–10.

Sandıkcı, Ö. and Ger, G. (2010) 'Veiling in style: How does a stigmatized practice become fashionable?', *Journal of Consumer Research*, 37 (1): 15–36.

Sassen, S. (2012) 'When the center no longer holds: Cities as frontier zones', *Cities*, 34: 67–70.

Sutton-Brady, C., Davis, T., and Jung, M. (2010) 'Perceived cultural spaces and cultural in-betweens: Consumption among Korean Australians', *Journal of Consumer Behaviour*, 9 (5): 349–66.

Takhar, A., Maclaran, P., and Stevens, L. (2012) 'Bollywood cinema's global reach: Consuming the "diasporic consciousness"', *Journal of Macromarketing*, 32 (3): 266–79.

Thompson, C.J. and Tambyah, S.K. (1999) 'Trying to be cosmopolitan', *Journal of Consumer Research*, 26 (3): 214–41.

Thompson, J. and Troester, M. (2002) 'Consumer value systems in the age of postmodern fragmentation: The case of the natural health microculture', *Journal of Consumer Research*, 28 (4): 550–71.

Tinson, J. and Nuttall, P. (2010) 'Exploring appropriation of global cultural rituals', *Journal of Marketing Management*, 26 (11–12): 1074–90.

Üstüner, T. and Holt, D.B. (2007) 'Dominated consumer acculturation: The social construction of poor migrant women's consumer identity projects in a Turkish squatter', *Journal of Consumer Research*, 34 (1): 41–55.

Vikas, R.M., Varman, R., and Belk, R.W. (2015) 'Status, caste, and market in a changing Indian village', *Journal of Consumer Research*, *42* (3): 472–98.

Wallendorf, M. and Reilly, M.D. (1983) 'Ethnic migration, assimilation, and consumption', *Journal of Consumer Research*, *10* (3): 292–302.

Ward, S. (1974) 'Consumer socialization', *Journal of Consumer Research*, *1* (2): 1–14.

Wilk, Richard (1995) 'The local and the global in the political economy of beauty: From Miss Belize to Miss World', *Review of International Political Economy*, *2* (Winter): 117–34.

World Bank (2016) *Reports on Migration and Remittances*, 3rd edn. Washington, DC: World Bank Group.

PART FOUR

The Ideological Shaping of Consumption Practices and Consumers' Co-creative Appropriations

11
NEOLIBERALISM AND CONSUMPTION

Ela Veresiu, York University, Toronto
Markus Giesler, York University, Toronto

CHAPTER OVERVIEW

- Neoliberalism is a highly influential political-economic system or ideology that promotes free-market competition, deregulation, privatization, and individual responsibility.
- Since the 1970s, neoliberalism has become a dominant way for governments to address key social issues such as poverty, global warming, and chronic illness.
- Following the ideology of neoliberalism, governments form partnerships with corporations to encourage all citizens to become active and responsible consumer subjects.
- Responsible consumers are obliged to help solve pressing social issues through their everyday consumption choices.
- Some of the responsible consumption projects include green consumption and bottom-of-the-pyramid consumption.

INTRODUCTION

Neoliberalism is a dominant political-economic system, also known as a political ideology, used to organize societies (the people occupying a geographical area) and manage economies (the wealth and resources of a region). An ideology is defined as a set of ideas and ideals that influence the economic and political decisions of a particular country (e.g. the United States of America) or political region (e.g. the European Union). The ideology of neoliberalism encourages free-market competition, deregulation, privatization, and individual responsibility. At its core, neoliberalism complements market capitalism by favoring individual (private) interests over collective (public) goals. For example, profit maximization and wealth accumulation are private interests, whereas an equitable distribution of resources across a population is a public goal.

Supporters of neoliberalism believe that a free market without any restrictions enables unprecedented social and economic prosperity worldwide, from which everyone benefits. Neoliberalism's critics, however, believe that it widens the gap between the rich and the poor, and exposes consumers to higher risks (see the Critical Reflection in Box 11.1 for more details about criticism of neoliberalism versus support). Despite these concerns, neoliberalism has become the dominant way through which important social issues, such as poverty, global warming, and chronic illness are addressed by governments forming partnerships with corporations. Through these public–private partnerships, citizens are encouraged to become more active and responsible consumer subjects to help solve global social issues.

A social issue is defined as a major problem that affects a large number of people. In the past, these concerns were solely the responsibility of the state (aka governments). In our neoliberalized present, however, individual consumers are not only made to feel responsible for social issues, but also to help minimize them through their everyday consumption choices. Therefore, the overarching questions that guide this chapter are (1) how have social issues been reframed in market terms to make consumers feel responsible for their solution through their consumption choices? And (2) what new responsible consumption projects result from such neoliberal undertakings? To help provide some context to these overarching chapter questions, refer to the Critical Reflection in Box 11.2 for an overview of consumer culture research on the topic of politics in consumption.

Box 11.1:   Critical Reflection

Criticism of neoliberalism vs. its support

According to the United Nations' World Mortality Report (www.un.org/en/development/desa/population/theme/mortality/index.shtml), the worldwide shift from public (government-based and available to all) to private (market-based and available only to those who can afford it) healthcare delivery systems since the 1970s has left approximately 5.6 billion consumers without access to proper medical care and led to more than 47 million preventable deaths. Consider the following scenarios or social issues that have occurred since the 1970s across the world: a decline in the quality and availability of healthcare and education due to privatization; the disappearance of social safety nets for poor, disabled, and otherwise vulnerable populations; the undoing of food, health, and safety regulations; the exposure of consumers to increased risk and uncertainty in global financial markets; the disappearance of local agriculture systems in developing countries; reduced consumer access to basic necessities such as clean water and energy in developing countries; a surge in environmental disasters ranging from tsunamis to hurricanes to forest fires; and rising inequalities among men versus women (gender issues), visible minorities versus white citizens (race issues), and rich versus poor people (economic issues).

Remarkably, only a small number of activists, critical scholars, and researchers across the world view these events as evidence of neoliberalism's failure. For the majority of policy-makers, researchers, and even regular citizens, they believe that the best way to solve these social issues is through more neoliberalism or market-based reforms to further privatize healthcare, education, immigration, resource distribution, environmental protection, etc. Therefore, such global events and trends that create tensions in society set a specific neoliberal process in motion through which governments form partnerships with corporations. These public–private partnerships shift the responsibility for social, economic, and environmental wellbeing away from the state to self-governing consumer subjects. Consumers, in turn, are made to feel individually responsible to help solve these issues through their everyday consumption choices. Regardless of whether the benefits of responsible consumers' consumption projects are ever realized or not, the political ideology of neoliberalism nonetheless has remained the dominant way for governments to organize societies and manage economies worldwide.

Box 11.2:   Critical Reflection

Overview of consumer research on politics in consumption

To provide some context for this chapter, we briefly explore the relationship between politics and consumption in consumer culture research. Previous consumer research investigating how politics influence consumer culture, and therefore people's consumption choices and projects, has focused on three key topics. One research area is consumer activism, which documents individuals' and groups' quests to instigate real changes in existing product offerings, market practices, and advertising campaigns. One prominent type of consumer activism focuses on how products, brands, and advertisements negatively impact humans, animals, and the environment. Past examples of this form of consumer activism project include calls to boycott brands such as Nike, when it was discovered that its running shoes were produced in sweatshops with subpar conditions; McDonald's, when it became blatantly clear through documentaries such as Morgan Spurlock's film *Super Size Me* (2004) that it leads to obesity; Hummer cars that were known as gas guzzlers polluting the environment; or L'Oreal, due to the continued use of animal testing for its cosmetics.

When a corporation is found to jeopardize the health and wellbeing of people and the planet, consumer activists first publically shame it, especially online through social

(Continued)

(Continued)

media platforms such as Twitter and Facebook. They then make emotional and moral appeals for others to join the cause and stop purchasing products from the company under public scrutiny. Another type of consumer activism research considers consumer strategies beyond boycotts that are used to change existing market offerings. Examples range from Napster users, who fought for music to be shared and downloaded online, to plus-size women, who continue to fight for fast-fashion companies, such as H&M and Zara, to increase the sizes of their clothing lines.

A second political area of interest for consumer researchers is commonly referred to as consumer resistance. This research deals with individuals' critiques of, often Western, brands and consumer culture as a consequence of anti-corporate, anti-globalization, anti-branding, and voluntary simplicity political movements. For instance, voluntary simplicity, or simple living, is a way of life that rejects high-consumption projects and the materialistic lifestyles of Western consumer cultures in favor of downsizing and downshifting. One popular example is the tiny house movement, where people chose to build and live in the tiniest, mobile homes possible even if they can afford regular houses. Individuals engage in this type of political consumption project to demonstrate that humans can live healthy and fulfilling lives without owning so much stuff and occupying a lot of space. Another type of consumer resistance concerns consumer groups politicizing brands in order to motivate public resistance and rallies around particular causes (see Chapter 13 for detailed examples).

Lastly, a third research area investigates how the market tends to have depoliticizing effects by transforming political movements and revolutionary ideas into commodities and consumption projects, which is the exact opposite of their original intentions. Consider, for example, the Burning Man Festival that was created in 1986 as an anti-market celebration. This arts festival was designed to physically distance people from their regular lives and everyday consumption practices by spending a week in the dry, desolate desert. Instead of achieving this main goal, the festival has grown more commercial, expensive, and exclusive every year since its inception. By 2017, it was even reported in the popular press that Google employees attending the event dined on lobster in the middle of nowhere (Nevada's Black Rock desert). A second prominent example of market forces depoliticizing a political movement is the organic food market. This market was created by co-opting and commercializing the community-supported agriculture political movement, which, along with the ecological goals of reducing the amount of pesticides released into the environment and preserving topsoil, sought to form communal relations between farmers and consumers, improve economic outcomes for farmers, shift consumers' diets away from heavily processed (and resource-intensive) foods, and, last but not least, foster consumer autonomy from the corporate controlled food system. However, organics have become a lucrative branding strategy for major agribusiness firms who offer a broad range of highly processed foods using organic ingredients and shipped across the globe. This corporatization of organics maintains much of the high carbon footprint of conventional branded foods and has shifted the meaning of organics from a public critique of corporate power and ideals of social responsibility to privatized arguments related to ideals of healthiness and other individuated benefits. However, what remains understudied in this body of consumer research is the ways in which the political ideology of neoliberalism shapes people's consumption projects.

TRACING THE HISTORY OF NEOLIBERALISM

How has the political ideology (set of ideas and ideals) of neoliberalism come to dominate the way governments organize societies and manage economies? To answer this question, we must travel back in time to the first half of the 18th century, when a crucial change took place in the Western world (Europe and North America): the rise of the market society. During this time, a shift occurred from countries having a subsistence economy embedded in an agrarian (farming) society, where people simply wanted basic necessities such as food, water, shelter, and safety, to an industrial society embedded in an economy of gain, where people now wanted to make as much profit as possible. According to over-view historical studies, this shift in societies and economies, which is often referred to as *The Great Transformation*, gave rise to two opposing political ideologies: one advocating the protection of the market from society, known as market liberalism, and the other demanding the protection of society from the market, called social protectionism. Next, we briefly review these contradictory political ideologies. After that, we show how histori-cal tensions between them gave rise to the political ideology of neoliberalism.

Market Liberalism

One fundamental political ideology that emerged during the first half of the 18th century in the Western hemisphere is market liberalism. Market liberalism is defined as a political theory positing that markets should develop without any interference. In a nutshell, mar-ket liberalism supports a so-called free or self-regulating market, where prices for products and services are determined by unrestricted competition among privately owned compa-nies, by advocating that such an unregulated economy also leads to personal liberty, basic human rights, and collective interests. Overall the political ideology of market liberalism valorizes individual freedom, self-reliance, and choice.

Market liberalism emerged as a challenge to the absolute control and power first of monarchies, known as feudalism, then of states, known as mercantilism, which were the two main styles of government up until the 18th century. Feudalism is defined as a political system where power is dispersed between kings and nobles. Specifically, the nobility was given land from monarchies in return for their military service to defend kings and their kingdoms. At the same time, the nobility also protected the peasants who farmed their lands in exchange for them supplying the lords with food and other resources. However, feudalism had very negative consequences for the majority of people who were not kings or lords, since it forced them to live in squalid conditions at the mercy of the nobles, it spread diseases such as the bubonic plague, and it did not allow peasants to become educated.

Hence, by the end of the Middle Ages (15th century) Europe transitioned from a mostly agrarian and feudal system to one that was increasingly money- and state-based. As a consequence, a new political theory became influential, named mercantilism. Mercantilism posits that the prosperity of a country depends on its supply of capital, and that the global volume of trade is unchangeable. It can be thought of as a collection of political policies designed to keep the state (government) prosperous through heavy economic regulation. Through mercantilism, the economy is understood as a zero-sum game. This means that any gain by one party requires a loss by another. The state therefore exerts strict control over commercial practices. In other words, the state governs the market. Furthermore, mercantilism imagines the market as a means to arrange people and things so that the state becomes wealthy, strong, and powerful. As such, mercantilism was the cause of frequent wars among European nations at the time, and motivated colonial expansion in Africa, Asia, and the Americas.

Owing to too many expensive voyages and wars, mercantilism eventually lost its influence. In its place emerged the political ideology of market capitalism, which is defined as an economic and political system in which a country's trade and industry are controlled by private owners for profit. The rise in popularity of market capitalism also coincided with the rise of the nation-state as the most appealing way to organize people in the modern world. A nation-state is a type of political organization under which a relatively homogenous group of people inhabits an independent piece of land. Nation-states therefore merge the political idea of a sovereign territory with the cultural idea of a sacred homeland. Thus, by claiming a physical piece of land and associating it with a particular way of life and a common history (culture) nation-states solidified their way of organizing people and things over other competing forms of organization.

Pushing the idea of market capitalism even further, the political theory of market liberalism steadily gained currency in prominent political and cultural circles. Its aim was to realize the ideal of the self-regulating market using laissez-faire methods (no government intervention) and free trade among sovereign (independent) nation-states. Building on the idea that humans have an inborn moral sense of liberty, equality, responsibility, opportunity, and private property that guides their struggle for liberation from oppressive forces, such as the monarchy or the state, influential economists like Adam Smith (1723–1790) – a Scottish economist and philosopher widely regarded as the founder of modern economics – argued that the market functioned as a free zone of self-regulating exchange. Moreover, Adam Smith proposed that governments should not interfere in this free zone precisely to let the so-called invisible hand of the market automatically provide social benefits for the group from individual self-interest. Through market liberalism, the economy is understood as a non-zero-sum game of mutual enrichment. Hence, market liberalism interprets the market as a self-organizing system where individual and collective interests align. Following the idea of market liberalism, the state governs through the market, and the winning formula to do so is for the state to protect the market from any rules and regulations so that society can reap the natural benefits of exchange.

Social Protectionism

Whenever a political ideology is very pervasive, it inevitably leads to oppositional voices or counter-movements forming to criticize and try to change it. In the case of market liberalism, the opposite political ideology is social protectionism. Social protectionism is defined as a political theory positing that governments should manage the market economy in order to ensure that the welfare of society is not trammeled by the quest for profit maximization. In other words, society needs to be protected from the excesses of the free market. These protections can take the form of environmental regulations, consumer rights and safeguards, minimum wage laws, worker protection regulations, tariffs and price controls, product labeling requirements, and mandated product testing and safety certification processes, among others. Overall the political ideology of social protectionism valorizes social justice, solidarity, and community.

Social protectionism emerged during the second half of the 18th century. Individuals whose health and wellbeing had been negatively impacted by the self-regulating (aka free) market embraced social protectionism. This included the working class, peasants, and merchants, who worked non-stop in insufferable conditions for insufficient compensation. Specifically, some of the devastating consequences of market liberalism included disease and death caused by overcrowded cities with no sanitation codes, dangerous and dirty work conditions, and child labor. As a consequence, social protectionism proposed new methods for governments to introduce worker's rights, minimum wages, etc. These methods included passing binding laws for social protection and resource redistribution, as well as creating restrictive associations such as worker unions.

The political ideologies of market liberalism and social protectionism endorse contradictory ideas about how to achieve a prosperous economy and society. Therefore, the tradeoffs inherent in governments following one of these ideologies have precluded either one from gaining a clear advantage over the other. For instance, in the 19th century market liberalism was the more influential political ideology. This led to the creation of economic zones with no government intervention in several European nations. However, governments' lack of care about any social outcomes caused inequalities between the rich and the poor, worker oppression, social turmoil, and ultimately wars in countries such as France and England. However, solely following the ideas of social protectionism also created chaos and turmoil in countries like Germany, Italy, and Russia. For example, attempts to counteract the negative consequences of the free market through more extreme measures of social protection and retribution in the beginning of the 20th century led to the fascist crisis in Italy and the emergence of Nazism in Germany and communism in the Soviet Union, where people were once again severely oppressed and endangered by a political system. In the end, history proved that too much market freedom and too little government protection could be as aversive to social wellbeing as too much government protection and too little market freedom.

Neoliberalism

The need for governments to find an alternative solution to both market liberalism and social protectionism intensified after World War II. The first proposed political solution to rebuild countries' economies and societies was known as Keynesian economics. Although this theory was developed by the British economist John Maynard Keynes (1883–1946) during the 1930s as an attempt to understand and counteract the Great Depression, it picked up steam at the end of the war in 1945. The Great Depression (1929–1939) is known as the worst global economic downturn in the history of the industrialized world, which began with the infamous stock market crash of October 1929 in New York. Using Keynesian economics, governments sought to once again play a more directive and interventionist role in the market through means such as price controls and managing the supply and demand of commodities that they deemed essential, like foodstuffs, medicine, and fuel. These interventions were undertaken in an effort to maintain full employment and create a social safety net so that citizens would not have to again grapple with catastrophic economic downturns, like the Great Depression. Keynesian policies produced a welfare state: that is, a political system whereby the government takes a proactive role in protecting its citizens' health and wellbeing. A key policy feature of the welfare state is that it redistributes resources – via higher taxes on corporations and more affluent members of society – to provide benefits to less affluent citizens, via grants, pensions (such as Social Security in the US context) health care, child support, and other such state-sponsored benefits.

At the same time, however, a group of influential European and US economists warned that Keynesian economics and the welfare state model moved too much in the direction of social protectionism. They were afraid that too much state power exerted by governments meddling with the market would once again lead down the dangerous political path towards Nazism or communism. In 1947, these individuals, who included Noble Prize winners in Economic Sciences Friedrich Hayek (1899–1992), Milton Friedman (1912–2006), and George Stigler (1911–1991), formed a think tank – a body of experts providing advice on political and economic problems – named the Mont Pelerin Society (https://www.montpelerin.org/). Members of the Mont Pelerin Society were convinced that the central values of civilization were in danger and that only a global alliance of economic elites – individuals residing in the 90th percentile of income distribution or higher including scholars, politicians, and industrialists – committed to defending the competitive aspect of the market could defeat the threat of communism and other totalitarian political regimes. The aim of the think tank was to reform governments and corporations across the world through a revised political ideology: neoliberalism. The Mont Pelerin Society is therefore thought of as the birthplace of neoliberalism.

The Mont Pelerin Society argued that the Great Depression had been first and foremost a moral crisis rather than an economic crisis. Hence, they believed that it could be overcome by embracing the social Darwinist notion of competition or survival of the fittest as a dual economic and moral virtue. This idea of competition is central to the ideology of neoliberalism. These early proponents of neoliberalism asserted that competition among people enhances the global efficiency of economies by allowing the best individuals to contribute the most to prosperity. Competition also rewards individuals according to their merits, brings out the best in people, and allows them to better themselves.

Hence, neoliberalism is defined as a political theory positing that national governments should not interfere in the market economy, except to ensure that free-market competition is not compromised by collusions, monopolies, or localized restrictions (such as protectionist measures that impede the free flow of goods across borders). In other words, the state should govern for the market. Through neoliberalism, the economy is understood as a non-zero-sum game, similar to market liberalism, but of a constantly growing pie. The key difference between market liberalism and neoliberalism is that the former maintains that competition happens naturally among people, whereas the latter holds that competition is not a naturally occurring phenomenon of human nature so it must be continuously encouraged. Overall the political ideology of neoliberalism valorizes individual competition, responsibility, and opportunity seeking. As such, neoliberalism is particularly beneficial for corporations. Rather than designing the market in ways that cushion consumers from social, economic, environmental, and other such risks, governments advocate the transformation of all citizens into active, self-responsible entrepreneurs, otherwise called responsible consumer subjects.

However, while leading economists promoted the ideology of neoliberalism across the world through academic journals and think tanks such as the Mont Pelerin Society, it nonetheless remained a peripheral political view until the 1970s, when a new global financial crisis hit. Between 1973 and 1979, a dramatic increase in the world oil prices catapulted the 'First World' – the industrialized countries of Western Europe, North America, Japan, Australia, and New Zealand – into a severe economic recession, the 'Second World' – the former communist block countries of the Soviet Union and Eastern Europe – into an economic tailspin that eventually led to the dismantling of communism, and the 'Third World' – the developing countries of Asia, Africa, and Latin America – into a debt crisis giving rise to a condition of international aid dependency that continues to this day.

The political ideology of neoliberalism filled the void created by the breakdown of Keynesian policies. Governments hoped its ideals of competition, self-responsibility, and entrepreneurship would end the economic crises of the 1970s. Some of the first government leaders to adopt neoliberalism, and therefore set examples for the rest of the world, were the first female British Prime Minister Margaret Thatcher (1979–1990) and the 40th US President Ronald Reagan (1981–1989). The early success of their neoliberal policies during the 1980s, in turn, fostered a series of more moderate neoliberal transformations of traditionally social-democratic countries such as Canada, New Zealand, and Germany. Neoliberal reforms also occurred in South America, most notably in Chile through the military ruler Augusto Pinochet (1973–1990). Chile's success story persuaded transnational organizations and governments that neoliberalism is the ideal way to solve the problems of developing economies in South America. US-influenced multilateral agencies like the International Monetary Fund (IMF) and the World Bank soon began tying loans for Third World countries to the implementation of neoliberal reforms. Similarly, the IMF demanded neoliberal reforms as a precondition for the successful integration of post-apartheid South Africa and post-communist Eastern-European societies into the world economy.

These neoliberal reforms called for all governments to defend competition by putting moral pressure on individuals to act in self-governing and entrepreneurial ways. Furthermore, neoliberalism requires social problems to become a shared responsibility among governments, corporations, and citizens. In this new political-economic landscape, groups that traditionally protected society such as governments and trade unions did not become obsolete, but rather formed partnerships with nongovernmental organizations, charities, and corporations. One successful example of such a public–private partnership is the World Economic Forum (WEF). The WEF is a powerful think tank or international organization for public–private cooperation, whose mission statement is cited as 'committed to improving the state of the world by engaging business, political, academic, and other leaders of society to shape global, regional, and industry agendas' (www.weforum.org/). Refer to the Real World Scenario in Box 11.3 for more details about the WEF.

Box 11.3:   Real World Scenario

The World Economic Forum

Originally founded in 1971 by Geneva business professor Klaus Schwab, the World Economic Forum (WEF) has since established itself as one of the most influential global political and economic agenda setters in the contemporary world. For one week in January of each year, the forum gathers leaders from the top 1,000 transnational corporations, representatives from 100 of the most influential media groups, key policy-makers from national and regional governments and from international organizations, and select academics, experts, and activists from political, economic, scientific, social, and technological fields for their so-called annual meeting in the exclusive ski resort of Davos, Switzerland. WEF members then develop multilateral policy visions that shape global, regional, and industry agendas on a vast array of key social issues including poverty, global warming, chronic illness, education, and financial security. The World Economic Forum also facilitates meetings among governments and corporations throughout the year and produces reports on how to solve key social issues. Visit the following website for a video introduction of the WEF: https://youtu.be/LWP9kPzaBBo.

By embracing the ideology of neoliberalism, governments transformed themselves from regulators to facilitators, and began to consult, trade, and compete over the deployment of flexible guidelines that instill an ethos of personal consumer responsibility in their citizens. As a consequence of this historical trajectory, today key social issues that cause tensions and turmoil in society, such as poverty and global warming, almost invariably trigger a government intervention into society in the name of competition. Feeling called upon to defend the principle of competition, economic elites, such as those found at the World Economic Forum including government leaders, emphasize the increased ethical responsibility of individual consumers as the key to the solution of a spotlighted global problem. These responsible consumer subjects understand the social risk in question no longer as an obligation of the government to solve but rather as a self-care problem to manage. To examine this new type of responsible consumer subject, we will now unpack two cases of responsible consumption projects from the World Economic Forum.

Box 11.4: Case Study

Bottom-of-the-pyramid consumption

One major social issue on the rise and of interest to members of the World Economic Forum during our research of this think tank was poverty. The United Nations' announcement to 'cut the proportion of people living in extreme poverty in half by the year 2015', after shockingly revealing that roughly 4 billion people in the world were actually forced to live on less than one dollar a day (www.un.org/millenniumgoals/) was a key event that put new pressure on governments and corporations to address the many manifestations of severe poverty. These included poor labor conditions, energy infrastructure, and sanitation conditions. It also stimulated demands among poverty activists, poor consumers, development experts, and socialist politicians to curb market freedoms (market liberalism) in service of better social protection and redistribution (social protectionism).

To help address these issues, the WEF began inviting a broad array of experts related to severe poverty, including economists, development agencies, politicians, and celebrities. WEF members re-focused the solution of severe poverty to the level of shared responsibility. From this perspective, public and private stakeholders should acknowledge that merely focusing on the simple opposition between rich and poor or the world of social compassion and the world of business could never account for the diversity of poor consumers' individual aspirations. Consequently, ending poverty required a new beginning, a fundamental moral commitment among all involved stakeholders, and a new spirit of partnership.

Scientific expert formulations, most notably those delivered in Prahalad's (2004) research about 'wealth at the bottom of the pyramid', provided a crucial basis for establishing this neoliberal ideal. For example, Prahalad tirelessly argued in Davos sessions that businesses, governments, and donor agencies should stop thinking about the poor as victims and, instead, emphasize the need for public–private partnerships that support 'resilient and creative entrepreneurs and value-conscious consumers' (Prahalad 2004: 1). From this perspective, the key to eradicating poverty was to be found in understanding that the poor are not just a homogenous mass but rather a diverse community ripe with entrepreneurial, and hence responsible, consumers eager to have more and better choices. What made Prahalad's expert contribution particularly resonant was that his presentations already featured a number of concrete models for how the fortune of the bottom-of-the-pyramid could be unleashed and poverty could be eradicated, including microcredits, business and community partnerships, and microfranchise concepts.

Guided by this bottom-of-the-pyramid logic, the WEF organized multiple roundtables and task forces developing scalable marketing initiatives and tools for nurturing consumer values such as self-determination, independence, resilience, creativity, and entrepreneurship in poor consumers. Our field notes reveal a shared enthusiasm among WEF members about pioneers of microlending such as Grameen bank CEO Muhammad Yunus, who showed how his virtuous social entrepreneurship had brought prosperity to local communities. Further emanating from these initiatives were taskforce reports showing how every business could benefit from attracting bottom-of-the-pyramid consumers. Consider next how one of our interviewed WEF members adopted this moral ethos in his own marketing activities:

> Grameen Danone is a social business we started in 2006. Our objective is to bring health through nutrition to as many children as possible and to have a positive social impact on poor local communities by creating employment, income, and skill. ... The problem is that children in Bangladesh didn't have many healthy snacking options. ... Through the Grameen Danone initiative, we contribute to local development by offering a product that has high nutritional value and is affordable to the poorest of individuals. ... Shokti Doi ['that which builds strength'] is a huge success-story for everyone since it is a local development story. The yoghurt is locally sourced and sold and contains zinc, iron, vitamin A, and iodine. It is distributed either through local shops or through Grameen Danone ladies – a network of micro-entrepreneurs who are trained by our staff.

In 2002, Danone CEO Franck Riboud presented his company as a regular corporation mainly interested in its own bottom line and leaving social issues entirely for governments to solve. In 2007, he re-appears as an enlightened moral entity. His company has become a virtuous social entrepreneur who understands its duty to help resolve severe poverty by engaging the bottom-of-the-pyramid consumer with healthier snacking options. Note how this moralistic approach dismantles any justification for top-down (aka government) measures to promote poverty alleviation. Such classic approaches can only come from ignorant bureaucrats who are not interested in giving consumers healthier options and instead construct them as a mass of anonymous victims. Whereas a government solution forces consumers into accepting whatever humanitarian intervention higher-order authorities deem right, Danone is giving consumers the freedom to shape their own destiny.

The tendency to paint traditional means of poverty alleviation as immoral and, thus, inherently undesirable also extends to other traditional policies of social protectionism, including fostering long-term employment and upholding labor rights. These measures are rejected by WEF members as ineffective as they would foster structural dependency, disempower consumers, undermine self-esteem, and hamper consumers' ability to invest into their own talents as social market entrepreneurs. Instead, as Maximilian (37, CEO, energy company) and Michael (44, CEO, cosmetics company) stress, poverty can only be resolved when companies respond to poor consumers' desire for innovation and entrepreneurial creativity:

> There are approximately two billion people on this planet who live without access to reliable and affordable power. Most of these consumers are living in villages so it's very difficult to reach them. ... Governments [in countries with poor energy

(Continued)

(Continued)

infrastructure] often subsidize low quality energy through environmentally damaging kerosene lanterns, which puts people's health at risk. ... So we created an affordable solar lamp that allows these consumers to enjoy energy at a low cost. ... We serve markets in India, China, and Africa. In these markets, we have empowered over 10 million consumers.

Traditionally, we are a global cosmetics company. But in this context we operate as a micro-franchising coordinator to stimulate public health and community development. By giving poor consumers new roles, we are also a veritable source of economic development. The secret is that we don't view our consumers as helpless victims. ... Taking micro-franchise seriously as a sustainable and scalable solution to eradicating poverty means understanding the true power of social entrepreneurship. So we don't view our consumers as passive recipients of welfare. To us they are resilient entrepreneurs and value-conscious consumers who work very hard to help improve public health and wealth. They are healthy and productive individuals who serve their villages. They act as mothers, friends, market researchers, businesswomen, and sometimes even as nurses. We provide them with the basic resources, for which they are responsible, and it's their choice how much they want to sell.

Maximilian and Michael (synonyms used upon request) help improve poverty by liberating poor consumers from so-called shackles of oppression. In Maximilian's quote, the shackle is public energy infrastructure – a dirty, disempowering, dangerous, and dependency-inducing social prison. Business-delivered solar lamps, on the other hand, are not only clean and cutting-edge innovations. They also allow consumers to cultivate a sense of freedom and independence from the state. Michael's quote depicts social entrepreneurship in the positive light of a market-based feminism. From this perspective, by reducing all poor citizens to welfare recipients, public health is blind to, and thus also reinforces, some of the existential struggles poor women are facing in traditionalist settings rather than giving them opportunities to emancipate themselves by combining multiple identity projects such as mother, friend, market researcher, businesswoman, and nurse. The idea that bottom-of-the-pyramid business is the best solution can also be seen in Matthew's (61, CEO, global bank) intention of bringing poor consumers' startup talents to fruition:

The microloan partnerships we develop are firmly rooted in the conviction that we really need antidotes to the paternalism that is inherent to traditional poverty alleviation approaches. ... We strive for a radical change of minds. The old mindset was that all poor consumers are inherently vulnerable, weak, and unable to decide for themselves. This is a really patronizing and arrogant standpoint that has long stood in the way of poverty eradication because it pretends that there is no potential whatsoever. But there is a lot of potential. ... So in sharp contrast to the old view, let's instead build on the idea that all the decision power lies actually with the poor, not with government or higher-order stakeholders. I believe that poor consumers have what it takes to empower themselves, that they can be creative and flexible decision-makers, and that the problem is the lack of opportunities to perform rather than a lack of willingness.

From a neoliberal standpoint, Matthew's microloan solution must be superior to classic debt relief as it allows poor consumers to approach themselves as empowered market entrepreneurs who view their own situation as a business opportunity. Rather than treating all poor consumers as anonymous welfare recipients, he offers a solution that can be flexibly and creatively tailored to individual cases and situations. In sharp contrast, traditional debt relief mechanisms not only reinforce the contradiction between business and social goals. They also fail to recognize and develop consumers' individualized entrepreneurial talents and innovative capabilities.

Owing to these and other initiatives, a significant shift has occurred in the ways governments and corporations understand poverty. Whereas these institutions previously approached poverty through the lens of social rights and structural inequality, now 'the overall aim will be to ensure that markets work better for the poor as entrepreneurs, wage employees, and consumers' (https://business.un.org/en/documents/5702). Similarly, development is no longer understood as a state-level concern for protection but is rather viewed as an enterprise of promoting bottom-of-the-pyramid innovation. This means that responsible poor consumers can now strategize for themselves among various market options ranging from microcredits, mobile capital plans, microfranchise regimes, and low-cost energy solutions to end their own poverty rather than relying on social protection from governments.

Box 11.5:   Case Study

Green consumption

A second social issue prominently addressed at the World Economic Forum is global warming. Around 2003, climate experts began announcing a panoply of shocking environmental developments such as melting ice caps, rising sea levels, skyrocketing carbon emissions, fading ozone layers, and a growing number of extreme weather events such as hurricanes, monsoons, floods, and dire heat waves all over the world. Not only did these reports emphasize a new scientific consensus that climate change was in fact occurring and that human activities were the primary driver, they also documented the existence of

(Continued)

(Continued)

a strong discrepancy between rich and poor countries, with the latter category being hit hardest by the consequences of climate change.

Traditionally, environmental protection had been linked to public policy and government strategies. From this top-down command and control perspective, corporations were legally mandated by the state to subjugate their business activities to larger goals of environmental protection and safety. Paying environmental taxes, upholding environmental standards, and paying for environmental damages had been routine elements in the environmental policy mix. The global warming crisis increased the political pressure to curb extant market freedoms, which stood in an uneasy relationship with corporate agendas admonishing greater fidelity to the competitive logic and warning of the impact of extended environmental protection on economic productivity. Furthermore, the Kyoto protocol, thus far the only global regulatory instrument, was soon expiring and some countries' hesitancy to ratify the treaty foreshadowed the difficulty of finding a new democratic compromise.

In 2004, the WEF officially joined the war against global warming when WEF executive chairman Klaus Schwab invited more environmental leaders to the summit. Since then, new groups of environmental stakeholders have arrived in Davos every year, including national and regional ministers of the environment, Greenpeace activists, and large groups of climate experts, advocates, and ecologically active celebrities. The rationale behind these invitations was that global warming was much too pressing to continue petty fights. On the contrary, solving the problem of global warming was everybody's business. Representatives of the world of environmental protection should work with representatives of the business community as well as individual consumers and other important political agents to improve the state of the world. Still, initial deliberations among these opposing stakeholder groups were characterized by the traditional arguments of 'devise much stricter environmental laws' (social protectionism) versus 'do not sacrifice economic growth' (market liberalism), making it seem as though a solution was impossible.

To overcome this deadlock, the WEF contrasted these political quarrels with the importance of a shared commitment to individual neoliberal values such as innovation, creativity, flexibility, and entrepreneurial spirit. Accordingly, WEF members promoted a particular problem-solving agent, the green consumer, around which a new spirit of partnership and multilateral collaboration could materialize. From this perspective, political disagreements between opposing public and private agendas sustained themselves mainly on the basis of both sides assuming an anonymous mass of citizens, thereby neglecting the diversity of consumer abilities and ambitions to contribute to the solution of global warming. Instead of wasting valuable time by defending their respective interests, opposing camps had a profound moral obligation to help foster these individual ambitions and to create the partnerships needed to cultivate consumers' environmental consciousness.

One key instrument in establishing this moralistic framing was the academy-award-winning documentary *An Inconvenient Truth* by former US Vice President and long-time WEF member, Al Gore. Building on a rich basis in cutting-edge environmental, economic, and psychological science, Gore made the case that climate change was 'really not a political issue, so much as a moral one' and that the solution of global warming was about a passionate commitment from all involved stakeholders to become a society in which 'each one of us is a cause of global warming, but each of us can make choices to change that with the things we buy, with the electricity we use, the cars we drive' (Gore 2006). The new framing promulgated in Gore's documentary not only made it clear that the Kyoto protocol could only be replaced with a moral covenant focused on changing individual mindsets. It also revealed that businesses who partnered up with others to nurture a green consumption mindset would be both economic and moral leaders, thereby synthesizing the longstanding discrepancy between opposing environmental and economic-growth goals into a strong business case for green consumption. Along these lines, Gore's film already presented a number of examples of how small initiatives had made a big difference.

Emboldened by Gore's moralistic-problem-solving approach, the WEF organized multiple task forces and agenda councils committed to translating the need for green consumption into a number of scalable market solutions. Each report not only emphasized the need to move outside of static policy mechanisms, the 'failed' Kyoto protocol being the most prominent example, and instead foster green growth partnerships. It also demonstrated how corporations could reap significant economic and ecological benefits by engaging consumers through green innovations, partnerships, and technological market solutions. Consider next how interviewed members have adopted the WEF's sustainability ethos:

> People here understand the need to drill deeper, on a psychological level. That's the spirit of Davos. That's what makes this gathering so special. ... We're all passionately committed to implementing absolute sustainability. Absolute sustainability in the sense of nurturing an entirely new set of water consumption habits and attitudes in people, in short, creating a fundamentally new generation of water consumers who readily connect environmental issues with their personal water lifestyles and what they aspire to as individuals. ... Let me take you through one of our current initiatives. ... With the ['Aquameter'], for example, we give South-African consumers a technology that they can use to take stock of the amount of water they have saved each time they run the tap or take a shower. We also provide cool facts and tips, like here. So this one says ... purified bottled water contains ten times more minerals than regular tap water ...

Note how the shift from viewing water security as a passive and superficial government concern to the pursuit of individual-level green consumption as a 'deeper' and individual attitude-shifting enterprise imbues Jeff's (56, sustainability manager, soft drink company) call for 'absolute sustainability' with heightened moral significance. In their adaptations of green consumption, WEF members like Jeff not only portray themselves as

(Continued)

(Continued)

mindset-changing heroes who partner up with other leaders to help consumers live more sustainable lives. They also portray classic means of environmental protection inherently depraved. These initiatives are problematic for two main reasons. By establishing a straightjacket of inflexible environmental regulations, they readily discourage managers like Jeff from playing an active role in the fight against global warming. And second, they also fail to inspire consumers to actively question and re-evaluate their own ambitions, interests, desires, and habits. Both of these themes are also evident in Tina's quote (28, business student, young global leader):

> I'm focused on the millennials, that's my generation. I feel very responsible for helping create my generation's sustainable legacy. ... I'm proud in terms of the progress we've made so far. ... Together with [a US energy company] we have created a program to get students to take greater care of their own ecological footprint on campus by sending phone alerts to them at bedtime. ... In colleges participating in our program, heating costs in dorms have gone down by almost thirty percent. ... Next, we want to develop a mobile phone app that people can use not only to monitor their own energy consumption but also to sign up with more sustainable energy providers.

As Tina's quote suggests, embedding energy companies within a body of stricter environmental laws is a dangerously anti-creative, anti-innovative, and iniquitous move. It would stifle corporate motivation to create cutting-edge green consumption technology and solutions, and, worst of all, government policy mechanisms can never alone encourage consumers to act. Consider, as a case in point, Steve (48, Chief Sustainability Officer, IKEA Group):

> People want to act on climate change, but it needs to be easy for them to do so and they also need to feel that others are doing something too. People feel their actions only make a difference if they are part of something much bigger. ... With Prime Minister Tony Blair and a wide group of NGO and corporate partners in the UK, and later beyond, we launched the 'Together' campaign. Each partner made commitments to help customers reduce CO_2 emissions – a phone tariff without the need to buy a new phone, discounted loft insulation and affordable energy saving light bulbs. The campaign itself was successful, saving an estimated 1 million tons of CO_2 at the same time as helping billions of consumers collectively save 200 million pounds off their energy bills.

As these quotes illustrate, the WEF's green growth ethos has produced a significant shift in the ways powerful national and international institutions such as United Nations or the World Bank, but also national governments and NGOs such as Greenpeace and the World Wide Fund for Nature (WWF) approach global warming. These institutions no longer understand their role as rigorous watchdogs and strict regulators of global corporate practice to the collective benefit of citizens. Rather, they intervene into society on behalf of the market through policies 'stressing that consumption habits had to change if people really wanted to address the growing environmental crisis, civil society representatives called on all sectors of society to use more responsible and green consumption and production practices' (United Nations 2011). Sustainable development is good for business and business is good for sustainable development, provided some minimal responsible requirements of individual consumers. Global warming would thus continue, not because capitalism would be inherently unsustainable, but only because continuing environmental bureaucracy or individual ignorance prevented the blossoming of a green consumption lifestyle.

Box 11.6:   Extended Case Study

World Health Organization

The World Health Organization or WHO (www.who.int/en/), founded in 1948, is a specialized agency of the United Nations concerned with international public health. In 2006, it publicly announced that infectious diseases such as malaria, HIV/AIDS, and tuberculosis, which were though to no longer pose an imminent threat, were instead making a dangerous comeback. Moreover, the WHO also reported a rapid rise across the world in non-communicable, yet chronic diseases like cardiovascular disease, chronic respiratory disease, cancer, diabetes, obesity, and mental health. This report (WHO 2006) cited a number of reasons for this development, ranging from work stress and antibiotics resistance to environmental factors and the worldwide dismantling of state-regulated healthcare and vaccination regimes since the 1970s.

Questions

1. How would governments following the ideology of social protectionism deal with the rise in chronic illness?
2. How would governments adhering to market liberalism address the problem?
3. How would members of the World Economic Forum, who comply with the ideology of neoliberalism, attempt to solve the global rise of chronic illnesses?
4. How does consumption factor into a solution to help combat chronic illness?
5. What tradeoffs exists among potential options?
6. What unintended consequences to societies and economies exist among the different proposed solutions?

CONCLUSION

In this chapter we have highlighted the role of neoliberalism in shaping responsible consumer subjects, and hence responsible consumption projects. We started by tracing the history of neoliberalism as a political ideology meant to replace both market liberalism (which urges governments to protect the market from society) and social protectionism (that encourages governments to protect society from the market). Then, we explored how governments are forming partnerships with corporations to create responsible consumers. Members of these public–private partnerships known as economic elites, such as those of the Mont Pelerin Society or the World Economic Forum, work towards convincing individual consumers to help fight pressing social issues, such as severe poverty and global warming, through their everyday consumption choices. In the end, the political ideology of neoliberalism shifts responsibility for solving social issues away from governments to individual consumers.

RESEARCH DIRECTIONS

We highly encourage future research to verify the success or failure of the two types of responsible consumption projects outlined in this chapter: green consumption and bottom-of-the-pyramid consumption. Did these responsible consumption projects actually lead to measurable and verifiable decreases in global warming and poverty? How would a research project be designed to measure the effect of consumers' responsible consumption projects on helping find a solution to key global social issues? What types of data would need to be collected for such a critical endeavor?

Furthermore, future research can investigate if the different responsible consumption projects were more successful in certain countries than in others. For example, was the bottom-of-the-pyramid consumer more successful in helping get him/herself out of poverty in India than in South Africa? Moreover, future research can investigate what other types of responsible consumption projects exist beyond the two outlined in this chapter and what specific social issues they may address. Finally, from a more critical perspective, future research can explore the unintended consequences of the political ideology of neoliberalism on economies and societies more generally, as well as on consumers' consumption projects more specifically. For example, are there any negative consequences on individuals who are made to feel responsible for solving the world's problems through their consumption choices? Does this responsibility negatively impact their mental and emotional health and wellbeing?

RECOMMENDED READING

Giesler, Markus and Veresiu, Ela (2014) 'Creating the responsible consumer: Moralistic governance regimes and consumer subjectivity', *Journal of Consumer Research*, 41 (October): 840–57.

Harvey, David (2007) *A Brief History of Neoliberalism*. Oxford: Oxford University Press.

Polanyi, Karl (1945) *The Great Transformation*. New York, NY: Farrar & Rinehart.

REFERENCES

Gore, Al (2006) *An Inconvenient Truth*. Lawrence Binder Productions/Participant Productions.

Prahalad, C.K (2004) *Fortune at the Bottom of the Pyramid: Eradicating Poverty Through Profits*. Upper Saddle River, NJ: Pearson Prentice Hall.

United Nations (2011) 'Sustainable production, consumption practices key to combating environmental degradation, inequality, say round table participants', Press Release 5 September. www.un.org/press/en/2011/ngo732.doc.htm.

WHO (2006) 'Influenza pandemic and chronic non-communicable diseases are major causes for concern'. WHO Press Archive. www.emro.who.int/press-releases/2006/influenza-pandemic-and-chronic-non-communicable-diseases-are-major-causes-for-concern.html.

12
SOCIAL DISTINCTION AND THE PRACTICE OF TASTE

Zeynep Arsel, Concordia University
Jonathan Bean, University of Arizona

CHAPTER OVERVIEW

- Taste is practice that is performed reflexively.
- Taste practices reflect and reinforce symbolic boundaries because they are a reflection of one's early socialization and life conditions.
- People use marketplace resources to develop competencies in specific domains of taste.
- Mediated culture, social media, and the Internet have displaced the central role of tastemakers and intermediaries.
- Taste practices take new forms across the globe because taste is grounded in local culture and idiosyncratic meaning systems.

INTRODUCTION

The concept of taste describes one's ability to make judgments about aesthetic objects. Philosophers have been discussing taste since the ancient Greek philosopher Aristotle wrote about the senses. Most obviously, taste applies to the realm of food and drink, where the term gustatory taste is used to differentiate taste as one of the senses. This chapter considers taste as something you do. Taste, in this sense, is engaged when you laugh at a meme shared on social media or appreciate art in a museum. Across cultures and social classes, taste is an inseparable component of even the simplest everyday practices. Take drinking coffee as an example. Do you choose Starbucks or Dunkin Donuts, make instant coffee at home, or head to the independent shop with reclaimed wood tables? Do you prefer drip coffee, cold brew, or a regional variation, such as Turkish coffee?

What type of vessel do you think appropriate for your coffee? Is it a Styrofoam or paper cup, a reusable stainless steel coffee mug, or a delicate filigree porcelain cup? Do you Instagram your latte art? While gustatory taste is certainly a part of drinking coffee, it is but one of many aspects of taste. Taste requires us to make choices that reveal and reinforce our preferences.

This everyday practice of taste, from ordinary to spectacular, is of interest to scholars because of the way these seemingly small acts can tell us a lot about consumers and the culture in which they live. What might you be able to infer about a person who will drink nothing but organic coffee from a reusable mug versus another who proudly clutches a paper Starbucks cup containing a Venti cappuccino with extra foam? All judgments about the aesthetic properties of objects, such as when and how a designer on a home improvement television show talks about how a house has 'good bones' or 'clean lines', are expressions of taste. These judgments are frequently theorized as a reflection of social hierarchies, and in fact, theorists and philosophers have long seen taste as trickling down from the attitudes and behaviors of the upper classes. Social mobility, globalization, and digital culture, however, have led scholars to consider ways that taste is transforming in contemporary consumer culture. This chapter provides an overview of these transformations and discusses the implications of scholarly work on taste for management practices such as branding and segmentation. We focus on theories that come after the German philosopher Immanuel Kant's (1987) work on aesthetic judgment, because this is the stream of thought that has generated the most interest among consumer culture scholars. If you are interested in reading further about aesthetics, art, and taste, the philosophy of aesthetics is a good starting point. Reviewing the work of Kant, Hegel, Heidegger, and other philosophers and scholars who engage with taste will open the door to many new perspectives.

TASTE AS SOCIAL DISTINCTION

Sociologically, taste is seen as an activity that reaffirms social hierarchies because it reflects how members of a society have differential access to economic, cultural, and social resources (also see the chapter on social class in this book). Because the practice of taste often results in the accretion of material goods, it creates a condition where previous opportunities and choices continually shape one's present preferences and future possibilities. For example, choosing a sturdy, cushioned, and oversized chair prioritizes physical comfort and durability. This logic tends to be valued by people with modest incomes who are unfamiliar with the sort of aesthetic deliberations cultivated by those with more cultural and economic capital. People with specialized aesthetic knowledge, time, and money have the privilege of worrying about style. As sociologist Pierre Bourdieu claims, the upper classes are bestowed with what he calls *freedom from necessity*, which shapes their lifelong preferences for delicate objects, ascetic and stylized food, and luxury products (1984). Meanwhile, working classes develop a *taste for necessity*, preferring durable objects, gratifying and heavier food, and objects that are versatile. For example, Tuba Üstüner and Douglas Holt (2010) have discussed how Turkish upper-class consumers, who are culturally conditioned to exercise restraint, look down on middle-class consumers who eat large quantities of food at all-you-can-eat buffets.

A scholar must resist the old adage 'there is no accounting for taste.' Taste is not idiosyncratic, personal, and subjective. Rather, taste is the product of socialization and, regardless of your position in the social hierarchy, it is impossible to escape its consequences. These consequences are different depending on your resources and position. As the example at the beginning of this chapter draws out, even the seemingly innocuous act of drinking coffee can become a big deal, not only for the person choosing and drinking the coffee, but also for those who see and judge the coffee and the person who chose it. Practicing taste is a prime opportunity to establish symbolic boundaries. Sociologist Michéle Lamont (1992), who compared French and American upper-class men, found that cultural distinctions expressed through morals, manners, and aesthetic preferences are primary markers that set apart classes. People use symbolic boundaries to determine who does and does not belong to a group. Some symbolic boundaries, such as religious affiliations, are inscribed in laws or regulations, while other symbolic boundaries, such as who is allowed to show tattoos in the workplace, are unwritten. Some who transgress these boundaries, such as the person at a fancy restaurant who does not know which fork to use for the salad, are simply seen as lacking taste and manners. For others, such as the person who tries to wear a bathing suit at a traditional Japanese bath where one is expected to bathe naked, the violation of a symbolic boundary is grounds for removal or exclusion.

Because taste is a reflection of social class, it also continuously underlines class differences in everyday interactions. Therefore, Pierre Bourdieu describes taste judgments as social weapons – acts of symbolic violence – that reinforce hierarchies. People tend to internalize deeply these hierarchies. When Üstüner and Holt (2007) studied squatters in Turkey, they found an interesting generational difference among these people of limited means. Whereas older women in the community sought to maintain the tradition of knitting and wearing wool garments, the younger generation of women were embarrassed, even repulsed, by the thought of wearing hand-knit sweaters, which they associated with rural poverty and deviance from middle-class Western fashion norms. The older generation sought to insulate themselves from the influences of modernization and Western culture, while the younger generation of socio-economically marginalized squatters internalized what the dominant culture deemed to be 'good' taste.

This negation of self-worth is frequently reinforced by the way symbolic meanings and social hierarchies are performed in market spaces. For example, Delphine Dion and Stéphane Borraz (2017) discuss how French luxury stores deliberately manage status differences between different groups of customers and exercise symbolic violence to maintain exclusivity and make customers understand their position in the social hierarchy. This is done not only by the way the stores are designed and the goods are ordered (such as through silence, emptiness, and a lack of visible price tags), but also through training service personnel in the strategic use of subtle intimidation. For example, staff are allowed to employ a dismissive or even rude attitude towards customers that management deems unfit, whereas they are encouraged to be helpful and courteous to the 'right' category of customers. This type of service design can reinforce symbolic boundaries and perpetuate social exclusion. Dion and Borraz's findings show how the marketplace uses taste as an agent to perpetuate and highlight inequality. These are not new practices, nor specific to the French context; in the 1850s the designers of New York City's Central Park elevated the pathways for horse-drawn carriages so that working-class people, who could not afford to keep a horse or buy a carriage, would literally have to look up to those in the upper class, with the expectation that the less fortunate would aspire to emulate the wealthy (Cranz 1982).

However, note that it is neither an object itself nor its outward appearance that gives people status. You do not gain status simply by purchasing a Mercedes, nor is Mercedes' three-pointed star inherently more classy than Chevrolet's bowtie-shaped logo. To this point, class boundaries are maintained not simply through purchase but instead by how people make sense of these objects of consumption and the kinds of social interactions in which these expressions of taste are embedded. For example, Holt (1998) explains how two people with different backgrounds may enjoy the same mass-market film, such as Marvel's *The Avengers*, but in very different ways. Those who have high cultural capital (see Chapter 7 on social class) would consume the film in a more intellectual manner – such as evaluating the caliber of the acting or cinematography or interpreting the film as an allegory for some broader existential or societal question. In contrast, those who possess lower levels of cultural capital are more likely to focus on their emotional responses to the film – was it exciting or funny, etc. – and to what extent they could personally identify with key characters.

Thus, social distinctions are not conveyed so much by which objects consumers consume, but how they consume these objects (Holt 1998). A related implication is that the distinctions conveyed by goods and brands can be highly dependent upon the cultural and social contexts in which they are brandished. For example, consumers can sometimes interpret brands as luxury symbols precisely because they are seen to evade the status system: think of Tom's Shoes (see http://www.toms.com/). In fact, high fashion regularly borrows styles from the mass market and working class. The Vetements brand sells plain yellow t-shirts with the logo of the shipping company DHL for £185. The luxury fashion house Balenciaga introduced a $2145 leather bag with an uncanny resemblance to the decidedly un-stylish, blue reusable shopping bag IKEA sells for about $1. Similarly, those who claim to reject trends by expressing a taste for durability or timeless style have found themselves in the epicenter of a culture that values cast iron skillets, classic Mercedes diesels, linen shirts, and $350 artisanal axes (Bean et al. 2017). The artist Rebecca Modrak has lampooned the artifice and impracticality of these aesthetic preferences by creating a parody brand (see remadeco.org) featuring artisanal toilet plungers and related accessories, such as a raw leather holster to carry the plunger (Modrak 2015). This is another example of how working-class aesthetics, which within one context could be seen as unrefined by the upper classes, have been appropriated to become a means of social distinction.

Viewing taste as primarily a mode of distinction suggests that it is very difficult for people to escape their class position. In this view, people do not decide what they like. Rather, what they like is decided for them by way of rigid social mechanisms reinforced by the market. Social class structures taste, and taste in return reaffirms class differences. While this theoretical perspective rings true in some realms, forces including globalization, digital culture, and increasing mobility suggest we might instead think of taste as a fluid phenomenon instead of a static category. For example, globalization is characterized by the free flow of information and goods across international borders and cultural boundaries, forces which reshape consumers' ideas about taste and continually expand the material resources that can be used to express taste. Digital culture further increases the rate of information flow and has also increased the consumption of immaterial objects such as images on Instagram. Among other things, digital culture provides consumers the possibility to express taste while spending very little, if any, money. Finally, the role of taste is inescapable when it comes to social mobility, which describes upward and downward movement in the class structure. This creates challenges for global brands in places such as China, where social mobility is increasing, and in the United States, where it is stagnating, as we further discuss in our case study.

Box 12.1:   Critical Reflection

Marketplace encounters and symbolic violence

When American cultural commentator David Brooks wrote an article titled 'How we are ruining America' much controversy followed. He wrote:

> Recently I took a friend with only a high school degree to lunch. Insensitively, I led
> her into a gourmet sandwich shop. Suddenly I saw her face freeze up as she was

confronted with sandwiches named 'Padrino' and 'Pomodoro' and ingredients like soppressata, capicollo and a striata baguette. I quickly asked her if she wanted to go somewhere else and she anxiously nodded yes and we ate Mexican.

American upper-middle-class culture (where the opportunities are) is now laced with cultural signifiers that are completely illegible unless you happen to have grown up in this class. They play on the normal human fear of humiliation and exclusion. Their chief message is, 'You are not welcome here.'

Consider Brooks' anecdote along the lines of Bourdieu's theory. Why did Brooks relate his choice to take his friend to a gourmet sandwich shop as insensitive? Why is the educational attainment of Brooks's friend ('only a high school degree') relevant in this story? What is the significance of the Italian terms? Now also think about how Brooks resolved the situation by choosing to avoid conflict rather than, for example, explaining that soppressata and capicollo are types of preserved meats and that striata is a chewy bread? Taste is reflected not only in what we prefer, but also in the types of interpersonal interactions one finds appropriate and comfortable. Finally, consider Brooks' story alongside Dion and Borraz's work. Is there a way to manage market segmentation without being exclusionary, or is this an inescapable characteristic of markets?

TASTE IS REFLEXIVE, EVERYDAY PRACTICE

While theories on the structuring property of taste prevail, of late scholars are showing that taste can be liberatory and productive. However, other work remains entrenched in a tradition of showing how taste reinforces social hierarchies. By acknowledging the impact of social class in aesthetic dispositions, this more recent stream of research looks at how people within class positions perform taste reflexively, that is to say, self-consciously, over objects of interest, either individually or collectively. The concept of reflexivity is a way of thinking about human action that considers individuals as both aware of the structural conditions that enable and constrain their choices and capable of working to reshape the systems in which they are embedded. Rather than continuing to focus on domination and conflict between classes, these scholars inquire about how, within social structures, people continuously perform taste. This work follows Antoine Hennion's theorization of taste as 'reflexive work performed on one's own attachments' (2007: 25) to emphasize how individual projects, such as learning how to appreciate wine, increase people's cultural bodily, sensory, and linguistic competences. In their study of beer connoisseurs, Maciel and Wallendorf (2017) discuss this as a process of *taste engineering*, a deliberate strategy of action to master aesthetic faculties. When you learn with others to appreciate the taste of a virgin olive oil or an extra-hoppy beer, you experience a special sense of closeness courtesy of those shared perceptions.

Box 12.2: Real World Scenario

Blue Apron and taste engineering

Figure 12.1 Blue Apron Box (Source: Blue Apron Press Kit)

Blue Apron is an American meal-kit delivery service. Customers receive a box of pre-measured, ready to cook ingredients and detailed instructions for how to prepare a specific dish (see Figure 12.1). The instructions include a photograph and description of the dish, as well as a suggested wine pairing (see Figure 12.2). Although Blue Apron also runs a wine delivery service, the recommendation is more than cross-promotion. Blue Apron's advice guides customers through the tricky world of wine pairing, outlining an accompaniment that is both tasty and tasteful to accompany the dinner the customer will assemble from the meal kit. Gustatory taste is obviously relevant here because Blue Apron delivers boxes of food and wine. But if tasty food were all that customers wanted, they would have ordered delivery! The real value proposition is outsourcing the drudgery of meal planning and preparation – and the provision of taste. Far more than just dinner, Blue Apron provides an easily consumable package that gives its subscribers the resources to increase their taste competencies, both in terms of the bodily competencies related to cooking procedures, such as sautéing a chicken breast that is tender rather than tough, or knowing only by smell that flour has been incorporated into a sauce and will no longer taste raw. Blue Apron also helps its consumers gain aesthetic competencies, such as pursuing new and unusual flavors and ingredients rather than repeating the same basic dish again and again. Blue Apron puts new food practices in a box, providing its customers with the means to better not only their dinner, but also their cultural capital.

Cumin-Sichuan Shrimp Fried Rice

with Bird's Eye Chile & Marinated Radish

PREP TIME: 15 minutes
COOK TIME: 25-35 minutes
SERVINGS: 2

Tonight's shrimp fried rice gets its delicious heat from two special ingredients: bird's eye chile and cumin and Sichuan peppercorn sauce. First, we're sautéing the chile with garlic and scallion as a base for the dish. Later, we're stirring the sauce in with our rice, building another layer of warm, aromatic flavor. A topping of vinegar-marinated purple daikon radish completes each bowl with a bit of refreshing crunch—and a splash of gorgeous color. (Be sure to slice your radish very thinly, so that it softens a bit as it marinates!)

 BLUE APRON WINE PAIRING:
Benziger Sauvignon Blanc, 2015
Order wine and view other perfect pairings at blueapron.com.

Figure 12.2   A sample recipe card with wine pairing (Source: Blue Apron Press Kit)

Blue Apron rides on the wave of a broader cultural shift towards food (sometimes described as *foodie culture*), especially in upper and upper middle classes around the globe. One can see this shift in our preoccupation with TV shows about food, celebrity chefs, and ever-changing food fads, dietary practices, and the growing popularity of niche products such as the fermented beverage kombucha. Blue Apron targets novice cooking enthusiasts with significant disposable income but not a lot of cultural capital around food (for a discussion on cultural capital, please see Chapter 7 on social class). The beautifully photographed step-by-step instructions that Blue Apron provides are a good example of taste engineering because the service provides training wheels for people who want to increase their bodily and aesthetic competencies in the domain of cooking. Through repeated practice, they can increase their bodily skills, linguistic competencies, and aesthetic competencies relating to food, and perhaps eventually dare to cook without outsourcing these skills. Until then, some food aficionados will look down on them, because they are not 'real foodies' capable of making decisions without guidance from others.

The *taste regime* is a foundational concept in consumer research that defines taste as a practice. This concept builds on two interrelated qualities of the term regime. Regime describes a systematic way of doing things. It also describes how outcomes become predictable and regular. For example, taking on a new workout regime suggests that you will adopt a new way of exercising. At the same time, adopting an exercise regime also encompasses the expectation that your body will change in a predictable way as a result of your engagement. This kind of linkage between aesthetic and action is at the heart of the taste regime concept. Taste regimes shape the ways individuals relate to the objects in their world, what those individuals and objects do, and the systems of meaning embedded in these relationships (Arsel and Bean 2013). Put another way, a taste regime continuously orchestrates the objects, doings and meanings that organize and make legible an aesthetic system. Taste regimes enroll people in three related practices (see Figure 12.3). First, a taste regime sets a person up to *problematize* their own material surroundings and possessions by comparing them to the regime's core meanings. Think about all of the different colors cars come in: what's the cultural meaning of a beige car? A red motorcycle? Second, taste regimes reinforce the habits and routines that achieve these end goals through *ritualization*. For example, take an American who likes how black cars connote luxury in that culture. This person may take pains to wash and wax their own black car frequently to emphasize its color. The third practice, *instrumentalization* connects objects and doings with the taste regime's meanings. Thus, every time the car owner drives that shiny, black car, they experience luxury.

The taste regime concept also works to span the scales at which taste operates. Taste regimes impact culture at the macro level, for example in the circulations of ideas in political campaigns, ideals of healthy and unhealthy food, and mass-market fashion trends,

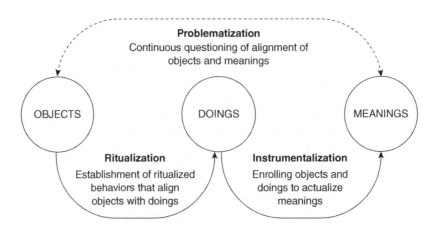

Figure 12.3   Taste regimes orchestrate practices (adapted from Arsel and Bean 2013)

such as torn jeans and leggings. At the meso level, taste regimes are visible in groups such as book clubs, university sororities and fraternities, social clubs, and consumption communities such as greyhound dog rescuers. Furthermore, taste regimes also operate at the micro level, for example in magazines, online discussion groups such as Reddit, and idiosyncratic practices passed from one generation of a family to another, such as the 'proper' way to fold towels or put toilet paper on the holder, which pass from one generation to the other. Furthermore, modes of interaction structured by media platforms such as Tumblr, Instagram, and Facebook have influenced the emergence and direction of taste regimes specific to those platforms: think about the last time you heard someone exclaim 'that's so instagrammable!'. What made that moment recognizable as belonging to an aesthetic system? Kozinets and his colleagues discuss how the popular practice of 'food porn' is governed by networked taste regimes that participants frequently transgress and extend, for example by adding gratuitous amounts of bacon to milkshakes, cakes, and other desserts. As many scholars have noted, the power of taste lies in its reach, invisibility, and tacit nature. Taste becomes second-nature, which gives it the ability to reconfigure even the most ordinary aspects of our lives.

Box 12.3:　Real World Scenario

Authentic, artisan, and cool: is taste mediated or collaboratively constructed?

Kinfolk magazine launched in 2011 and quickly became a central point of reference for an aesthetic that has since spread worldwide. *Kinfolk* constituted an aesthetic system that linked reclaimed wood, old-timey light bulbs with visible filaments, potted succulent plants, muted colors, and natural fibers with cultural narratives about durability, authenticity, and close social ties. From 2012 to 2013, circulation skyrocketed from 2,000 to 70,000, while the influence of *Kinfolk* became visible elsewhere in popular culture and especially on social media. Summer Allen, reflecting on the tension between *Kinfolk*'s claim to authenticity and the sudden ubiquity of the *Kinfolk* aesthetic, started a tumblr blog to catalog the magazine's influence on Instagram. As she explains:

> I started the The Kinspiracy tumblr after I noticed a pattern emerging from dozens of Instagram users – my own personal *Beautiful Mind* moment. It was suddenly so clear: Every account cultivating that *Kinfolk* look seemed to follow a specific formula. Every account had a photo (or several) of the following: A latte with a foam leaf design, a fresh piece or two of citrus, a glimpse of a pair of small feet – often in a well-worn pair of boots – an ice cream cone, weather permitting, some glasses here and there, twine, the occasional fixed-gear bike. And always, in every damn

(Continued)

(Continued)

account, *Kinfolk. The Kinspiracy* catalogs the brown shoes, piles of wood, American flags, twine scissors, and Wes Anderson-like lined up objects arranged just so. I collect four photos from the same account to create what is basically the same thing over and over again. (Summer Allen/gawker.com 2015)

Figure 12.4 The *Kinspiracy* lampoons the taste regime of *Kinfolk*

Check out the images in the screenshot of thekinspiracy.tumblr.com (Figure 12.4) or visit the website for yourself. Readily apparent is the limited universe of things represented at *The Kinspiracy* or in *Kinfolk*: the ice cream cone, leather shoes, and wood piles that Allen noticed, many of which share the twee, contrived style familiar to viewers of Wes Anderson films such as *The Grand Budapest Hotel* or *The Royal Tenenbaums*. But think also about the doings represented. Notice how *Kinfolk* is not only a resource for *what* to consume, but also *how* to consume. For example, in *Kinfolk* and on *The Kinspiracy* ice cream cones typically appear in the center of the frame. They are photographed before they are eaten, and often held by a carefully manicured hand grasping only the bottom of the cone. Visual repetition such as this example is one way that the *Kinfolk* taste regime problematizes the relationships between objects and meanings. Ice cream is to be savored not only for its flavor, but also appreciated for its transitory aesthetic quality. The overwhelming quantity of similar images on *The Kinspiracy* is evidence of the related processes of instrumentalization and ritualization. Every carefully composed shot of a foam latte heart, for example, is a mode through which the person taking and posting the image further turns themselves into a subject of the *Kinfolk* taste regime.

TASTEMAKING, CO-OPTATION, AND MEDIATED INFLUENCE

Theoretical models of taste have long contended that certain people, or groups of people, often referred to as tastemakers, wield disproportionate power over the ideas and aesthetic patterns seen as desirable in a given culture. In American culture, prototypical examples of tastemakers include *House Beautiful* editor Elizabeth Gordon, who cultivated a preference for a softer, gentler form of modernism during the 1950s (Penick 2017) and Martha Stewart, who built a powerful brand around the ideal of domestic perfection in the 1990s (Golec 2006). Tastemakers serve as personified articulations of taste regimes, establishing normative references for people who seek for market resources to outsource or develop their taste competencies. Additionally, tastemakers have the power to shape fashion systems and the symbolic boundaries that are established within. This power relies on the fact that taste is oppositional. Any definition of good taste is always predicated on a construction of someone else's taste as being bad. As we have discussed earlier, this opposition reinforces hierarchies. When tastemakers declare that one thing is out and another is in, the oppositions they create fuel fashion cycles and trends. For example, Jacob Östberg (2012) has explored how for many style-conscious men the choice of socks – which had been not really a choice, as dark socks were the only acceptable mode – exploded in the early 2000s into a breakneck cycle. Colorful socks became the way to show good taste as opposed to boring dark socks. But when everyone started wearing colorful socks, wearing dark socks became the way to exhibit independence. Finally, white socks, which had long been outré, came into fashion. The value of what Östberg calls a 'sock semiotic meltdown' is that socks became a powerful way for stylish men to signal social status and assert their power. Another consequence of this, at the meso level, how fashion cycles drive markets to evolve. Making a choice outside the mainstream is a way to assert power by saying 'those rules don't apply to me; I can do something else.' Non-mainstream taste is typically diluted by the process of co-optation, which describes how outsiders borrow and adapt meaning. For example, Zeynep Arsel and Craig Thompson's (2010) research discusses how the so-called indie aesthetic became appropriated and mass marketed, ultimately becoming a parody of itself, a joke.

But who has the power to decide what is good taste? Traditionally, tastemakers were a very few who achieved status by rising to the top of their fields or who were ascribed with this status through birth. As McQuarrie, Miller, and Philips (2012) discuss in their work on fashion bloggers, however, the Internet has made it possible for ordinary people to bypass the traditional gateways to influence, acquire an audience, and exert cultural influence. Through social media, the traditional model of the tastemaker is becoming increasingly unstable. Mediated communication not only accelerates and fuels the cycle of taste, but also allows a much larger group of players to enter the field to play with – and contest – what had been a largely static and dominant set of taste regimes. In some areas, such as the wine industry, a top-down system has prevailed for a number of structural and institutional reasons, and it remains the case that a small number of tastemakers influence the choices available on the consumer market. But considered in the aggregate, taste has become far more participatory than ever before. As Dolbec and Fischer discuss (2015), the accumulated effects of micro-level actions of connected consumers, even without coordination or intent, can shape aesthetic markets.

Box 12.4:   Critical Reflection

Can one escape the hierarchy of taste?

You might recall (or find online) the memorable scene in the movie *The Devil Wears Prada* where Miranda Priestly, played by Meryl Streep, schools her not-yet-fashionable assistant Andy Sachs, played by Anne Hathaway, over the origin of the blue sweater she is wearing after Hathaway's character dismisses fashion as 'stuff.' Here is Miranda's soliloquy:

> MIRANDA: This ... 'stuff'? Oh. Okay. I see. You think this has nothing to do with you. You go to your closet and you select ... I don't know ... that lumpy blue sweater, for instance, because you're trying to tell the world that you take yourself too seriously to care about what you put on your back. But what you don't know is that that sweater is not just blue, it's not turquoise. It's not lapis. It's actually cerulean. And you're also blithely unaware of the fact that in 2002, Oscar de la Renta did a collection of cerulean gowns. And then I think it was Yves Saint Laurent ... wasn't

it who showed cerulean military jackets? ... And then cerulean quickly showed up in the collections of eight different designers. And then it filtered down through the department stores and then trickled on down into some tragic Casual Corner where you, no doubt, fished it out of some clearance bin. However, that blue represents millions of dollars and countless jobs. And it's sort of comical how you think that you've made a choice that exempts you from the fashion industry when, in fact, you're wearing the sweater that was selected for you by the people in this room from a pile of 'stuff'.

Think about this explanation of the origin of Andy's sweater in light of what we have discussed so far. What concepts can you see in operation? Why does the difference between blue, turquoise, lapis, and cerulean matter? What is the relationship between the brands Oscar de la Renta and Casual Corner? How does Miranda's position reflect the theory that taste is a mechanism of distinction? If you have seen the movie, how are the concepts of agency and reflexivity reflected in Andy's subsequent transformation? In your own experience as a user of social media, does Miranda Priestly's claim that Andy's sweater was selected for her hold up?

CONCLUSION

In this chapter, we summarized recent conceptualizations of taste in consumer research and have shown them in operation in real life contexts. At this point, you have gained a clearer understanding of taste as a boundary-making mechanism and a way of creating distinction that is influenced by your position in a culture, and that is not biologically innate. In addition, you also have gained an understanding of taste as a reflexive practice and as an ever-evolving, increasingly distributed mechanism of market change. We have presented several cases in which marketplace offerings have provided resources for people to perform taste and develop taste competencies. When you pick up a magazine, watch a television, like a post on Instagram, or go to the grocery store, watch for the ways in which taste regimes bind together the material qualities of objects, their meanings, and the things people do. Further reading about the theories we have discussed – both within consumer culture theory and in the broader realms of philosophy, anthropology, and sociology – will help better your understanding of how and why consumers consume. For managers, taste is an accessible window into the socio-cultural bases for segmentation. Because it is so closely related to status, taste is also a window to consider the important ethical implications related to class-based segmentation, as we discussed in the Critical Reflection in Box 12.1.

Box 12.5:   Extended Case Study

The two Buicks

In the United States, Buick has long had a reputation as a car for 'geezers', which is American slang for cranky old people. In 2005, the CEO of GM, which owns Buick, described it as a 'dead brand'. At that time, Buicks were large, comfortable, and con-servatively styled cars bought almost exclusively by older people likely to remember the heyday of the brand in the 1950s and 1960s. Back then, Buick was renowned for making quiet, durable, and powerful cars that more subtly communicated status than a flashy Cadillac or Lincoln. Today, Buick actively fights its stereotypical associations in the United States to convince younger consumers that its cars are stylish and exciting. A 2017 Superbowl ad featuring American football player Cam Newton ended with the punchline 'If that's a Buick, then I'm a supermodel' (www.youtube.com/watch?v=Nx2PMnSzCB4). Meanwhile, in China, Buick has found success as a luxury car for the business elite. There, Buick's history recalls not the stodgy car of yesteryear, but instead the stately and prestigious cars driven by government officials in the 1930s, when China was begin-ning to open up to the world. The same material qualities that establish Buick as a safe, conservative, and reliable brand in the United States communicate its position as an aspirational product in China. Buick has retained its organic and rounded styling even after most other brands, following Volkswagen and Ford, adopted a trend for more squared-off, machined shapes. In the United States, organic and rounded styling made Buicks feel dated. But GM's design director asserts in an interview that this same styling helped propel Buick sales in China because 'Buicks have a lot of flow in their design and Chinese artwork and calligraphy have a lot of flow' (Waldmeir 2011). While this rationale might suggest stereotypical images, rounded, organic forms have long been considered more auspicious than shapes with sharp edges in Chinese culture because of deeply rooted cultural ideals about the order of the universe. For example, smooth and rounded shapes are related to the importance of water in Chinese culture. Water is understood to bring good luck. Buick worked that idea into a concept car built for the Chinese market with flowing lines, and named it the Riviera, bringing back a name last used in the United States in 1999. In doing so, Buick tied together an appeal to Chinese cultural values with a nod to its American heritage. This has been a potent recipe for Buick's success in China.

Both the use of Buick's cars and the users of Buick's cars differ across the two coun-tries. In China, Buick cars are status symbols for executives and the upwardly mobile. Minivans, which are Buick's best-seller category, are used as chauffeured rolling con-ference rooms by executives and government officials, whereas in the United States minivans are typically purchased by families with multiple children to haul their multi-ple children and friends to after-school activities. Of course, that customer segment is very small in China, where couples are limited to having only one or two children and the dominant after-school activity is working on homework. In the United States Buick has sold only one model of minivan, and it was discontinued in 2007 after its third year on the market. Sales were poor because Buick found few families with young children among its geriatric customer base. Consider also that China has quickly become the largest car market in the world. Its streets are clogged with traffic and labor costs are relatively low. Chinese consumers who can afford a car often employ a driver. This is not only a way to show status, but also a practical way to turn an hour stuck in traffic into productive work time or quality family time. All that traffic means there is little reason to own a fast car, but a quiet, comfortable cabin is a valuable feature. Whereas its competitor Ford made a strategic blunder by emphasizing power, speed, and the quality of the driving experience (Madsbjerg 2017), GM understood these taste regimes and reoriented the Buick brand to even better align with Chinese practices, doubling down on curvy, organic design, quiet interiors, and spacious back seats. As a result, Buick now outsells BMW and Mercedes in the luxury category in China.

Questions

1. Discuss how the same material elements can be integrated with distinct taste regimes in different cultures. How has the Chinese cultural context shaped Chinese consumers' interpretation of the Buick brand? How has Buick adapted its use of the constituent elements of taste regimes – objects, meanings, and doings – for the Chinese market?

2. Do some background research to learn more about Chinese culture and governance in the 1930s and how it compares to middle-class Chinese culture today. Think about how the shift from communism to capitalism relates to Buick's positioning in the Chinese market. Discuss how Buick can improve its customer experience by further taking account of localized meanings and taste regimes. In what ways can Buick change its products (objects and doings) or communication strategies (meanings)?

3. A recent newspaper article discusses how Chinese consumers are not aware of the American stereotypes about Buick owners, but they are familiar with the brand through product placement in American television shows and movies. Therefore, Chinese consumers associate the brand with elite professionals and 'bosses'. Do you think Buick can manage two product lines and two branding strategies that appeal to two very different global segments?

RESEARCH DIRECTIONS

As we move forward, scholars and practitioners can further inquire about issues that are becoming increasingly salient in the current global context. Here we propose five examples and arenas for future research:

1. What role does taste play in the sharing economy and the platform economy, for example in the case of Uber or Airbnb?
2. How do taste, power, gender and politics intersect? For example, think of the reaction on Twitter to US president Donald Trump's preference for well-done steak and ketchup; Turkish president Tayyip Erdogan's 1,150 room presidential residence, former US Vice president Al Gore's infamous $400 haircut; or the gender politics of former US Senator Hillary Clinton's pantsuits vs. the conspicuously abysmal style of UK Labour leader Jeremy Corbyn (as *Vogue* reported, 'very Vetements' – remember the DHL t-shirt?).
3. What happens at the intersection of taste and religion – such as the high-level prohibition against the representations of deities in Muslim and other traditions, or the historical relationship between decoration and austerity in Catholic versus Protestant traditions?
4. How does taste inform how we think about sustainability? For example, the social anthropologist Annette Henning (2005) found that people in Sweden were reluctant to put solar panels on their homes because they did not want to signal difference from their neighbors.

RECOMMENDED READING

Arsel, Zeynep and Bean, Jonathan (eds) (2018) *Taste, Consumption and Markets*. London: Routledge.

Arsel, Zeynep and Bean, Jonathan (2013) 'Taste regimes and market-mediated practice', *Journal of Consumer Research*, 39 (5): 899–917.

Bourdieu, Pierre (1984) *Distinction: A Social Critique of the Judgement of Taste*. Cambridge, MA: Harvard University Press.

Hennion, Antoine (2007) 'Those things that hold us together: Taste and sociology', *Cultural Sociology*, 1 (1): 97–114.

Highmore, Ben (2016) 'Design, daily life, and matters of taste', in Penny Sparke and Fiona Fisher (eds), *The Routledge Companion to Design Studies*. London: Routledge.

Holt, Douglas B. (1998) 'Does cultural capital structure American consumption?', *Journal of Consumer Research*, 25 (1): 1–25.

Johnston, Josée and Baumann, Shyon (2015) *Foodies: Democracy and Distinction in the Gourmet Foodscape*, 2nd edn. New York: Routledge.

Kant, Immanuel (1987) *Critique of Judgment* (trans. Werner S. Pluhar). Indianapolis: Hackett.

Maciel, Andre. F. and Wallendorf, Melanie (2016) 'Taste engineering: An extended model of consumer competence constitution', *Journal of Consumer Research*, 43 (5): 726–46.

Warde, Alan (2005) 'Consumption and the theory of practice', *Journal of Consumer Culture*, 5 (2): 131–54.

REFERENCES

Arsel, Zeynep and Bean, Jonathan (2013) 'Taste regimes and market-mediated practice', *Journal of Consumer Research*, 39 (5): 899–917.

Arsel, Zeynep and Thompson, Craig J. (2010) 'Demythologizing consumption practices: How consumers protect their field-dependent identity investments from devaluing marketplace myths', *Journal of Consumer Research*, 37 (5): 791–806.

Bean, Jonathan, Khorramian, Avid, and O'Donnell, Kelsey (2017) 'Kinfolk magazine, anchoring a taste regime', *Consumption Markets & Culture*, 1–11.

Bourdieu, Pierre (1984) *Distinction: A Social Critique of the Judgement of Taste*. Cambridge, MA: Harvard University Press.

Cranz, Galen (1982) *Politics of Park Design. A History of Urban Parks in America*. Boston: MIT Press.

Dion, Delphine and Borraz, Stéphane (2017) 'Managing status: How luxury brands shape class subjectivities in the service encounter', *Journal of Marketing*, 81 (5): 67–85.

Dolbec, Pierre-Yann and Fischer, Eileen (2015) 'Refashioning a field? Connected consumers and institutional dynamics in markets', *Journal of Consumer Research*, 41 (6): 1447–68.

Golec, Michael J. (2006) 'Martha Stewart living and the marketing of Emersonian perfectionism', *Home Cultures*, 3 (1): 5–20.

Henning, Annette (2005) 'Equal couples in equal houses', in Simon Guy and Steven A. Moore (eds), *Sustainable Architectures: Cultures and Natures in Europe and North America*. London: Taylor & Francis. pp. 89–104.

Hennion, Antoine (2007) 'Those things that hold us together: Taste and sociology', *Cultural Sociology*, 1 (1): 97–114.

Holt, Douglas B. (1998) 'Does cultural capital structure American consumption?', *Journal of Consumer Research*, 25 (1): 1–25.

Kant, Immanuel (1987) *Critique of Judgement* (trans. Werner S. Pluhar). Cambridge, MA: Hackett.

Lamont, Michèle (1992) *Money, Morals, and Manners: The Culture of the French and the American Upper-Middle Class*. Chicago, IL: University of Chicago Press.

Maciel, Andre F. and Wallendorf, Melanie (2017) 'Taste Engineering: An extended consumer model of cultural competence constitution', *Journal of Consumer Research*, 43 (5): 726–46.

Madsbjerg, Christian (2017) *Sensemaking: The Power of the Humanities in the Age of the Algorithm*. New York and Boston: Hatchette Books.

McQuarrie, Edward F., Miller, Jessica, and Phillips, Barbara J. (2012) 'The megaphone effect: Taste and audience in fashion blogging', *Journal of Consumer Research*, 40 (1): 136–58.

Modrak, Rebekah (2015) 'Learning to talk like an urban woodsman: An artistic intervention', *Consumption Markets & Culture, 18* (6): 539–58.

Östberg, Jacob (2012) 'Masculinity and fashion', *Gender, Culture, and Consumer Behavior,* 253–81.

Penick, Monica (2017) *Tastemaker: Elizabeth Gordon, House Beautiful, and the Postwar American Home*. New Haven, CT: Yale University Press.

Üstüner, Tuba and Holt, Douglas B. (2007) 'Dominated consumer acculturation: The social construction of poor migrant women's consumer identity projects in a Turkish squatter', *Journal of Consumer Research, 34* (1): 41–56.

Üstüner, Tuba and Holt, Douglas B. (2010) 'Toward a theory of status consumption in less industrialized countries', *Journal of Consumer Research, 37* (1): 37–56.

Waldmeir, Patti (2011) 'China's influence on car design accelerates', *Financial Times,* 18 April. www.ft.com/content/e4ee68e8-69da-11e0-89db-00144feab49a.

13

CONSUMER RESISTANCE AND POWER RELATIONSHIPS IN THE MARKETPLACE

Dominique Roux, University of Reims Champagne-Ardenne
Elif Izberk-Bilgin, University of Michigan–Dearborn

CHAPTER OVERVIEW

- Why do consumers resist? Power as the driver for resistance.
- What are consumers opposing/escaping? From macro to micro targets of resistance.
- How is resistance manifested? Examining overt and covert resistance.
- Sketching the future of consumer resistance.

INTRODUCTION

The term 'consumer resistance' sometimes has been used interchangeably with anti-consumption and broadly applied to encompass a variety of consumer practices from voluntary simplicity, culture jamming, to boycotts. Simply put, to resist means standing up against what is perceived as a power, a pressure, an influence, or any attempt to act upon one's conduct. In the marketing literature, Peñaloza and Price (1993: 123) seminally used this construct to describe 'the way individuals and groups practice a strategy of appropriation in response to structures of domination'. The first noteworthy thing about this seminal definition is that resistance involves action, not only thought or intention. Second, it alludes to many conventional marketing practices such as market studies, advertising, sales techniques, shop fitting, loyalty programs, etc. that may be perceived as operations of power. For example, using pleasant scents in a store to prompt consumers to buy more is one of the many marketing techniques individuals may perceive as influencing their behavior. When consumers come to regard those practices as manipulative, exploitive, or restrictive, the basis for resistance to power is created. Hence, power is central to understanding resistance, which is the outcome of power. We further explore the resistance/power dynamic in the next section.

In the marketplace, power can be exerted on individuals or groups through discourses. For example, corporations and industry organizations have the resources and the marketing expertise to create marketplace myths (e.g. advertising that using deodorant liberates one from the shame of unpleasant underarm odor) to serve their financial interests. Consider the infant food advocacy campaigns of the 1960s–70s backed by industry leaders including Nestlé. These campaigns promoted formula as more nutritious than breast milk and hence their adopters as 'good' mothers. In portraying breast feeding as a nuisance to the modern woman and riding the coattails of the feminist movement back then, pro-formula marketplace myths played an influential role in consumers' early adoption of breast milk substitutes. However, as a perfect example of the power/resistance dynamic, these discourses subsequently triggered a counterculture reaction. This led to the 1980s breastfeeding movement as well as the proliferation of non-profit breast milk banks and today's popular online platforms for mom-to-mom breast milk exchange. As seen in this case, marketplace discourses can impose norms, prescribe certain behaviors, and convey ideologies that are resisted. In turn, resistance can be transformative, creating change in marketplace discourses, practices, and power relationships.

Additionally, power can also be exercised through material arrangements, techniques, and marketing tools that are variously dedicated to surveillance, categorization, and broadly speaking, to the government of people's lives. For example, many companies utilize information, assessing economic significance of consumers' search engine histories and digital data to pinpoint not only what the consumer needs, but also his/her location, friends, and other personal details. Based on this information, marketers can send digital coupons, make product or service recommendations, and post stalker ads – those ads that follow the consumer wherever he goes online – on the websites that the consumer is browsing.

Overall, consumer reactions to such marketplace discourses or tactics are likely to result in multiple actions such as opposing, thwarting, escaping or circumventing marketing techniques and powers, i.e. resisting. Consumer resistance may be expressed individually or collectively, in an audible or silent way, by fighting certain powerful market players and/or by (re)creating alternative ways of producing, provisioning, and consuming. In addition to being consumers, individuals perform many roles in society as citizens, workers, producers, and family members. As such, they take issue with the economic, social, cultural, and ethical dimensions of both the consumption and production of goods and services. Hence, consumer resistance is fundamentally political in the sense that it has to do with how people envision to behave, to consume, and to define what is good versus bad for them, their families, their countries, or the planet. Since the dawning of modern consumer culture in the post-World War II era, journalists, politicians, and social scientists have argued that consumers are passive puppets of advertising and other modes of marketing control. More recently, business leaders and marketing academics have portrayed consumers as compliant co-producers. In other words, consumers were seen as using brands to facilitate their own identity projects and, in the process, helping companies promote their brands (Holt 2002). However, we believe that today's consumers are better characterized as cultural entrepreneurs, who critically and creatively observe, reform, and transform markets, and in so doing, challenge the status quo. However, consumer resistance is by no means something new; questioning and resisting power are as old as human history. Therefore, consumer resistance is an exemplary case and an interesting construct to highlight what sustains a continuous change in the markets. This construct is thus highly critical to consumer researchers and marketing practitioners interested in market dynamics. Understanding consumer resistance bears significant implications for companies, consumers, and policy-makers given that consumers' active participation in reshaping markets redefines not only companies' future strategies, but also the regulations and the scope of political action.

The rest of this chapter is organized into four sections. The first section introduces theories of power and resistance. The second section examines how consumer resistance has evolved over time and which macro- and micro-level targets are the focus of consumer resentment and resistance. The third section unpacks how resistance is manifested, from overt ways of voicing discontent to covert activities of bypassing, escaping, and reshaping the marketplace. Finally, the fourth section sketches some perspectives on the future of consumer resistance. The chapter concludes with some research directions about new forms of consumer resistance, its possible amplification and impact on market system dynamics, and consumer competency.

RESISTANCE AND POWER

From classical to critical philosophers, like Plato to Marx, who have tackled the questions of politics and the arts of governing people, theories of power have been anchored in a political framework. In these approaches, power is conceived of as the state's monopoly on the legitimate use of violence. In particular, the war of all against all characterizes the state of nature and commands people to submit to the sovereign, to whom they delegate authority. Thomas Hobbes (1588–1679), an English founding father of modern political philosophy, was the most influential promoter of the 'social contract', a theory that suggests that people abandon certain freedoms in exchange for the protection of the state. Such a view, however, equates power with domination and implies that the political power is endowed with the monopoly of legitimate violence and the right to exert control on subjects who consent to obey. This traditional conceptualization of power has then been largely developed by Max Weber (1864–1920), a German sociologist, philosopher, and political economist, who extended such a proposition to organizational thinking and bureaucracy. For Weber, power is the probability that some will be in the position to carry out their own will despite resistance, and regardless of the basis on which this probability rests. Such a perspective clearly envisions power as vertical (exerted from above by political power), substantive (reflected in having particular resources such as status, money, authority), structural (reified by ruling classes and dominant institutions of the political sphere), and repressive (mostly exerted through restraint, control, and castigation if need be).

Enriching this conceptualization, other political theorists like Antonio Gramsci (1891–1937), an Italian Marxist theorist, argued that repression is possible mainly because domination rests on ideological underpinnings that underlie the legitimization of violence. In other words, if power wants to succeed, it must create an upstream consensus that can only be achieved through persuasion, and the perpetuation, or naturalization, of its dominance in the general population. Following the same line of thinking, Louis Althusser (1918–1990), a French Marxist philosopher, developed the idea that the repressive and hegemonic dimensions of power are located in and reproduced by the state's various ideological apparatuses such as churches, school systems, laws, political parties, trade unions, media, and cultural organizations. These 'micro-powers' – by contrast with the macro-political power – do not operate on the same basis. Macro-political power defines rules – i.e., sets out the law – and exercises a repression of a legal type. Differently, micro-powers rely on norms. Norms are behaviors that are consistent with the majority or at least with an average conduct. They thus refer to what should be or to an ideal model to be reproduced. Micro-powers define normative landmarks and use techniques of normalization to rule conducts, each ideological apparatus – churches, school systems, laws, political parties, trade unions, media, etc. – operating on its own basis. However, all micro-powers circulate know-how and behavioral patterns that everyone is expected to internalize and follow.

From a different angle, in challenging the equation between power and violence in the political field, Hannah Arendt (1906–1975), a German-born American political philosopher, provided a radical shift in the political conceptualization of power. More precisely, she contended that power should not be reduced to the domination of man over man, and could rather be envisioned as a 'power-in-common' – or power of a group – that may be exerted by people coherently as long as the group is not divided. As a result, Arendt's view of power makes it a contingency: power is exercised but cannot be possessed or kept forever; also, it exists only through action. For example, a rebellion against a political authority may acquire an irresistible (still temporary) power, even if the authority has an overall superiority of material forces.

Bridging together these conceptualizations of power, Michel Foucault (1978), a contemporary French philosopher and social theorist, challenged the general idea that power should be a unidirectional process between an entity that commands and subjects who obey. On power, Foucault (1978: 92) makes the following observation:

> It seems to me that power must be understood in the first instance as the multiplicity of force relations immanent in the sphere in which they operate and which constitute their own organization; as the process which, through ceaseless struggles and confrontations, transforms, strengthens, or reverses them; as the support which these force relations find in one another, thus forming a chain or system, or on the contrary, the disjunctions and contradictions which isolate them from one another; and lastly, as the strategies in which they take effect, whose general design or institutional crystallization is embodied in the state apparatus, in the formulation of the law, in the various social hegemonies.

By arguing that power is not one and unique, Foucault thus decentered and disseminated its presence everywhere in the sense that power may be anywhere and come from everywhere. In his conceptualization, power is not found in a single center, nor is it exerted by a single actor; rather it should be viewed as a moving set of forces continually inducing states of power through inequalities and asymmetries. Hence, power is not a binary opposition between the dominant and the dominated, nor is it some kind of strength that some actors could be endowed with, but it is the capacity of action some may have on the action of others.

Next, we summarize how power and resistance have been discussed with respect to consumption and markets by offering two contrasting views from the social science literature in the Critical Reflection in Box 13.1.

Box 13.1:   Critical Reflection

Enslaved vs. empowered consumers?

Even though consumers have considerable power to influence business practices and public policy through boycotting, buycotting, and a host of other forms of activism, the consumers' role in the marketplace has been somewhat downplayed in the literature. For example, early social scientists portray the consumer as a victim of capitalist interests and mindlessly trapped in a consuming spiral. This portrayal of the consumer as exploited and enslaved is best reflected in the writings of Karl Marx, Max Horkheimer and Theodor Adorno, and Jean Baudrillard. Marx (1818–1883), a Prussian-born economist and sociologist, for instance, holds that industrialization and capitalism have brought about a new social order, in which labor is commoditized and individuals are alienated from the very things they produce. According to Marx, in a market economy individuals can no longer claim a fair share from the goods they produce, rather they are paid a fraction of the market value of these products as wages. Moreover, the capitalist system further exploits

(Continued)

(Continued)

individuals by luring them with expensive goods and services that they can hardly afford. Hence, the capitalist interests of the bourgeoisie render the workers entrapped in a work–spend cycle. Building on Marx, Horkheimer (1895–1973, a German sociologist) and Adorno (1903–1969, a German sociologist) suggest that consumerism is a powerful ideology, which reduces the meaning of life to buying things and confines the meaning of freedom to having numerous brands to choose from in the marketplace. Even artists are entrapped by consumerism; according to Horkheimer and Adorno, artistic work that is created with market expectations in mind is no longer free. Adding to this line of thinking, Jean Baudrillard (1929–2007, a French sociologist) concludes that resistance to such a powerful ideology (i.e., breaking from the work–spend cycle) is not possible because individuals have come to believe that satisfaction and social equality in a market society can be attained by merely acquiring the 'trendy' or the 'cool' thing. Yet, what is 'cool' is constantly redefined by marketers and other cultural intermediaries (e.g. fashion designers, technology companies).

Some anthropologists and philosophers have challenged this representation of the consumer as a mindless dupe with a dramatically different perspective. In this alternative view, consumption is a means for self-expression through which individuals play with the objects they acquire to change their meanings or use them in creative ways that would counter the producers' intentions. In other words, consumption is defined as an empowering exercise; far from being mindless consumers, individuals enact agency through consumption by assigning their own meanings and coming up with creative uses for objects. The proponents of this celebratory view of consumption include Mary Douglas, Pierre Bourdieu, Michel de Certeau and James Scott. Douglas (1921–2007, a British anthropologist) encourages scholars to look at how people use consumption objects to communicate taste, status, or even protest. Together with economist Baron Isherwood, Douglas notes in *The World of Goods* (1979) that consumption is a ritualistic activity; individuals use goods in constellations to create meaning systems, or an intelligible universe with goods. These constellations of goods also serve as social boundaries, which structure social relationships.

Along a similar vein of thought, renowned French sociologist Pierre Bourdieu (1930–2002) notes that what one decides to consume and how one consumes it can be a resource, or in Bourdieu's terms, cultural capital. Cultural capital allows individuals to socially distinguish themselves from others. Therefore, cultural capital can be deployed through consumption to reproduce or transcend social status. Adopting a pragmatic view, Michel de Certeau (1925–1986, a French philosopher) pays attention to how individuals play with rules and imposed structures, showing that people engage in bricolage, that is creative acts to reinterpret the meaning of goods or use them in unintended ways to resist established norms and meanings. For example, a paperclip can be creatively repurposed as a screwdriver to fix small screws or as a jewelry clasp. In *Domination and the Arts of Resistance* (1990), James Scott (1936 – present, an American anthropologist) develops a similar perspective by showing how subordinate groups may silently and covertly subvert existing order, what he terms infrapolitics. According to Douglas, Bourdieu, de Certeau, and Scott, consumption can thus counteract power relations by using micro-level tactics and imperceptible gestures of disobedience.

In summary, the two paradigms summarized above differ significantly in the way they view the roles of the consumer and the market as well as the possibility of resistance in modern market societies. The first perspective as reflected in the writings of Marx, Horkheimer and Adorno, and Jean Baudrillard conceptualize the marketplace as the realm of dominance and manipulation. Consumers are mesmerized and passivized by the ideology of consumerism that instills individuals with the belief that happiness, accomplishment, and satisfaction can be attained through consumption. In this view, the consumer's role in society is reduced to a spectator; they watch as marketers and other cultural intermediaries first invent false needs and then create products and services that promise to satisfy those false needs, thus leaving the consumers with a sense of false empowerment at the end of the day. Resistance to consumerism is highly unlikely in this view. However, the second perspective, as reflected in the writings of Douglas and Bourdieu in particular, conceptualizes the market as a realm of self-development and a rich resource for constructing an identity. Consumers are seen as the masters of the field of consumption, creatively constructing new meanings and re-purposing marketers' offerings to mark status, order social relationships, and even contest the influence of consumer culture. Therefore, according to this second view that affords a greater agency to the consumer, it is possible to resist and transform the social order within the marketplace.

For a more detailed review of these two perspectives and full references to the cited works in this section, see Izberk-Bilgin (2010).

EVOLUTION OF CONSUMER RESISTANCE AND ITS CHANGING TARGETS

The Critical Reflection in Box 13.1 highlights how researchers portray resistant consumers. Both perspectives show that scholars have been making normative or ideological judgments on what consumers either should do (the enslaved consumer) or are likely to do (the empowered consumer). But what consumers *actually do* is a question that requires examining which power(s) they challenge in practice. Furthermore, even though consumer resistance is an emerging term in the marketing literature, historically, the collective expression of consumer resentment and resistance in the marketplace is not new. More precisely, resistant actions date back to the non-importation movement that took place between 1764 and 1776 during the American colonial era (Witkowski 1989). Also known as the Boston Tea Party, the movement was a politically motivated boycott of British goods and manufacturers in response to imperial taxation policies. The boycott was intended to place economic pressure on British manufacturers, who would, in turn, force the British parliament to retract the imposed duties on British merchandise that the colonialists grew accustomed to consuming as symbols of novelty and high status. Boycotts, thereafter, became the tactic of the seemingly powerless and oppressed throughout history. From the 1905 Swadeshi movement that shunned the use of British cloth and eventually led to the end of colonial rule in India, to the Montgomery bus boycotts of 1950s that ignited the civil rights movement and helped end segregation laws in the United States, boycotts have been effective tools of social change.

The turn of the 20th century, however, witnessed a shift in the drivers and tactics of boycotts. The later protests increasingly targeted multinational corporations and their global brands, rather than commodities like tea and clothing, and were concerned with issues like unethical business practices, corporations' indirect support of undemocratic regimes, and exploitation of natural resources. Between 1975 and 2000, Nestlé, Coca-Cola, Bristol-Myers, Campbell Soup, General Electric, Procter & Gamble, and PepsiCo were among the corporations and brands that became targets of consumer boycotts, some of which lasted more than seven years. Today's 21st-century consumers are also sophisticated in their utilization of digital technology and social media to communicate their goals to both the public and the corporate world. Boycotts continue to be an effective means for raising public awareness about ethical, social, and environmental causes such as the Nike boycott against working conditions and child labor in Asia or the present #grabyourwallet boycott against Trump-brand businesses and retailers selling Trump family products. In the new millennia, individuals are increasingly leveraging their consumer role by pressuring multinationals for social and environmental change, largely because citizens have lost faith in local governments to find solutions to global concerns and corporations have become more financially powerful than some nation-states.

CCT research has been closely following the changing nature, agenda, and practices of consumer resistance. Below, we synthesize and present research on macro- and micro-level concerns that have drawn consumer resentment and led to acts of resistance. First, we discuss research on how globalization and ideologies have spurred consumer resistance against global brands. Next, we discuss how some marketing techniques and tools that try to govern consumers' conducts at a micro-level prompt acts of resistance.

Brands, Globalization, and Marketplace Ideologies

Today's consumers are concerned about macro-level sociohistorical, economic, and political trends that have significant consequences on everyday life primarily through the way companies function and the marketplace operates. One such enduring trend is globalization (see Chapter 6). Advances in technology and globalization of business have promised companies faster and cheaper access to resources, new geographical markets, and more consumers worldwide. Yet almost five decades of intense, albeit uneven, globalization have also brought about critical environmental, sociocultural, political, and economic problems. For example, multinational companies' pursuit of cheaper resources has resulted in not only growth of sweatshops in industrializing nations (like Vietnam or Bangladesh) and loss of jobs in economically advanced countries, but also environmentally unsound manufacturing practices, which are believed to aggravate global warming. As awareness about human, environmental, and cultural consequences of globalization has increased, these concerns have culminated in massive resistance demonstrations, such as the Seattle World Trade Organization and G8 Summit protests, as well as the global Occupy Movement organized by non-governmental organizations (NGOs), labor unions, and student organizations.

CCT research has explored antiglobalization sentiments in less developed countries and has revealed the complex role of ideology on consumer resistance in the backdrop of East–West tensions and colonial history. These studies suggest that, from the perspective of low-income and postcolonial consumers, globalization is just a fancy neoliberalist term for colonialism. For example, Varman and Belk (2009) reveal that the British colonial rule that ended 70 years ago continues to mark the collective memory of contemporary Indians. As the authors show, activists and consumers in India draw from and synthesize their collective colonial memory with their lived experiences of asymmetrical globalization to mobilize a modern Swadeshi movement against multinational companies like Coca-Cola. In doing so, the Indian anticonsumerist activists summon nationalist ideology and patriotic tactics of resistance (e.g. advocating national drinks like *lassi*) to create a discursive and performative space for Indian nationhood and national identity. On the other hand, Izberk-Bilgin (2012) shows that religious teachings, when combined with ideology, can turn into a powerful antiglobalization rhetoric that motivates consumer resistance to global brands. Her study finds that lower-income Turkish consumers, who subscribe to a political view of Islam, protest the cultural influence of multinational corporations by characterizing global brands as 'infidels'. Waging a boycott against Western consumerism, Islamist consumers substitute foreign brands that are perceived to embody immorality, injustice, and inequality with local, particularly Islamist, alternatives. In doing so, these consumers seek to moralize the marketplace and re-construct a society that is compatible with their religious ideals.

Collectively, these studies reveal the complex socioeconomic and historic tensions involved in global–local encounters and the important role that religious and political ideologies play as a critical cultural resource in assembling an anticonsumerist identity, forging local reflexivity, and mobilizing consumer resistance (see further illustrations in the Real World Scenario in Box 13.2). They also reveal the symbiotic relationship between consumption and ideology in that ideologies require a material form or expression to exist. In turn, resisting certain market offerings – be they Coca-Cola drinks, Hummer cars, or genetically modified foods – gives anticonsumerism the ability to be showcased and performed effectively on an everyday basis.

Box 13.2:   Real World Scenario

The political consumer: macro-social issues and resistance

As indicated earlier, ordinary people have always been using consumption to express discontent. As the digital era has provided various means to spread information and opinions, the media plays a growing role in raising public awareness about political, social, and environmental problems unfolding anywhere in the world. Apart from ecological and health concerns that nowadays constitute a key issue (see the Real World Scenario in Box 13.3), other issues that can be found at the intersection between production, consumption, and labor fuel consumer resistance. More specifically, some consumers are not only focused on the product they buy (including its environmental impact) but also the conditions in which workers are treated within the production process, particularly in emergent countries. Such questions are at the heart of the controversial Michael Moore documentary *Roger and Me* (1989) that sought to raise awareness about the dramatic economic and social consequences of General Motor plant closings in Flint, Michigan. Another movie by Moore, *The Big One* (1998), took issue with the human consequences of globalization, unveiling the unethical labor practices and poor social responsibility records of multinational companies.

Likewise, David Redmon's documentary *Mardi Gras made in China* (https://vimeo. com/143373618) aptly captures similar issues of unethical production and employees' poor social conditions. The documentary presents a virtual dialogue mediated by the filmmaker between Chinese teenage workers from a small factory in Fuzhou, China, producing Mardi Gras beads, and New Orleans Mardi Gras revelers consuming them. The film shows that the Mardi Gras celebrators have no idea about the teenagers who manufacture the beads, the hard working conditions under which these necklaces are produced, or the 25 million pounds waste that accumulates each year at the end of the celebration when the beads are abandoned in the streets.

Global awareness of inhumane working conditions has also increased with the media reports of the 2013 Rana Plaza disaster in Bangladesh where a building housing a contract manufacturer of H&M, Primark, Benetton, and Calvin Klein collapsed, resulting in the death of 1,129 workers and around 2,500 injuries. The tragedy culminated in protests around the world led by advocacy groups, politicians, researchers (e.g. the NYU Stern Center for Business and Human Rights issued a 2014 report entitled 'Business as Usual is Not an Option: Supply Chains & Sourcing after Rana Plaza') and consumers as well. Indeed, widely diffused information on scandals and serious violations of social and safety rights do increase consumers' understanding that consumption is fully intertwined with globalization. It makes clear how the free movement of goods, capital, services, technology, and information fuel private financial interests and economic imbalance.

Questions

1. Could you provide other examples of how economic globalization fosters and/or hampers consumer resistance?
2. Which other issues could you mention as triggers of resistance related to labor conditions and economic inequalities?

Techniques, Tools, and Discourses for Governing Consumers' Conduct

Broadly speaking, most marketing techniques are sources of tension when consumers feel these are trying to influence their behavior. For example, when sales staff insist on giving advice and pressure the consumer to buy, or when telemarketers engage in cross-selling or up-selling, they may persuade people to buy what they did not want, or more than they needed, or at a higher price than they had originally planned, thus raising resistance to marketing techniques. Aside from such direct persuasion attempts, advertising is another marketing tool frequently perceived as intrusive and pervasive. At an individual level, resistance may be expressed by putting a STOP PUBLICATION sticker on the mailbox to prevent junk mail, watching or listening to commercial-free channels, muting the sound during commercials, installing adblockers on the computer or even new software bypassing anti-adblocker technology. At a collective level, resistance tactics against advertising may be enacted in a more coordinated and enduring manner by groups of activists like Adbusters. This anticonsumptionist group implements guerrilla communication, culture jamming, Buy Nothing Day (BND) initiatives, and other forms of protest that aim at preventing the colonization of public and mental space by advertising and more generally at *subvertizing* consumerism. In the same vein, resisting the spread of the marketing panoply across all aspects of social life may be the drive for engaging in ephemeral anti-market activities like the Burning Man festival, where commercial activities are banned and replaced by socializing and gift-giving practices (Kozinets 2002).

In addition to sales techniques and advertising, other marketing tools may, surprisingly, become targets of resistance. In the retailing field, using in-store ambient elements such as lighting, music, scent, and temperature is expected to induce positive mood and provide pleasant shopping experiences. Yet, design and retail marketing techniques may be viewed as modes of discipline and influence when consumers themselves notice that atmospherics are purposively used to make them buy more or stay longer in the shops, or when retailers – IKEA one prototypical example – shape the consumer journey by purposively constraining him/her to follow a pre-designed and imposed path in the shop. Similarly, a long tradition of literature in the domain of Customer Relationship Management (CRM) has supported the merits of loyalty programs, both for companies and their customers. However, such approaches have misrepresented the fact that these relational tools are powerful technologies directed at governing consumers' conducts who, in turn, may seek to bypass or avoid enticements to join. In many Western countries where loyalty programs have globally spread, people may possess loyalty cards but not use them or express dissatisfaction about membership. For example, in France where the penetration of loyalty programs is close to saturation, half of the consumers feel frustrated by what they get from companies. The reason is not only financial, but appears to be grounded in non-monetary arguments such as a lack of privacy and of freedom to shop wherever they want. In addition, some consumers quit loyalty programs or even refuse to join because they claim the calculation game in which retailers invite them to participate is not interesting.

In light of the enslaved/empowered consumer model, these behaviors, however, point out an important issue. They demonstrate that, in order to resist, consumers must perceive marketing techniques, tools, and discourses as powers that are exerted on them. Because many such marketing tools, and especially the role played by objects and material arrangements, have been largely overlooked, they deserve increased attention. As shown by El Euch Maalej and Roux (2012), loyalty programs assemble heterogeneous elements that seek to bind the consumer to the company. But often times the consumer remains unaware of their potential influence because they are incorporated into existing practices. As such, they have the peculiarity, like chameleons, of being somehow imperceptible and 'naturalized'. Hence, resistance may be suspended to the condition of 'denaturalizing' incorporated routines and of questioning determinations that are most of the time taken for granted. Such posture is obviously aligned with the Marxian approach, which seeks to raise consumers' awareness. But it is also supported by the 'emancipatory school that emphasizes individuals' ability to deploy reflexive and creative modes of resistance in everyday practices. For example, greater evidence of their ability to destabilize existing institutional structures and to reconfigure conventional markets can be found in the way marginalized groups may exert pressure on big companies to thwart their hegemony and/or to be recognized as legitimate market segments. Consumer empowerment is also perceptible through the way progressive groups push forward new – more sustainable, local, social – initiatives as exemplified by the so-called sharing economy. Likewise, at an individual level, consumers have been shown to be cultural producers likely to challenge cultural codes and to contradict authoritative discourses when shopping for food, deciding how they dress, choosing what type of entertainment and leisure activities they endorse, and even challenging other cultural – patriarchal, medical, sexual, social – powers *through* consumption. Hence, the marketplace should be envisioned not solely as a space for consumer resistance, but also a resource base providing means for identity construction and identity expression in the face of other micro-powers that are exerted within the society.

In sum, CCT research has explored various aspects of anticonsumption and consumer resistance behavior. Some key works highlighted in this section have uncovered the various factors that drive for consumer resistance and the myriad forms in which it materializes.

THOUSAND AND ONE WAYS FOR CONSUMERS TO RESIST: OVERT AND COVERT FORMS OF RESISTANCE

The previous section has outlined various macro- and micro-level issues that spur resistance. This section develops the many ways by which resistance is enacted. Schematically, audible, visible, and often collective forms of resistance have been largely investigated, in particular because they not only make salient what is contested in the marketplace, but also try to legitimize other grounds against dominant powers. Apart from this overt resistance, however, less noticeable resistant activities have been brought to light in consumer research, illustrating Scott's (1985) 'weapons of the weak' and how consumers play covert games that hamper dominant actors' activity or provide palliatives to offset market failures.

Overt Resistance: Voicing Discontent

Forms of resistance that have been studied early and extensively are boycotts and buycotts. While the former aims at prompting consumers to withhold their participation and patronage in order to denounce market abuses and bring about change, the latter urges people to support companies and brands that align with people's economic, political, and social concerns. As discussed earlier, boycotts and buycotts are old forms of consumer activism that date back to the 18th century. Since then, they have become a pervasive means for consumers to 'vote with their wallets' in various industrialized and even emergent countries. While the early wave of Western consumer activism tended to merge workers' and consumers' interests in fighting against capitalism, the next stage of consumerism was more about educating consumers to get the best value for money and increase their buying power (Lang and Gabriel 2005).

At a time when social networks and media resonance amplify consumer protests, the way resistance is organized has also changed through Internet-based activities (online only) as well as Internet-supported actions (online and offline). Online petitions, virtual sit-ins, email bombing, or cyber-attacks against targeted websites not only enrich the repertoire of traditional offline protest actions, but also change the way traditional social movements operate. In particular, online activism enables the transnationalization of the activists' causes by spreading the word about consumers' concerns quickly and far beyond their local point of origin. Further, online activism transforms the way activists reconfigure political action. For instance, while New Social Movements (NSM) used to adopt a top-down, vertical, and hierarchical structure, cyber protests offer a horizontal, a-hierarchical and open-access functioning that resembles a 'swarm' with no clear decisional center. However, fluid cultural groups sharing common – political, environmental, social, ethical – interests may constitute dormant networks that quickly unite and mobilize isolated individuals when something threatens their status. For example, websites dedicated to a particular topic are instances of such intermediary organizations capable of providing an arena for protestors' grievances, in particular in situations when freedom of speech is threatened and peer-to-peer online sharing is prosecuted.

Covert Resistance: Bypassing, Escaping, and Reshaping the Marketplace

While not every consumer is compelled to participate in a boycott, many consumers may still resist the marketplace discourses and marketing strategies by simply practicing little gestures of everyday resistance (see the Real World Scenario in Box 13.3 below). Such resistance acts usually involve avoiding the targeted company's brands. For example, Sandıkcı and Ekici (2009) show that consumers reject certain brands and avoid buying products from companies that convey questionable political ideologies such as predatory globalization, chauvinistic nationalism, and religious fundamentalism. Such 'politically motivated brand rejection' remains more expressive at an individual level than transformative at a societal level, and some may even turn rejection tactics into a lifestyle by becoming activists and evangelizing other consumers to boycott companies (Kozinets and Handelman 2004).

Similarly, Thompson and Arsel (2004) show that some consumers refuse to patronize Starbucks stores to protest unfair treatment of coffee farmers and corporate homogenization of the authentic coffee shop experience. Likewise, Hummer antagonists not only demonize the brand, but also publicly chastise Hummer owners for their wasteful, irresponsible, and conspicuous fascination for oversized and polluting vehicles (Luedicke et al. 2010). Although consumer resistance is mostly targeted at brands and commercial companies, it may also be directed towards public actors. For example, passing on one's ticket to another consumer in the underground, car parks, or city package tours – known as the 'la repasse' phenomenon – bears a strong resistant ethos. This practice contravenes the rules of public/private market actors operating in parking, public transportation, or tourism, while initiating at the same time a 'token gifts' ritual in commercial places.

Likewise, consumers may dispose of unwanted items on the curbside to help 'gleaners' to retrieve somehow reusable objects while avoiding their premature and unnecessary destruction. In both cases, the need to help others while subverting the system is obvious, thus illustrating infra-political resistant tactics aiming at correcting for market dysfunctions through micro-scale initiatives (Scott 1985).

Box 13.3:   Real World Scenario

Little gestures of everyday resistance

Overall, consumer resistance is about change. It may be radical and dissenting at the collective level or reformist and transformative at the individual level. The issue of environmental and health concerns is an interesting one to exemplify various levels and forms of resistance. Let us consider first how some political leaders are undertaking enduring action about climate change and raising awareness about the consequences of unbridled consumption. More than 10 years have passed since Al Gore's documentary film *An Inconvenient Truth* (2006) was launched. The former Vice President of the United States now gives an update to these growing concerns with a second film (*An Inconvenient Sequel: Truth to Power*, 2017; www.youtube.com/watch?v=-2 wwsdMt6Po). This new documentary aims to urge individuals to take serious action for more sustainable production and consumption while disproving discourses that deny global warming. With a different angle, the French documentary *Demain* ('Tomorrow', 2015) shares optimistic stories and practical, local solutions addressing sustainability issues in agriculture, energy, and economy. The documentary was well received globally, attracting over a million viewers across 27 countries. Likewise, the ACR video 'Changing Consumer Behavior in Diet and Health' (Hu and Haugtvedt 2011) demonstrates how popular initiatives like 'Local Matters' may reconnect people – children in particular – with local farming and healthy diets, while educating them to avoid processed food and obesity. These three documentaries are all exemplary of initiatives that raise people's awareness of consumer resistance and motivate them to reflect on societal concerns. Using video contents, they draw attention to issues about the wellbeing of humanity such as health and environment, while offering suggestions *and* highlighting consumer initiatives that mobilize audiences.

Questions

1. What other issues could be mentioned as illustrations of the growing scope of consumer resistance?
2. Which alternative channels and modes of communication/interaction may be used to prompt consumers to change their consumption?

Generally consumer resistance tactics that are enacted in everyday practices include 'reject, restrict, or reclaim' behaviors. This is because environmental concerns, distaste with over-spending, over-consumption and materialism, and sensitivity to economic as well as social inequalities are significantly growing among well-educated consumers. As a result, some of them try to downsize their lifestyles and minimize their ecological footprint by reclaiming and reusing, or engaging in 'custodian behaviors' to counter waste and materialism. Others, who take issue with the use of genetically modified foods (natural products such as fruit, vegetables, or cereals whose genetic material (DNA) has been altered in order to give them 'better' properties, e.g. resistance to diseases and better conservation), the absorption of the organic foods movement by agricultural conglomerates, and the unethical aspects of industrial farming, may restrict their dependence on mainstream retailers by participating in community-supported agriculture communities.

To summarize, consumer resistance may be manifested through many different ways, overtly or covertly, at an individual, communal, and/or collective level. Overt resistance seeks to voice concerns, mostly at a collective level, to achieve significant and prompt changes through boycotts and cyber protests. Covert resistance is enacted at an individual or communal level, in everyday practices, trying to consume differently and make micro-changes that will be impactful in the long run. Overt and covert resistances are by no means disconnected. People involved in everyday critical changes are also aware of major collective actions undertaken at a broader level to push forward the cause for which they fight. Yet, the extent to which these multiple forms of resistance are truly effective deserves examination. The Critical Reflection in Box 13.4 below addresses some of the ambiguities that run through postures of resistance.

Box 13.4:   Critical Reflection

Resisting the resistant ethos?

Owing to its orientation toward struggle, opposition, denunciation, and the innate will to rectify inequality or injustice, resistance is often viewed as a heroic posture. This is all the more obvious when 'emancipatory-oriented' scholars emphasize the identity-construction processes through which individuals, groups, and communities seek to correct imbalance in the marketplace by creating new spaces for production, consumption or exchange. At first sight, there seems no doubt that the participants at the Burning Man festival, or various supporters of consumer activist movements, such as Nike boycotters, or anti-Coca-Cola and anti-Starbucks consumers are fully involved in the cause over which they fight. Likewise, downsizing possessions and lifestyle in search for a simpler and better life is obviously perceived as an authenticating act of reclaiming power over one's consumption choices.

Yet, taking consumer resistance at face value is problematic because it can hardly be disentangled from the market logic it seeks to challenge. It may be noted, for example, that certain anti-market initiatives take a stand against the capitalist ethos, which they ironically reproduce in their communication strategy or even in their basic functioning (for example, the Burning Man festival that started as a counterculture annual event to denounce commercial culture and celebrate artistic expression turned into a global spectacle, which now charges entrance fees comparable to Disney theme parks). Likewise, as exemplified by the French online sharing platform Mutum, people are prompted to freely share objects that they do not use, a drive that is consistent with the collaborative ethos. Yet, in order to generate a critical mass of users, and hence to secure its own viability, Mutum has tried to encourage people to lend as many objects as they can. This has been achieved by creating a virtual internal currency, which is called Mutum: participants earn 'Mutums' in proportion to the number of objects they propose; they then set the 'price' (in Mutums) of their object, which can align (or not) with the price suggested by the platform for the same standard object; in turn, they are debited Mutums when they borrow something. Hence, while such system aims at eliminating calculation – a core principle of the market ethos – and at reestablishing pure forms of gifts and counter-gifts between individuals, it finally restates one of its most significant components through the pricing of goods. One direct and most obvious consequence of such a system is that participants who intend to borrow something are prompted to carry out a financial calculation. Indeed, in order to balance the cost of borrowing, they must either multiply the number of objects to rent or overprice them. Such discrepancies between the anti-market purposes of many initiatives of the sharing economy and the way they operate practically are legion. Schor et al. (2016) also examines in four different contexts – a time bank, a food swap, a makerspace, and an open-access education site – how seemingly egalitarian initiatives and so-called openness of these new circuits of exchange in fact conceal distinction and exclusion mechanisms that are brought and perpetuated into sharing sites.

Many other examples could be provided about how so-called resistant initiatives both provide their supporters a sense of freedom, accomplishment, and transformative power, while being imbued with great ambivalence, if not simply recreating the old demons they were tracking the moment before. As Mario Campana's ethnographic work on the Brixton Pound, a local currency alternative to the British Pound, shows, such resistant initiatives can create tensions among local stakeholders. For we have stressed earlier how power and resistance are coextensive phenomena, and because markets are dynamic systems in which the distribution of power is constantly redefined, neither their demonization, nor the heroism of consumer resistance are viable options. Rather, understanding their material and discursive interplay is likely to better account for how the redistribution of power between various actors is shifting over time.

SKETCHING THE FUTURE OF CONSUMER RESISTANCE

Consumer resistance is not a new phenomenon, but rather a new concern on the part of consumer researchers, companies' executives, NGOs' workers, and public policy-makers to name a few. Although these various stakeholders' interests are not the same, they testify to the need to better understand what drives consumer resistance, how it evolves, and to what extent its dynamics impact consumption and market actors. For consumer resistance and the marketplace are fully entangled; the former as well as the latter are evolving coextensively. How will forms and targets of consumer resistance change over time? Regarding forms, part of the answer lies in how power and which type of power is/will be exerted. Addressing this question means examining which technologies and techniques will be implemented by market actors and how their systemic effects will be likely to be thwarted by consumers. For example, market segmentation based on the analysis of 'big data' raises immediate concerns about privacy and the prospect of private and governmental sectors merging for purposes of population surveillance and control – that is in itself a problem for which consumers are helpless at their own level. Less obviously, however, big data tracking of consumers' preferences and habits has the potential to reshape how consumers understand their identities and how they interact with the marketplace. Furthermore, the use of big data to track and target voter groups is exacerbating an ongoing transformation in political life as voters increasingly become akin to consumers and candidates are marketed as brands who speak to consumer-voters' aspirations and needs for identity affirmation, rather than focusing on the resolution of pressing social problems.

Tracing back to the glorious days of the consumption society in the 1960s which was liberating women from burdensome household drudgery not to mention giving them more control of their bodies, as more and more marketplace solutions intervene in everyday life, we now face crucial questions of social and personal wellbeing. We witness an epidemic of obesity, for example, and loss of productive competency in basic activities like healthy eating. Hence, consumer resistance at large will for sure evolve with marketplace technologies, infrastructures, and knowledge, these likely being both triggers and weapons of resistance.

Regarding targets, the other part of the answer suggests that the scope of consumer resistance will also evolve. As globalization poses cross-cutting issues in terms of equality, wealth distribution, and growing environmental threats, consumption will become the arena where dramas are likely to take place. The question of sharing resources, managing populations, massive economic inequality, and reducing waste are already at stake for NGOs and political activists/leaders like Al Gore (see Real World Scenario, Box 13.2). This suggests a clear broadening of consumer resistance and its growing dedication to enacting micro/macro changes in a wider range of consumption fields.

Box 13.5:   Extended Case Study

Digital consumer resistance – an example from the United States

Social media proves to be a powerful platform for consumer resistance and an influential means for spreading the word about important political or social causes to masses. Also known as digital resistance, this type of activism is relatively new and its impact in bringing about social change is still debatable. Nonetheless, easier and faster mobilization of consumer movements over online platforms like Facebook and Twitter renders digital resistance worthy of study.

One recent case of digital activism that has garnered a lot of international attention is the Grab Your Wallet Movement launched in reaction to Donald Trump's comments about groping women without their consent. Following these offensive remarks, Shannon Coulter, a small business owner, started as a simple website that lists around 50 retailers that carry Trump merchandise such as Macy's, Nordstrom, and Amazon.com for consumers to boycott.

Coulter's call to consumers to protest Trump by showing their economic muscle has quickly received attention, with two million website visits every month and 496,000 engagements (i.e., Facebook likes, retweets, and Instagram posts that include #grabyourwallet) according to Captiv8, a firm that studies social media influence (washingtonpost.com). In response, many businesses, including the retail giant Nordstrom, has stopped carrying Trump products. The movement has even prompted perhaps the first boycott app ever – also known as the Boycott Trump App, which lists all Trump affiliated businesses – that has been downloaded more than 350,000 times.

Similar digital resistance tactics have been used recently by other individuals and organizations. For example, a Twitter-based group named Sleeping Giants has targeted advertisers that support the Trump political agenda. The group simply asks its followers to take screenshots of ads posted on racist websites such as Breitbart (edited by a former White House strategist and Donald Trump's friend) and tweet that screenshot to the advertised company along with a message asking it to stop supporting hateful discourse. Likewise, journalist and activist Naomi Klein, well known for her book *No Logo*, has published a video on the Internet urging individuals to target the Trump brand by making reservations at Trump hotels and canceling them at the last minute or jamming the phone lines of his companies. Lastly, Corporate Backers of Hate, another online campaign co-launched by an immigrant rights group and the Center for Popular Democracy, has targeted large financial institutions like Wells Fargo and JP Morgan Chase for lending money to the Trump campaign and investing in Trump-backed projects like the Dakota Access Pipeline that would cross through Native Indian tribal lands. Specifically, the Corporate Backers of Hate website allows visitors to send messages directly to top executives expressing their criticism (salon.com).

(Continued)

(Continued)

Despite the wide media attention these types of digital resistance acts receive, their effectiveness is still debated. Professor Marshall Ganz from Harvard University remarks that digital tools have made it very easy and cost-effective for individuals to start their own initiatives. In turn, the proliferation of many campaigns leads to the fragmentation of resistance movements. Another criticism of digital activism is that it does not require consumers to engage in effortful acts characteristic of traditional boycotts such as picketing or marching. Therefore, digital activism has sometimes been mockingly called slacktivism. More research is needed on the economic impact of digital consumer resistance and its potential to bring about social change.

Questions

1. What are some strengths and weaknesses of digital activism compared to traditional forms of activism?
2. What other examples of digital activism do you observe online?
3. With the advance of technology, particularly with the formation of crowdsourcing platforms such as change.org, does online consumer resistance hold the potential for social change?

CONCLUSION AND RESEARCH DIRECTIONS

In short, consumer resistance comprises a wide range of reactions to various forms of power that are exerted on individuals and groups in the marketplace. As we have shown, many instances of how consumer resistance may express itself have been suggested above, either at a macro-level against the effects of globalization, multinational strategies, and marketplace ideologies, or at a micro-level against marketing techniques, tools and discourses aiming at governing individuals' conducts. What could we expect for the future?

Amplification vs. Weakening of Resistance

Consumer resistance will persist as long as power continues to be exercised over individuals and groups. In principle, therefore, there is no reason why it should disappear. Yet, one could expect it to change according to the nature of the powers it confronts. Injustice and economic imbalance could be one of the ongoing issues related to globalization, and especially struggles that may appear about the unequal distribution of essential resources such as water, food, clean air, etc. From another perspective, invisible tools of surveillance and the inappropriate use of big data could trigger consumer desire to avoid disclosure of sensitive information.

New Forms of Consumer Resistance?

The Internet has enriched the means for protesting and spreading dissent. Parallel to voicing concerns, ways of exiting the marketplace may develop as a more radical response to moral condemnations of irresponsible brands and companies. In addition, new forms of resistance may appear, such as a networked shared resistance between consumers and salespeople, workers, or populations (including animals, plants, and things) whose rights are still denied. While different groups of stakeholders – consumers, workers, citizens – are mostly expected to defend their own particular interests and remain isolated in their social class, an alliance of shared interests may unite these actors more tightly in the future.

Market System Dynamics

Evolution, or the continuous development and transformation, of markets is also a prime example to study consumer resistance (e.g., consider the drastic change in the music industry and how digital consumption of music threatened established ways of music production and distribution). Indeed, the changes in any industry or market involve multiple actors such as producers, distributers, consumers, and regulators, who often have different perspectives and even contrasting agendas. Therefore, market transformation can generate various tensions and involve the resistant acts of different stakeholders. For example, the growing popularity of alternative medicine has been changing the way consumers seek diagnosis and treatment. Instead of visiting physicians, some consumers have been turning to chiropractors, phytotherapists, and acupuncturists, who treat patients through natural ways such as herbal remedies and manipulation of the spine. Threatened by the financial impact of these health practices on their bottom-line, large pharmaceutical companies and some physicians have responded by degradingly labeling natural medicine 'alternative', thereby portraying these practices as secondary and implicitly inferior to modern medicine. Big Pharma continues to undermine the growing influence of natural medicine by lobbying the US Federal Drug Administration to pass legislation that would require highly expensive clinical trials of each herbal ingredient used in supplements. If passed, this legislation could make natural remedies inaccessibly expensive and force many producers out of business. As we see in this example, markets can change drastically through the oppositional acts of power exerted by various market actors whether they are companies, legislators, or consumers. Studying the counteracting discourses and actions of these stakeholders may provide ideal material for understanding cultural changes over the long run within and across societies.

Consumer Competency

Consumer resistance, as we have shown, is about perceiving the action of power. Therefore, a lack of information about how power operates may hamper consumer resistance as long as people ignore how brands, companies, and market actors in general shape their environment, act upon their conduct, or pursue activities that have socially or environmentally detrimental effects. Conversely, circulating information and increasing consumer knowledge are key issues for consumer resistance regarding its possible intensification. In turn, this may require more transparency and accountability on the part of companies and brands to protect their reputation.

RECOMMENDED READING

Foucault, Michel (1978) *The History of Sexuality: An Introduction*. London: Penguin Books.

Izberk-Bilgin, Elif (2010) 'An interdisciplinary review of resistance to consumption, some marketing interpretations, and future research suggestions', *Consumption Markets & Culture, 13* (3): 299–323.

Kozinets, Robert V. and Handelman, Jay M. (2004) 'Adversaries of consumption: Consumer movements, activism, ideology', *Journal of Consumer Research, 31* (3): 691–704.

Lang, Tim and Gabriel, Yannis (2005) 'A brief history of consumer activism', in Rob Harrison, Terry Newholm, and Deirdre Shaw (eds), *The Ethical Consumer*. London: Sage. pp. 39–53.

Scott, James C. (1985) *Weapons of the Weak: Everyday Forms of Peasant Resistance*. New Haven, CT: Yale University Press.

REFERENCES

El Euch Maalej, Mariem and Roux, Dominique (2012) 'Regimes of critique and conflicts of 'worlds': A conventionalist approach to loyalty programs', *Recherche et Applications en Marketing*, English Edition, *27* (4): 59–93.

Foucault, Michel (1978) *The History of Sexuality. An Introduction*. London: Penguin Books.

Holt, Douglas B. (2002) 'Why do brands cause trouble? A dialectical theory of consumer culture and branding', *Journal of Consumer Research, 29* (1): 70–90.

Hu, Anne and Haugvedt, Curtis (2011) 'Changing consumer behavior in diet and health: A video case study on local matters', Association for Consumer Research. https://vimeo.com/groups/136972/videos/41395962.

Izberk-Bilgin, Elif (2010) 'An interdisciplinary review of resistance to consumption, some marketing interpretations, and future research suggestions', *Consumption Markets & Culture, 13* (3): 299–323.

Izberk-Bilgin, Elif (2012) 'Infidel brands: Unveiling alternative meanings of global brands at the nexus of globalization, consumer culture, and Islamism', *Journal of Consumer Research*, *39* (4): 663–87.

Kozinets, Robert V. (2002) 'Can consumers escape the market? Emancipatory illuminations from Burning Man', *Journal of Consumer Research*, *29* (1): 20–38.

Kozinets, Robert V. and Handelman, Jay M. (2004) 'Adversaries of consumption: Consumer movements, activism, ideology', *Journal of Consumer Research*, *31* (3): 691–704.

Lang, Tim and Gabriel, Yannis (2005) 'A brief history of consumer activism', in Rob Harrison, Terry Newholm, and Deirdre Shaw (eds), *The Ethical Consumer*. London: Sage. pp. 39–53.

Luedicke, Marius K., Thompson, Craig J., and Giesler, Markus (2010) 'Consumer identity work as moral protagonism: How myth and ideology animate a brand-mediated moral conflict', *Journal of Consumer Research*, *36* (6): 1016–32.

Peñaloza, Lisa and Price, Linda (1993) 'Consumer resistance: A conceptual overview', *Advances in Consumer Research*, *20* (1): 123–8.

Sandıkcı, Özlem and Ekici, Ahmet (2009) 'Politically motivated brand rejection', *Journal of Business Research*, *62* (2): 208–17.

Schor, Juliet B., Fitzmaurice, Connor, Carfagna, Lindsey B., and Attwood-Charles, Will (2016) 'Paradoxes of openness and distinction in the sharing economy', *Poetics*, *54*: 66–81.

Scott, James C. (1985) *Weapons of the Weak: Everyday Forms of Peasant Resistance*. New Haven, CT: Yale University Press.

Thompson, Craig J. and Arsel, Zeynep (2004) 'The Starbucks brandscape and consumers' (anticorporate) experiences of glocalization', *Journal of Consumer Research*, *31* (3): 631–42.

Varman, Rohit and Belk, Russell W. (2009) 'Nationalism and ideology in an anti-consumption movement', *Journal of Consumer Research*, *36* (4): 686–700.

Witkowski, Terrence H. (1989) 'Colonial consumers in revolt: Buyer values and behavior during the nonimportation movement', *Journal of Consumer Research*, *16* (2): 216–26.

14
CONCLUSION

Linking CCT and Consumer Research: Consumers' Mobilization of Co-created Resources

Craig Thompson,
University of Wisconsin–Madison
Debbie MacInnis,
University of Southern California
Eric Arnould,
Aalto University Business School, Helsinki

Grant McCracken's (1986) theorization of the relationship between culture and consumption is one of the foundational works in the consumer culture theory (CCT) canon. Drawing from anthropology, McCracken argues that material goods encode or substantiate cultural meanings, ideals, and values. When people consume these goods, they are then able to practically integrate these substantiated meanings into their everyday lives. As McCracken conceptualized this relationship in his highly influential 'meaning-transfer' model, goods, brands (and we add services) are most of all carriers of cultural meanings. McCracken emphasized the role of cultural intermediaries – most particularly entertainment media and advertising – in forging these associations between the material and symbolic realms. In subsequent years, CCT research – as demonstrated in this book's chapters – have placed greater emphasis on the role that consumers play in co-creating these meanings. For example, recall the example from Chapter 8 (Visconti, Maclaran, and Bettany) detailing how women's biker groups re-appropriated the macho meanings conveyed by Harley–Davidson motorcycles and transformed these hellacious machines into sources of female empowerment and liberation from constraining gender norms (see Martin et al. 2006). Despite such conceptual revisions, McCracken's core insights remain: goods, services, and brands materialize (or substantiate) abstract cultural meanings and consumers then put these substantiated meanings into everyday use and integrate them into their identity projects though consumption practices.

Though the chapters in this book address a broad range of topics and theoretical perspectives, all demonstrate that consumer culture is fundamentally a material culture (see for example Marcoux 2017 on the ways in which objects and artifacts associated with the 9/11 terrorist incident selectively encode cultural memories). Consumption's fundamental materiality is made more evident when we consider that even seemingly ephemeral goods like digitized music, films, and social media are still dependent for their effects upon material networks of storage mediums, servers, and globally linked power and communication grids. iTunes has little meaning or value without an iPhone or a like technological medium. Increasingly we can also argue that these materials have certain agentic abilities that act on we humans. Consider how your Fitbit structures your time or your iPhone battery meter sends you running to the charging station.

The idea that goods substantiate meanings also implies that production does not end when a product leaves an assembly line because a good's 'cultural biography' (Kopytoff 1986) consists of meanings and values it acquires and conveys subsequent to physical production. Accordingly, consumers are fundamentally involved in this ongoing production and transformation of the cultural meaning substantiated in goods. Although McCracken recognized this co-creative process in his model, its broader implications remained underdeveloped. To correct this shortcoming, several theorists have developed the alternative conceptions of prosumption and prosumers (Cova and Cova 2012; Ritzer and Jurgenson 2010). These concepts combine production and consumption to convey two, interrelated ideas.

First, the distinction between production and consumption that arose in the 18th and 19th centuries in the West had culturally coded the public sphere as the work site and the home as the private site of consumption. Contemporary socio-economic and technological developments have thoroughly effaced this distinction. While this public/production versus private/consumption dichotomy has always been questionable from a socio-cultural standpoint, it provided a powerful heuristic for how marketers understood consumers and their lifestyles. In this orthodox view, companies provided goods and brand symbols to consumers who, in turn, purchased these meaning-infused goods and consumed the various utilities they contained (ranging from functional benefits to social linking value to identity value; Cova and Cova 2002; Holt 2002). Thus, the public–private distinction harbored an implicit metaphor that represented a product/brand as a container of meanings or values, which consumers dutifully unpacked. In this metaphor, consumers have some degree of freedom to rework the meanings that producers inscribed in their products. However, these practices of co-creation were understood as being quite limited in scope. Ultimately, the co-creation of meaning and value was constrained by the simple fact that 'consumers' did not control the 'means of production'.

This traditional view may have once offered marketers a useful heuristic. It is now glaringly at odds with contemporary consumer culture and the intensified influence that 'consumers' can now exert on the means of production or their capacity to outright take over these productive capacities (Woermann 2012). Individually and collectively, consumers have power; a multifaceted resource that encompass competencies, social and cultural capital, and interpersonal influences (such as the 'expert power' exerted by so-called market mavens (see Feick and Price 1987)). Using a definition of power as a feeling of influence and control over others, Rucker and Galinsky (2008) found that a lack of this resource encourages compensatory status-seeking behaviors and preferences for status-oriented goods. In a parallel study, Rucker and Galinsky (2009) report that high power consumers resonate with functionally oriented ad appeals while low power consumers are more responsive to status-oriented campaigns. The military recruiting case in Chapter 7 of this book largely aligns with these findings. The Rucker and Galinsky study also aligns with sociologically oriented CCT studies which find that higher cultural capital consumers, *vis-à-vis* lower cultural capital ones, eschew ostentatious modes of status signaling in favor of consumption practices that they deem edifying, authentic, and that serve autotelic identity goals (Holt 1998). However, we note that such higher cultural capital consumers are not immune from status competitions and status-seeking aims (see Üstüner and Holt 2010); rather, they are competing in social fields where symbolic capital (i.e. status) accrues from displays of cosmopolitan sophistication and understated tastes that are valued for their intellectual, aesthetic, and technical merits (as in 'geek culture').

Digital technologies that are now integrated into people's everyday lives and other disruptive technologies that will soon be – such as 3D printers (Desai and Magliocca 2013) – are another kind of empowering resource. Enabled by these decentralized, DIY technologies, prosumers, on their own time and not following the directives of a firm – may undertake a vast array of productive activities. Consumers can create personal brands (as exemplified by one's social media profile) and distribute these productions across a network of connections, whether through an Instagram feed or digitized exchange systems like eBay, Etsy, or Threadless. These transformations have also greatly amplified consumers' power to reward or punish firms for their branding initiatives in real time, such as in the case of Pepsi's social media-driven withdrawal of its now notorious Kendall Jenner 'ends racism' ad (Smith 2017; see case study in Weinberger and Crockett, Chapter 3).

The second related implication of this conceptual turn to prosumption is that the process of consumer co-creation is extensive and encompassing (Cova and Cova 2012;

Ritzer and Jurgenson 2010). Prosumers create experiences out of commercial goods by way of cognitive devices such as filling narrative gaps, recontextualizing current and remembered experiences, and imagining. Knowledge, including literacy, is a resource that consumers can use to their advantage (Adkins and Ozanne 2005; McGregor 2011; Sujan 1985; Viswanathan et al. 2005). Prosumers also exhibit a broad range of behavioral competencies that range from the complex costumed role playing of cosplay (Seregina and Weijo 2017) to the development of new markets (Martin and Schouten 2014; and see Scaraboto and Karababa, Chapter 5). Collectively, prosumers can radically transform markets (see Roux and Izberk-Bilgin, Chapter 13) and, sometimes merely by intense following and retweeting on social media (Arvidsson et al. 2016), alter the nexus of meanings that circulate within consumer culture.

The crucial issue is not whether one uses the terms 'consumer' or 'prosumer' but that one recognizes the divergent assumptions and implications that follow from these contrasting terms. We tend to associate 'consumer' with a passive social role in which one accepts or adapts to the market offerings advanced by producers. Alternative active identities apply to those who engage in collaborative consumption practices (see Cova and Shankar, Chapter 4); those who critically interpret marketplace signs and symbols; those who leverage their collective power to mobilize against problematic or exclusionary market actions (see Roux and Izberk-Bilgin, Chapter 13; Coskuner-Balli and Thompson 2013; Denegri-Knott et al. 2006; Scaraboto and Fischer 2012); and, those prosumers who create market resources that serve identity and collective goals when established commercial channels do not provide them (see Weinberger and Crockett, Chapter 3).

From this standpoint, a 'prosumerist' reformulation of McCracken's meaning-transfer model portrays the commercial marketplace as a complex, globally distributed system of co-created resources. Whether purchased through Alibaba, Amazon or Taobao, collaboratively created in an emergent market, shared through peer-to-peer networks, or self-produced in one's home, material goods and services are resources that allow individuals to pursue a broad spectrum of identity goals. Prosumers enact an ideal of family togetherness where the symbolic and experiential resources offered by Disney or Club Med are recruited into a family's particular vision of their family vacation ideal (see Epp and Thomas, Chapter 2) or by assembling an ideal Thanksgiving feast from a mix of branded and unbranded raw ingredients (Wallendorf and Arnould 1991). Such enactments enhance feelings of social connectedness, which psychologists recognize as a cognitive resource important to emotional health, self-esteem, and identity (Lee and Robbins 1998). Prosumers perform an imagined or idealized identity as fans of KPop phenomenon ETS (see Schau, Chapter 1). Prosumers can also participate in a community as *Star Wars* devotees; Tough Mudder enthusiasts or avid distance runners, who are linked by collectively galvanizing marketplace resources (see Cova and Shankar, Chapter 4; Kozinets 2001; Thomas et al. 2013).

MARKETPLACE RESOURCES AND THEIR IDENTITY VALUE

We propose that marketplace resources facilitate consumers' personal and collective identity projects by providing two types of value: material-practical value and perform-ative-ideological value. We can think of value to consumers as consisting in meaningful distinctions that refine identities and 'count' as significant achievements. This value emerges from what people do; that is to say, the social pursuit of those meaningful dis-tinctions typically through the exchange and use of resources (Arnould 2014).

Material-practice value resembles what some term functional benefits. For example, an individual cannot readily enjoy 'flow' and communion with nature offered by activities such as white water river rafting or mountain biking without an array of material goods to support those activities. Furthermore, technological advancements can improve the quality of those experiences but also democratize them by making them more accessible to a broader range of participants. For example, the consumer-driven development of the Minimoto market enabled risk-averse consumers to participate in the sport of motor cross on smaller, less powerful (and less dangerous) motorbikes and, in the process, to gain a range of pleasurable new experiences (Martin et al. 2014; also see Scaraboto and Karababa, Chapter 5). Of course, the democratization of material-practical value can create rifts in a consumption community if experienced members view new, technologically enabled par-ticipants as interlopers who spoil a sacred experience, as Canniford and Shankar (2013) discovered in their study of big wave surfers.

The cultural scope of material-practical value is broader than the conventional view of functional utilities. Functional utility treats functional capacities as attributes inherent in the product, such as the case of an automobile that offers better fuel efficiency. This attribute would seem to be an objective resource that exists independently of consum-ers' goals. However, asking one simple question: 'Why would consumers want a more fuel-efficient vehicle?' exposes the limitation of this common sense, marketing view. The answers to this question range from saving money (enacting a thriftiness value) to repre-senting oneself as responsible consumer (enacting an environmentally responsible value). In these cases, functional utility – and the non-trivial fact that the marketer promotes it as an important consumer value and point of competitive differentiation – cannot be separated from the consumer identity goals that motivate consumers to interpret certain features or qualities as desirable benefits. Products and attributes presumed to have func-tional value may well provide other symbolic meanings; reflecting or communicating values central to one's actual or ideal self (Markus and Nurius 1986).

The often taken-for-granted enabling role of resources in affording material-practical value is illustrated by Bardhi, Eckhardt, and Arnould's (2012) analysis of 'global nomad' consumers – a segment of professional workers who revel in their global mobility (see

Sharifonnasabi, Bardhi, and Luedicke, Chapter 10). These consumers prize possessions that are transportable, disposable, and relatively immaterial (digital photos, music, books). Global nomads' detached and flexible 'liquid' relationship to possessions also presupposes that they possess particular forms of cultural capital, which is itself a resource. Recall cultural capital consists of a person's social assets (education, intellect, style of speech and dress, specialized knowledge, etc.) that promote social mobility in a stratified society (see Henry and Caldwell, Chapter 7). Global nomads possess cultural (and social) capital, which allows them to readily and regularly attain well-paying short-term employment – facilitating their serial re-locations around the world. Other material enablers of their lifestyle include expensive market resources such as air travel, dining out, and myriad services. Without their requisite volumes of cultural and economic capital, these consumers would be unable to act upon the identity goal of being a global nomad, and the capacities of these material resources – airlines, condos, LinkedIn and other job networking services, digital technologies – to enable such a lifestyle would remain dormant. Thus, functional benefits are distributed throughout the basic infrastructure of consumer culture and we often take them for granted. Thus, we casually flip on a light switch and rarely question where the electricity comes, how much it might affect our pocketbook, or the ecological toll of mining the natural gas or the CO_2 emissions generated at the power plant.

However, the case of taken-for-granted institutionalized material-practical values embedded in airlines, condos, LinkedIn, and digital technologies generally, also reminds us that not all consumers have equal opportunity to enact their identity goals. Such is the case with those at the bottom of the economic development pyramid (Martin and Hill 2011; Üstüner and Holt 2007); the homeless (Hill and Stamey 1990); those in prisons (Hill et al. 2015); or those in forced internment (Klein and Hill 2008), where access to an enabling background of resources is blocked.

From the case of global nomads, we segue to the second type of value afforded by marketplace resources – performative-ideological value. Being nomadic liberates consumers from the burdens of material goods, freeing up the precious resource of space. Here, we are using 'performative' in a sense pioneered by gender theorist Judith Butler (see Chapter 8, Visconti, Maclaran, and Bettany) and by the sociologist Erving Goffman's (1959) influential analysis of social life as performances intended to gain a favorable impression from an intended audience (i.e. social group). From this perspective, identities enact cultural ideals and archetypes and these performances can generate social rewards if satisfactorily performed. Deviations from these socially shared and normatively enforced expected scripts can result in forms of social punishment, such as stigma and rejection (Brickell 2003).

For example, consider some consumer identity/lifestyle types – the hipster, the nerd, the mall 'rat', the socially responsible consumer, the helicopter parent. Each of these consumers acts out a set of social expectations and social norms that popular culture already prefigures. We know them when we see them, whatever local form they may take, right? In performing their identities, global nomads, hipsters, or socially responsible consumers reiterate the ideals and archetypes, and conform and reinforce pre-existing cultural codes. The hipster with her fancy coffee; the nerd with her app hack; the mall rat with her trendy bags and bundles; the socially responsible consumer with his second-hand clothes and food obtained from dumpster diving; the helicopter parent endowing her child with a complement of IKEA furniture. Of course, consumers may self-consciously deviate from the performative stereotype (i.e., the suburban mom who drives a Porsche Cayenne to avoid identification as a typical 'soccer mom'). One can resist the culturally prevalent performative script, creating some type of distinctiveness amid stereotypical expectations (creating what psychologists call 'optimal distinctiveness', Brewer 2003; see also Bellezza et al. 2013; Berger and Heath 2007). Here, one's identity is still being shaped by the meanings and expectations being defied. For example, the male-dominated Porsche brand community stigmatized the Porsche Cayenne precisely for being the car for soccer moms who did not want to look like 'soccer moms' (see Avery 2012). Similarly, Turkish immigrants sought to conform to Austrian culture by driving BMW automobiles, but Austrians branded drivers of certain model BMWs as foreigners (see Chapter 10; Luedicke 2015). What we see across all these examples is how consumer goods serve as performative-ideological resources.

Consumer identity goals are embedded in value systems that shape how we understand the categories of social class, gender, ethnicity, and age (consider the stereotypes that frame the identity position of being a millennial) (see Coskuner-Balli and Ertimur, Chapter 6; Thomas, Cross, and Harrison III, Chapter 9; Veresiu and Giesler, Chapter 11). Consumers can interpret and perform cultural and ideological codes in a vast variety of ways – treating them as natural aspects of their identities, or as aspirations, or as constraining norms that they should contest and challenge (Weinberger and Crockett, Chapter 3). Marketplace resources enable consumers to co-creatively adapt or transform ideological codes while the codes nonetheless exert a shaping influence on consumers' identities and the goals they pursue. Whether in the overtly performative character of roller derby competitor (brandishing roller skates, fishnet stockings, short shorts, tattoos, piercings, and colorfully streaked punk rock hair) or the more naturalized role of corporate global nomad dressing for success, individuals choose goods and brands whose symbolic meanings align with the broader ideological codes they are seeking to perform. For example, McAlexander et al. (2014) analyze the identity transformations among consumers who decided to abandon the prohibitions enforced within the Mormon Church, such as those forbidding the consumption of coffee and alcohol products. In this context, the act of drinking a cup of coffee with a co-worker breached their prior religiously framed identity performance as a Mormon, and simultaneously signaled that they had reconstructed their identity in ideological alignment with dominant North American consumer tastes.

One major source of performative-ideological resources, though little discussed in this book, will surely feature more prominently in future editions – digital technology. However, digital technologies are not merely resources, but material actors that can reciprocally exert power and influence. Consider self-tracking apps and devices that constantly nudge consumers to consume calories, time, and energy in accordance with norms inscribed in their customized algorithms. Consider also the way in which Twitter redefines popularity, influence, inclusion, and exclusion through consumers' use of hashtags, and retweets, often enmeshed with fashion and pop culture brands (Arvidsson et al. 2016; McQuarrie and Phillips 2014). When you ask a young teen about their popularity and self-esteem, the resource they turn to is their Snapchat or Instagram feeds. Through Facebook likes, Instagram follows and Twitter retweets anyone can assess their popularity in an instant on the condition one accepts the power and resource that social media exert.

CONSUMPTION AND THE STRUCTURE–AGENCY PROBLEM

A consequential theoretical and social issue raised by consumers' use of marketplace resources and the co-creation of performative-ideological value is: how much flex is there in the social system? Some accounts of consumer culture suggest that consumers have considerable latitude to choose and construct their identities through active participation in consumer communities (Cova and Shankar, Chapter 4; Schau, Chapter 1). Other chapters in this book suggest that sociological conditioning and the power relations that stratify the distribution of socio-economic resources along the lines of social class, gender, and race, while not unchanging, are entrenched and not easily escaped (Thomas, Cross, and Harrison III, Chapter 9; Henry and Caldwell, Chapter 7; Visconti, Maclaran, and Bettany, Chapter 8; Weinberger and Crockett, Chapter 3).

Sociologists refer to this tension as the structure versus agency problem; that is, how much of human behavior (including consumption) is a function of one's social conditioning and the normative demands and expectations that are enforced by social institutions (i.e., the family, the workplace, religious organizations, and even consumption communities) and how much reflects autonomous actions that are not predetermined by these structural influences and constraints (Giddens 1984). This book can help you consider these issues for yourself.

In making sense of the relationship between the classic problem of conditioning and domination vs. freedom and self-determination, we first suggest that there is no definitive or absolute resolution to these divergent theoretical and political positions. We call this contrast in perspective the structure–agency problem. Overall, social science points to the ambiguous conclusion that some non-significant portion of our identity is determined by social structures and some of it is a function of choices that are not determined by these structural influences. However, the balance of these two dimensions seems to vary across social, institutional, and technological contexts in ways that defy generalization. Consider the repeated, unpredicted, and unprecedented worldwide expressions of pro-democracy sentiment against undemocratic political regimes since 2011's Arab Spring. Absent consumers' widespread adoption of mobile technologies, similar mass movements for self-determination and empowerment would have been less effective.

Given this complexity, we suggest that the work of sociologist Pierre Bourdieu (see Arsel and Bean, Chapter 12; Henry and Caldwell, Chapter 7; Weinberger and Crockett, Chapter 3) offers a useful way to think about the structure–agency conundrum. Bourdieu posits that, in many instances, our identities enact taken-for-granted meanings and norms. Thus, we take culturally contingent characteristics as immutable traits we happen to possess by virtue of personality or even biology. Hence, your taste, your preferences, your demeanor are treated as being akin to your height or eye color, that is, as something innate and natural rather than cultural. This sense of having a naturalized identity also encourages people not to question the social hierarchy that governs their lives and limits their life opportunities: someone may strive to move up the hierarchy but, in so doing, accepts as the natural order of things the social inequities it reproduces (see Henry and Caldwell, Chapter 7 for an extended discussion).

However, consumers can become aware of ways in which these supposedly natural aspects of their identity have been culturally and ideologically shaped. This reflexive awareness creates an opening for more purposeful reconstructions of identity, via consumer choice making that can mobilize a host of different resources. However, the extent of these changes can vary considerably depending on one's particular resource endowments and circumstances.

According to Bourdieu (1984), the impetus for states of reflexive awareness generally ensues from significant socio-economic or cultural shifts that disrupt normal routines and orthodox social hierarchies, such as a political upheaval. Less dramatically, for many college students, entering into the world of university life heightens awareness of different beliefs, identity positions, and lifestyle orientations that can, in turn, spark critical reflection on their taken-for-granted identity practices and expand their horizon of possibilities.

Consumer culture, and the array of marketplace resources, can spark reflexive self-awareness and open a space for various modes of identity experimentation. In this regard, one of the key sources of performative-ideological value that marketplace resources provide is cultural capital (see Arsel and Bean, Chapter 12; Henry and Caldwell, Chapter 7; Weinberger and Crockett, Chapter 3). By participating in particular consumption communities, or 'taste cultures' (Gans 1999), consumers gain access to specific forms of cultural capital, such as specialized knowledge about indie music, Chinese high fashion, manga and anime, automobile racing, craft beer, the soft modernist aesthetic in architecture, or vegetarianism to name a few (Arsel and Bean 2013; Arsel and Thompson 2011; Cronin et al. 2014; Maciel and Wallendorf 2017). Acquired performative-ideological resources may be discrepant from a consumer's given stock of cultural capital and related tastes acquired through his/her socialization in a particular society and social class. The reconfiguration of a consumers' habitus (taken-for-granted performances) may most directly be reflected in altered preferences – suddenly you are choosing short-run craft beer produced at a local Danish 'ghost' brewery rather than industrially produced Carlsberg (Kjeldgaard et al. 2017), or Mariage Frères green tea rather than Lipton Yellow label, for instance. Such new tastes also tend to situate one in a different social group and send different signals about the kind of person one is. Thus, consumption of novel performative-ideological resources may precipitate social-symbolic transformations, which in turn, can also precipitate different kinds of identity goals and performative orientations than had been associated with one's prior tastes.

Thus, reflexive awareness leading to changes in preferred material-practice and performative-ideological resources sparked by participation in a particular consumption community or taste culture can enable a consumer's performative identity transformation, albeit one grounded in a specific system of cultural meanings (see Arsel and Bean, Chapter 12; see also Solomon 1983). As we said in the introduction to the book, commentators and thought leaders tend to think that consumer culture is reproduced over time through individual choice among consumption goods. We might say instead, that the reproduction and unfolding complexity of consumer culture hinges on a dialectic. Constraints built in to our systems of norms and values and our performative capacities are the mirror image of each other. To build competencies in one consumer community, one taste culture, or even one family is to forgo options to build other kinds of capacities and to pursue other kinds of consumer identities. The meanings that we derive from marketplace resources that allow us to perform an identity are also the meanings that subsume our actions within a sociological web of normative demands and constraints. These ideas may shed light on the fairly recent trend of 'cultural omnivorousness' (Lizardo and Skiles 2012), which refers to consumers' cultivating tastes that cut across the mass market versus 'high culture' divide (for example, one might enjoy McDonald's fries and haute Asian-Peruvian fusion cuisine). Cultural omnivorousness is perhaps one way that consumers seek to resist structural tradeoffs, and, in effect, become more fluid or liquid in their identities (see Bardhi, Luedicke, and Sharifonnasabi, Chapter 10). But even here, one can ask if the conspicuous cultural omnivore is not just another identity produced by our neoliberal market economy, an economy that is increasingly reliant upon a culturally adaptable and cosmopolitan workforce (see Veresiu and Giesler, Chapter 11).

FURTHER LINKS TO CONSUMER PSYCHOLOGY

This book focuses on the socio-cultural aspects of consumption and the ways in which a host of sociological, cultural, and ideological forces shape consumers' individual and collective identity projects, and their prosumption of marketplace resources. One often unstated implication in CCT is that these socio-cultural factors influence the choices consumers make from the potpourri of marketplace resources available to them, and how they subjectively experience the marketplace. Consumer psychologists have historically studied consumer behavior from the standpoint of decision-making. Generative topics have concerned the micro-level goals that drive consumer choice, the emotional implications of goal fulfillment (Bagozzi et al. 1999; Baumgartner and Pieters 2008), the extent to which consumption decisions involve extensive vs. limited effort (Petty 1983), the processes by which choices are made (Bettman et al. 1998), and whether attitudes predict choices (Ajzen 2008). Recent work acknowledges not just the role of acquiring consumer goods, but also how such goods are used, and how they are sensorily experienced through music and other sounds, taste, touch, smell, and sight (Kellaris 2008; Krishna 2012). Advances in neuroscience promise additional insights into traditional and emerging topics studied by consumer psychologists (Plassmann and Karmarkar 2015).

Whereas CCT research undertakes analyses that operate at more macro (i.e. broader socio-historical trends) and meso (i.e., meanings that are collectively shared among a particular social group) levels, the CCT community and that of consumer psychologists shows signs of convergence, at least in terms of a few substantive topics.

The macro (anthropological, sociological, historical) perspective of CCT research is now being supplemented by work in consumer psychology that considers the evolutionary roots of consumption (Griskevicius and Kenrick 2013). Some work in the CCT tradition has complemented psychologically oriented analysis, such as by showing how prominent cultural ideals, myths, and societal norms shape consumers' decision-making process and their emotional responses to choice options (Allen 2002; Fischer et al. 2007); their experiences of satisfaction (Arnould and Price 1993; Fournier and Mick 1999), and their perceptions of market risks (Fischer et al., 2007; Thompson 2005; Wong and King 2008).

Moreover, consumer psychologists are increasingly studying the identity domain, examining how consumption can signal identities (Gal 2015) and restore threatened identities (Gao et al. 2008; Park and John 2011). CCT researchers recognize that paradoxes in the marketplace and threats to one's identity project requires coping resources. Consumer psychologists are similarly studying how consumers cope (Han et al. 2015), not just with unsatisfactory consumption experiences, but also with consumption paradoxes and significant experiences, like natural disasters (Ferraro et al. 2011), their own mortality or those of their children (Botti et al. 2009; Ferraro et al. 2005), and the identity implications of loss.

CCT researchers have studied the role of cultural intermediaries as sources that influence brand meaning as noted above. Consumer psychologists similarly examine influencers of brand meaning, though they have focused more on personal meanings developed through reference group affiliations (Escalas and Bettman 2005; White and Dahl 2007), childhood socialization experiences (Roedder John 1999), and brand relationships (Fournier 1998; Park et al. 2010).

With increasing overlap in the substantive topics studied by CCT and psychological researchers, we see evidence of the potential for the concept of resources to further integrate the two approaches to consumer behavior (MacInnis 2017). Consumer psychologists define a resource as any asset that an individual values and feels is important to happiness (Dorsch et al. 2017). This definition is largely compatible with Bourdieu's influential theorization of capitals discussed above or practice theory in consumer sociology that defines consumption practices in terms of rule-based knowledge, tacit knowledge, and affective commitments (Warde 2005).

RESOURCES AS CONCEPTUAL LINKING POINTS BETWEEN CCT AND CONSUMER PSYCHOLOGY

Earlier in this chapter, we have seen references to different types of resources that consumers can deploy in pursuit of their identity goals, including *cultural capital*, *social capital* and *interpersonal influence* (i.e., one mode of power), *status*, *marketplace goods*, and *consumer knowledge*. Consumer psychologists study additional resources, including *time* (Bellezza et al. 2016; Hornik 1984; Leclerc et al. 1995), *money* (e.g., Garbinsky et al. 2014; Mogilner and Aaker 2009; Lasaleta et al. 2014), and *health* (Bolton et al. 2008; Keller et al. 2011; Moorman and Matulich 1993). For a long time, the consumer marketplace has functioned as a source of *hope*. Consumer psychologists have shown that hope is an emotional resource that sustains commitment to consumption goals in domains as far flung as cosmetics to fertility treatments (MacInnis and deMello 2005). Hope is the wellspring of consumers' desire to attain a more ideal self or lifestyle (Belk et al. 2003).

Attention and mental capacity are cognitive resources that are often and regularly depleted as the marketplace becomes more complex, global, and connected (Schwartz 2004; Wu 2016). When these cognitive resources are exhausted, consumers are more likely to give in to temptation, buying and consuming goods that bring immediate pleasure at the expense of long-term welfare (Agrawal and Wan 2009; Hoch and Loewenstein 1991; Vohs and Faber 2007). Deliberation thus gives way to gratification. Marketplace resources offer a conceptual thread that can facilitate further synthesis and dialogue between the consumer psychology and CCT perspectives.

While having knowledge and access to information provides consumers resources that enhance their decision-making, cyber-attacks and interlinking databases are raising concerns about who has access to personal information, in turn, raising the importance of information *privacy* and *security* as resources in marketplace decisions.

Although CCT researchers and consumer psychologists tend to investigate different kinds of questions and topic areas, a resource perspective offers the chance to align CCT research and consumer psychology. This conceptual shift reflects, in small part, the influence of CCT on consumer psychological theorizations (see Berger and Ward 2010; van Laer et al. 2013). It also ensues from innovations in the marketing literature, again echoing certain CCT precepts, which conceptualize the marketplace as a domain in which consumers deploy 'operant' and 'operand' resources in exchange with complementary resources deployed by firms (Arnould 2007; Vargo and Lusch 2004). While the psychological variations of this concept might address some of the performative-ideological values of marketplace resources, and they could readily encompass the material-practice (i.e. enabling functions) and hence provide a conceptual bridge between these two theoretical approaches to analyzing consumption.

Up to now, people who study one type of resource, for example time, might not look at papers published by others who focus on a different resource – say attention, or power, identity or status. But thinking broadly about all of these entities as 'resources' makes the notion of 'resources' a construct that can link disparate research areas. *It makes the construct of resources highly foundational to the study of consumer behavior.* We can envision a number of research implications that follow from re-visioning consumer research from a resource-oriented perspective.

Resources and Markets

An expanded view of consumer resources brings types of markets that might not always be so obvious into focus. Among them, we could include the dating market (which involves the exchange of money and time for relationships) and the market for experimental drugs (for which money is exchanged for purposes of hope and health). The spirituality market offers hope for everlasting happiness, in exchange for time and monetary donations (O'Guinn and Belk 1989). The philanthropy market involves the transfer of money (economic resources) for purposes of status enhancement (self-esteem and social resources). The market for contributions to political campaigns involves the exchange of money for the promise of power and perhaps social capital. The expanded view of resources also extends to markets where what the 'giver' gives may be non-monetary. Social recycling, the process of donating unwanted used goods to non-profit organizations, enhances resources like personal space and perceived social connectedness, while also acting in environmentally friendly ways (Donnelly et al. 2017). Other examples include the endorser market, where the endorser gives status and knowledge, the organ donor market, where the donor gives a healthy body part, and the volunteer where individuals donate time in exchange for social connections with others whose identity and values converge.

This notion of resources and consumer behavior is not new (Bagozzi 1975; Brinberg and Wood 1983; Foa and Foa 1980; Levitt 1972; Levy 1959), but perhaps it was an idea ahead of its time. Indeed, a focus on resources not only connects CCT researchers and consumer psychologists, it can extend to novel areas of research that go beyond the notion of exchanges in a marketplace. What else does an expansive view of 'resources' offer to consumption research?

How Resources are Valued and Evaluated

In order to consider what consumers are willing to give and get in marketplace exchanges, researchers must assess how resources are valued, and how different types of resources can be conceptualized on a common metric of value. What is 'time' worth? How much will people pay to get 'status'? What's more important, money or health? When will consumers value nature over technology? By thinking broadly about what constitutes a 'resource', we can explore comparative questions that can help us understand whether all resources operate in similar ways. Chris Janiszewski and Luc Warlop co-edited a special issue of *Journal of the Association for Consumer Research* focusing on the topic of how consumers value resources (Janiszewski and Warlop 2017). Some articles in the special issue illustrate that many transactions are not simple exchanges of one resource for one benefit. Instead, transactions often involve exchanges of a combination of resources for a combination of benefits, wherein the value of each resource is contingent on the other resources involved in the transaction. Other articles explore the social utility of relationships and the socially malleable value of things as well as the socially variable nature of money as a resource, all themes well explored in consumer culture theory and consumer sociology. Finally, a number of the studies in this special issue show that the value of a resource is malleable and interacts with cognitive resources like memory, the importance of the goals individuals pursue, and the mental energy available to evaluate the attractiveness of a good. Together the articles in this special issue open up fruitful avenues for consumer psychology but of potential cross-fertilization between consumer psychology and consumer culture theory. CCT research has also explored this interdisciplinary terrain (Arnould 2014; Arsel 2015).

The valuation of resources is clearly impacted by things like resource scarcity, resource dependence, and resource saving. For example, resource scarcity clearly impacts how much consumers are willing to pay to get more of the resource (Thaler 1985), not to mention how people relate to others. Witness the behavior of American consumers on Black Friday, when retailers offer steep markdowns in anticipation of the end of year holiday season.

Some consumers risk being trampled by other shoppers and will pay exorbitant prices to obtain the hot new toy that everyone wants but few can find. Also, being faced with restricted resources has deleterious effects on one's self concept (Bone et al. 2014). Yet, resource scarcity is complicated. Not having enough resources makes us plan and stretch our resources, which we see as rather painful and costly (Fernbach et al. 2014). Scarcity can increase creativity as it requires us to think more broadly about what we can do to accomplish the goals we have (Mehta and Zhu 2015). Although there are situations in which scarcity prompts people to be selfish, there are other situations in which it prompts people to behave generously (Roux et al. 2015). Uncertainty in resources, whether it is time, money, power or health, influences whether and how we anticipate resource demands in the future, and how we plan for resource availability (Bosmans et al. 2010). A number of the above-referenced papers address the effects of monetary scarcity on consumption. Are similar effects observed when consumers are depleted of other types of resources, like cultural capital or social connections?

Whereas being dependent on others for resources can sound like a bad thing, we're learning that consumption communities are preserved when community members depend on others for resources like social and economic support (Thomas et al. 2013). Does dependency on others for resources similarly preserve bonds when the resource on which one depends is cultural capital or hope? We have also learned that consumers spend money differently on boys vs. girls, depending on whether economic resources are tight or more abundant (Durante and White 2015). Does a similar effect operate for time? Interesting questions can also be asked about how consumers build and stockpile different types of resources (Shen et al. 2014; Ülkümen et al. 2008). Do people think about time or social capital as resources that they can build?

Sharing and Donating Resources

Sharing resources seems somehow different than spending resources (Belk 2009), though spending and sharing resources both have the potential to lead to resource depletion. Interesting questions can be addressed about why, and how, people share resources with others, whether it's sharing information on social networking sites (Berger and Milkman 2012), sharing money by donations to charitable organizations (Fennis et al. 2008), or sharing (vs. owning) consumer goods (Bardhi and Ekhardt 2012).

Categorizing Resources

We already know that consumers behave differently depending on how resources are categorized. We behave differently when we categorize time as 'work time', 'leisure time', 'personal time', or 'family time' (McCracken 1990). We budget money differently when we categorize a year as involving 12 months or 365 days (Ülkümen et al. 2008). Categorizing money in terms of larger vs. smaller denominations (e.g., a $10 bill vs. ten $1.00 bills) affects how consumers spend their money (Raghubir et al. 2017). Categorizing relationships as 'communal' vs. 'exchange' has a huge impact on whether we expect immediate reciprocity from an exchange partner or not, as well as expectations of reciprocity of the same resource vs. a different one (Aggarwal 2004; Fiske 1992). Do consumers have mental categories for things like health (e.g., health preservation vs. health prevention), status (achieved vs. ascribed), or power (benevolent vs. malevolent)? How would mentally accessing these different categories change consumption behavior?

Resources as Drivers of Consumer Decision-Making

A resource perspective also makes the lens through which consumers view the world more focal. That is, it emphasizes what's happening in the *consumer's world*, not what's happening in the marketplace. It forces us to consider that product availabilities in the marketplace may drive consumer choices less than do the resources about which consumers feel deprived or flush. This perspective contrasts sharply with classic decision-making models, which are premised on the idea that consumers' choices involve the comparison of brands along a set of features or attributes and where preferences are driven by logically evaluating these discrete features on their relative importance. In fact, it is easy to imagine various consumer choices that have nothing to do with the characteristics of a brand or even the competitive landscape in which that brand operates. A consumer may refuse to buy a new car and to instead get around using Lyft and public transportation. Recalling our earlier example about brand choice, this decision is not based on the lack of good brands on the market. Rather, it is based on the fact that from the consumer's standpoint, this decision preserves time, money, identity, and perhaps greater feelings of power, more so than buying a car does. A broader consideration of the resources consumers do and do not have might lead to insights about how resource abundance and deficiencies drive consumer choices.

Resource Paradoxes and Tradeoffs

Resource endowments, surfeits or deficits, can have paradoxical effects on other resources. For example, it's clear that investments in technology can make us more connected to others in a virtual environment. Consider how much time consumers spend texting, posting, and photosharing. However, such investments can come at a cost of weakening other resources, like close interpersonal relationships. To appreciate this paradox, one only needs to witness how many people are glued to their phone at dinner, even while sitting next to a partner. Complicating the picture is the fact that abundance or lack of a given resource can enhance perceptions of another. Such is the case, for example, when being extremely busy (e.g., having little to no time) becomes a status symbol (e.g., Bellezza et al. 2016). Having more stuff also means having less space (Bardhi et al. 2012), such that consumer goods trade off with the resource of space. Having more stuff means bigger houses on larger lots, which, in turn, means less opportunities to form relationships with neighbors, weakening the resource of social connections (Pieters 2013). Outsourcing childcare obligations to others saves time, but it can be costly in terms of money and connections with one's family (Epp and Velagaleti 2014). Acquiring information on the web often means giving up aspects of our privacy, which can leave us feeling less secure (Miyazaki, and Fernandez 2001). These tradeoffs may be making consumer decision-making even more complex, as consumers need to consider more resource categories in making their decisions. As such, we surmise that *a broader set of resource considerations are figuring more prominently into consumers' decisions.*

Resource Portfolios

If resource abundance and deficits do indeed drive consumers' marketplace choices, our knowledge of consumer behavior may be enhanced by focusing on how consumers subjectively perceive the cluster of resources that characterize their current resource portfolio. Those with an abundance of cultural capital but deficits in time will surely behave differently from consumers with the reverse profile. Life circumstances can also radically alter perceived resource abundance or deficiencies, demarcating new life projects for which resource investments are needed. Learning that a child is disabled or that a parent has Alzheimer's disease can highlight new deficiencies in knowledge, social support, time, and financial resources (see for example, Henkel et al. 2017). Considering the portfolio of resource available to consumers also contrasts sharply with the prevailing paradigm. Marketers and consumer psychologists have historically thought about resources *in terms of a specific transaction* – that is, what the consumer is willing to give up in order to get a resource in return. Conceptualizing consumers as bundles of resources clarifies that transactions are made in a larger life context where consumers must balance a portfolio of resources.

The Role of Technology in Resource Valuation

Technology can clearly be regarded as a resource as it has the potential to contribute to happiness. Yet, one wonders how changes in technology alter what resources are valued or the means by which deficient resources are rectified. For example, could social capital become so readily quantified by 'likes' that it eventually replaces monetary capital as a medium of exchange. A recent episode of the TV Show *Black Mirror* (the episode titled Nosedive) eerily portrays what such a consumer world would look like. We know that consumers anthropomorphize products and brands, imbuing them with human-like qualities, motives, and traits (MacInnis and Folkes 2017). Will advances in robotics enable environments where connections with robots, who seem to know our voice, face, preferences and the like, are as powerful as human connections in contributing to human happiness? Could connections with robots become even more valued than human connection because robots 'know' us better and offer greater predictability with less 'maintenance'?

Resources and Happiness

Consumer researchers are increasingly studying happiness. A focal question of many is whether material or experiential purchases bring consumers more happiness (e.g., Mogilner 2010; Nicolao et al. 2009). Thinking about consumer behavior in terms of one's portfolio of resources also has the potential to help us understand what it means to be happy. Whereas one might argue that we are most happy when we have a surplus of all types of resources, the paradoxical nature of resources suggests that such a state is impossible to achieve. Maybe happiness is not a state marked by having more of every resource. It's a state of equilibrium where one's current portfolio of resources leaves us not wanting for more.

CONCLUSION

This chapter has discussed two related ideas. Consumer culture can be viewed as a heterogeneous constellation of marketplace resources, which consumers proactively and co-creatively utilize in a multitude of ways that reflect their identity goals, capacities, and enabling resources such as time, money, social connections, health and wellbeing. Seen in this light, consumers are perhaps better conceptualized as prosumers – a term that blurs the traditional boundaries between consumption and production. Conversely, marketplace resources (i.e., goods, services, brands, media) themselves have latent capacities that are realized when prosumers render them as (manifest) enabling resources through their co-creative practices. In so doing, prosumers draw from their own embodied stock of capacities, most prominently skills and knowledge (i.e., cultural capital), cognitive aptitudes, and emotional intelligence, to draw out the material-practical and ideological-performative value afforded by these enabling marketplace resources as they seek to realize their particular identity and lifestyle goals. Though these dynamic interactions take place through institutionalized market systems and platforms, prosumers can also be transformed by the marketplace resources that they are ostensibly using as tools for identity work. For example, interactions with products often lead to the acquisition of new skills and knowledge, which become integrated into one's existing stock of embodied capacities. Figure 14.1 summarizes this circuit of prosumption.

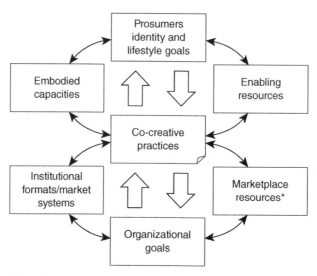

* Material-practical value
* Performative-ideological value

Figure 14.1 The circuit of prosumption

We close by noting that this dawning era of prosumption also harbors myriad potentials for conflict as prosumers come to believe that they have some degree of legitimate ownership over their co-created resources. In the meantime, companies maintain considerable legal control over their commercial offerings and they often view consumer co-creation simply as a means to gain increased profit from expropriating the free labor of consumers, as in the case of the Build-A-Bear workshops (see Zwick et al. 2008; also Cova et al. 2015). Firms may also view prosumers' creative outputs as resources on which they can capitalize, as exemplified by the business models of Facebook, YouTube, and other social media gathering points (see Ritzer and Jurgenson 2010). Conflict may also arise when media companies provide prosumers a platform for producing creative remixes and mash-ups of their copyrighted resources but claim exclusive rights to this fan-generated content (Chapter 4, Cova and Shankar).

In the end, prosumption, while often celebrated in marketing narratives as fostering higher levels of 'customer engagement', is a de facto struggle over the control of marketplace resources and whether consumers and corporations can find viable compromises when their respective interests collide. Whether in terms of complex policy debates over 'net neutrality' and its effects on consumers' ability to access information through the internet or peer-to-peer sharing networks, like Bit torrent, that enable consumers to circumvent copyright laws, the future shape of our prosumerist society will be shaped by political and legal forces, as well as cultural and technological ones. As McCracken (1986) noted long ago, in 'hot' (i.e., dynamic) societies, the pace of cultural change and technological innovation tends to evolve much faster than do regulatory and legal systems and dominant social norms and mores. In the end, consumer culture often provides pressures for broader societal changes and the era of prosumption promises to be no different.

REFERENCES

Adkins, Natalie Ross, and Ozanne, Julie L. (2005) 'The low literate consumer', *Journal of Consumer Research, 25* (December): 93–105.

Aggarwal, Pankaj (2004) 'The effects of brand relationship norms on consumer attitudes and behavior', *Journal of Consumer Research, 31* (1): 87–101.

Agrawal, Nidhi and Wan, Echo Wen (2009) 'Regulating risk or risking regulation? Construal levels and depletion effects in the processing of health messages', *Journal of Consumer Research, 36* (3): 448–62.

Ajzen, Icek (2008) 'Consumer attitudes and behavior', in Curtis P. Haugtvedt, Paul M. Herr, and Frank R. Kardes (eds), *Handbook of Consumer Psychology*. New York: Erlbaum. pp. 525–48.

Allen, Douglas (2002) 'Toward a theory of consumer choice as sociohistorically shaped practical experience: The Fits-Like-a-Glove (FLAG) Framework', *Journal of Consumer Research, 28* (March): 515–32.

Arnould, Eric J. (2007) 'Service-dominant logic and consumer culture theory: Natural allies in an emerging paradigm', in Russell W. Belk and John F. Sherry Jr (eds), *Consumer Culture Theory*, Bingley, UK: Emerald Group Publishing. pp. 57–76.

Arnould, Eric J. (2014) 'Rudiments of a value praxeology', *Marketing Theory, 14* (1): 129–33.

Arnould, Eric J. and Price, Linda L. (1993) 'River Magic: Extraordinary experience and the extended service encounter', *Journal of Consumer Research, 20* (June): 24–45.

Arsel, Zeynep (2015) 'Assembling markets and value', in Robin Canniford and Domen Bajde (eds), *Assembling Consumption*. New York and London: Routledge. pp. 32–41.

Arsel, Zeynep and Bean, Jonathan (2013) 'Taste regimes and market-mediated practice', *Journal of Consumer Research, 39* (February): 899–917.

Arsel, Zeynep and Thompson, Craig J. (2011) 'Demythologizing consumption practices: How consumers protect their field-dependent identity investments from devaluing marketplace myths', *Journal of Consumer Research*, *37* (5): 791–806.

Arvidsson, Adam, Caliandro, Alessandro, Airoldi, Massimo, and Barina, Stefania (2016) 'Crowds and value. Italian Directioners on Twitter', *Information, Communication and Society*, *19* (July): 921–39.

Avery, Jill (2012) 'Defending the markers of masculinity: Consumer resistance to brand gender-bending', *International Journal of Research in Marketing*, *29* (4): 322–36.

Bagozzi, Richard P. (1975) 'Marketing as exchange', *Journal of Marketing*, 32–9.

Bagozzi, Richard P., Gopinath, Mahesh, and Nyer, Prashanth U. (1999) 'The role of emotions in marketing', *Journal of the Academy of Marketing Science*, *27* (2): 184.

Bardhi, Fleura and Eckhardt, Giana M. (2012) 'Access-based consumption: The case of car sharing', *Journal of Consumer Research*, *39* (4): 881–98.

Bardhi, Fleura, Eckhardt, Giana M., and Arnould, Eric J. (2012) 'Liquid relationship to possessions', *Journal of Consumer Research*, *39* (3): 510–29.

Baumgartner, Hans and Pieters, Rik (2008) 'Goal-directed consumer behavior: Motivation, volition and affect', in Curtis P. Haugtvedt, Paul M. Herr, and Frank R. Kardes (eds), *Handbook of Consumer Psychology*. New York: Erlbaum. pp. 367–92.

Belk, Russell (2009) 'Sharing', *Journal of Consumer Research*, *36* (5): 715–34.

Belk, Russell W., Ger, Guliz, and Askegaard, Søren (2003) 'The fire of desire: A multi-site inquiry into consumer passion', *Journal of Consumer Research*, *30* (December): 326–52.

Bellezza, Silvia, Gino, Francesca, and Keinan, Anat (2013) 'The red sneakers effect: Inferring status and competence from signals of nonconformity', *Journal of Consumer Research*, *41* (1): 35–54.

Bellezza, Silvia, Paharia, Neeru, and Keinan, Anat (2016) 'Conspicuous consumption of time: When busyness and lack of leisure time become a status symbol', *Journal of Consumer Research*, *44* (1): 118–38.

Berger, Jonah and Heath, Chip (2007) 'Where consumers diverge from others: Identity signaling and product domains', *Journal of Consumer Research*, *34* (2): 121–34.

Berger, Jonah and Milkman, Katherine L. (2012) 'What makes online content viral?', *Journal of Marketing Research*, *49* (2): 192–205.

Berger, Jonah and Ward, Morgan (2010) 'Subtle signals of inconspicuous consumption', *Journal of Consumer Research*, *37* (4): 555–69.

Bettman, James R., Luce, Mary Frances, and Payne, John W. (1998) 'Constructive consumer choice processes', *Journal of Consumer Research*, *25* (3): 187–217.

Bolton, Lisa E., Reed, Americus, Volpp, Kevin G., and Armstrong, Katrina (2007) 'How does drug and supplement marketing affect a healthy lifestyle?', *Journal of Consumer Research*, *34* (5): 713–26.

Bone, Sterling A., Christensen, Glenn L., and Williams, Jerome D. (2014) 'Rejected, shackled, and alone: The impact of systemic restricted choice on minority consumers' construction of self', *Journal of Consumer Research*, *41* (2): 451–74.

Bosmans, Anick, Pieters, Rik, and Baumgartner, Hans (2010) 'The get ready mind-set: How gearing up for later impacts effort allocation now', *Journal of Consumer Research*, *37* (1): 98–107.

Botti, Simona, Orfali, Kristina, and Iyengar, Sheena S. (2009) 'Tragic choices: Autonomy and emotional responses to medical decisions', *Journal of Consumer Research*, *36* (October): 337–52.

Bourdieu, Pierre (1984) *Distinction: A Social Critique of the Judgment of Taste*. London: Routledge and Kegan Paul.

Brewer, Marilynn B. (2003) 'Optimal distinctiveness, social identity, and the self', in M.R. Leary and J.P. Tangney (eds), *Handbook of Self and Identity*. New York: Guilford Press. pp. 480–91.

Brickell, Chris (2003) 'Performativity or performance? Clarifications in the sociology of gender', *New Zealand Sociology*, *18* (2): 158–78.

Brinberg, David and Wood, Ronald (1983) 'A resource exchange theory analysis of consumer behavior', *Journal of Consumer Research*, *10* (3): 330–8.

Canniford, Robin and Shankar, Avi (2013) 'Purifying practices: How consumers assemble romantic experiences of nature', *Journal of Consumer Research*, *39* (5): 1051–69.

Coskuner-Ball, Gokcen and Thompson, Craig (2013) 'The status costs of subordinate cultural capital: At-home fathers' collective pursuit of cultural legitimacy through capitalizing consumption practices', *Journal of Consumer Research*, *40* (June): 19–41.

Cova, Bernard and Cova, Véronique (2002) 'Tribal marketing: The tribalisation of society and its impact on the conduct of marketing', *European Journal of Marketing*, *36* (5/6): 595–620.

Cova, Bernard and Cova, Véronique (2012) 'On the road to prosumption: Marketing discourse and the development of consumer competencies', *Consumption Markets & Culture*, *15* (2): 149–68.

Cova, Bernard, Pace, Stefano, and Skålén, P. (2015) 'Marketing with working consumers: The case of a carmaker and its brand community', *Organization*, *22* (5): 682–701.

Cronin, James M., McCarthy, Mary B., and Collins, Alan M. (2014) 'Covert distinction: How hipsters practice food-based resistance strategies in the production of identity', *Consumption Markets & Culture*, *17* (1): 2–28.

Denegri-Knott, Janice, Zwick, Detlev, and Schroeder, Jonathan E. (2006) 'Mapping consumer power: An integrative framework for marketing and consumer research', *European Journal of Marketing*, *40* (9/10): 950–71.

Desai, Deven R., and Magliocca, Gerard N. (2013) 'Patents, meet Napster: 3D printing and the digitization of things', *Georgetown Law Journal*, 102: 1691–720.

Donnelly, Grant E., Lamberton, Cait, Walker Reczek, Rebecca, and Norton, Michael I. (2017) 'Social recycling transforms unwanted goods into happiness', *Journal of the Association for Consumer Research*, *2* (1): 48–63.

Dorsch, Michael J., Törnblom, Kjell Y., and Kazemi, Ali (2017) 'A review of resource theories and their implications for understanding consumer behavior', *Journal of the Association for Consumer Research*, *2* (1): 5–25.

Durante, Kristina M., Griskevicius, Vladas, Redden, Joseph P., and White, Andrew Edward (2015) 'Spending on daughters versus sons in economic recessions', *Journal of Consumer Research*, *42* (3): 435–57.

Epp, Amber M. and Velagaleti, Sunaina R. (2014) 'Outsourcing parenthood? How families manage care assemblages using paid commercial services', *Journal of Consumer Research*, *41* (4): 911–35.

Escalas, Jennifer Edson and Bettman, James R. (2003) 'You are what they eat: The influence of reference groups on consumers' connections to brands', *Journal of Consumer Psychology*, *13* (3): 339–48.

Feick, Lawrence F. and Price, Linda L. (1987) 'The market maven: A diffuser of marketplace information', *The Journal of Marketing*, *51* (1): 83–97.

Fennis, Bob M., Janssen, Loes, and Vohs, Kathleen D. (2008) 'Acts of benevolence: A limited-resource account of compliance with charitable requests', *Journal of Consumer Research*, *35* (6): 906–24.

Fernbach, Philip M., Kan, Christina, and Lynch Jr, John G. (2014) 'Squeezed: Coping with constraint through efficiency and prioritization', *Journal of Consumer Research*, *41* (5): 1204–27.

Ferraro, Rosellina, Edson Escalas, Jennifer, and Bettman, James R. (2011) 'Our possessions, our selves: Domains of self-worth and the possession–self link', *Journal of Consumer Psychology*, *21* (2): 169–77.

Ferraro, Rosellina, Shiv, Baba, and Bettman, James R. (2005) 'Let us eat and drink, for tomorrow we shall die: Effects of mortality salience and self-esteem on self-regulation in consumer choice', *Journal of Consumer Research*, *32* (1): 65–75.

Fischer, Eileen, Otnes, Cele, and Tuncay, Linda (2007) 'Pursuing parenthood: Integrating cultural and cognitive perspectives on persistent goal striving', *Journal of Consumer Research*, *34* (December): 425–40.

Fiske, Alan P. (1992) 'Four elementary forms of sociality: Framework for a unified theory of social relations', *Psychological Review*, *99*: 689–723.

Foa, Edna B. and Foa, Uriel G. (1980) 'Resource theory: Interpersonal behavior as exchange', in Kenneth Gergen, Martin S. Greenberg, and Richard H. Willis (eds), *Social Exchange: Advances in Theory and Research*. New York: Plenum Press.

Fournier, Susan (1998) 'Consumers and their brands: Developing relationship theory in consumer research', *Journal of Consumer Research*, *24* (4): 343–73.

Fournier, Susan and Mick, David Glen (1999) 'Rediscovering satisfaction', *Journal of Marketing*, 25 (2): 15–23.

Gal, David (2015) 'Identity-signaling behavior', in Michael I. Norton, Derek D. Rucker, and Cait Lamberton, (eds), *The Cambridge Handbook of Consumer Psychology*. New York: Cambridge University Press. pp. 257–81.

Gans, Herbert J. (1999) *Popular Culture and High Culture: An Analysis and Evaluation of Taste*, 2nd edn. New York: Basic Books.

Gao, Leilei, Wheeler, S. Christian, and Shiv, Baba (2008) 'The "Shaken Self": Product choices as a means of restoring self-view confidence', *Journal of Consumer Research*, 36 (1): 29–38.

Garbinsky, Emily N., Klesse, Anne-Kathrin, and Aaker, Jennifer (2014) 'Money in the bank: Feeling powerful increases saving', *Journal of Consumer Research*, 41 (3): 610–23.

Giddens, Anthony (1984) *The Constitution of Society: Outline of the Theory of Structuration*. Berkeley, CA: University of California Press.

Goffman, Erving (1959) *The Presentation of Self in Everyday Life*. New York: Doubleday.

Griskevicius, Vladas and Kenrick, Douglas T. (2013) 'Fundamental motives: How evolutionary needs influence consumer behavior', *Journal of Consumer Psychology*, 23 (3): 372–86.

Han, Dahee, Duhachek, Adam, and Agrawal, Nidhi (2015) 'Coping research in broader perspective: Emotions, threats, mindsets and more', in Michael I. Norton, Derek D. Rucker, and Cait Lamberton (eds), *The Cambridge Handbook of Consumer Psychology*. New York: Cambridge University Press. pp. 282–308.

Henkel, Alexander P., Boegershausen Johannes, Ciuchita, Robert, and Odekerken-Schröder, Gaby (2017) 'Storm after the quiet: How marketplace interactions shape consumer resources in collective goal pursuits', *Journal of the Association for Consumer Research*, 2 (1): 26–47.

Hill, Ronald Paul and Stamey, Mark (1990) 'The homeless in America: An examination of possessions and consumption behaviors', *Journal of Consumer Research*, 17 (3): 303–21.

Hill, Ronald Paul, Rapp, Justine M., Capella, Michael L., and Gentlemen, Gramercy (2015) 'Consumption restriction in a total control institution: Participatory action research in a maximum-security prison', *Journal of Public Policy and Marketing*, 34 (2): 156–72.

Hoch, Stephen J. and Loewenstein, George F. (1991) 'Time-inconsistent preferences and consumer self-control', *Journal of Consumer Research*, 17 (4): 492–507.

Holt, Douglas B. (1998) 'Does cultural capital structure American consumption?', *Journal of Consumer Research*, 25 (June): 1–26.

Holt, Douglas B. (2002) 'Why do brands cause trouble? A dialectical theory of consumer culture and branding', *Journal of Consumer Research*, 29 (June): 70–90.

Hornik, Jacob (1984) 'Subjective vs. objective time measures: A note on the perception of time in consumer behavior', *Journal of Consumer Research*, 11 (1): 615–18.

Janiszewski, Chris and Warlop, Luk (2017) 'Valuing resource valuation in consumer research: An introduction', *Journal of the Association for Consumer Research, 2* (1): 1–4.

Kellaris, James J. (2008) 'Music and consumers', in Curtis P. Haugtvedt and Paul M. Herr (eds), *Handbook of Consumer Psychology*. New York, NY: Psychology Press. pp. 837–56.

Kjeldgaard, Dannie, Askegaard, Søren, Rasmussen, Jannick Ørnstedt, and Østergaard, Per (2017) 'Consumers' collective action in market system dynamics', *Marketing Theory, 17* (March): 51–70.

Klein, Jill G. and Hill, Ronald P. (2008) 'Rethinking macro-level theories of consumption: Research findings from Nazi concentration camps', *Journal of Macromarketing, 28* (3): 228–42.

Kopytoff, Igor (1986) 'The cultural biography of things: Commoditization as process', in Arjun Appadurai (ed.), *The Social Life of Things: Commodities in Cultural Perspective*. New York: Cambridge. pp. 64–94.

Kozinets, Robert V. (2001) 'Utopian enterprise: Articulating the meanings of Star Trek's culture of consumption', *Journal of Consumer Research, 28* (June): 67–88.

Krishna, Aradhna (2012) 'An integrative review of sensory marketing: Engaging the senses to affect perception, judgment and behavior', *Journal of Consumer Psychology, 22* (3): 332–51.

Lasaleta, Jannine D., Sedikides, Constantine, and Vohs, Kathleen D. (2014) 'Nostalgia weakens the desire for money', *Journal of Consumer Research, 41* (3): 713–29.

Leclerc, France, Schmitt, Bernd H., and Dube, Laurette (1995) 'Waiting time and decision making: Is time like money?', *Journal of Consumer Research, 22* (1): 110–19.

Lee, Richard M. and Robbins, Steven B. (1998) 'The relationship between social connectedness and anxiety, self-esteem, and social identity', *Journal of Counseling Psychology, 45* (3): 338–45.

Levitt, Theodore (1972) 'Production-line approach to service', *Harvard Business Review, 50* (September/October): 41–52.

Levy, Sidney J. (1959) 'Symbols for sale', *Harvard Business Review, 37* (July/August): 117–24.

Lizardo, Omar and Skiles, Sara (2012) 'Reconceptualizing and theorizing "omnivorousness": genetic and relational mechanisms', *Sociological Theory, 30* (4): 263–82.

Luedicke, Marius K. (2015) 'Indigenes' responses to immigrants' consumer acculturation: A relational configuration analysis', *Journal of Consumer Research, 42* (June): 109–29.

Maciel, André F. and Wallendorf, Melanie (2017) 'Taste engineering: An extended consumer model of cultural competence constitution', *Journal of Consumer Research, 43* (5): 726–46.

MacInnis, Deborah J. (2017) *'Musings on our collective journey'*, ACR Fellows Address, San Diego, CA, Association for Consumer Research.

MacInnis, Deborah J. and De Mello, Gustavo E. (2005) 'The concept of hope and its relevance to product evaluation and choice', *Journal of Marketing, 69* (1): 1–14.

MacInnis, Deborah J. and Folkes, Valerie S. (2017) 'Humanizing brands: When brands seem to be like me, part of me, and in a relationship with me', *Journal of Consumer Psychology*, *27* (3): 355–74.

Marcoux, Jean-Sébastien (2017) 'Souvenirs to forget', *Journal of Consumer Research, 43* (6): 950–69.

Markus, Hazel and Nurius, Paula (1986) 'Possible selves', *American Psychologist, 41* (9): 954–69.

Martin, Kelly D. and Hill, Ronald Paul (2011) 'Life satisfaction, self-determination, and consumption adequacy at the bottom of the pyramid', *Journal of Consumer Research, 38* (6): 1155–68.

Martin, Diane and Schouten, John W. (2014) 'Consumption-driven market emergence', *Journal of Consumer Research, 40* (5): 855–70.

Martin, Diane M., Schouten, John W., and McAlexander, James H. (2006) 'Claiming the throttle: Multiple femininities in a hyper-masculine subculture', *Consumption Markets & Culture, 9* (3): 171–205.

McAlexander, James H., Leavenworth Dufault, Beth, Martin, Diane M., and Schouten, John W. (2014) 'The marketization of religion: Field, capital, and consumer identity', *Journal of Consumer Research, 41* (3): 858–75.

McCracken, Grant (1986) 'Culture and consumption: A theoretical account of the structure and movement of the cultural meaning of consumer goods', *Journal of Consumer Research, 13* (June): 71–84.

McCracken, Grant (1990) *Culture and Consumption*. Indianapolis: University of Indiana Press.

McGregor, Sue (2011) 'Consumer acumen: Augmenting consumer literacy', *Journal of Consumer Affairs, 45* (2): 344–57.

McQuarrie, Edward F. and Phillips, Barbara J. (2014) 'The megaphone effect in social media: How ordinary consumers become style leaders', *GfK-Marketing Intelligence Review, 6* (November): 16–20.

Mehta, Ravi and Zhu, Meng (2015) 'Creating when you have less: The impact of resource scarcity on product use creativity', *Journal of Consumer Research, 42* (5): 767–82.

Miyazaki, Anthony D. and Fernandez, Ana (2001) 'Consumer perceptions of privacy and security risks for online shopping', *Journal of Consumer Affairs, 35* (1): 27–44.

Mogilner, Cassie (2010) 'The pursuit of happiness: Time, money, and social connection', *Psychological Science, 21* (9): 1348–54.

Mogilner, Cassie and Aaker, Jennifer (2009) 'The time vs. money effect': Shifting product attitudes and decisions through personal connection', *Journal of Consumer Research, 36* (2): 277–91.

Moorman, Christine and Matulich, Erika (1993) 'A model of consumers' preventive health behaviors: The role of health motivation and health ability', *Journal of Consumer Research, 20* (2): 208–28.

Nicolao, Leonardo, Irwin, Julie R., and Goodman, Joseph K. (2009) 'Happiness for sale: Do experiential purchases make consumers happier than material purchases?', *Journal of Consumer Research, 36* (2): 188–98.

O'Guinn, Thomas C. and Belk, Russell W. (1989) 'Heaven on earth: Consumption at Heritage Village, USA', *Journal of Consumer Research, 16* (2): 227–38.

Park, C. Whan, MacInnis, Deborah J., Priester, Joseph, Eisingerich, Andreas B., and Iacobucci, Dawn (2010) 'Brand attachment and brand attitude strength: Conceptual and empirical differentiation of two critical brand equity drivers', *Journal of Marketing, 74* (6): 1–17.

Park, Ji Kyung and Roedder John, Deborah (2010) 'Got to get you into my life: Do brand personalities rub off on consumers?', *Journal of Consumer Research, 37* (4): 655–69.

Petty, Richard E., Cacioppo, John T., and Schumann, David (1983) 'Central and peripheral routes to advertising effectiveness: the moderating role of involvement', *Journal of Consumer Research, 10* (2): 135–46.

Pieters, Rik (2013) 'Bidirectional dynamics of materialism and loneliness: Not just a vicious cycle', *Journal of Consumer Research, 40* (4): 615–31.

Plassman, Hilke and Karmarkar, Uma R. (2015) 'Consumer neuroscience: Revealing meaningful relationships between brain and consumer behavior', in Michael I. Norton, Derek D. Rucker, and Cait Lamberton (eds), *The Cambridge Handbook of Consumer Psychology*. New York: Cambridge University Press. pp. 152–79.

Raghubir, Priya, Capizzani, Mario, and Srivastava, Joydeep (2017) '"What's in your wallet?" Psychological biases in the estimation of money', *Journal of the Association for Consumer Research, 2* (1): 105–22.

Ritzer, George and Jurgenson, Nathan (2010) 'Production, consumption, prosumption: The nature of capitalism in the age of the digital "prosumer"', *Journal of Consumer Culture, 10* (1): 13–36.

Roedder John, Deborah (1999) 'Consumer socialization of children: A retrospective look at twenty-five years of research', *Journal of Consumer Research, 26* (3): 183–213.

Roux, Caroline, Goldsmith, Kelly, and Bonezzi, Andrea (2015) 'On the psychology of scarcity: When reminders of resource scarcity promote selfish (and generous) behavior', *Journal of Consumer Research, 42* (4): 615–31.

Rucker, Derek D. and Galinsky, Adam D. (2008) 'Desire to acquire: Powerlessness and compensatory consumption', *Journal of Consumer Research, 35* (2): 257–67.

Rucker, Derek D. and Galinsky, Adam D. (2009) 'Conspicuous consumption versus utilitarian ideals: How different levels of power shape consumer behavior', *Journal of Experimental Social Psychology, 45* (3): 549–55.

Scaraboto, Daiane and Fischer, Eileen (2013) 'Frustrated fatshionistas: An institutional theory perspective on consumer quests for greater choice in mainstream markets', *Journal of Consumer Research, 39* (April): 1234–57.

Schwartz, Barry (2004) *The Paradox of Choice: Why More is Less*. New York: Harper Collins.

Seregina, Anastasia and Weijo, Henri A. (2017) 'Play at any cost: How cosplayers produce and sustain their ludic communal consumption experiences', *Journal of Consumer Research*, *44* (June): 139–59.

Shen, Luxi, Fishbach, Ayelet, and Hsee, Christopher K. (2015) 'The motivating-uncertainty effect: Uncertainty increases resource investment in the process of reward pursuit', *Journal of Consumer Research*, *41* (February): 1301–15.

Smith, Alexander (2017) 'Pepsi pulls controversial Kendall Jenner ad after outcry', *Newsweek*, 5 April. www.nbcnews.com/news/nbcblk/pepsi-ad-kendall-jenner-echoes-black-lives-matter-sparks-anger-n742811.

Solomon, Michael R. (1983) 'The role of products as social stimuli: A symbolic interactionism perspective', *Journal of Consumer Research*, *10* (3): 319–29.

Sujan, Mita (1985) 'Consumer knowledge: Effects on evaluation strategies mediating consumer judgments', *Journal of Consumer Research*, *12* (1): 31–46.

Thaler, Richard (1985) 'Mental accounting and consumer choice', *Marketing Science*, *4* (Summer): 199–214.

Thomas, Tandy Chalmers, Price, Linda L., and Schau, Hope Jensen (2013) 'When differences unite: Resource dependence in heterogeneous consumption communities', *Journal of Consumer Research*, *39* (5): 1010–33.

Thompson, Craig J. (2005) 'Consumer risk perceptions in a community of reflexive doubt,' *Journal of Consumer Research*, *32* (September): 235–48.

Ülkümen, Gülden, Thomas, Manoj, and Morwitz, Vicki G. (2008) 'Will I spend more in 12 months or a year? The effect of ease of estimation and confidence on budget estimate', *Journal of Consumer Research*, *35* (2): 245–56.

Üstüner, Tuba and Holt, Douglas B. (2007) 'Dominated consumer acculturation: The social construction of poor migrant women's consumer identity projects in a Turkish squatter', *Journal of Consumer Research*, *34* (June): 41–56.

Üstüner, Tuba and Holt, Douglas B. (2010) 'Toward a theory of status consumption in less industrialized countries', *Journal of Consumer Research*, *37* (June): 37–56.

Van Laer, Tom, De Ruyter, Ko, Visconti, Luca M., and Wetzels, Martin (2013) 'The extended transportation-imagery model: A meta-analysis of the antecedents and consequences of consumers' narrative transportation', *Journal of Consumer Research*, *40* (5): 797–817.

Vargo, Stephen L. and Lusch, Robert F. (2004) 'Evolving to a new dominant logic for marketing', *Journal of Marketing*, *68* (January): 1–17.

Viswanathan, Madhubalan, Rosa, Jose Antonio, and Harris, James Edwin (2005) 'Decision making and coping of functionally illiterate consumers and some implications for marketing management', *Journal of Marketing*, *69* (1): 15–31.

Vohs, Kathleen D. and Faber, Ronald J. (2007) 'Spent resources: Self-regulatory resource availability affects impulse buying', *Journal of Consumer Research*, *33* (4): 537–47.

Wallendorf, Melanie and Arnould, Eric J. (1991) '"We gather together": The consumption rituals of Thanksgiving Day', *Journal of Consumer Research*, *18* (June): 13–31.

Warde, Alan (2005) 'Consumption and theories of practice', *Journal of Consumer Culture*, *5* (2): 131–53.

White, Katherine and Dahl, Darren W. (2007) 'Are all out-groups created equal? Consumer identity and dissociative influence', *Journal of Consumer Research*, *34* (4): 525–36.

Woermann, Niklas (2012) 'On the slope is on the screen: Prosumption, social media practices, and scopic systems in the freeskiing subculture', *American Behavioral Scientist*, *56* (4): 618–40.

Wong, Nancy and King, Tracey (2008) 'The cultural construction of risk understandings through illness narratives', *Journal of Consumer Research*, *34* (5): 579–94.

Wu, Tim (2016) *The Attention Merchants: The Epic Scramble to Get Inside our Heads*. New York: Alfred A. Knopf.

Zwick, Detlev, Bonsu, Sammy, and Darmody, Aron (2008) 'Putting consumers to work: Co-creation and new marketing governmentality', *Journal of Consumer Culture*, *8* (2): 163–96.

INDEX

Page numbers in *italics* refer to figures and tables; those in **bold** indicate boxes.

Made in the USA
Monee, IL
23 September 2020

43262525R00203